DECODING ANNE LISTER

This is the first edited collection of essays on the nineteenth-century diarist Anne Lister. Now recognised as a UNESCO world heritage document, Lister's 5-million-word diaries are paradigm-shifting in terms of their range of material, from social commentary and local and global politics to breath-taking travel accounts. However, they have become best known for their explicit descriptions of same-sex practices, which were written in code and constitute a significant portion of their content. The collection addresses the full variety and interdisciplinary quality of Lister's diaries: her complex negotiations with her own 'odd' identity, her multiple same-sex relationships, her involvement in local politics, her travel accounts and her lifelong thirst for knowledge. It also addresses how Lister studies have crossed over to the realm of popular culture through the successful *Gentleman Jack* BBC-HBO series, and includes an interview with Sally Wainwright and a foreword by author Emma Donoghue. This title is part of the Flip it Open Programme and may also be available Open Access. Check our website Cambridge Core for details.

CHRIS ROULSTON is Professor of Gender, Sexuality, and Women's Studies and French Studies at the University of Western Ontario. She has been a leading Lister scholar for the past decade. Her essays on Lister's relationship with Eliza Raine, classical literature, queer sexuality, marriage and *Gentleman Jack* have appeared in *Eighteenth-Century Studies* (2022), the *Journal of Lesbian Studies* (2013, 2022) and the *Journal of the History of Sexuality* (2021).

CAROLINE GONDA is College Associate Professor and Director of Studies in English at St Catharine's College, Cambridge. She was the first person appointed to the post of LGBTQ+ Fellow at a Cambridge College. With John Beynon, she co-edited the pioneering collection *Lesbian Dames: Sapphism in the Long Eighteenth Century* (2010). She writes and teaches on literature, gender and sexuality, particularly lesbian narrative and queer reception.

DECODING ANNE LISTER

From the Archives to 'Gentleman Jack'

EDITED BY

CHRIS ROULSTON

University of Western Ontario

and

CAROLINE GONDA

St Catharine's College, Cambridge

CAMBRIDGE
UNIVERSITY PRESS

CAMBRIDGE
UNIVERSITY PRESS

Shaftesbury Road, Cambridge CB2 8EA, United Kingdom

One Liberty Plaza, 20th Floor, New York, NY 10006, USA

477 Williamstown Road, Port Melbourne, VIC 3207, Australia

314–321, 3rd Floor, Plot 3, Splendor Forum, Jasola District Centre, New Delhi – 110025, India

103 Penang Road, #05-06/07, Visioncrest Commercial, Singapore 238467

Cambridge University Press is part of Cambridge University Press & Assessment, a department of the University of Cambridge.

We share the University's mission to contribute to society through the pursuit of education, learning and research at the highest international levels of excellence.

www.cambridge.org
Information on this title: www.cambridge.org/9781009280730

DOI: 10.1017/9781009280723

First published 2023

A catalogue record for this publication is available from the British Library.

Library of Congress Cataloging-in-Publication Data
NAMES: Roulston, Chris, editor. | Gonda, Caroline, editor.
TITLE: Decoding Anne Lister : from the archives to 'Gentleman Jack' / edited by Chris Roulston, University of Western Ontario and Caroline Gonda, St. Catharine's College, Cambridge.
DESCRIPTION: Cambridge, United Kingdom ; New York, NY : Cambridge University Press, 2023. | Includes bibliographical references and index.
IDENTIFIERS: LCCN 2022062063 (print) | LCCN 2022062064 (ebook) | ISBN 9781009280730 (hardback) | ISBN 9781009280747 (paperback) | ISBN 9781009280723 (epub)
SUBJECTS: LCSH: Lister, Anne, 1791-1840. | Lesbians–England–Biography. | Lesbians–England–History–19th century. | Sex role–England–History–19th century.
CLASSIFICATION: LCC HQ75.4.L57 D43 2023 (print) | LCC HQ75.4.L57 (ebook) | DDC 306.76/63092 [B]–dc23/eng/20230209
LC record available at https://lccn.loc.gov/2022062063
LC ebook record available at https://lccn.loc.gov/2022062064

ISBN 978-1-009-28073-0 Hardback

Contents

Figures

Contributors

CAROLINE BAYLIS-GREEN is an independent postdoctoral researcher and visiting lecturer at the University of Sussex, specialising in long nineteenth-century poetry and life writing, with a particular focus on links between queer theory, identity and women's writing. She has published on closeting and decoding in long nineteenth-century poetry, material culture and the Victorian short story form, and previously taught nineteenth-century literature as an associate lecturer at Manchester Metropolitan University, where she completed her PhD. She also teaches on film, performance art and drag.

ANGELA CLARE has more than fifteen years' experience working in museums and heritage, including eight years at the Royal Armouries Museum in Leeds and the Tower of London working on various interpretation projects and exhibitions. She has worked for Calderdale Museums, which manages Shibden Hall and Bankfield Museum in Halifax, for several years now, completing various collection projects, gallery changes and developments, a wide range of exhibitions, publications and films, all to improve access and engagement with collections and history, and she has written non-fiction articles and publications on a range of topics including Anne Lister of Shibden Hall.

ANNA CLARK is the author of *Alternative Histories of the Self: a Cultural History of Sexuality and Secrets* (2017), which includes a chapter on Anne Lister that rethinks her original article, 'Anne Lister's Construction of Lesbian Identity', *Journal of the History of Sexuality* (1996). She is also the author of *Desire: a History of European Sexuality* (2008), *Scandal: the Sexual Politics of the British Constitution* (2004), *The Struggle for the Breeches: Gender and the Making of the British Working Class* (1995) and *Women's Silence, Men's Violence: Sexual Assault in England* (1987). She is a professor at the University of Minnesota.

EMMA DONOGHUE is a writer of fiction, drama, screenplays and literary history. Born in Dublin, she did a PhD on eighteenth-century English fiction at Cambridge University before settling in Canada. She is best known for *Room* – the novel (2010; shortlisted for the Man Booker Prize and the Orange Prize), the film (nominated for four Oscars) and the play. Her latest novel, *Learned by Heart* (2023), is about Eliza Raine and Anne Lister at the Manor School.

CAROLINE GONDA is College Associate Professor and Glen Cavaliero Fellow in English at St Catharine's College, Cambridge University, where she is also the college's first official LGBTQ+ Fellow. She is the author of *Reading Daughters' Fictions, 1709–1834: Novels and Society from Manley to Edgeworth* (1996), and has published articles on lesbian and queer representation in the eighteenth and early nineteenth century in *Women's Writing*, *Journal for Eighteenth Century Studies*, *Journal of Lesbian Studies* and *The Cambridge Companion to Lesbian Literature*. She is the co-editor of *Queer People: Negotiations and Expressions of Homosexuality, 1700–1800* (2007) and of *Lesbian Dames: Sapphism in the Long Eighteenth Century* (2010), the first collection of scholarly essays on desire between women in this period.

SUSAN S. LANSER is Professor Emerita of Comparative Literature, English and WGS at Brandeis University. She has written widely on topics of sexuality and gender in the eighteenth century, most extensively in *The Sexuality of History: Modernity and the Sapphic, 1565–1830* (2014), winner of the American Historical Association's Joan Kelly Prize and runner-up for the Louis D. Gottschalk Prize, and her essays have appeared in journals such as *Eighteenth-Century Studies*, *ECTI*, *Eighteenth-Century Life*, *PMLA*, *Feminist Studies* and *Narrative*. She is a past president of the American Society for Eighteenth-Century Studies and the International Society for the Study of Narrative.

KIRSTY MCHUGH is Curator of the John Murray Archive and Publishers' Collections at the National Library of Scotland and has recently completed her PhD at the University of Wales Centre for Advanced Welsh and Celtic Studies. Trained as an archivist, she is interested in the use of manuscript sources for studying the history of travel writing, and the interaction of manuscript and print. Her interest in Anne Lister grew out of her doctoral research on tours of Scotland and Wales in the Romantic period, and she published the first study of Anne Lister's 1828 tour of Scotland in *Studies in Travel Writing* in 2019.

CHRIS ROULSTON is Professor of Gender, Sexuality and Women's Studies and French Studies at the University of Western Ontario. Her books include *Virtue, Gender and the Authentic Self in Eighteenth-Century Literature* (1998) and *Narrating Marriage in Eighteenth-Century England and France* (2010). She has recently published on marriage in *A Cultural History of Marriage in the Age of Enlightenment* (2020), on Mme de Graffigny in *Françoise de Graffigny: femme de lettres des Lumières* (2020) and on Anne Lister in *After Marriage in the Long Eighteenth Century* (2018), *Journal of the History of Sexuality* (*JHS*), *Journal of Lesbian Studies* (*JLS*) and *Eighteenth-Century Studies*. Her current project, *School Daze: Queer Nostalgia in Modern British Girls' Boarding School Narratives*, focuses on queer sexuality in girls' boarding school novels, with recently published articles on Rosemary Manning's *The Chinese Garden* in *Twentieth-Century Literature* (2019) and on Dorothy Strachey's *Olivia* in *Modernism/Modernity* (2020).

LAURIE SHANNON is Franklyn Bliss Snyder Professor of Literature at Northwestern University and a historian of ideas. Her first book, *Sovereign Amity: Figures of Friendship in Shakespearean Contexts* (2002), assesses the impact of classical friendship on the political imaginary of the long sixteenth century. Her second, *The Accommodated Animal: Cosmopolity in Shakespearean Locales* (2013), analyses cosmic membership and the species concept before Descartes, earning the Elizabeth Dietz Memorial Prize for its contribution to literary studies of the English Renaissance. Projects underway include *Frailty's Name: Shakespeare's Natural History of Human Being* and *Anne Lister's Hand*, an account of Lister's hospitable theory of nature.

ANGELA STEIDELE has written several books about LGBTQ+ lives in the eighteenth and nineteenth centuries. *Love Story: Adele Schopenhauer and Sibylle Mertens* (2010) was shortlisted for the NDR Kultur non-fiction prize, and she won the Gleim Literature Prize for *In Men's Clothes* (2004, revised edition 2021), her biography of Catharina Linck, and the Bavarian Book Prize for her novel *Rosenstengel* (2017). Her biography of Anne Lister, *Gentleman Jack* (2019), was longlisted for the Portico Prize and praised by the *Guardian* as 'a triumph of truth over fantasy'. Her latest book, *Enlightenment. A novel* (2022), was shortlisted for the prestigious Leipzig Book Fair Prize. In 2023 she gained the Klopstock Prize for her entire literary work.

STEPHEN TURTON is a Research Fellow in English at Gonville and Caius College, Cambridge. He specialises in the history of English dictionaries from 1600 to the present, with a particular interest in their representations of marginalised sexualities, genders and linguistic varieties. His essay 'The Confessional Sciences: Scientific Lexicography and Sexology in the Oxford English Dictionary' was awarded the Vivien Law Prize by the Henry Sweet Society for the History of Linguistic Ideas in 2019. His first book, *Before the Word was Queer: Sexuality and the English Dictionary, 1600–1930*, is forthcoming from Cambridge University Press, and he is co-editing a digital edition of the letters of Sir James A. H. Murray, the first chief editor of the *Oxford English Dictionary*, at www.murrayscriptorium.org.

CASSANDRA ULPH is a specialist in British women's fiction and non-fiction of the eighteenth and nineteenth centuries, with particular focus on literary and artistic professionalism, women's intellectual identity and sociability. Her publications include articles on Frances Burney, Hester Piozzi and Anne Lister. She was a Research Associate in Reading Practices at the University of Manchester on *Unlocking the Hamilton Papers*, a major AHRC-funded project to reconstruct, digitise and transliterate the correspondence and other writings of bluestocking diarist and courtier Mary Hamilton. She works at the University of Leeds as the Digital Development Officer for the Digital Creativity and Cultures Hub in the Brotherton Library, University of Leeds.

SALLY WAINWRIGHT, OBE, is a Yorkshire-born television writer, producer and director, who started as a scriptwriter for the BBC Radio 4 drama *The Archers* before launching her television career in 2000 with the television series *At Home with the Braithwaites* (2000–3). In 2009, she won the Royal Television Society's Writer of the Year Award for her mini-series *Unforgiven*. She is also the creator of ITV's *Scott & Bailey* (2011–16) and the BBC's *Last Tango in Halifax* (2012–20) and *Happy Valley* (2014–23), the last two winning the British Academy Television Awards (BAFTAs) for Best Drama Series in 2013 (*Last Tango*), 2015 and 2017 (*Happy Valley*). In 2016, she wrote and directed a two-hour drama series for the BBC on the Brontës, *To Walk Invisible: the Brontë Sisters*, and in 2019, created season one of the BBC/HBO television series *Gentleman Jack*, with season two airing in 2022. She was made a Fellow of the Royal Television Society in 2016.

HELENA WHITBREAD, MBE, is a writer, born in Halifax, West Yorkshire in 1931, whose education was cut short at the age of fourteen, before, in 1965, she gained a BSc (Hons) at Bradford University and a PGCE in Further Education. Following the discovery of the journals of Anne Lister in 1983, she spent five years transcribing extracts from them. The edited extracts have been published in her two books, *The Secret Diaries of Miss Anne Lister* (2010) and *The Secret Diaries of Miss Anne Lister, vol. II: No Priest but Love* (2020). She has been employed as a consultant on the following television productions: *A Skirt through History*, episode one (BBC; 1994), the documentary *Revealing Anne Lister* (BBC; 2010) and the first season of *Gentleman Jack* (BBC/HBO; 2019). She was also on *The One Show* (2019), a live BBC TV interview with Suranne Jones and Sophie Rundle. She is presently working on a biography of Anne Lister's early life (1791–1826). In January 2023 she was awarded an Honorary D.Litt. from the University of Sheffield for her research and publications on Anne Lister's diaries. A short biographical film of her life entitled 'The Helena Whitbread Story', filmed at Shibden Hall, Halifax in November 2022, was released on April 3rd 2023.

Foreword

Emma Donoghue

'I dare to say I am like no one in the whole world,' Anne Lister wrote in her diary in 1823. A 'curious genius' from the cradle on, a prodigy known as the 'Solomon' of her school, Lister grew up to be an individual remarkable for, and self-aware about, her individuality – what she called her *oddity*. She knew her 'softly gentleman-like' manners were distinctly 'peculiar', and sounded wryly amused about the *odd freak* Nature must have been in when she made Lister.

These phrasings aren't just euphemisms for – though they include – gender nonconformity and lesbian desire. Anne Lister was singular in many ways, and even when she could be seen as a type (self-educated lady, say, or Tory landowner on the border between yeoman and gentry), she combined her affiliations unpredictably. Those of us who have been drawn to Lister over the past two centuries, to investigate and write about her, have found different aspects of her most urgently interesting, but I think we all treasure her queerness, in the broadest sense.

In the twenty-first century, Lister has become so much more than an individual. Her archive has bloomed into a cultural phenomenon that includes not just one of the longest diaries in the English language, plus letters, travel journals, and reading and lecture notes, but prose, theatrical and televisual fictions of her life and times, most notably the TV series *Gentleman Jack*, which has provoked everything from Yorkshire tourism to online community and controversy.

As someone who has been fascinated by Anne Lister and written about her on and off for more than three decades, I am delighted to see the ripples made by her life spread farther and farther. I appreciate her not just

Figure 1 Anne Lister portrait (*c.*1822). West Yorkshire Archive Service, Calderdale, SH:2/M/19/1/1.

for her own odd self but for the peephole her eloquent diaries cut into a hidden world of sociability and sexuality; not just for the path she negotiated through early nineteenth-century English society but for the ways that her some dozen lovers and crushes lived their varied lives. Lister logged everything from prices to gossip to coal mining to masturbation with a relentless hunger for understanding that I can only call libidinal, so her writing throws shafts of new light in all directions.

A free spirit who defied gender norms, but also a conservative snob, coldblooded as often as she was passionate, Lister boasted of her consistency, but could be inconsistent to the point of hypocrisy. She vaunted her candour, but lied to her family, friends and intimates, and used fictional techniques to rework the past in her diary. Long after her 'crypt hand' code was broken and her handwriting puzzled out, Lister's paradoxes require interpretation; like an onion, she has layers all the way down.

Perhaps quarrels over which descriptive labels to choose for Anne Lister on plaques marking key locations in her life will always have something absurd about them, because this protean, polymorphous figure would need a mile-wide plaque to begin to describe her properly. This book – the long-overdue first collection of research essays on Lister – is an excellent start at making sense of a phenomenon that will still be demanding decoding for centuries to come.

Acknowledgements

The editors would like to thank Emma Donoghue for her knowledge of and enthusiasm for Anne Lister and her encouragement and ongoing support of this project; Sally Wainwright for bringing Anne Lister to a much broader audience and supporting the digitisation project that has made it possible for scholars to delve more deeply into the diaries; Harriet Monkhouse for her enthusiastic support and encouragement; and Helena Whitbread for her lifelong commitment to Anne Lister and for bringing the first coded sections of the diary into publication. Both editors are also deeply grateful to all the volunteer transcribers who have given their time and energy to making the Anne Lister diaries available online.

Note on the Text

No critical edition of any Anne Lister papers (diaries and correspondence) exists, so citations from the diaries and the correspondence come from a range of different sources: the West Yorkshire Archive Service diary transcriptions, available online but not yet complete; published extracts from the diaries by Helena Whitbread and Jill Liddington, available in original and reprinted editions; published extracts from the correspondence by Muriel Green; and individual websites where transcribers have pursued their own Lister interests. Contributors to this volume have made use of all these sources, which are clearly referenced in the endnotes of each chapter. In general, italicized passages represent the coded sections of the diaries, but not all contributors have distinguished between the coded and non-coded sections. We have also provided a select bibliography of Lister references which we hope will prove useful in navigating this complex archive.

Introduction

Chris Roulston

The diaries of Anne Lister (1791–1840) challenge our understanding of the history of sexuality, and of the social, economic and political contexts of nineteenth-century society. Containing twenty-six bound volumes from 1816 to 1840, as well as loose pages from 1806 to 1810, the Lister archive is more than five million words long (three times the length of Samuel Pepys's diary), with 15 per cent written in Lister's 'crypt hand' or code, detailing her intimate and sexual relationships with women. The importance of the Lister diaries has gained increasing recognition in recent years. This is the first volume of essays to bring together an international range of scholars and researchers working on the Anne Lister archive. It showcases the burgeoning and dynamic field of Anne Lister Studies both within and beyond academia.

The diaries' survival is nothing short of miraculous. They were first discovered in the 1880s by John Lister when he inherited Shibden Hall. Once he cracked the code with the help of an antiquarian friend, Arthur Burrell, and realised what it contained, he placed the diaries behind wooden panels. What followed over the next hundred years was sporadic interest in the diaries from historians who never alluded to the coded sections.[1] In the 1980s, the Lister diaries were finally properly catalogued and made available to the public as an accessible archive, one hundred years after they were first discovered.[2] The history of the diaries as a material artefact, with their repeated return to the literal and proverbial closet, reflects the complicated trajectory of queer history itself, with its legacy of shame, occlusion and censorship.

An archive that pushes the boundaries of the social, sexual and gendered norms of early nineteenth-century Britain, the Lister diaries refuse to fit neatly into available scholarly categories. This has often resulted in their placement in an outlying class of their own. As Susan S. Lanser has argued, the Lister diaries form part of a broader narrative of how pre-twentieth- and twenty-first-century intimacies between women were 'entangled with

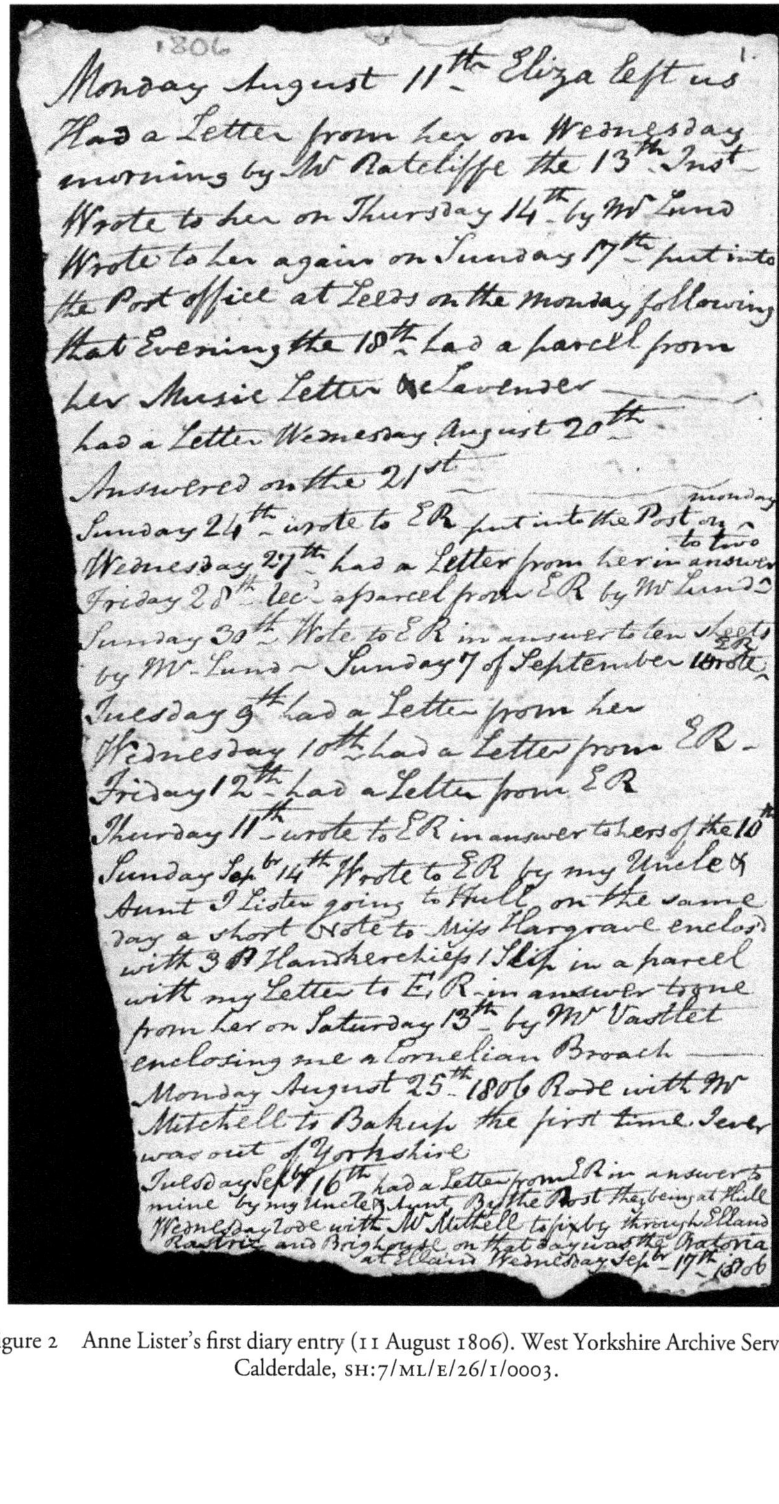
1806
Monday August 11th Eliza left us
Had a Letter from her on Wednesday
morning by Mr Ratcliffe the 13th Inst
Wrote to her on Thursday 14th by Mr Lund
Wrote to her again on Sunday 17th put into
the Post office at Leeds on the monday following
that Evening the 18th had a parcel from
her Music Letter & Lavender
had a Letter Wednesday August 20th
Answered on the 21st
Sunday 24th wrote to ER put into the Post on monday
Wednesday 27th had a Letter from her in answer to two
Friday 28th recd a parcel from ER by Mr Lund
Sunday 30th Wrote to ER in answer to ten sheets
by Mr Lund ~ Sunday 7 of September wrote ER
Tuesday 9th had a Letter from her
Wednesday 10th had a Letter from ER
Friday 12th had a Letter from ER
Thursday 11th wrote to ER in answer to hers of the 10th
Sunday Sepbr 14th Wrote to ER by my Uncle &
Aunt J Lister going to Hull on the same
day a short Note to Miss Hargrave enclos'd
with 3 Pr Handkerchiefs 1 Slip in a parcel
with my Letter to E.R. in answer to one
from her on Saturday 13th by Mr Vastlet
enclosing me a Cornelian Broach
Monday August 25th 1806 Rode with Mr
Mitchell to Bakeup the first time I ever
was out of Yorkshire
Tuesday Sepbr 16th had a Letter from ER in answer to
mine by my Uncle & Aunt By the Post they being at Hull
Wednesday rode with Mr Mitchell to Rixley through Elland
Rastrick and Brighouse on that day was the Oratoria
at Elland Wednesday Sepbr 17th 1806

Figure 2 Anne Lister's first diary entry (11 August 1806). West Yorkshire Archive Service, Calderdale, SH:7/ML/E/26/1/0003.

contests about authority and liberty, power and difference, desire and duty, mobility and change, order and governance',[3] yet the Lister diaries cannot be seen as representative in that they have no comparable analogue.[4] Writing soon after publication of the first extracts from the diaries, Martha Vicinus cautioned against using them as a yardstick by which to measure other queer/lesbian histories.[5] While not claiming the Lister diaries as a reference point, the chapters in *Decoding Anne Lister* nevertheless explore how this unusual archive intervenes in histories of the nineteenth century and helps us to redraw and reimagine the constantly evolving fields of gender and sexuality as well as those of life writing and the role of women in social and political life. They also ask in what ways the social, political and economic conditions of early nineteenth-century Britain enabled the emergence of a figure such as Anne Lister. And what potential the material history of the diaries can unearth as we continue to engage with, uncover and interpret their extraordinary content.

The global significance of the Lister diaries was marked by their inclusion in UNESCO's Memory of the World Register in 2011. The diaries are also reaching far beyond the world of scholars and archivists and generating a dialogue among genealogists, amateur historians, diary transcribers and avid fans of the BBC/HBO *Gentleman Jack* series. A community has evolved around the figure of Anne Lister that is engendering a broader and more public discussion about our understanding of queer sexuality, gender variance and women's roles from the nineteenth century to the present. As the controversy over the plaque commemorating Lister's union with Ann Walker at Holy Trinity Church, York, reveals, the Lister diaries have striking relevance to our current conversations around public history and memorialisation, and to how we shape those conversations in the light of the suppressed and occluded queer, lesbian and gender nonconforming past.[6]

The Lister diaries bear out the idea that if attended to correctly, the past can redirect our understanding of the present. The chapters in this collection reflect the encounter between past and present by showing how Lister's transgression of gender and sexual boundaries not only marked and shaped every aspect of her lived experience, but also challenges our understanding of the evolution of sexual and gendered narratives up to the present. *Decoding Anne Lister* includes interviews and essays on Lister's queer sexuality and gender variance, her role as a diarist, her pushing of gender barriers through her involvement in local politics and in the managing of her Shibden Hall estate, her adventurous and at times gender-defying travels through Britain, Europe and the Russian

Caucasus, and the highly successful adaptation of the Lister diaries into the BBC/HBO series *Gentleman Jack*. Revealing not only the life of an exceptional woman but also the local and global world in which she lived, the Lister diaries reconfigure the more traditional trajectories of nineteenth-century histories of gender and sexuality, and of social and political life.

Lister was keeping her diary at a time of extreme political, social and economic transformation and upheaval. Key events included the Napoleonic wars (1803–15), the expansion of the British empire, the Industrial Revolution (1760–1840), the Peterloo Massacre (1819) and the 1832 Reform Act, several of which are commented on in the diaries.[7] Within this public history, Lister navigated and challenged the codes, rules and norms of genteel society while also being very much of her time, participating in class and institutional privilege, wanting to advance her own social connections and seeking the advantages afforded her by her landowner status once she inherited Shibden Hall in 1836.[8] As much as they defy sexual and gender norms, the diaries also document a need and desire for social and political belonging, foregrounding a tension that is itself a constitutive part of queer, lesbian and gender nonconforming archival histories.

The bound volumes of the diaries begin in 1816, towards the end of Jane Austen's life and at the start of Charlotte Brontë's, and Lister herself made occasional references to having literary aspirations.[9] However, in contrast to published literary works of the period, Lister's private diaries have provided frank and explicit observations on romantic and sexual queer intimacies, gender nonconformity, social belonging and exclusion, and invaluable social commentary on class and local politics. Lister's status as a woman of privilege who was simultaneously operating outside the normative codes of her class provides a unique insight into the norms of nineteenth-century society as well as how those norms could be contested. The diaries help us to understand how, among the many transformative effects of the Industrial Revolution, the radical separation of the private and public spheres within an increasingly influential and economically powerful bourgeois class contributed to create a space for a queer figure such as Anne Lister. As Sharon Marcus has shown, the separation of the gendered spheres meant that, rather than being a thing apart, female intimacy was encouraged and supported. Both married and unmarried women were free to develop romantic female friendships, with the underlying assumption that homosociality would never slide into homosexuality. Marcus argues that these relationships were intricately woven into nineteenth-century society, so that 'female friendships peaceably coexisted with heterosexual marriages and moreover, helped to promote them'.[10] This active encouraging of female friendship left the field relatively open for those women who chose to cross the unspoken boundary between sentimental friendship and sexual intimacy, Lister and her lovers being among them.

In her diaries, Lister becomes a key liminal figure who exposes the boundary crossings of her society. For if Lister was herself exceptional in terms of her gender nonconformity and her refusal of the codes of femininity, her many lovers were less so. How, in this homosocial world of separate spheres, did Lister manage to seduce so many women who did not question their gender identity or sexuality to the same extent as she did? Lister's tales of seduction would suggest that the boundary between the homosocial and the homosexual in bourgeois and aristocratic Britain was fluid in ways that were tacitly acknowledged if never explicitly stated. If this is the case, Marcus's analysis suggests that this fluidity actively created a space for Lister rather than positioning her as an entirely exceptional subject.

Lister does belong to a larger group of pre-sexological nineteenth-century gender-nonconforming women who formed intimate sexual relationships with one another, among them the Ladies of Llangollen, Anne Damer, Emily Faithfull, the Michael Fields, Minnie Benson, Ethel Smyth and Frances Power Cobbe.[11] Yet the Lister diaries engage with questions of sexuality, sexual pleasure and gender nonconformity in a unique manner. Broadly speaking, historical scholarship dealing with desire between women has had to develop ways of understanding this desire outside of empirical modes of representation. Lanser has argued that there was a dissonance between the relatively few known examples of female same-sex eroticism prior to the twentieth century and 'the larger space and excessive language accorded it in print'.[12] She shows how the Sapphic circulated as a discourse denoting subversion and threat in inverse proportion to its embodied reality. Other scholars have argued that because of their elusive quality, sexual relationships between women cannot be 'revealed' through historical proof, but rather approached through what Judith Bennett has called their 'definitional uncertainty' and explored in terms of the 'not said' and the 'not seen'.[13]

In contrast, in terms of sexuality the Lister diaries stand out as remarkably explicit, self-aware and hyper-visible.[14] Although Lister used her 'crypt hand' to record her intimate relationships and sexual experiences, she described sex with anatomical precision. Here, for example, is Lister's account of having an orgasm with Mrs Barlow in Paris in 1824: 'I had kissed & pressed Mrs Barlow on my knee till I had had a complete fit of passion. My knees & thighs shook, my breathing & everything told her what was the matter.'[15] Lister's ongoing fascination with anatomy and the workings of the human body as well as her eclectic reading practices appear to have given her the psychological and intellectual confidence to name and describe her sexual practices and experiences in ways that would have been unthinkable for most women of her era. In Ann Walker's newly discovered diary from 1834 to 1835, comparisons can be made between Walker's and Lister's same-day entries to show that Walker never discussed sex in the way Lister did.[16] As we have seen, this explicitness led to the diaries being repeatedly returned to the closet, and upon publication of the first extracts in 1988, rumours circulated that the Lister diaries must be a hoax.[17]

Ground-breaking as the Lister diaries have been, their openness has complicated how we think about queer/lesbian and gender nonconforming histories, in that they have established a standard of 'proof' that is yet to be found in other comparable archives. The status of Lister's gender variance, alongside her unwavering erotic interest in women, has also helped to shape Lister scholarship. Jack Halberstam's identification of Lister as an example of 'female masculinity'[18] finds ample evidence in the diaries. From her early decision in 1817 'always to wear black',[19] to having 'drawers put on with gentlemen's braces'[20] and to arranging her hair 'curled . . . like the crest of a helmet at the top of [her] head',[21] Lister repeatedly defied the dress codes of traditional femininity. She also occasionally fantasised about having a penis, as in an entry from 7 May 1821, 'Supposing myself in men's clothes & having a penis.'[22] She engaged in traditionally masculine interests, such as opening her own coal pit and having a sophisticated knowledge of pistols, which she did not hesitate to use when needed. Lister was also quite often mistaken for a man, both at home – 'The people generally remark, as I pass along, how much I am like a man'[23] – and, on one occasion, three times in one day as she travelled through Strasbourg.[24] She understood herself as having 'manners like those of a gentleman'[25] and would often explicitly perform masculinity in the way she held her cane or twirled her watch. These performative gestures and identifications with masculinity extended to her seduction practices, where she often consciously adopted the role of husband, as with Eliza Raine and Mariana Belcombe, and she also tended to fall for conventionally attractive, feminine women.

Lister's self-presentation in the diaries can therefore be framed in terms very similar to the behaviours of the eighteenth-century female husband, whom Jen Manion describes as having an 'ability to flirt, charm, and attract female wives' and whose gender embodiment demonstrated that 'gender was malleable and not a result of one's sex'.[26] Lister's explicit descriptions of sexual desire and sexual practices also fit into Ula Klein's analysis of representations of female cross-dressers as able to teach 'readers how to recognize the realistic, pleasurable, and serious possibility of female same-sex desires that are not apparitional but, rather, tangible, visible, and embodied'.[27] To this extent, Lister's performative and embodied expressions of masculinity correspond to the cross-dressing or trans model more closely than to the elusive or apparitional 'lesbian' one.

At the same time, while certain of Lister's lovers or women she was interested in claimed to wish she were a man, often so that they could share a more public life with her – Miss Browne, a potential love interest, tells Lister in February 1819 that 'she could not help thinking she wished I had been a gent'[28] – Lister herself resisted a full identification with masculinity. Her occasional 'wish to be a gent'[29] seems to have coincided with her desire to be freer to seduce her female lovers, rather than to inhabit a masculine identity in any permanent way. For example, her Parisian lover, Mrs Barlow, tells Lister: 'It would have been better had you been brought up as your father's son,' to which Lister firmly replies: 'No, you mistake me. It would not have done at all. I could not have married & should have been shut out from ladies' society. I could not have been with you as I am.'[30] In this key exchange, Mrs Barlow's wish that Lister had been brought up as her 'father's son' is repudiated. It seems rather that Lister sought the freedom afforded by nineteenth-century homosocial culture to delight in the intimacy of female society where she could be, in her words, 'as I am'. Yet this simple phrase reveals the complexity of Lister's relationship to her gender, one with which scholars continue to grapple and which leaks into our current-day debates on gender identity and sexuality. In a more ambivalent entry from 1830, at the age of thirty-eight, Lister wrote: 'Said I to myself as I came in this evening, alas I am as it were neither man nor woman in society.'[31] Not only does this entry reveal Lister's understanding of gender as a mode of constraint imposed by a set of social conventions, but it also exposes her sometimes melancholic relationship to her gender variance.

Lister consistently refused to envisage heterosexual marriage, even a marriage of convenience, repeatedly claiming that she 'never intended to marry at all'[32] and that any kind of sexual contact with a man aroused in her feelings of revulsion. This placed her at odds with several of her female lovers, especially with Mariana Belcombe – whom Lister described as the love of her life – who married Charles Lawton in 1816, largely because she had no other means of financial support. The question of marriage haunts the diaries and brings with it the ongoing conundrum of Lister's gender identity. Far from being a radical, Lister was a product of her gentried class and wanted a marriage on her own terms, in which she would take on the role of husband married to a wife. Finally claiming a marital-style partnership in 1834 with a neighbour, heiress Ann Walker, Lister achieved a lifelong goal. This is the narrative that has served as the basis of the *Gentleman Jack* TV series, once again connecting past and present, and speaking to our current global struggles over LGBT+ marriage equality.

In the diaries, the governing normative frameworks of gender and sexuality and Lister's subversion of them underwrite every other aspect of her lived experience. Whether Lister was confronting the local coal baron, Mr Rawson, expanding and renovating her Shibden Hall estate, climbing the highest peaks in the Pyrenees or mastering Greek and Latin more competently than her tutors, she refused to be constrained by the imposed limits of femininity, claimed her gender variance and asserted her right to desire whom she pleased, even if this produced moments of shame, humiliation and exclusion. The essays and interviews in this volume show how Lister's fascination with her own 'oddity' and her desire to understand herself were inseparable from her drive and ambition, which in turn paradoxically foreground the opportunities as well as the constraints of her nineteenth-century society.[33]

Increasingly, the Lister diaries are being interpreted as a liminal archive that touches on multiple disciplinary fields, including life writing, travel writing, social history, women's writing and women's history as well as queer, lesbian and gender nonconforming histories of sexuality. *Decoding Anne Lister* is divided into five parts with a foreword by the award-winning Irish Canadian author, Emma Donoghue, who, upon discovering Helena Whitbread's edition of the extracts in 1990, wrote the first play based on the Lister diaries.

By focusing on key aspects of the Lister archive, each section shows how the diaries shed new light on questions of gender, sexuality, identity construction and sociability, and on the social, political and economic frameworks of nineteenth-century society. *Decoding Anne Lister* also examines how this archive from the past intervenes in our present. The opening and closing interviews with Helena Whitbread and Sally Wainwright discuss the emergence of the Lister archive from its near-total obscurity to its status as an iconic prime-time television series. Caroline Gonda's interview with Helena Whitbread engages with the challenges of how to bring an archive such as the Lister diaries to public attention, what obstacles were encountered, and what a transformative role the diaries played, and continue to play, for local histories and for queer and women's histories in general.

Although Lister had ambitions 'in the literary way' and 'a wish for a name in the world',[34] the diaries themselves were a personal, private document, never intended for the mass public readership they have acquired today. Extracts of the coded sections of the diaries finally saw the light of day in 1988, when Virago published *I Know My Own Heart*, edited by Whitbread, at that time a Yorkshire-based independent scholar. Whitbread then published a second volume in 1992, *No Priest but Love*, with extracts covering Lister's time in Paris between 1824 and 1826. Jill Liddington has also published three volumes of extracts from the diaries: *Female Fortune* (1998), with extracts from 1833 to 1836, *Nature's Domain* (2003), with extracts from 1832, and *As Good as a Marriage* (2023), with extracts from 1836–8. These published extracts enabled Sally Wainwright to conceive and develop the *Gentleman Jack* series, a project which, as Wainwright's interview shows, took many years to be funded by the BBC.

Emma Donoghue's interview with Sally Wainwright at the end of our volume reveals the journey the diaries have made since the 1980s. Both Donoghue and Wainwright have had a longstanding interest in the Lister diaries and have contributed to their adaptation for a broader audience. Donoghue's interview with Wainwright focuses on the complicated process of adaptation for television and how to 'stay true to [the diaries'] spirit and texture'. Wainwright also discusses the challenges of navigating the overwhelming richness of the source text to extract the content needed to shape and fashion a queer historical television drama. Alongside the published extracts, Wainwright immersed herself for months in the Lister archive, initially doing her own transcriptions and wanting to understand this exceptional diarist from the source.

In Part I, '"Nature was in an odd freak when she made me": Lister, Sexuality, Gender and Natural History', Laurie Shannon and Anna Clark engage more closely with Lister's understanding of her 'odd' sexuality by unpacking and analysing what kinds of resources were and were not available to help her craft her narrative of the self. While access to the classics and their frank references to same-sex erotic practices offered an invaluable resource for Lister, Shannon argues that Lister's interest in natural history played an equally key role in providing an ethical as well as a scientific framework for her self-understanding as an 'oddity', giving her 'permission' and 'authorisation' to be who she was. Shannon's analysis of Lister reverses the binary between the natural and the unnatural or deviant, arguing that Lister saw herself as 'following natural prescriptions' rather than perceiving herself as a 'freak' of nature. Calling Lister's approach 'queerly traditional', Shannon argues that Lister's understanding of the questions of nature and the natural continues to be relevant in how we understand sexuality today.

Clark's chapter explores Lister's engagement with anatomy and unpacks her desire to grasp the workings of the human body, particularly as it relates to sexuality. While Lister understood the sensations of sexual pleasure in a scientific way, she recorded discovering the clitoris for the first time in 1831. Clark analyses this late discovery by contextualising it within debates about the relative importance or irrelevance of the clitoris in contemporary medical texts and examines Lister's own sources for learning about female anatomy. Clark argues that little work has been done on nineteenth-century understandings of female anatomy and that Lister's studies in France with Georges Cuvier and Geoffrey Saint-Hilaire – recently made available as online diary transcriptions – allow us to compare British and French understandings of female anatomy during this period.

Lister's forays into natural history and anatomy were part and parcel of her thirst for knowledge. That thirst is reflected in her intimate diary writing and in her interest in the power of language more generally. Part II, '"My spirit's oil": Lister Reading, Lister Writing', examines how both Lister's creation of lexicons and her use of the diary form were central to her self-construction and to her knowledge acquisition. Fascinated by words in all their variety, Lister compiled lexicons from different languages that helped her to develop a knowledge base about sexuality. As Stephen Turton argues, by the time Lister turned thirty, 'she had compiled her own private glossary of erotic and anatomical terms as a means of making sense of her sexuality'. Lister's 'imaginative use' of dictionaries and her compilation of lexicons provide us with further insights into her use of language, and her idiosyncratic adaptation of certain terms shows how she challenged the linguistic norms of her day. Turton shows how Lister's close attention to lexicography formed a crucial part of her self-understanding and enabled her to expand linguistic possibilities in terms of non-normative approaches to gender and sexuality.

Lister's diary writing, in turn, was as much a map of the social world as a form of personal record keeping. She meticulously recorded others' comments about her, for example how acquaintances found her 'deep-toned voice ... very singular'[35] and how she was seen as a bluestocking. She would also on occasion turn the conversation to '[her] own oddities'[36] to gauge how her friends and acquaintances reacted. Lister's diary also formed her most intimate relationship, the place where she could unburden herself, analyse her feelings and share her private thoughts, as well as comment on politics, her various business practices, her travels and other more pragmatic concerns. Lister repeatedly recorded how the act of writing had a therapeutic effect, making her feel calmer after a crisis: 'It is always a relief to me to write down what I feel & after I have done, I am, as it were, satisfied.'[37] Because of her status as a gender and sexual outlier, diary writing for Lister was less a genteel occupation than a necessary way of caring for the self. She needed her diary as a survival tool that enabled an ongoing and indispensable dialogue between her public and private identities: 'I owe a good deal to this journal. By unburdening my mind on paper I feel, as it were, in some degree to get rid of it; it seems made over to a friend that hears it patiently, keeps it faithfully, and by never forgetting anything, is always ready to compare the past & present & thus to cheer & edify the future.'[38]

Caroline Baylis-Green examines the discursive strategies in Lister's diary writing and how Lister negotiated the relationship between her crypt hand and her plain hand. Challenging the 'lesbian continuum' model that certain scholars have applied to Lister, Baylis-Green approaches Lister's crypt hand from a different perspective, arguing that the diaries reveal a relationship between coding and closeting. She argues that the diaries' coded sections 'subvert assumptions about disclosure and latency', allowing Lister to explore the liminal space between her crypt hand and her plain hand, what Baylis-Green calls 'the edge of her own closet/s'. Paradoxically, the coded sections of the diaries ultimately function as the most open and transparent ones in their ability to discuss sexuality frankly, whereas the uncoded sections follow a more public script and participate in a depersonalised 'public closet'.

Lister's private self-construction as a diarist was also inextricably meshed with her very visible and public persona. In Part III, '"Born at Halifax": Lister's Politics, Local and Global', Lister is considered in terms of her public role and her relationship to political discourse. Susan S. Lanser, Cassandra Ulph and Angela Clare each explore Lister's engagement with the public sphere, revealing a figure who refused to be defined by the constraints of domestic femininity, even if her visibility led to occasional incidents of harassment and public humiliation. Lanser's contribution broadens the question of Lister's politics in terms of Tory party affiliation and considers how she reacted to the great political events and upheavals of her day. Lanser asks what Lister most cared about and how she responded to her era's 'national and global tumult', as well as to notions of Englishness in the context of both her public and private identities. Specifically, Lanser analyses how Lister's Protestantism, conservatism and more general 'quest for status' might be interpreted as a 'constitutive' element of her sexual self-fashioning.

Cassandra Ulph, in turn, explores Lister's more local 'engagement in associational activity', as a way of understanding 'women's participation in civic and intellectual life' during the early nineteenth century. Ulph argues that Lister's gender nonconformity and her position as proprietor of Shibden Hall gave her an exceptional status within her Halifax community, enabling her to 'deploy traditionally patriarchal forms of power' in promoting particular civic projects, such as the 'Lit and Phil' society. Ulph suggests that rather than turning her into a social outlier, Lister's unusual status provided her with an influence that was itself exceptional for a woman of her class during this period.

In the final chapter in this section, Angela Clare, the Collections Manager for Calderdale Museum Service, focuses on Lister in the context of local belonging and the evolving significance of the Shibden Hall estate. Clare analyses how Shibden Hall connects past and present, from its initial status as a heritage 'hidden gem' to its current place as a 'literary house' equivalent to the Brontës' Parsonage at Haworth. Clare shows how this new designation reflects Lister's own deep investment in Shibden Hall and how Shibden cannot be understood as a heritage site without an understanding of the imprint Lister left on it. The increased visibility of the Anne Lister diaries and the *Gentleman Jack* series, in turn, has played a critical role in how Shibden Hall is now being contextualised and interpreted.

Lister's intellectual and physical restlessness pushed her to expand her horizons well beyond her Yorkshire community. Refusing the limits generally placed on women during this period, she became an avid traveller from early on. Part IV, '"Curious scenes": Lister's Travels', examines Lister's crossing of geographical boundaries, which in certain contexts can be mapped on to her crossing of gender boundaries, in that she went on journeys no other European women had previously attempted. Between 1826 and 1832, Lister spent only a few weeks in Shibden Hall, repeatedly returning to the continent on tours that included France, northern Italy, Switzerland, Belgium, Germany, Denmark, the Netherlands and the Pyrenees. Prior to these, she also visited Scotland and Wales, with a particularly evocative visit in 1822 to Eleanor Butler and Miss Ponsonby, known as the Ladies of Llangollen, a renowned female couple who had escaped their Irish families in 1780 in order to live together in Llangollen, North Wales, and who had achieved a certain notoriety, captured in a sonnet by Wordsworth. A generation older than Lister, they served as role models in her diaries, representing the kind of long-term companionship she dreamed of achieving.

However, over her lifetime Lister did not limit herself to the conventional European tour. As an accomplished hiker and mountaineer, she climbed some of the highest peaks in the Pyrenees: among them, in August 1830, Mont Perdu or Monte Perdido (3,335 m) – the Pyrenees' third highest peak on the French–Spanish border. She also made the first 'official' ascent of the Vignemale (3,298 m), the highest peak of the French Pyrenees, noting in her journal in August 1838: 'I have made each ascent for my pleasure, not for éclat. What is éclat to me? What is éclat to anyone?'[39] In tribute to her achievement, a section of the route was named the Col Lady Lister.

Lister's most adventurous trip, however, began in 1839 with her 'wife', Ann Walker. Setting off from Shibden in June with Walker and two servants, the group travelled through France, Denmark and Sweden into Russia, arriving in Saint Petersburg in September and then reaching Moscow in October 1839. From there they travelled south along the frozen Volga river to the Russian Caucasus. Very few Western European travellers had ventured as far into this remote landscape and it was virtually unheard of for any Western European women to make such a journey. Not only was the expedition physically challenging, but because of unrest among the local population against the Tsarist regime, at times they needed a military escort. While Lister often recorded in her diaries visits to 'oddities' that included the display of giants and 'Esquimaux', here she and her party became the objects on display: 'The people coming in to look at us as if we were some strange animals such as they had not seen the like before.'[40] It was during the last leg of this journey to western Georgia in 1840 that Lister died of a fever near Kutaisi. Walker was faced with the task of returning her body to Shibden Hall. Until recently, it was assumed that Walker accompanied the coffin home over the course of six months, but newly discovered documents show that she in fact returned earlier on a different ship.[41]

Kirsty McHugh and Angela Steidele examine Lister's travels through Great Britain and the Russian Caucasus respectively and consider the ways in which these parts of the diaries contribute both to travel writing and to the genre of autobiography. McHugh argues that we need to analyse the

Lister diaries more closely as life writing and travel writing. She shows how Lister's home tours in the 1820s have contributed to recovering female travel writing during this era, both for the study of tourism and in terms of female sociability – specifically Lister's visits to the Ladies of Llangollen and to the Scottish aristocrat Sibbella Maclean. By reading Lister through her travels and her interactions with place, we can achieve a deeper understanding of her complex relationship to class, sexuality and gender outside her local Yorkshire communities.

Steidele follows Anne Lister and Ann Walker's footsteps on their final journey from Saint Petersburg along the Volga to the Caucasus and to the scene of Lister's death in Kutaisi. Noting the ways in which the Russian landscape has been transformed since the early nineteenth century, Steidele travels through space in order to travel back in time and to reflect on the genre of autobiography. She asks what it means to use geography in order to understand history. She also contemplates Lister's own role as autobiographer, particularly through her travel diaries, which broke new ground in terms of how far these two British women were able to get off the beaten track. McHugh and Steidele consider not only the ways in which travel expanded Lister's self-understanding, but also how these journeys add a new critical dimension to our comprehension of the possibilities of travel for women during this period.

The Lister archive is evolving on an almost daily basis as more transcriptions are completed and shared. This, in turn, is a direct result of the diaries' expansion beyond the realm of academia into that of popular culture, fandom and crowdsourcing. Notoriously impenetrable on account of Lister's unreadable handwriting and the sections in 'crypt hand', the full archive is now becoming available online through a volunteer Digitisation and Transcription Project run by the Calderdale Museum and West Yorkshire Archive Service (WYAS) and funded by a generous donation from Sally Wainwright's Wellcome Trust Screenwriters Fellowship. Lister herself refused to be contained within boundaries – intellectual, physical or sexual – and it is fitting that her archive is no longer confined to a handful of academics. In its boundary crossing and democratisation, the Lister archive and its unfolding narrative can also be read as a queering of traditional modes of knowledge acquisition and dissemination.

In Part V:, '"I beg to be remembered": Lister, Public History and Popular Culture', the volume's final section considers the effects and repercussions of the Lister diaries' shift beyond academia into mainstream culture and the ways in which such a transition creates new possibilities, unforeseen challenges, and unexpected and enriching dialogues that demand a rethinking of our own categories of gender and sexuality as well as those from the past. Caroline Gonda considers the ways in which Lister eludes modern-day attempts to classify her gender identity, a phenomenon particularly evident in the controversy over the plaque at Holy Trinity Church to celebrate the Lister–Walker union. The plaque initially labelled Lister as 'gender nonconforming', a description later replaced with the term 'lesbian'. Despite Lister's insistence on her own exceptionalism, Gonda explores how she sought role models, such as the Ladies of Llangollen, that were distinct from her narratives of seduction and closer to notions of female community. Like Shannon and Clark, Gonda argues that Lister's understanding of 'the naturalness of her desire for women' was key to how she inhabited her gender and sexual identities in ways that continue to resonate in a contemporary setting.

In the final chapter, Chris Roulston considers Lister's contemporaneity in terms of how the Lister diaries have entered popular culture through the BBC/HBO series *Gentleman Jack*. She analyses how the adaptation of the Lister diaries into a television series has produced a particular culture of fandom that has made viewers rethink their present in terms of a new relation to the past. She argues that Wainwright's refashioning of the Lister diaries for today's television audience has in fact led us back to the 'phenomenon' that Lister was in her own time and to a new understanding of the importance of Lister for today.

The chapters solicited for this collection showcase the ways in which the Lister archive complicates, disrupts and unsettles our expectations and our understanding of the sexual, gendered, social and political frameworks of early nineteenth-century Britain, as well as how this disruption creates new possibilities for the present. Extending in approach from in-depth analyses of the diaries' contents to their broader historical and contemporary influence, the contributors to this volume are expanding the scope and reach of Anne Lister Studies. Once the Lister diaries have been opened, they are difficult to put down, inspiring affective as well as intellectual engagement. We hope that this collection will reflect the dedication, enthusiasm, thrill and sheer surprise the diaries repeatedly manage to generate in their readers.

Notes

1 See J. Liddington, 'Anne Lister of Shibden Hall, Halifax (1791–1840): Her Diaries and the Historians', *History Workshop* 35 (Spring 1993), 45–77, for a comprehensive account of the history of the diaries.

2 See ibid., 57.
3 S. S. Lanser, *The Sexuality of History: Modernity and the Sapphic, 1565–1830* (Chicago: University of Chicago Press, 2014), p. 2.
4 Ibid., p. 15.
5 M. Vicinus, 'Lesbian History: All Theory and No Facts or All Facts and No Theory?', *Radical History Review* 60 (1994), 57–75, 66.
6 See 'Anne Lister: Reworded York Plaque for "first lesbian"', BBC News, 28 February 2019, www.bbc.com/news/uk-england-york-north-yorkshire-47404525, accessed 15 November 2021.
7 For an analysis of Lister's engagement with her historical period, see Lanser, this volume.
8 Anne Lister inherited a third of Shibden Hall in 1826, when her uncle James died. She inherited the rest of the estate in 1836, upon the death of her father, Jeremy Lister, and her aunt, Anne Lister. For an account of the history of Shibden Hall, see Clare, this volume.
9 See H. Whitbread (ed.), *The Secret Diaries of Miss Anne Lister* [hereafter *Secret Diaries*] (London: Virago, 2010), p. 96.
10 S. Marcus, *Between Women: Friendship, Desire, and Marriage in Victorian England* (Princeton: Princeton University Press, 2007), p. 2.
11 See ibid., p. 20.
12 Lanser, *Sexuality of History*, p. 4.
13 Vicinus, 'Lesbian History', 58.
14 J. Bennett, 'The L-Word in Women's History', unpublished papers (October 1990 and September 1993), quoted in Vicinus, 'Lesbian History', 57.
15 11 November 1824, H. Whitbread (ed.), *No Priest but Love: the Journals of Anne Lister from 1824–1826* (Otley: Smith Settle, 1992), p. 47.
16 See Baylis-Green, this volume, for a discussion of this comparison.
17 See A. M. Jagose, *Inconsequence: Lesbian Representation and the Logic of Sexual Sequence* (Ithaca: Cornell University Press, 2018), p. 14.
18 J. Halberstam, *Female Masculinity* (Durham, NC: Duke University Press, 1998).
19 1 June 1817, *Secret Diaries*, p. 18.
20 2 April 1817, *Secret Diaries*, p. 9.
21 17 September 1818, *Secret Diaries*, p. 76.
22 7 May 1821, *Secret Diaries*, p. 167.
23 28 June 1818, *Secret Diaries*, p. 60.
24 Lister records this on 22 June 1827. See A. Choma, *Gentleman Jack: the Real Anne Lister* (London: Penguin, 2019), p. 3.
25 29 November 1816, *Secret Diaries*, p. 6.
26 J. Manion, *Female Husbands: a Trans History* (Cambridge: Cambridge University Press, 2020), p. 1.
27 U. Klein, *Sapphic Crossings: Cross-Dressing Women in Eighteenth-Century British Culture* (Charlottesville: University of Virginia Press, 2021), p. 2.
28 18 February 1819, *Secret Diaries*, p. 92.
29 18 February 1819, *Secret Diaries*, p. 94.

30 25 October 1824, in Whitbread, *No Priest but Love*, p. 36.
31 26 January 1830, Anne Lister Papers, West Yorkshire Archive Service (WYAS), SH:7/ML/E/12/0153-0154.
32 28 May 1817, *Secret Diaries*, p. 17.
33 On 19 June 1824, Lister writes: 'Speaking of my oddity, Mrs Priestley … thought nature was in an odd freak when she made me', in *Secret Diaries*, p. 374.
34 3 March 1819, *Secret Diaries*, p. 96.
35 22 March 1820, *Secret Diaries*, p. 134.
36 2 July 1821, *Secret Diaries*, p. 172.
37 1 October 1819, *Secret Diaries*, p. 116.
38 22 June 1821, *Secret Diaries*, p. 171.
39 A. Pryce, 'Anne Lister: the Mountaineer', 'Packed with Potential' website, 20 December 2020, https://storymaps.arcgis.com/stories/3428e82114dd43fe810e814c09610f7e, accessed 3 April 2022.
40 24 February 1840, quoted in A. Steidele, *Gentleman Jack: a Biography of Anne Lister*, trans. K. Derbyshire (London: Serpent's Tail, 2019), p. 273.
41 See S. Crabtree's article on the 'Packed with Potential' website, *In Search of Ann Walker*, for details of Ann Walker's journey back to England from Kutaisi. The available documentation shows that Walker travelled home on a separate ship from the one containing Lister's body: https://insearchofannwalker.com/research-ann-walkers-return-to-shibden/, accessed 3 March 2022.

CHAPTER 1

Caroline Gonda in Conversation with Helena Whitbread

An interview with Helena Whitbread, the first editor of selections from the Anne Lister diaries.

CAROLINE GONDA Your work has been vitally important for decades now to those of us who study Anne Lister – historians of sexuality and gender, literary scholars and others. What took you to the archives in search of her?

HELENA WHITBREAD In 1976, at the age of forty-five, I decided to pick up my neglected education and enroll on a three-year degree course in politics, literature and the history of ideas at Bradford University. Following on from that, I thought I would like to write short articles with a view to publication in magazines, etc. Casting around for a subject, I remembered that Shibden Hall in my home town of Halifax had once housed a woman called Anne Lister, and one afternoon in 1983 I went to the Calderdale archives department to make inquiries about any material about her that might be lodged there.

CG What did you know about her already, and what did you expect to find?

HW I actually knew nothing at all about her, apart from a vague memory of an article in the local *Halifax Courier* many years ago which referred to John Lister, the last resident of Shibden Hall, having mentioned that her letters were still extant and were housed in the archives. So a bundle of her letters is what I expected to find on my first visit there.

CG What surprised you most?

HW Initially, on that first afternoon, the fact that she kept a journal was my first surprise. The archivist had shown me some of the letters – and to my dismay, I saw that many of them were crossed, giving a trellis-like pattern which looked exceedingly difficult to transcribe. When I expressed my doubts about this, he asked me if I knew that she had kept a journal. Of course, I didn't. He produced some of her journal pages on the reader-printer screen and my second surprise that day was to find that much of it was in a secret code. Fortunately, there was also a key to the code, so that afternoon I photocopied the key and the first fifty pages of the journal and took them home with me. I was curious to find out why this woman who had lived in my own home town almost two hundred years ago had felt the need to write sections of her journal in code. My biggest surprise was when the transcribed passages revealed her need for secrecy. Whatever I had speculated might be hidden in the crypt-hand sections, the fact that she was a lesbian had never occurred to me.

CG What was your process for working with the journals? How easy did you find them to transcribe?

HW It has to be remembered that in the 1970s the Computer Age was in its fledgling state of development, and in 1983 I certainly was not computer literate. In fact, it was Anne Choma who taught me to use a computer in the early 1990s. So, my initial process for working with the journals was very much a pen-and-paper system. Anne Lister used two strategies for recording her life on paper: plain hand, in which she wrote about her everyday life, and what she called her 'crypt hand' – the esoteric code she used to depict mainly her emotional and sexual life with women. Both types of writing threw up many textual difficulties. The plain hand was not easy to read, mainly due to Anne's cramped handwriting and her use of abbreviations for almost every other word – but with usage, one could read it on the page. The coded extracts needed a different technique. The lines of symbols give no indication whatsoever of any punctuation and, to add to the obfuscation which Anne obviously intended, there is no space between individual words. When every symbol in each extract had been decoded, symbol for letter, the transcriber is then left with long, unpunctuated lines of letters of the alphabet. It has to be the decision of the decoder to impose a structure on the sequence of letters – to define where words begin and end. Only then can a sense of what could be found in the crypt hand emerge. The next step is to form coherent sentences from the words until the full meaning of the coded passage emerges. With practice, it eventually became easier to read the un-transcribed crypt-hand passages than those in plain hand.

CG How early in the process of transcribing the journals and decoding Lister's crypt hand did you realise what you were dealing with? What was your reaction to that moment of realisation?

HW When I first saw the journal pages in the archives, I was under the impression that they began early in March 1817. The transcriptions of the early sections of crypt hand at this point in her life were certainly indicating Anne's keen interest in what was going on in the married life of Mariana and Charles Lawton – but there was little indication of any sexual tie between Anne and Mariana. It appeared she was bemoaning the loss of her best friend to a marriage which took her away from York. Had I had the 1816 journal (which was actually appended at the end of the whole body of the journals – after 1840), I would have discovered her lesbianism much sooner. As it was, I think the first indication I had, in her 1817 journal, was the fact of her cross-dressing, i.e. '*Began this morning to sit, before breakfast, in my drawers put on with gentleman's braces I bought for 2/6 on 27 March 1809 & my old black waistcoat & dressing gown.*' [Journal entry 2 April 1817] My reaction to that entry was, first of all, to go back and reread it – wondering if I had got the true sense of what she was doing with such a strange assembly of clothing! I think this was the clue to why she needed the necessity of the crypt-hand passages. Once the realisation of what I was dealing with truly sank in, although I will not pirate Tony Blair's 'I felt the hand of history on my shoulder', what I can say is I became conscious that Clio, the muse of history, must have joined me on that first visit to the archives and ordained that everything that followed was possible.

CG What was the point where you knew this needed to be a book?

HW My first reading through the first batch of fifty pages which I took home from that initial visit to the archives in 1983 dispelled any idea that a short article would ever do justice to Anne's enthralling life. As I worked through the pages and transcribed the crypt-hand passages, I soon formed the idea that a book was the necessary vehicle to convey an idea of the riches contained in her journals.

CG How easy was it to find a publisher for this material?

HW Amazingly easy! I looked through the *Writers' and Artists' Yearbook* in the library and decided that Virago was the obvious publisher for this amazing story of a nineteenth-century lesbian writing in a secret code about her love affairs. I sent them a short proposal and, I believe, a couple of chapters, and I got an almost immediate answer of acceptance. When I look back, I wonder why I never thought to find myself an agent!

CG How did Virago shape the book? What did they want from it?

HW On my submission of the completed manuscript, I was informed by my Virago editor that the word count was too high and she wanted me to go through it and make a good many deletions to trim it down. I demurred, and proposed instead to lift out a large section of the MS – all of which pertained to Anne Lister's stay in Paris. I knew that this could then form the basis for a second book – which it has done, i.e. *No Priest but Love*. Although at the time (1988), Virago declined to publish this second volume, it was published by Smith Settle in 1992 and eventually by Virago in 2020.

CG What was the response to that first volume, *I Know My Own Heart*, and was it what you expected?

HW I have to admit that I felt some trepidation when *I Know My Own Heart* was published. I had thought that there would be an outraged response locally, in my home town (and Anne Lister's) of Halifax. The Listers had been a well-respected family ever since they inherited Shibden in the 1400s and here was I, disclosing the best-kept secret in the town! However, there was very little local notice taken apart from the Halifax Antiquarian Society members and other readers of local history. In terms of media attention and in the world of academe, the book attracted a great deal of attention – but sales were modest. The first print run of five thousand copies took a while to sell and for the next three decades, until the *Gentleman Jack* series appeared in America, the book was well under the radar so far as sales went. Virago is to be commended for keeping it in print!

CG The emphasis of your work in the two volumes of *Secret Diaries – I Know My Own Heart* and *No Priest but Love* – falls more on Anne Lister's personal relationships with other women than on the economic and political aspects of her life. With such a mass of material to choose from, how did you decide on the focus and narrative shape for your selections from the diaries?

HW Obviously, faced with such a mass of material (five million words!), I knew that difficult choices had to be made. During those first five years (1983–8) of reading and transcribing, I was living in Anne Lister's Halifax of two hundred years ago – and it was enthralling! I was born and brought up in Halifax and I had walked the streets which she had walked before me. It is almost impossible to describe the thrill and the sense of wonder I felt as modern Halifax dissolved for me and Anne Lister's Halifax took over my life. The temptation to make the book as much about the town itself was almost overwhelming – but when the love stories emerged from the transcriptions of the crypt hand, the dilemma became acute. I then reasoned that, given the proliferation of articles, books and societies (such as the Halifax Antiquarian Society), there were many available resources to be had for the history of the town – but who knew about the intimacies and affairs of Halifax people in the past? Or the fact that a circle of women had formed a small lesbian community, the locus of which was our own Shibden Hall? The detailed accounts of Anne's private life in her crypt hand are riveting. All her angst over Mariana Belcombe's marriage to Charles Lawton is depicted in heartbreaking detail. She analysed her disenchantment in true Romantic fashion. Her sardonic appraisals, also in crypt hand, of the social scene in the small, provincial town of Halifax tucked away in the Pennine hills are hilarious. So, for me, it was this whole encapsulation of thwarted lesbian love and Anne's sardonic appraisals of the Halifax social world of the day contained in what I called 'the Halifax narrative' which I wished to work on and present to my readers.

CG I imagine those questions of focus and narrative shape are even more pressing when it comes to writing a biography of Anne Lister, as you have done. What has that process of writing Lister's biography been like, and what have you found most rewarding and most challenging about it?

HW The process of writing a biography of Anne Lister has been (and is) absorbing, enthralling, exhausting, tiring, exasperating and compelling. I have to say that picking out the tiny factual details in the journals and letters sometimes makes me feel as if I am engaged in the literary equivalent of single-handedly stitching the Bayeux tapestry!!

In my first two books I had worked more or less solely from the journals. That, of course, was too limiting for the necessary expansion which a full biography demanded. The first challenge, therefore, of writing the biography lay in that there was an extensive back-story to be told prior to Anne's life before her journals began, and this involved years of visiting the Calderdale Archives department – sitting for many hours reading documents and taking notes from them which the ever-willing and wonderful staff members produced for me on request. This was a far different cry from sitting at home with the pages of the journals decoding the crypt-hand passages and weaving the story by selecting relevant passages. In addition, the background reading has been immense – as my bookshelves and the footnotes in the biography will testify!

I began the story then with a prologue which covered the history of the Lister family and the involvement of Jeremy Lister (Anne's father) in the American War of Independence in the 1770s. From then on, chronologically, Anne's life unfolds from the day of her birth on 3 April 1791 to the day she inherits Shibden Hall in 1826.

CG I'm intrigued by Lister's statement that she has had thoughts of being a published author, perhaps under the name Constant Durer. Do you think she saw the diaries as in any way a preparation for that – either as raw material, or as a kind of regular writing practice?

HW It is true that Anne longed to become a published author and at various intervals, she confided her literary ambitions to her aunt: 'Spent all the evening talking to my aunt . . . *Talked of my ambition in the literary way, of my wish for a name in the world, all of which she will second. She really is very good & is surely fond & proud of me.*' [Journal entry 3 March 1819] But she was also very wary of drawing unseemly attention to herself. '*I would do many things if I could but at present I must be as careful as I can & study only to improve myself in the hope of a possibility of making something by writing.*' [Journal entry 30 October 1819] In 1822 she even went so far as to contemplate writing up her love affair with Mariana. '*Thought . . . I would write an account of my acquaintance with M[ariana}, surely, in a series of letters to a friend. Think of calling myself Constant Durer, from the verb, dure, to endure.*' [Journal entry 16 December 1822] So, my conclusion is that Anne's journal constituted both a regular writing practice and a therapeutic exercise in which she could analyse her deepest emotions about her love affairs and her angst about her sexual identity. '*Alas! I am neither man nor woman in society. How shall I manage?*' [Journal entry 26 January 1830.] Her choice of a book based on 'letters to a friend' would have been a much more circumspect publication than the too revelatory content of her journals.

CG Do you read the journals as unmediated outpourings of emotion, or is there a kind of self-consciousness to them even if they're not written to be read by anyone else?

HW I think there is a great deal of self-consciousness in Anne's journal writing. She had a finely honed sense of the dramatic, and the almost forensic examination of her own feelings is at the core of most of the crypt-hand entries. Consider the following entry, especially the last line, when Mariana had broken the news that Charles Lawton had proposed to her and she apparently asked Anne's permission to accept him: '*To sink January 1815 in oblivion! Oh, how it broke the magic of my faith forever. How, spite of love, it burst the spell that bound my very reason. Suppliant at her feet, I loathed consent but loathed the asking more. I would have given the "Yes" she sought tho' it had rent my heart into a hundred thousand shivers* [*sic*]. *It was enough to ask.* It was a coward love that dared not brave the storm &, in desperate despair, my proud, indignant spirit watched it sculk [*sic*] away.' [Journal entry 20 August 1823] Anne is fascinated by her own 'proud, indignant spirit'! She is carried away by the impact of the scene – and the carefully wrought language she uses is in the true Romantic idiom of the day:

'The chivalry of heart was gone. Hopes brightest hues were brushed away. Yet still one melancholy point of union remained. She was unhappy. So was I. Love scorned to leave the ruin desolate; & Time & he have shaded it so sweetly, my heart still lingers in its old abiding place.' [Journal entry 20 August 1823]

To that extent, I feel that her crypt-hand passages, in particular, are mediated to some extent by her desire to present the events almost as an onlooker despite her use of the first person. As one commentator said, 'Anne Lister's journals are a long love-letter to herself.'

CG With all the detail Lister gives about her life in the journals, are there nevertheless aspects of her life that you wish she'd said more about?

HW There is, I feel, a great deal more that could have been said about Anne's mother, Rebecca Lister née Battle; her background, her family connections, her unhappy marriage to Captain Jeremy Lister, her decline into alcoholism and the troubled relationship between her and Anne. Anne's mentions of her mother are brief. In my current biography I address this omission by providing a fuller picture than Anne's journal conveys, but from what can be gleaned, it is obvious that she has no respect for her mother and yet, despite their turbulent relationship, Anne was extremely saddened not to have arrived in time to be at her mother's side when her death occurred. Nine pages, covering the dates 13–21 November 1817 have been cut out of her journal, but a letter sent to her Uncle James at Shibden Hall, Halifax, dated 'Market Weighton, Friday morning 14th Nov. 1817', gives some indication of her feelings: 'Not to have had the satisfaction of seeing my mother ere she closed her eyes forever, has indeed been a shock to me which no language can describe.' The trauma of losing her mother before having the opportunity to make some sort of reconciliation remained with Anne for many years. More than ten years later, her emotions were still running deep on this issue. 'Looking over my journal of November 1817 – *Could not help crying over the account of my poor mother's death.*' [Journal entry 22 September 1828] The relationship with her sister, Marian, is also worth an in-depth analysis – which again can be addressed in the more capacious form of a biography.

CG Reading your work on Anne Lister, and hearing you talk about her, one thing that comes through very strongly is the sense of your affection for her. Has that ever wavered?

HW It is true that I do feel a sense of affection for Anne. She has been a constant companion for forty years of my life. From my first reading of her journal, I almost immediately found myself intrigued with her. I would not say I have ever really wavered in my affection for her – rather that I recognised that, like every human being, she was not without faults, some of them quite glaring, all of which added more ingredients to the complex brew of emotions which reading her journal engenders. Obviously her faults had to be weighed in the balance against the more positive aspects of her character, but the poignancy of her struggles to forge her own identity as a lesbian (although she never used that word in relation to her own sexuality) in an alien, binary world, plus her heartbreak over Mariana's defection into a heterosexual marriage, always touches me.

CG Has your view of her changed much over the years?

HW I can't really say that it has. The first five years of my reading and transcribing Anne's journal from start to finish implanted a strong impression in my mind of this remarkable woman which has never really been dislodged, despite all the scholarly articles, books and media representations which have proliferated over the years. All this additional work by others has been fantastic – and has added greatly to my initial understanding of Anne's character. I have collected every article and book, so far as I know, that has been written about her and been involved in every possible media outlet – radio, TV, film – in addition to giving talks and lectures in the UK and a number of European countries, yet I always return to the original view which those first five years of solitary reading formed.

CG Have there been times when you really disliked Lister?

HW I think the correct term here might be rather that I was 'dismayed' – by some of the less attractive facets of her personality. The crypt-hand entries which relate her sexual affairs frequently depict some reprehensible behaviour towards the women with whom she became involved. Mariana Lawton's marriage changed Anne's attitude towards women. She became more cynical – in one instance, speaking of a young woman, Miss Vallance, who was awaiting the return of her soldier sweetheart: '*I think I could have her in the meantime if I chose*' [Journal entry 28 September 1818] – and, as this indicates, more of a philanderer, as one of her friends, Miss Marsh, described her. When Miss Marsh 'quizzed' Anne about whether or not she had been in a young woman's room the previous night, Anne replied that she had not, '*but said I had been with her for an hour from seven this morning. Miss M[arsh] said it was like me. I was determined not to lose my philandering.*' [Journal entry 12 September 1823] It also has to be acknowledged that, as a member of the upper class, she had many of the less attractive features of her kind in that era. She was undemocratic in her political stance in that she was diametrically opposed to any form of radicalism in either politics or religion. She was unable to appreciate the innate justice of the demands of those who were denied a voice, or deprived of earning a decent living, in their own country. Reading a publication in the *Manchester Observer* by one James Wroe which favoured the reformers and the rights of women, she dubbed it 'a most seditious rousing article . . . what will not these demagogues advance, careless what absurdity or ruin they commit!' [Journal entry 6 December 1819] She was no flag-bearer for the higher education of women, despite her own rigorous programme of study. Indeed, she rather opposed than supported such educational ideals: '*I spoke against a classical education for ladies in general. It did no good if not pursued & if [it was] undrew a curtain better for them not to peep behind.*' [Journal entry 20 September 1824] Her snobbishness was also an unattractive feature and gained her a level of unpopularity in her home town of Halifax. It was obvious that she felt she had to make do with what she saw as an inferior set of people, the middle-class manufacturing families of the town, but, as she found out to her cost, many of them were well aware of her feelings of condescension towards them.

CG Did you ever imagine, when you started this work, that Anne Lister would one day be the subject of so much attention?

HW No, indeed I didn't! I was writing about a local historical figure in an obscure Yorkshire town who was unknown to the world. My ambitions for the future of my books were limited. I had hoped that she would become better known through the agency of those publications and this indeed did happen – as I have indicated above – but only in the world of (mainly lesbian) academics. The attention of the media was soon exhausted and the books dropped below the radar, so to speak, for the next twenty years. But I now understand the perspicacity of the remark made in 1988 by the headmaster of the school I was working at when my first book came out. He said, 'You have lit a slow fuse,' and now, thirty-five years later, thanks to Sally Wainwright's brilliant epic series *Gentleman Jack*, Anne Lister has become a global icon, particularly in the lesbian world. Anne Lister and the town of Halifax are firmly established on the world's cultural map, and her journals are on the United Kingdom Memory of the World Register for documentary heritage of UK significance.

CG What has it been like to go from those early days with fifty microfilmed pages at a time, to the developments of the past few years: the success of Sally Wainwright's *Gentleman Jack*, the commemorative plaques at Holy Trinity in York and at Shibden, the Anne Lister Research Summit, the Anne Lister Society, the transcription project with participants from around the globe, the founding of a college named after Anne Lister at the University of York, the unveiling of a statue of her at the Piece Hall?

HW It has been an astonishing four decades for me – a woman from a working-class background who left school at thirteen with no educational qualifications. As a child, I devoured books; as an adult, I yearned to immerse myself in highbrow literature. I had what Charles Dickens called 'the nagging consciousness of faculties unexercised'. My foray into the Anne Lister journals – which I privately entitle 'Entering the Labyrinth' – has quieted that pervasive sense of unfulfilled need, and I think that title conveys the sense of all that has happened since. This is all on a personal basis, of course. The greater picture lies in the worldwide response from lesbians around the world, and all the developments encapsulated in your summary above. Anne Lister has made the world a kinder and better place for many women, and I am truly grateful and humbled to know that my initial work was the catalyst – in the sense of 'an agent that provokes or speeds significant change or action' – for all that has taken place since. It is, of course, the effect of Sally Wainwright's *Gentleman Jack* which has caused the most significant escalation of interest in Anne Lister's story, and, because the series was based on the later years of Anne's life, I thought that my books, on her earlier years, would continue to exist on a very low-key scale. But people wanted to get back to the source of how all this interest in Anne Lister came about, and very quickly, after the screening of the first episode of *Gentleman Jack*, sales of my books rose considerably, fuelling all that has happened in my life to a dizzying degree!

CG What's been the best thing about your years with Anne Lister, and what are your hopes for the future?

HW In 2016, a young lesbian friend and I published, through Amazon, a small booklet entitled *Secret Diaries Past and Present: a Q&A with Helena Whitbread and Natasha Holme*. I addressed the above question in that book, saying that the first five years (1983–8) must count as the best experience of my involvement with the Anne Lister journals. No one, apart from my family and one or two trusted friends, really knew about what I was doing. I had Anne Lister and her magnificently detailed life all to myself. It was more or less my secret, and I loved the feeling of intimacy and quiet hours of studying the life of this remarkable woman. This never-to-be-recaptured idyll of quiet, scholarly work, untroubled by the demands of the outside world, has now, of course, to be balanced against the experience of the past two years – and how can one deny that the happiness and courage which lesbians around the globe have drawn from Anne's story must count as the best thing that has come from my years in the Labyrinth. Given all the wonderful achievements already in place, which you list above – i.e. the success of Sally Wainwright's *Gentleman Jack*, the commemorative plaques at Holy Trinity in York and at Shibden, the Anne Lister Research Summit, the Anne Lister Society, the transcription project with participants from around the globe, the founding of a college named after Lister at the University of York, the unveiling of a statue of her at the Piece Hall, and including the journals on the United Kingdom Memory of the World Register, part of Unesco's Memory of the World programme – my hopes for the future, on a personal basis, now rest mainly on getting the biography, dealing with Anne's life prior to the period depicted in *Gentleman Jack*, published in book form, so that a more complete account of Anne's life is available to the eager readership which already exists. On a general basis, I would hope that posterity will treat Anne Lister kindly, remembering her as a woman of courage and integrity who defied the world's opinion and remained true to her own mantra: 'I love and only love the fairer sex and thus, beloved by them in turn, my heart revolts from any other love than theirs.' [Journal entry 29 January 1821]

PART I

'Nature was in an odd freak when she made me': Lister, Sexuality, Gender and Natural History

CHAPTER 2

A Regular Oddity: Natural History and Anne Lister's Queer Theory of Tradition

Laurie Shannon

'call me an "oddity" if you please'

Anne Lister (1824)[1]

What might it mean to try to think forward to Anne Lister, instead of looking backwards to find her foreshadowing the present future? For that purpose, this inquiry brackets freighted keywords like 'identity' and even 'subjectivity', lest they retroactively colour her writing too much with preoccupations of our moment. What frameworks does Lister call on to write her own way forward? The ubiquitous phrase dubbing her 'the first modern lesbian' has surprisingly much to recommend it, but its three descriptors raise as many historiographic questions as they resolve.[2] Helena Whitbread precisely captures what *does* seem modern: Lister's articulation of an 'unswerving credo', '*I love & only love the fairer sex.*'[3] This chapter expands our picture of the non-modern idioms on which Lister drew as she forged an authority to live the remarkable way she did. In particular, her unwavering claim that 'Nature' authorised what she called her 'oddity' – itself so striking in the history of ideas – demands a closer account of its premises. If we read Lister predominantly within a metric of transgression or even nonconformity, we may miss the scope of her intellectual project (as well as some of the grounds for her storied confidence). For Lister stakes a claim to core cultural knowledge and textual traditions in order to make venerable ideas about Nature answer to her life. Embracing 'oddity' and composing a lifelong brief in its favour, Anne Lister *articulates a theory.*

Nature offers perhaps the most Protean concept in the history of ideas. Even so, Lister's improvisation made it mean something daringly new. This excavation of her claim on Nature locates it within the tradition of natural history, a durable mode of thought that (from early modernity to Darwin and beyond) mingled classical science and the Christian creation story. Natural history assumed a creator and dwelt more in the details; its close cousin, natural theology, moved in the other direction, proposing to prove God's existence retroactively from the order evident in those details. They share one archive.[4] Since the Renaissance, as the mostly Christian cultures of Europe assimilated ancient material ranging from Pliny's encyclopedic *Historia Naturalis* to Horace's aphorisms into vernacular writing, the related concepts of God and Nature converged. The two terms almost interchangeably named an artist-creator of the world's 'creatures', and classical and Christian origin stories alike emphasised earthly splendour as fit for direct moral contemplation.[5] So configured, this tradition aims not just to explain the variety of lifeforms, but to tarry with it. In natural history's embrace of original diversity, Lister found a mandate for her 'oddity'. It was 'regular' because it followed natural rules of creation.

The opening chapters of Genesis loomed large in the natural-historical archive and not only as theology. Its creaturely procession establishes differentiation itself as natural. Divine fiat grounds a quasilegal existence for the distinct kinds being formed. All are legitimate, in the most technical and absolute sense; this God is not making any mistakes. By virtual decree, all forms of life are enrolled and enfranchised to thrive, each according to their kind – to go their own ways, to persist in being as they were made, and so to spread their metaphorical and literal wings across earth's elemental spaces. The Genesis origin story, then, backs native diversity with the single, strongest warrant available to human thought: a godly mandate for all creatures great and small to continue 'as-built'. In colloquial terms, they are supposed to be themselves.

Anne Lister fully grasped the extraordinary authority that natural-historical discourses and the providential logic of Genesis combined to make available, not simply to justify her 'oddity', but to see a divine hand in it. So much so we can call her theory creationist, keeping in mind this was no flat-earth vision and the evolutionary models modern creationism arose to deny had not yet arrived. By contrast to modern creationism, this non-modern, creatures-and-creator logic endowed every one of the world's creatures with a native patent backed by divinity itself. In conjunction, natural-historical habits of mind favoured the ramifying enumeration of particulars over the clustered groupings of taxonomy.[6] Character approaches the singularity of a fingerprint. We might now associate the capaciousness of natural history (as a habit of thought at the cosmic level) with a tendency to open-ended lists and even a spirit of inclusivity. As we will see, Lister conscripted these perfectly traditional habits of thought to authorise her own, queer form of life; we can call her method *queerly traditional*. Providence provides.

The term 'queer', of course, marks a swerve, a surprise, a puzzle or a break – being akimbo to expectation instead of following an assumed or common path. But we should not yet set 'queer' in opposition to 'normal', because that scientistic term barely appears in print before rising in usage after Lister's death in 1840.[7] The word 'tradition', by contrast, indexes something that abides. It suggests an oppressive weight when marking a constraining tyranny from the past, 'handed down' regardless of the specific person on whom its burden falls. But 'tradition' derives from Latin *tradere* (to hand over, deliver, surrender, transfer or give up some possessory interest), and this fuller resonance suggests a more interesting practical dynamic of authority for so-called traditional transfers. They might be linear, they might even be lineal, but the line need not run straight or in prescribed directions. How did Lister, born to provincial Yorkshire gentry in 1791, engage the textual bedrock of her cultural inheritance? Fostered by her unmarried aunt and uncle in the free and queer domesticity of Shibden Hall above Halifax, and enjoying broad social and intellectual scope in York and Paris, Anne Lister took tradition queerly in hand.

This chapter traces Lister's bold theory that natural history and theology backed her 'oddity'. We have a powerful and growing sense of the role of erotic/obscene Roman writers and Romantic models like Byron and Rousseau in Lister's knowledge repertoire.[8] Scholars have shown she read Roman poetry and its annotated commentaries both forensically and for pleasure; they have also analysed how she deployed literary references in social situations to gauge/engage friends and lovers.[9] To extend our overall mapping of Lister's thought and citational range, this chapter adds natural-historical and theological discourses to the other resources she so keenly mined for sexual and related forms of knowledge. That context, in turn, enables us to take 'oddity' more seriously as the word Lister chose for herself across her decades of writing.

Lister was an erudite, multilingual collector of the vocabularies of sexual knowledge, from ancient poetry to dictionaries to contemporary anatomical sciences.[10] But whether recording exchanges with friends or musing, and across her crypt hand and plain hand alike, to gloss herself Lister chooses 'oddity'. Occasionally she calls herself '*an* oddity' (as in my epigram), but she embraces oddness mostly by the adjective 'odd', or as '*my* oddity', denoting a property she possesses. Indeed, even in crypt hand she tends to avoid nominalisation. In a telling encounter with Frances Pickford (the most similar 'oddity' Lister ever met), however, Lister classifies 'Pick' in just that way, calling her 'a regular oddity'.[11] Two 'regular oddities' will never be 'the same', but Chris Roulston has demonstrated how this encounter challenges Lister's justifying sense of singularity; Pickford's similarity 'threatens to obliterate Lister's own sense of uniqueness'.[12] Lister immediately differentiates herself, noting '*she supposes me like herself how she is mistaken!*'[13] For Lister, 'oddity' encodes irreducible singularity; there is nothing justificatory or confirming in doubles or likeness, let alone in some larger grouping.

By this same logic, for herself, she seems not to have adopted the classifications she assiduously gathered from her wide reading, notably the agentive nouns *tribade* (Gr.) and *fricatrice* (L.), drawn from the verb 'to rub'.[14] If we read her disinclination to adopt such categorical nouns alongside her 1823 transcription of Rousseau on singularity ('*Je ne suis fait comme aucun de ceux que j'ai vus; j'ose croire n'être fait comme aucun de ceux qui existent*' / I am not *made* like any of those I've seen; I dare to believe not *made* like any of those who exist), we can see how Lister's theory of being a singularly 'made' creature is not only non-identitarian, but anti-identitarian in effect.[15] While she does not quote the entire passage, Rousseau's paragraph immediately goes on to pose the question 'whether Nature did well or ill when she threw away the mould that *made* me', directly linking Romantic singularity to the older creationist discourse considered here.[16] What affordances might we moderns have missed by mistaking Lister's choice of 'oddity' for a quaint, vague, euphemistic or merely archaic usage?

As Susan Lanser has argued, 'oddity' along with terms like 'singular' and 'unaccountable' index lesbian/nonconforming behaviour; Caroline Gonda has further emphasised how such 'allusive codes' can expand 'our sense of the patterns and possibilities of lesbian narrative and lesbian history' in the period.[17] In usage, the heyday for 'oddity' runs from 1750 to 1899, neatly bracketing Lister's life.[18] Despite the commonplace that our prolific diarist lacked words for her experience, for Anne Lister 'oddity' answered. Continuing her invitation to Sibbella Maclean to 'call me an "oddity" if you please', Lister underscores it: 'I am odd, very very odd.'[19] 'Oddity' connected Lister's sense of social and sexual singularity with the providential force of a creation story, one that carried the imprimatur of godly backing. Conceptually, it derives from a natural-historical vision of creation that authorises variety and favours particulars; 'oddity' thus serves in a wider logic of ethical self-accounting and also navigates the apparent polarity (for us) between the queer and the traditional. Ultimately my inquiry aims to complicate notions of Lister's 'conservatism' by suggesting the larger traction of her argument: that authorising one's own life – necessarily, paradoxically – entails queer traditionality. Indeed, it seems impossible that the optimistic philosophical tradition compressed in Pope's phrase, 'Whatever IS, is RIGHT', has EVER been put to queerer or more radical purpose.[20]

The Past, On Time

If history arcs, it also loops. The monumental testimony of Lister's journals (from 1806 and continuously from 1817 to 1840) survived as a time-capsule literally immured at Shibden Hall. Their importance remained completely unknown until Helena Whitbread's paradigm-breaking volumes brought them out of the archive and into the world in 1988 and 1992.[21] In life, Lister traced thousands of peripatetic miles to and from Yorkshire, sojourning in European cities, scaling peaks from Ben Nevis and Mount Snowdon to the Pyrenees and the Alps, seeking world enough to match her investment in it. She died in distant reaches of the Russian empire, the farthest from Yorkshire she had ever been. Thanks to Sally Wainwright's drama *Gentleman Jack*, her story has (re)taken this sweeping stage, as Lister comes home again in the twenty-first century.

Even so, the *Gentleman Jack* project had to be pitched some twenty years before its proper 'time' arrived. Wainwright's 'exquisitely scripted show' and Suranne Jones's 'alchemical' performance as a 'force of nature' have given Lister a soundtrack of her own; the *Guardian*'s five-star review called it a disruptive 'masterpiece' that arrived at just the 'time' it was needed and 'one of the greatest British period dramas of our time'.[22] At once timely 'period drama' and 'of our time', the series establishes, for all time, the exclamation mark of Anne's all-black attire, her sustained romantic (but not sexual) disappointment, the tenacity of her hope, her cognitive firepower, her covert emotions of butch sentimentality, her polymorphous authority and her inexhaustible zeal. Suggesting the queer temporalities at stake in the show's many disruptions, Wainwright and her team aimed to represent Lister 'like she was from a different planet, *almost*'.[23]

In this time-twist between now and then, Lister's long occluded writings and emergence as an LGBTQ+ icon inspire contemporary enthusiasts practising their own queer traditionality.[24] New cultural practices have sprung up under Lister's banner, as she vaulted from the small screen into fan art, fiction, swag, blogs, social media groups, GIFs, memes, street art and growing institutional adoption. Within months of the 2019 airing of the show's first season, the West Yorkshire Archive Service launched a diary transcription project, recruiting 150+ international transcribers and earning a national award for volunteer engagement in 2020.[25] In 2021, Wainwright and Jones unveiled a bronze sculpture at the heart of Lister's home town and the University of York established Anne Lister College; town and gown moved beyond mere gestures of inclusion to incorporate LGBTQ+ history in permanent landmarks of our common culture.[26] In 2022, hundreds descended on Halifax for Anne Lister Birthday Week, and the Anne Lister Society's inaugural meeting showcased new research on the diarist.[27] Across this range of registers, Lister has been ardently embraced as a sudden, dazzling ancestor, one her enthusiasts never knew we had lost.

If notions of 'queer heritage' or 'queer tradition' seem paradoxical, they reflect Lister's own method: moving ahead partly by looking back. In Jones's words, Lister has landed, 'cutting through history to 2022'.[28] The world had become ready for a 'lesbian superhero'.[29] But history cuts both ways, and part of the force of Wainwright's writing springs from its care with the historical Lister's signature habits of thought and phrasing, making *Gentleman Jack* singular in the repertoire of television drama: a diary curation of its own.[30] The script incorporates Lister's own words, often in verbatim soliloquy, and the speeches of others she transcribed. Historically accurate, large-format journals appear, like characters, in Wainwright's indelible drama. What if the historical 'oddity' of Lister's 'proud spirit', leaping out from her emerging text, is part of her present power?[31] As bumper stickers proclaim – relaying a diary leitmotif in Lister's own hand, abbreviated style and optimism – '*ver. fine day*'.

The material specifications of Lister's journal are as singular as she was. In two partial volumes and then across twenty-four continuous volumes from a formal *incipit* (21 March 1817) until six weeks before her death in 1840, Lister inked an estimated five million words, roughly a sixth in unspaced, unpunctuated cipher. Pepys's diary is the closest precedent. Traversing the 1660s, it likewise bridges historico-political, household and frankly sexual matters (also using code). It too speaks in the charismatic voice of a particular personality. But at 1.25 million words, Pepys's diary is one-quarter the heft of Lister's. Measuring in European novels, Proust's *À la recherche du temps perdu* measures a tad longer than Pepys (1.26 million words); Richardson's 1748 *Clarissa* is shorter, at just under a million. Lister's journal chalks up to roughly five *Clarissa*s.

These staggering statistics cannot overshadow the even more extraordinary content of a text whose time has come.[32] UNESCO named the diaries a pivotal document in British history in 2011; for the history of sexuality, Emma Donoghue likened Whitbread's publications – without hyperbole – to the discovery of the Dead Sea Scrolls.[33] What this chapter proposes further is that we also understand Anne Lister's 'journal' as an emerging masterpiece of English writing, a monumental text to reckon with in literary, ethical, and intellectual terms as well as documentary and historical ones.[34] For Lister's diaries join the pantheon of self-accountings from the Stoic philosophers to Augustine, Montaigne, Rousseau and beyond. They command our attention as a highly engaged thinker's sustained analysis of the challenges her 'oddity' posed, but also as a spirited showing of why Lister's claim to proper cosmic membership is a rightful one. Choosing the path of greatest resilience – day upon day, year after year – Anne Lister's journal models one way to take life very seriously.

Scholars approaching the journals from whatever discipline (and it will take all of them) must contend with the intellectual confidence Lister summoned where nothing predicts it. Of course, this poses a constitutional, even metabolic question. Lister's anomalous situation, too, as the inheriting female member of a fading provincial line, was enviable. She well understood place has its privileges and eagerly expected her eventual inheritance to give her greater '*éclat*' – indeed, '*éclat enough to pass off my oddity*'.[35] But a journal like hers does not derive from any complacency about place. It stems from a non-modern and broadly theological imperative to grasp one's place. With the mental dedication of an ultramarathoner, Anne Lister took the time to muster a principled authority to live her way. She sometimes passes as libertine or transgressive, industrialist or 'entrepreneurial', stylistically imitative, and sometimes 'archly' conservative in religion or politics. The balance of this chapter, instead, analyses the learned resources of the queerly traditional Anne Lister who exhorted herself to 'never fear, learn to have nerve to protect myself & make the best of all things . . . & then face danger undaunted'; who affirmed simply, on the scrap of paper by which her code was cracked in the 1890s, 'in God is my *hope*'.[36] This Anne Lister gave new life to the storied Horatian line that still overlooks the housebody she renovated at Shibden Hall – *justus propositi tenax* (the just hold true to purpose) – as, of all things, a motto of queer confidence.

The Bias of Nature

To broaden our ethical and literary reckoning of the diaries and unfold Lister's queer traditionality, some precedents from natural history will situate what it means to claim a God-given nature in the nineteenth century's earliest decades. While Lister attended lectures with leading natural historians in late 1820s Paris, even befriending palaeontologist Georges Cuvier, these academic pursuits followed on intellectual ideas she had already framed from her own very wide reading at home in Yorkshire. The tradition of natural history approaches the world in a cornucopian spirit. Beginning with Aristotle, its open-ended encyclopedias collect lore about the world's creatures. The key figure in the historical relay of classical ideas – Pliny the Elder – captures this open attitude, musing, 'the more I observe nature, the less prone I am to consider any statement about her to be impossible'.[37] Pliny's sprawling, first-century classic, the *Historia Naturalis*, held a bursting treasury of not exclusively scientific details. From the sixteenth century, it served as a gateway text for Latin learning and continued to be cited, *pro et contra*, by scientific thinkers from Bacon to Linnaeus, Buffon, Cuvier, and Darwin. Lister was familiar enough with Pliny's compendium to record an October day in 1822 spent 'Till very nearly 4 looking over Pliny's natural history ... *having first put my hair in curl*'.[38] That December, she mused about translating this mammoth text herself.[39]

The ramifying, inclusive style of Pliny's classical natural history was absorbed into the enumerative aspects of the natural sciences by Lister's time. But the supervening biblical account gave further legitimising force to a vision of creaturely life as a matter of distributed, even prodigally scattered endowments.[40] As ancient natural history and Christian doctrine amalgamated during the Reformation and Anglican settlement, Genesis played a multivalent role, dressed in its new garb of vernacular translation; it signified as both natural history *and* scripture. The opening verses of Genesis enumerate a parade of creatures, rising in order of their creation. The emerging series of kinds (the fowl of the air, the fish of the sea, the beasts of the earth) shows distinct domains made proper to each. Each creature rightfully holds a divine endowment and *imprimatur*.

With the expansion of Latin learning and the Englishing of liturgy and theology, new archives of vernacular writing disseminated what it could mean to think of having an 'appointed' or God-given nature. As a core example, one of the *Sermons or Homilies to be Read in Churches* (1547) expands Genesis, using a poetry of lists:

> Almighty God hath created and appointed all things in heaven, earth, and waters ... al birdes of the aire ... earth, trees, seedes, plantes, herbes, corne, grasse, and all maner of beastes keepe them in their ordre ... all kyndes of fishes in the sea, rivers and waters, ... yea the seas themselfes, kepe their comely course ...[41]

Here we see natural history's enumerative style inflecting theology. This language instils each creature with an agency to continue, according to the arc of its own natural ways; the refrains stress how things have a delegated sovereignty to 'keep themselves' to their own 'comely [fitting] courses'. Although the Homilies were no longer read systematically in churches in Lister's time, they suffused English culture. Indeed, the catalogue for the posthumous sale of Lister's library lists her copy of the *Sermons or Homilies to be Read in Churches*.[42] Like her contemporaries, she routinely read sermons aloud at home when family were indisposed to attend church.

Meanwhile, another text from the Elizabethan vernacular mix of theology and naturalism remained a cornerstone of Anglicanism, with a major Oxford scholarly edition published in 1836. This treatise on church governance by Tudor theologian Richard Hooker found in these laws of Nature a *via media* between Puritanism and Catholicism. Hooker's account of a God-given nature pertains here: 'All things that are have some [natural] operation ... for unto every end, every operation will not serve. That which doth assign unto each thing the kind, that which doth moderate the force and the power, that which doth appoint the form and the measure, the same we term a law.' These kinds trace a 'course' established by Nature, as 'wonted motions', 'unwearied courses' and customary 'ways'.[43] Hooker explicates a theology of Nature in which created beings possess a signature arc or way of acting.

A detailed account of intervening developments exceeds my brief, but Pope's popular poem cited above, *An Essay on Man* (1734), faithfully rehearsed this older creationist vision in which everything across the natural world accrues sacred licence by its rightful share in divine intention. From our perspective, the poem's notorious line, 'Whatever IS, is RIGHT', sounds mainly complicit in the controlling hierarchies of a *status quo*. But in Lister's hands, this very logic shows itself ready to turn to queerer purposes. In scientific contexts, a theology of creation remained central during her life, and works like William Paley's widely read *Natural Theology* (1802) continued to propose that whatever exists can only have been intended to be. In 1859, Darwin would challenge natural theology's view of God as the direct author of each creature and its faith in the creaturely immutability that, as discussed below, anchored Lister's self-accounting. In Lister's lifetime, meanwhile, texts like the compendious *Dictionary of the Natural History of the Bible; or, A Description of All the Quadrupeds, Birds, Fishes, Reptiles, and Insects, Trees, Plants, Flowers, Gums, and Precious Stones Mentioned in the Sacred Scriptures* (published in Boston, London, Glasgow, and Dublin from 1793) worked to 'open new beauties in the sacred volume', even citing 'the natural history of foreign countries' as important for actual biblical understanding.[44] Natures are God-given; thus they teach and speak.

To begin turning to Lister's own textual improvisations on what it means to have a God-given nature, two Shakespearean pivots show how readily these traditional ideas could apply to *human* variety, particularly concerning gender and sexuality.[45] This creation model – in which an endowed bent is conferred by divine art or Nature's hand – shapes the two most intriguing close encounters between Nature and sex/gender in the canon. First, in the gender-bending Sonnet 20 ('A woman's face with nature's own hand painted'), the (male) poet imagines the process by which Nature creates his (male) beloved. Line ten proposes that 'nature, as she wrought thee, fell a-doting', randomly making the beloved male by a slip of her drifting hand. Nature's creatures, including humans, are 'wrought', or made, and the process contains enough free scope for a 'doting' Nature to vary her plans. Shakespeare casts sexual difference as something almost accidental – because Nature, as an artist, has her queer freedoms and moods.

The second instance is a textual crux in *Twelfth Night*, the most queerly convoluted of Shakespeare's comedies. When the cross-dressed boy actor playing Olivia, a female character who has fallen in love with another female character, Viola (who is also played by a boy, but spends most of the play disguised as a man), discovers these layered masks, another character (Viola's twin) naturalises the attraction between two likes. 'So comes it lady you have been mistook', he says, but, he explains, 'nature to her bias drew in that'.[46] The idea of Nature drawing to (keeping to) her bias comes from the game of bowls, where an inbuilt weight (the bias) directs the natural course of the ball as a bent or turn. By these lights, natural movement (life, hope, desire – all the creaturely prerogatives) bends or curves; no 'nature' can be straightened or confined against its own grain. This conception of nature encompasses both the freedom of Nature as an originating artist and distributed sovereign nature(s), which all naturally desire the self-constancy of staying 'true to purpose'. Every nature is endowed by a creator with a bias all its own.

It Was All Nature

Anne Lister does more than accept or explain that she is 'odd, very very odd'; she justifies it with arguments resting squarely on natural history's sense of this native, creaturely endowment. 'Oddity' bundles many things beyond sexuality, as Lanser and Gonda have shown, and Lister captures that range. Countless diary passages register other people's notions of her singularity. Of a London dressmaker, Lister writes, '*I think she understands me to be a character.*'[47] Flirting with Miss Browne, who asked about her youth, she explains in 1819, '*I was a curious genius & had been so from my cradle*'; to Maria Barlow, asking in 1824 what her servants made of her, she answers, '*Oh, merely . . . that I have my own particular ways.*'[48] Setting off from Shibden in 1832, she likens it to 'exile', considering how her 'own people . . . are accustomed to my oddities, are kind, & civilized to me'.[49]

Beyond these glancing instances, the diaries make clear her 'oddity' was a common topic of conversation; it is not too awkward to discuss and even supports flirtation. Indeed, Lister often notes that people like her that way. On 2 July 1821, for example, she describes being '*led into talking about myself . . . my figure, manner of walking & my voice; their singularity etc*' by Emma Saltmarsh, naming all these '*my own oddities*'. But crucially she adds that Emma '*does not appear to object[;] in fact she thinks me agreeable & likes me. So does her husband*'.[50] Another friend, Ellen Empson, '*said I was odd but hoped I would not change*'.[51] When Lister argues that her 'inquisitive, curious' gaze is *like* other people's, a new acquaintance in Paris counters, '*No . . . it is only like yourself. But I don't dislike it.*'[52] Though her beloved Aunt Anne wryly commented in 1832, 'Well, you're a queer one & I'll ask no more,' Lister is always answering for her 'oddity' – *the thing is*, with evident success.[53] Singular, odd, curious, particular, queer: that she has something to answer for is unsurprising. The surprise is the apparently persuasive weight of the answer she reliably gives. Putting it plainly, she explains to Mrs Barlow as their Paris intimacy proceeds apace, '*it was all nature*'.[54]

Indeed, we might add, it was all 'nature's bias' in the Shakespearean sense: Nature's embedded weight or guide directing a God-given 'inclination' or 'turn'. Across the years, Lister keenly prosecutes this natural and creationist theory of her native 'oddity', transcribing sustained dialogues with friends and lovers into her journal. Considering three of these by the lights of natural history shows both the erudition and the daring of Lister's experiment in queer traditionality. In a deft editorial decision, Whitbread's first volume opens with one such conversation, extending over two months in 1816. Tortured by the heterosexual marriage of her greatest love, Mariana Belcombe, Lister is brought into close quarters with Mariana's sister, Nantz; a dalliance ensues. Edging into the topic, Lister tells her '*I should never marry. Could not like men. Ought not to like women.*'[55] But she immediately undercuts the wrong implied in 'ought not' by accounting *'for my inclination that way by diverse arguments'*; Lister expounds on *'my penchant for the ladies. Expatiated on the nature of my feelings.'* Working by diverse arguments, expatiating on nature as an inclination or penchant – and succeeding with Mariana's sister – Lister then contends with Nantz's fear their sexual engagement is wrong. Sticking to the language of scholarly debate, Lister confidently writes, *'I* dexterously parried *all these points.'*

Distinguishing male homosexual acts from female (with the latter *'certainly not named'* in the Bible), Lister actually bends and expands scriptural logics in her favour. She transfers opprobrium from same-sex connections, per se, to the inconsistency of playing both sides instead. She calls it *'infamous to be connected to both sexes'*, but finds allowances for those who exclusively *'kept to one side of the question'*. Making her case to Nantz, Lister continues:

> *I urged in my own defence the strength of natural feeling & instinct, for so I might call it, as I had always had the same turn from infancy. That it had been known to me, as it were, by inclination. That I had never varied & no effort on my part had been able to counteract it. That the girls like me & had always liked me. That I had never been refused by anyone.*

These lines reverberate with keywords from across the 'nature's bias' tradition: instinct, a consistent 'turn' since birth, an unvarying 'inclination' so deeply planted it cannot be redirected. The 'feeling' is 'natural' – and defensible – because it is native. The absence of terms like 'lesbian' and related vocabularies aside, we are watching Lister forge a discourse of her own, seized from the heart of traditional texts, including the Bible.[56] Using marked rhetorical phrases ('for so I might call it' and 'as it were'), she musters older understandings of a bespoke endowment for every 'made' creature – and conscripts them queerly to make a peerless case for legitimacy. We may add, too, her 'oddity' having 'always' been liked and 'never' refused (essentially ratified by the world) chimes with Pope's logic, 'whatever IS, is RIGHT'.

A second episode extends the argument from Nature, as Lister takes Frances Pickford's measure. In 1823, she expands her earlier points. *'If it had been done from books & not from nature'*, she reasons, *'the thing would have been different. Or if there had been any inconsistency, first on one side of the question, or the other, but, as it was, nature was the guide.'*[57] Nature may wend, but it does not waver. Indeed, it is precisely this consistency principle that shapes the emphatic grammar built in to of one of the most singular declaratives in sexuality's long history: Lister's 1821 claim not just 'to love the fairer sex', but to '*love & only love the fairer sex*'.[58] With Pickford, Lister distinguishes 'the thing' (nature-based sex between women) from the notorious counterexample of whatever we decide goes on in Juvenal's racy Sixth Satire, which she knowingly critiques as both '*artificial & inconsistent*'.[59] The sexuality she justifies is, in sharp contrast, both '*the effect of nature*' and also '*always consistent with itself*'. Across these passages, nature rarely appears without its companion gloss, self-consistency. *Natura propositi tenax.*

A third conversation extends from Lister's meeting Maria Barlow in Paris in 1824 to their becoming lovers, giving another sustained meditation on 'the thing'. The same marks of argumentation and off-setting distinction recur. Lister takes up a '*vindicating style of conversation respecting myself*'. She explains: '*Said how it was all nature. Had it not been genuine the thing would have been different.*' Lister amplifies the earlier distinction between her own, authorised natural 'ways' and artificial or bookish ones. Here we find her disclaimer of '*Saffic regard*' or '*Sapphic love*' (glossed as the use of sexual devices) on the grounds that '*there was artifice in it. It was very different from mine.*'[60] By 1832, as Lister faced new challenges wooing Ann Walker, she writes of these naturalising arguments as long settled. Countering Walker's fear that the legal jeopardy male lovers would face implied that their connection too was wrong, Lister '*appealed to her reason & put my arguments on the basis of religion*'. She records what is by now shorthand for earlier arguments: '*I answered this in my usual way: it was my natural & undeviating feeling etc etc.*'[61]

Appealed to her reason? *On the basis of religion*? *Etc etc*? Across these textual cruxes, Lister's queer naturalisation of her 'oddity' draws on traditional intellectual resources to make a boldly original case for Nature's backing. At the same time, she sets a rigorous, even unforgiving, standard for the natural 'thing'. Both sexual artifice and inconsistency in sexual object choice stray from Nature into a zone she has no care to defend. Nature, as an inclination, a bent or a turn – instilled from birth and 'not put on' – is righteous, even ethical.[62] The Listerian path is not straight, but it is still narrow because it unfolds, ultimately, as an *ethical* construction. To round out this account of the intellectual resources Lister taps to justify her ways, we must add one more thread: the ethical tradition of Stoicism.

Whether drawn from Zeno, Epictetus, Diogenes, Horace or Cicero, the Stoic ethos appears in aphoristic maxims strewn across print and manuscript culture – in Greek, Latin and English garb. As Nicholas White describes, 'from the Renaissance until well into the nineteenth century, Stoic ethical thought was one of the most important ancient influences on

European ethics', especially due to 'the effect it had had in antiquity, and continued to have into the nineteenth century, on Christian ethic[s]'.[63] Stoic ideas infused discourses of consolation, its doctrines proposing that the ethical life and the happy one converge in a life lived 'according to' or 'in agreement with nature'. Let nature take its course; keep to Nature as your guide. Equipoise reigns between release and restraint. Lister herself highlighted a major *locus classicus* for this principle, inscribing it on the flyleaf of one of her volumes. Quoting Horace's aphorism (likely from memory, since it is good Latin but not exact), she writes: '*naturam expellas furcâ, licet usque recurret*'. In more fulsome English, it exclaims, 'Go ahead! Drive nature out with a pitchfork if you want to try, it will always rush back in.'[64] This nature is the same inextinguishable inclination, instinct, bent, genius, penchant, bias, or turn inscribed in bodies across the creationist traditions of natural history and theology.

In Shakespeare's phrasing of the inscription process, 'Nature as she wrought thee fell a-doting'. Lister's friend Eliza Priestley accounts for Anne's 'oddity' in exactly this way. '*Speaking of my oddity, Mrs Priestley said she always told people I was a natural, but she thought nature was in an odd freak when she made me.*'[65] In addition to taking 'oddity' as natural and making Nature its artist-creator, two further points stand out in both cases. First, Nature's creatures are not the only place where 'oddity' unfurls its flag; that 'odd' old girl Nature herself possesses it, as one of her freedoms, moods, or powers. Queerness is no exclusively human prerogative. Nature was in 'an odd freak', but Lister is not a 'freak of nature'. Second, questions were openly asked in Lister's environment, but (more surprisingly) not only Anne Lister, but even Mrs Priestley has an answer. When she records the answer Mrs Priestley says she 'always' gives to others who ask, Lister recounts: '*I looked significantly & replied the remark was fair & just & true.*' The extraordinary passage records what Anne Lister herself experienced as recognition, what she herself judges a 'fair & just & true' representation.

In the process of setting her creatures off with their odd scripts, *where* might we say Nature inscribes the 'bias'? Lister '*had thought much, studied anatomy, etc*', but she drew a confident conclusion: '*No exterior formation accounted for it*'; instead, '*It was all the effect of the mind.*'[66] My penultimate example of Lister's thought addresses the mind as the place where 'oddity' resides. In her journal's priceless treasury of women's engagements, Lister not only records live conversation, but often copies letters sent and received. In 1824, she transcribes a dialogue of letters with Sibbella Maclean, a much-understudied Scottish friend and lover whose poor health and Hebridean remoteness foreclosed one possible future for Lister.[67]

We find Maclean summoning the idea of Nature's bias to comprehend Anne and sending it back to her. Anne's ardent admiration had led Sibbella, who seems to have felt undeserving, to call Anne 'romantic', to which Anne objected. At a pivotal moment, Lister recounts 'Finished reading my letter by this morning's post from Miss Maclean . . . she is sorry she called me romantic.' Lister transcribes Maclean's apology:

> I shall never do so again, & am sorry I did so – I am convinced what you write, and how you will ever act is from *the natural bias of your mind* – I can assure you I thought not of affectation, or applying to you romance in the common acceptation of the word – your mind is not formed in the ordinary mould.[68]

Maclean repudiates the charge of affectation Lister heard in 'romantic', disclaiming artifice by invoking the larger discourse of Nature under discussion here. Assessing Lister by the mind and echoing Rousseau's idea of Nature throwing away 'the mould that made me', Maclean affirms that Lister writes and acts – and 'will ever act' – both with constancy and in accord with 'the natural bias of [her] mind'. In this friendly terminological negotiation, we find (once again) Nature conjured as the authorising figure.

What are the consequences, then, of Anne Lister's queerly traditional claims on Nature to justify her 'oddity'? For one thing, she defies the grip of charges against 'unnatural' behaviour. The charge goes back to Romans 1:26, about women abandoning 'the natural use for what is against nature', a passage with which she was highly conversant.[69] In later historical circumstances, *fin-de-siècle* and modern writers like Oscar Wilde and Vita Sackville-West would have their reasons to embrace this language, articulating homosexuality *against nature*. Lister instead outflanks the narrow biblical charge, reversing Pauline condemnation to insist on the wider theological perspective in which Nature is on *her* side. Rather than seeing herself turning from Nature or violating its laws, she claims exactly the opposite. She and her method too are 'odd', surely, and 'queer' in all the senses – but not 'deviant'. She is supposed to be here – as such, and as-is; she is, in other words, 'a *regular* oddity'.

'When we leave nature, we leave our only steady guide, and from that moment become inconsistent with ourselves.'[70] Wresting this impeccable maxim from the pedigreed resources of the past, Lister reads that tradition queerly – which ironically includes taking it literally. Nothing in that archive prepares us to think it includes 'a capital grubbling' or 'right middle finger up queer', as she writes with such indelible economy. But with this argument, she dares natural history, theology, and philosophy – on their own terms – to say otherwise. A second consequence of Lister's end-run on her own time, then, is a revised sense of ours as somehow the crowning goal of some less perfect past. Walking alongside Anne Lister as she thinks her way up the mountain of a nineteenth-century life offers an ethical resource to us, as we clamber about in the twenty-first. Consider what she knew about surviving. Contemplating her bold experiment in queer traditionality, we moderns might hope to catch up with her fluency in the everyday work it takes to live 'undaunted'. If Anne Lister posed 'an enigma even to [her]self', as she mused in a letter to Sibbella, we should also pause to note that she seems to have solved it.[71]

Notes

My thanks to Caroline Gonda and Chris Roulston for their leadership in Lister Studies and to Helena Whitbread, Mary Fairclough and the Centre for Eighteenth-Century Studies at the University of York, Anne Choma, and Jenny Wood of the West Yorkshire Archive Service for supporting this research. Special thanks to Jan Radway, Susan Shannon McCreadie, Julia Stern, Pat Esgate, Margreta de Grazia, Sally Wainwright, and the late Lauren Berlant for encouraging me to *try to keep up* with Miss Lister.

1 Anne Lister, letter to Sibbella Maclean, 10 July 1824, *Anne Lister Papers*, West Yorkshire Archive Service (WYAS) [hereafter *Lister Papers*], SH:7/ML/142.

2 The gloss often appears in quotes without attribution. R. Norton, 'Anne Lister: the First Modern Lesbian' (1 August 2003), www.rictornorton.co.uk/lister.htm, accessed 12 February 2021. Norton himself was the first to moderate this claim, noting 'the absence of a political consciousness'. We should also note that Lister voices no *desire* for 'political community' as we understand that idea.

3 H. Whitbread, 'Initiations, Explanations, Discrimination: Anne Lister's Strategies of Seduction', in M. McAuliffe and S. Tiernan (eds.), *Tribades, Tommies, and Transgressives* (Newcastle: Cambridge Scholars Publishing, 2008), pp. 109–27, p. 110. The force of her exclusive emphasis ('*& only love*') is detailed below. Lister inked this credo on 29 January 1821 (*Lister Papers*, SH:7/ML/E/4/0122).

4 See, for example, William Paley's much-republished *Natural Theology: or, Evidences of the Existence and Attributes of the Deity, Collected from the Appearances of Nature* (London: J. Faulder, 1802), which Lister extracted in her reading notes (*Lister Papers*, SH:7/ML/EX/1). Lister's neighbour, Eliza Priestley, was Paley's daughter. On Darwin and natural theology, see A. Clifford, 'Darwin's Revolution in *The Origin of Species*: a Hermeneutical Study of the Movement from Natural Theology to Natural Selection', in

R. J. Russell (ed.), *Evolutionary and Molecular Biology: Scientific Perspectives on Divine Action* (Vatican City: Vatican Observatory, 1998), pp. 281–302.

5 By longstanding interpretation, the created world held edifying value. In the 'two-books tradition', creation (the 'Book of Nature') relayed the same verities as scripture (the 'Book of Revelation'), following Romans 1:20: 'For the invisible things of him from the creation of the world are clearly seen, being understood by the things that are made.' On this tradition in the nineteenth century, see D. Linicum, 'Criticism and Authority', in J. Rasmussen et al. (eds.), *The Oxford Handbook of Nineteenth-Century Christian Thought* (Oxford: Oxford University Press, 2017), pp. 72–88, p. 75.

6 On natural history's preference for enumeration over reducing lifeforms into fewer categories, see B. Ogilvie, *The Science of Describing: Natural History in Renaissance Europe* (Chicago: University of Chicago Press, 2006).

7 'Normal', Google Books NGram Viewer (a broad search engine for word frequency in English print), analysing 1700–2019: https://books.google.com/ngrams/graph?content=normal&year_start=1700&year_end=2019&corpus=26&smoothing=3&direct_url=t1%3B%2Cnormal%3B%2Cc0#t1%3B%2Cnormal%3B%2Cc0, calculated 20 May 2022.

8 Lister herself notes the role of Rousseau's *Confessions*: 'I read this work so attentively for the style's sake. Besides this it is a singularly unique display of character'; H. Whitbread (ed.), *The Secret Diaries of Miss Anne Lister, vol. II: No Priest but Love* (London: Virago, 2020), p. 148. On Lister's classical and Romantic self-fashioning, see A. Clark, 'Anne Lister's Construction of Lesbian Identity', *Journal of the History of Sexuality* 7.1 (1996), 23–50. On Byronic style, see C. Tuite, 'The Byronic Woman: Anne Lister's Style, Sociability and Sexuality', in G. Russell and C. Tuite (eds.), *Romantic Sensibility: Social Networks and Literary Culture in Britain, 1770–1840* (Cambridge: Cambridge University Press, 2002), pp. 186–210.

9 See especially S. Colclough, '"Do You Not Know the Quotation?": Reading Anne Lister, Anne Lister Reading', in J. Beynon and C. Gonda (eds.), *Lesbian Dames: Sapphism in the Long Eighteenth Century* (Farnham: Ashgate, 2010), pp. 159–72.

10 On Lister and anatomy, see Clark, this volume. On Lister and dictionaries, see S. Turton, 'The Lexicographical Lesbian: Remaking the Body in Anne Lister's Erotic Glossary', *Review of English Studies* 73.310 (June 2022), 537–51.

11 28 February 1823, *Lister Papers*, SH:7/ML/E/6/0097.

12 C. Roulston, 'Sexuality in Translation: Anne Lister and the Ancients', *Journal of the History of Sexuality* 30.1 (January 2021), 112–35, 130.

13 28 February 1823, *Lister Papers*, SH:7/ML/E/6/0097.

14 To my knowledge, no instance has been found where Lister applies the name *tribade* or *fricatrice* to herself; she actively disidentifies with what she calls '*Sapphic regard*' (discussed below).

15 20 August 1823, *Lister Papers*, SH:7/ML/E/7/0055 (quoting Rousseau's *Confessions*; emphases mine).

16 Rousseau, *Confessions*; www.rousseauonline.ch/Text/les-confessions-de-jj-rousseau.php/, accessed 20 May 2022 (my translation).
17 S. S. Lanser, '"Queer to Queer": the Sapphic Body as Transgressive Text', in K. Kittredge (ed.), *Lewd and Notorious: Female Transgression in the Eighteenth Century* (Ann Arbor: University of Michigan Press, 2003), pp. 21–46, p. 39; C. Gonda, 'The Odd Women: Charlotte Charke, Sarah Scott and the Metamorphoses of Sex', in Beynon and Gonda, *Lesbian Dames*, pp. 111–25, p. 125.
18 'Oddity', Google Books NGram Viewer, analysing 1700–2019; www://books.google.com/ngrams/graph?content=oddity&year_start=1700&year_end=2019&corpus=26&smoothing=3, calculated 21 May 2022.
19 *Lister Papers*, SH:7/ML/142.
20 Alexander Pope, *An Essay on Man*, in J. Butt (ed.), *The Poems of Alexander Pope* (London: Methuen, 1963), Epistle I, line 294, p. 515. Lister cites the phrase 13 April 1834 and *passim*. On classifying Lister's politics, see Lanser, this volume.
21 Whitbread's editions of the diaries were published in 1988 and 1992; citations are to the republished volumes. *The Secret Diaries of Miss Anne Lister, vol. I: I Know My Own Heart* (London: Virago, 2018) and *The Secret Diaries of Miss Anne Lister, vol. II: No Priest but Love* (London: Virago, 2020).
22 'Gentleman Jack Series Two Review: One of the Greatest British Period Dramas of our Time', *Guardian*, 10 April 2022, www.theguardian.com/tv-and-radio/2022/apr/10/gentleman-jack-series-two-review-one-of-the-greatest-british-period-dramas-of-our-time, accessed 10 April 2022.
23 S. Wainwright, quoted in E. Vincentelli, 'In Vigil, Suranne Jones Sounds the Murky Depths', *New York Times*, 21 December 2021, accessed 12 June 2022 (my italics).
24 J. Lea, *The Gentleman Jack Effect* (Santa Fe: Laurel House Press, 2021); 'BBC Factual Announces New BBC One Documentary, Gentleman Jack Changed My Life', 9 May 2022, www.bbc.com/mediacentre/2022/gentleman-jack-changed-my-life, accessed 12 June 2022.
25 WYAS, Anne Lister Transcription Project, www.wyascatablogue.wordpress.com/exhibitions/anne-lister/anne-lister-diary-transcription-project/.
26 'Statue of Anne Lister, TV's Gentleman Jack, Unveiled in Halifax', *Guardian*, 26 September 2021, www.theguardian.com/artanddesign/2021/sep/26/statue-of-anne-lister-tvs-gentleman-jack-unveiled-in-halifax, accessed 27 December 2021; 'New University of York College to Be Named after Yorkshire Diarist Anne Lister', University of York News, 24 January 2021, www.york.ac.uk/news-and-events/news/2021/campus/lister-college-naming/, accessed 27 December 2021.
27 Anne Lister Birthday Week, 1–10 April 2022, www.annelisterbirthdayweek.com, accessed 2 May 2022; Anne Lister Society Inaugural Meeting, 8–9 April 2022, www.english.northwestern.edu/about/anne-lister-society/als-inaugural–2022.html, accessed 2 May 2022.
28 Suranne Jones, in 'Look Who's Back! It's Gentleman Jack', *Diva Magazine*, 25 March 2022; *Diva* dubs Lister and spouse Ann Walker 'our favourite historical WLW icons'.

29 'Gentleman Jack: the BBC/HBO Series about a 19th-Century Lesbian Landowner is a sparkling Delight', *Financial Times*, 31 May 2019, www.ft.com/content/32732f40-81fb-11e9-9935-ad75bb96c849, accessed 4 May 2022.

30 Wainwright made diary digitisation possible, in an incalculable boon to research that also enabled the diary transcription project to proceed.

31 Whitbread, *Secret Diaries, vol. I*, p. 317.

32 Jones concisely described the shock of first encounter: 'It was like seeing someone's brain on the page': 'I put all the bad stuff to one side, and worked and worked', Guardian, 11 May 2019, accessed 18 January 2021.

33 E. Donoghue, cover citation for Whitbread's I Know My Own Heart, republished as *The Secret Diaries of Miss Anne Lister* (London: Virago, 2012): 'The Lister diaries are the Dead Sea Scrolls of lesbian history; they changed everything.'

34 I am (so far) unaware of Lister using the term 'diary'. She consistently refers to 'my journal', occasionally capitalising it (e.g. 20 May 1835, *Lister Papers*, SH:7/ML/E/18/0037).

35 26 July 1825, *Lister Papers*, SH:7/ML/E/8/0171. See also 17 September 1823: with '*éclat*', she '*could do with impunity what I could not do now*'. Whitbread, *Secret Diaries, vol. 1*, p. 321.

36 1 October 1819, *Lister Papers*, SH:7/ML/E/3/0099. John Lister and Arthur Burrell cracked Lister's code in the 1890s. Arthur Burrell, Letter to Halifax Librarian, 12 December 1936, *Lister Papers*, SH:7/JN/B/74/6.

37 *Historia Naturalis*, II.6, in M. Beagon, *Roman Nature: the Thought of Pliny the Elder* (Oxford: Clarendon Press, 1992), p. 9.

38 26 October 1822, *Lister Papers*, SH:7/ML/E/6/0063.

39 Whitbread, *Secret Diaries, vol. 1*, p. 252 ('*Thought I myself would fit myself to translate Pliny*').

40 For the early modern development of this syncretic vision, see my *The Accommodated Animal: Cosmopolity in Shakespearean Locales* (Chicago: University of Chicago Press, 2013).

41 'On Good Order, and Obedience to Rulers', in R. B. Bond (ed.), *Certain Sermons or Homilies (1547) and A Homily against Disobedience and Wilful Rebellion (1570)* (Toronto: University of Toronto Press, 1987), p. 161.

42 Item 19, Catalogue of the Shibden Hall Library sold by auction at Northgate Hotel, 1846, *Lister Papers*, SH:3/L/92. One of the few books remaining at Shibden Hall from Lister's great library is an 1829 Clarendon Press imprint of the *Book of Common Prayer*, a gift from another of Lister's love interests, Vere Hobart – testifying not only to the quotidian importance of liturgical material in Lister's life, but also to the powerful resonance of books as gifts in her circle.

43 R. Hooker, in A. S. McGrade (ed.), *Of the Laws of Ecclesiastical Polity* (Cambridge: Cambridge University Press, 1989), pp. 54, 60. See also J. Keble (ed.), *The Works of the Learned and Judicious Divine, Mr Richard Hooker ... A New Edition* (Oxford: Oxford University Press, 1836). On Hooker's influence, see D. McCullough, 'Richard Hooker's Reputation,' *English Historical Review*, 117.473 (September 2002), 773–812.

44 T. M. Harris, *A Dictionary of the Natural History of the Bible* (London: Thomas Tegg, 1824), Preface, pp. ii–iii.
45 I explored these early modern logics in '"Nature's Bias": Renaissance Homonormativity and Elizabethan Comic Likeness', in *Religion, Gender, and the Writing of Women: Historicist Essays in Honor of Janel Mueller* (a special issue), *Modern Philology* 98.2 (2000), pp. 183–210. References to Shakespeare are to D. Bevington, (ed.), *The Complete Works of William Shakespeare* (New York: Pearson, 2012).
46 *Twelfth Night*, 5.1.272.
47 Whitbread, *Secret Diaries, vol. I*, p. 243.
48 Whitbread, *Secret Diaries, vol. I*, p. 402, n.2; *vol. II*, p. 50.
49 16 December 1832, *Lister Papers*, SH:7/ML/E/15/0164.
50 Whitbread, *Secret Diaries, vol. I*, p. 172.
51 Ibid., p. 82.
52 Whitbread, *Secret Diaries, vol. II*, p. 36.
53 Whitbread, *Secret Diaries, vol. I*, p. 181.
54 Whitbread *Secret Diaries, vol. II*, p. 69.
55 All quotations for this episode are from Whitbread, *Secret Diaries, vol. I*, pp. 2–5.
56 On the unorthodox theology of Lister's rereading of Eve, see my 'Apples and Etymologies: Anne Lister Reading Genesis', unpublished paper delivered at the Anne Lister Society Meeting, 8 April 2022.
57 Whitbread, *Secret Diaries, vol. I*, p. 296.
58 29 January 1821, *Lister Papers*, SH:7/ML/E/4/0122 (my emphasis).
59 On the pivotal importance of later commentaries like those Lister analysed closely in her extract books, see M. Schachter, 'Lesbian Philology in Early Print Commentaries on Juvenal and Martial', in J. Ingleheart (ed.), *Ancient Rome and the Construction of Modern Homosexual Identities* (Oxford: Oxford University Press, 2015), pp. 39–55.
60 Whitbread, *Secret Diaries, vol. II*, p. 68.
61 27 November 1832, *Lister Papers*, SH:7/ML/E/15/0155.
62 Whitbread, *Secret Diaries, vol. II*, p. 50.
63 Epictetus, *The Encheiridion*, ed. N. White (Indianapolis: Hackett, 1983), Introduction, pp. 1–11, p. 1.
64 Lister, citing 'Hor. Lib. 1. Epist. 10', 9 June 1824, *Lister Papers*, SH:7/ML/EX/5, flyleaf.
65 Whitbread, *Secret Diaries, vol. I*, p. 374.
66 Whitbread, *Secret Diaries, vol. II*, p. 68.
67 I am very grateful to Anne Choma for pointing me to this exchange.
68 18 January 1824, *Lister Papers*, SH:7/ML/E/7/0099 (my italics).
69 Whitbread, *Secret Diaries, vol. II*, p. 44.
70 Lister, letter to Maclean, 10 July 1824, *Lister Papers*, SH:7/ML/142.
71 Lister, letter to Maclean, 21–22 June 1824, *Lister Papers*, SH:7/ML/140.

CHAPTER 3

Anne Lister's Search for the Anatomy of Sex

Anna Clark

In October 1814, when she was twenty-two, Anne Lister wrote 'clytoris' on a scrap of paper.[1] But she did not find the clitoris 'distinctly for the first time' until 1831, when she was forty.[2] Why did it take so long? She had clearly been experiencing pleasure through the clitoris and giving pleasure to other women. She attended lectures in Paris on anatomy and read many medical texts. Yet until 1831, when she tried to find the clitoris on her own and her lovers' bodies, she seems to have confused the cervix with the clitoris.

Where could she find information about the clitoris and how did she interpret it? Famously, anatomist Renaldo Columbus claimed to discover the clitoris in 1559, and declared it was the seat of women's pleasure. Furthermore, popular anatomy books asserted that women could not conceive without an orgasm, so as the source of women's pleasure, the clitoris was rather important. At the same time, popular anatomists traditionally regarded the vagina as analogous to the penis, which made things somewhat confusing. By the late eighteenth and early nineteenth century, historian Thomas Laqueur argues, scientists began to understand that female orgasm was not necessary for conception; thus, the clitoris became less important, and some medical texts began to leave it out.[3] Other historians have criticised this chronology as too simple. Recently, Alison M. Moore has argued that in fact nineteenth-century medical texts did include the clitoris.[4] However, aside from Laqueur, these recent articles skip from the seventeenth and early eighteenth century to the 1840s, leaving out the early nineteenth century, Anne's time. By looking at Anne's reading about the clitoris, we can illuminate the debate about what nineteenth-century people could know about the clitoris and when they knew it.

Anne's diaries reveal that it was not enough for a medical or popular book simply to mention the clitoris. Anatomy could be difficult to understand: even medical experts could find it hard to understand the anatomist

Vesalius's text and images.[5] Studies focus on what medical experts wrote and thought, not how women themselves interpreted them. If such an erudite and sexually experienced woman had such difficulty accurately finding it on her own body, other women would face even greater confusion. Lister's diaries provide a rare opportunity to examine a woman's detailed exploration of her own body and of anatomy texts, therefore contributing to the historiography about how people understood their own bodies and interacted with popular and official medical knowledge.[6] A few historians have shown that eighteenth- and nineteenth-century people read popular medical tracts and learned about folk medicine, and the literate middle class also had access to books about anatomy and even venereal disease in circulating libraries.[7] With Anne's diaries, we can trace how she understood anatomy in detail. Conveniently, Anne noted each book and article she read, so that we can track where she found certain words and concepts.[8]

Because these texts often buried the clitoris in confusing and abstruse detail, Anne practised 'queer reading' to interpret them. In other writings, I use this term to explain how she found obscure references to sex between women, researched them down the rabbit hole of commentaries and used them for her own ends.[9] She also had to ignore negative depictions of women who had sex with each other. I have previously written about how she read deeply in Latin classical works that scornfully depicted women who had sex with each other as 'tribades'. Similarly, she loved the Romantic poet Byron, famed as 'mad, bad, and dangerous to know', and emulated his libertine persona to create a sense of self as a romantic hero, even though she denounced him as improper to her acquaintances.[10] In this chapter, I will argue that she read anatomy books in a similarly queer way, disregarding condemnations and warnings to find sexual information fascinating and arousing.

For instance, Anne also 'queerly' read *Onania*, Samuel Tissot's anti-masturbation tract.[11] Lister had decried her own masturbatory practice (indicated as a cross in the margin of her diary) as 'self-pollution', as 'shameful' and a 'vile habit'. Yet she never stopped masturbating, and after 1825, she no longer expressed guilt about it.[12] Like many such tracts, *Onania* titillated in condemning by conveying information about sex, even sex between women. Although Anne only lists reading up to page 102 in *Onania*, further in the book the author reprints a letter supposedly from another woman who recounts how she learned pleasure with other girls in boarding schools. The book also mentions anatomist Regnier de Graaf's theories that some women have enlarged clitorises that they use with other women.[13]

Two years later, Anne discussed the 'sin of Onan' with Mrs Barlow, her sexually experienced lover in Paris. Anne generally kept her queer reading interpretations very private: in conversations with others, she did not directly discuss sex; instead, she hinted obliquely until the other woman had implicated herself with her own knowledge. To get the sexually experienced widow Mrs Barlow to admit first to her own knowledge of female desire, Anne then '*made her believe how innocent I was all things considered*', until Mrs Barlow implicated herself by saying she thought there was 'little harm' in such things. Mrs Barlow then showed Anne a French book, *Voyage à Plombières*, which contains a brief and oblique condemnation of lesbian eroticism. Then, she was able to discuss with Mrs Barlow that the sin of Onan – spilling his seed or semen on the ground to avoid conceiving a child with his brother's widow – was how French husbands themselves avoided conceiving. *Onania* also mentioned the biblical condemnation in Romans 1:26–27 (KJV) that 'even their women changed the natural use into that which is against nature', implying this meant sex with each other. She and Mrs Barlow creatively decided that this meant women having sex with men contrary to nature (anal sex), and that the passage did not apply to women having sex with each other.[14]

Anne developed a secret language and code to record her sexual encounters both solitary and social. While she shared her code with a very few lovers, her sexual symbols seem to have been secret. Transcribers Steph Galloway and Livia Labate have also identified Anne's sexual vocabulary and the symbols for her sexual practices she noted in the margins of her daily entries (which Anne sometimes defined in her journals).[15] During her teenage relationship with Eliza Raine, Anne noted 'felix' (Latin for happy) in her diaries, apparently when they had sexual encounters – and also when she masturbated, for she noted 'felix' in her journal when Eliza was not there.[16] In her diaries, she wrote when she gave or received a 'kiss', using the word in 1816 if not earlier.[17] While she uses the word, as we would, simply to mean a kiss, it is very clear that this also meant a genital sexual encounter, perhaps deriving from the French *baiser*, which could mean kiss or sexual intercourse.[18] But it might also mean an orgasm: for instance, in 1817 she wrote '[Mariana] had a very good kiss last night mine was not quite so good but I had a very nice one this morning'.[19] Her lovers also gave her a kiss when they 'got close' or pressed together. She also used the more technical term vagina in the medical context.[20]

Anne seems to have worked on developing this sexual vocabulary even more intensively between 1818 and 1820, when she became embroiled with several lovers around the same time (sometimes on the same day). It is possible that some of these words were shared, and then these young women were aware amongst each other about the possibility of mutual sexual pleasure. For instance, Eliza Belcombe, Mariana Belcombe's sister, claimed she saw Anne lick Mariana's neck and that another girl grabbed her in bed at night, and alluded knowingly to 'using the fingers'. But Anne disapproved of this open conversation.[21] Instead, she seems to have preferred to invent or modify her own terms. She used 'queer' or 'quere' as her term for the female genitals, perhaps derived from 'quim', a slang term for them. She first used this term when she initiated sex with Miss Vallance in October 1818.[22] In her diaries, she described how she 'grubbled' women, reaching up under their petticoats and stroking and penetrating them with her fingers (she specified which finger she used); to grubble is defined in Johnson's dictionary as 'to feel in the dark, as in Dryden', and was used in Dryden's translation of *Ovid's Art of Love*, as 'to grubble, or at least to kiss'. It also meant 'grope' in earlier times, and perhaps later in northern parts such as Scotland.[23] Anne Lister first used this term on 19 October 1820, at a time when she was engaged in fervid sexual exploration with several women, and also when she had begun reading in the classics, such as Juvenal, to find obscure Latin references to sex between women.[24]

Anne's particular spelling of 'clytoris' also provided a clue that she found anatomical information in *Aristotle's Masterpiece*. This particular spelling of clitoris was found most often in some editions of the work, and in 1817, 1819, 1820 and 1821, her journal mentions reading it.[25] *Aristotle's Masterpiece*, a popular sex guide printed on cheap paper and sold by pedlars in several versions, was not an academic treatise but a compendium of many sources that often contradicted each other, as Mary Fissell has found.[26] It is impossible to note exactly which edition of many it was that Anne read, but I have cited a 1717 version of *Aristotle's Masterpiece* that contains this spelling of 'clytoris' and mentions other points cited by Anne. Like *Onania* and other popular medical and erotic literature, it intentionally had to be read against the grain: for instance, the introduction links 'the mutual delight [men and women] take in the act of Copulation' to the wonders of generation, and apologises that this information might 'stir up their Bestial Appetites, yet such may know, this was never intended for them', but only to help married couples procreate. Of course, not only married couples read it: Anne obtained her copy from her aunt, who had seized it from a maid.

Aristotle's Masterpiece did not have illustrations depicting the location of the clitoris, and it described female anatomy in three rather confusing instances. First, just after a paragraph on the nymphaea, or labia, the 'clytoris' is described as the 'seat of venereal pleasure', and as 'like a yard [in] Situation, Substance, Composition and Erection, growing sometimes out of the Body two Inches, but that never happens unless thro' extream Lust, or extraordinary Accidents'. In another chapter, it compares the clitoris to the penis, claiming its 'outer end' is like the penis or glans in men. In the third instance, the work describes the 'neck' of the womb, and goes on to say, 'near unto the Neck there is a prominent Pinnacle, which is called of Montanus, the Door of the Womb, because it preserveth the Matrix from Cold and Dust. Of the Grecians it is called Clytoris, of the Latins Proputium Muliebre [penis muliebre], because the Jewish Women did abuse this Part of their own mutual Lusts, as St Paul speaks Rom. 1:26.' The *Masterpiece* also referred to the theory that women's genitals were like men's but turned inside out, so that by extension, the penis resembled the vagina. Of course, this is very confusing if the clitoris is also analogous to the penis, but this may explain why Anne thought that the clitoris was located in the vagina.[27] *Aristotle's Masterpiece* does not define the cervix, so it is possible that Anne thought that this fleshy knob in the vagina was the clitoris, or the door of the womb.

It may be that the overall frame of thinking about sex during her time, as well as in the Latin authors she read, was still so phallic and focused on penetration that it shaped her assumptions about sex. Anne came of age during the Regency period, when prudishness competed with public sexual jokes, and the upper-middle class and gentry people with whom she socialised often told erotic jokes. Anne herself often disapproved of such public 'indecency' of men and even the 'gross language' of female friends, but she also regaled female lovers with wild sexual tales. Although Mr Empson kept 'indecent' books in his drawer, his wife did not understand the joke Anne told her about the Wexford oyster as 'rough without, moist within, and hard to enter'. This was a joke from *Yorick's Jests*, a collection of mildly smutty and highly phallic *bon mots.*[28]

In her diaries, we can see how Anne did not clearly understand the location of the clitoris. In 1820, she mentions the clitoris – spelled 'clytoris' – to her lover Miss Vallance. Miss Vallance recounted that a doctor told her that 'something came too low down and blocked the passage', and she feared she should not marry as 'she could not bear much and could never make anyone happy'. In response, Anne told her 'the clytoris had slipped down too low from illness anxiety etc'.[29] This resembles the discussion in *Aristotle's Masterpiece* of the 'dropping of the mother', or when the cervix and uterus sag into the vagina, what is now called a prolapsed uterus.[30] Anne seems to have been confusing the clitoris with the cervix. She also noted in her code that she was able to feel Miss Vallance's 'stones of ovaria' with her fingers.[31]

Anne continued these explorations with Mrs Barlow in Paris. She penetrated Mrs Barlow and reported that this enabled her to feel 'her clitoris all the way up just like an internal penis'. But Anne herself did not like anything 'inside her'; although she tried to find her own internal clitoris, she said it hurt and did not give pleasure, and with other women, it made her feel too much like a woman.[32] Instead, she decided to 'incur' a cross in her 'old way by rubbing the top of the queer' – no doubt the clitoris.[33] In 1821, she tried penetrating herself with a finger after managing to use a uterine syringe, but mentioned, 'anything of this sort would never give me pleasure or a kiss the latter is produced on the surface'.[34]

Aristotle's Masterpiece and Anne's studies in anatomy can also illuminate the wider debate about Anne's masculinity and whether she should be seen as a potentially trans subject. As Laqueur writes, popular anatomy often depicted the vagina as like a penis turned inside out, by implication comparable in substance and function, and possibly able to turn outside in. While texts sometimes told stories of boys who turned into girls or vice versa, this does not mean that early modern people saw gender as easily fluid or reversible.[35] For instance, *Aristotle's Masterpiece* presented a debate between ancient Greek physicians about this. Galen is quoted as saying that a man

> is different from a woman in nothing else, but having his genital members without his body, whereas å woman has them within. And this is certain, that if nature, having formed a male, should convert him into a female, she hath no other task to perform, but to turn his genital members inward, and so to turn a woman into a man by the contrary operation.[36]

The *Masterpiece* states, however, that Galen's model refers to possible gender confusion in the womb, when an imbalance of humours might make a boy become effeminate and shrill, or a girl too strong and masculine, rather than to allow a total transformation. Yet the text quotes Severus Plineus as regarding men's and women's genitals as utterly different, and states that apparent transformations of girls into boys and vice versa were merely cases of mistaken identity, of boys with very small penises who were mistaken for females or females with 'overfar extension of the Clytoris'.[37]

Unfazed, Anne took from *Aristotle's Masterpiece* the possibility that the clitoris could grow larger. She discussed with Mrs Barlow whether her attraction to women was based on her own anatomy. She declared that this attraction was 'all nature': 'I had thought much, studied anatomy, etc. Could not find it out. Could not understand myself. It was all the effect of the mind. No exterior formation accounted for it.' Evoking *Aristotle's Masterpiece* quoted above on women's genitals as like men's turned inside out, she 'alluded to there being an internal correspondence or likeness of some of the male or female organs of generation'. Mrs Barlow even tried 'To examine if I [Anne] was made quite like her but she merely observed that Anne had smaller breasts and narrow hips'. Anne also noted that rumours had spread that her physician thought there was a 'small difference between my form and that of women in general'. She made a parallel between men with undescended testicles and the possibility that she had something internal, alluding 'to the stones not slipping thro' the ring till after birth, etc'.[38] This most closely resembles the discussion of the development of the foetus in Blumenbach's 1817 work on anatomy;[39] Lister later visited him in Germany. But she may have also learned it from Guillaume Dupuytren, a famed French physician whom she visited for treatment for her presumed venereal disease, who explained to her that men with only one testicle had the other one undescended in the abdomen. She had been asking questions about Charles Lawton, husband of her lover Mariana.

Instead of becoming a man, Anne hoped that she could enlarge her clitoris and therefore 'copulate with women'. In 1825 she mused to Mrs Barlow: 'I felt as if something might come farther out and that perhaps if I had an operation performed I might have a little thing – half an inch would be convenient. It would enable me to have my drawers made differently – that is to make water more conveniently.' She allowed Mrs Barlow to imagine that her doctor, Mr Simmons, had said this was possible.[40] A few months later, she wrote in her diary that she 'began putting up my left middle finger to bring down the clitoris, wishing it come so as to be able to copulate with women'.[41] Around the same time, she worried that 'I cannot do enough for Mrs B[arlow]. I cannot give her pleasure in any way but with my finger, and this does not suit. If I had a penis an inch or two long, or the clitoris down far enough I could manage.'

Mrs Barlow never expressed any discontent about this, and in fact said that she had more pleasure with Anne than with men.[42]

More reputable sources than *Aristotle's Masterpiece* did not prevent Anne from confusing the cervix and the clitoris. In 1821 she read Cheselden's *Anatomy* on the genital parts of men and women; it described the clitoris as the 'chief seat of pleasure' for women in coition, as the glans is in men. Anatomically, Cheselden described the clitoris as a 'small spongy body, bearing some analogy to the penis in men'. But the description of its place is highly technical, stating 'it begins with two crura from the ossa ischia': although he does mention that this 'proceeds to the upper part of the nymphaea', this text did not help Anne understand the location of the clitoris.[43]

With both Mariana and Mrs Barlow, she tried to reach the 'orifice of the womb', but it is unclear whether she meant the hymen or cervix.[44] She was intent on 'devirginating' Mariana, or breaking her hymen, in a way to triumph over Charles, her husband, who had not been able to accomplish the act. In 1825, she penetrated Mariana with her finger and was surprised to find no entrance into the womb; she did not understand, therefore, the nature of the tightly closed cervix. At other times, Mrs Barlow complained that Anne pressed so far against the 'orifice of the womb' that it was painful.[45]

The theory of male and female seed also fascinated Anne, who was very aware of female wetness during sex. To Mrs Barlow, she said, 'in copulation I always used my finger to keep the parts open so that I could give them what came from me'.[46] She and Mrs Barlow speculated what it would be like if Anne had a penis: 'she said I must excuse her saying so but she thought if I had a little one meaning a penis what I emitted was not good enough to beget children it was too thin not glutinous enough to which I agreed'.[47] One night in 1834, her partner, Ann Walker, complained, 'I gave her no dinky dinky that is seminal flow.'[48] This is interesting because it referred to debates about generation at the time. Earlier anatomy books, and especially popular works, debated whether the male or female fluids contained the seed that formed the embryo. By the 1820s new anatomical studies were proving the latter theory wrong; however, their work was still hotly contested.[49]

Anne also read widely to try to find more sophisticated and scientific understandings of anatomy than *Aristotle's Masterpiece*. This was not just because she was searching for the clitoris: she was intensely interested in the body and in the medical treatment of her relatives, and followed the symptoms of her ailing aunt and uncle very closely. Although she never published anything, she was insatiably curious about science and pursued a systematic course of reading and lectures. As early as 1819 she wrote to the famed anatomist Cuvier and asked if she could study with him in Paris.[50] By the 1820s, she was also very concerned that she had contracted venereal disease from her great love, Mariana, who in turn had contracted it from her husband, Charles Lawton. While this may have been simply thrush or another similar infection, Anne sought out experts, such as Guillaume Dupuytren, for treatment, including mercury.

In 1824 Anne asked local doctors in Yorkshire what she should read about, and they recommended Andrew Fyfe's *Anatomy* and John Bostock's *Physiology*.[51] In contrast to the centuries-old *Aristotle's Masterpiece*, and earlier more scientific anatomists, these newer books often ignored or slighted the clitoris. For earlier anatomists, the clitoris was interesting because its erectile tissue was similar to that of the penis. As Laqueur points out, the change in the understanding of fertilisation meant that the clitoris became less important, and also once the idea of female seed was discredited, then female sexual pleasure was also less significant.[52] Fyfe's *Anatomy* focused on the process of generation and buried the clitoris in a paragraph about the labia, noting that it produced the same sensation as the penis but without referring to pleasure. Unlike *Aristotle's Masterpiece*, Fyfe began his description with the uterus, for he saw it as more important in the process of conception and birth. He also described the cervix in a way that might confuse it with the clitoris, which in other works was often compared to the penis. Fyfe claims 'the under part of the Cervix projects into the Vagina, somewhat in form of the Glans Penis'.[53] Similarly, while Alexander Monro, whom Anne read, mentions the clitoris in highly technical terms, he describes the womb and vagina first, and only mentions the function of the clitoris as 'sensibility'.[54] Bostock was up on the latest science. Trained in Edinburgh, he became fascinated by the chemical functions of the human body and trained in chemistry as well as medicine.[55] Bostock was a physiologist, which meant that he was concerned with the mechanical, that is muscular or contractile, and nervous functions of the body, rather than simply describing anatomy. Although Bostock presented the debates about generation in detail, he was not concerned with sexual pleasure; he did not mention the clitoris.[56]

By 1828 Anne returned to Paris to attend lectures on anatomy, as well as botany, geology, zoology and mineralogy. In 1829–31 she wrote, 'Surely my taste is decidedly for anatomy tho' every part of science gives me so much pleasure I have always had difficulty in choosing that which seemed really to suit my natural inclination best.'[57] Her studies also provided a welcome distraction from her romantic entanglements with three women, and she wrote, 'What is there like gaining Knowledge? all else here below is indeed but vanity and vexation of spirit – *I am happy among my books.*'[58]

She purchased a skeleton for her rooms, and even dissected human body parts and foetuses, employing a medical student to teach her. Dissecting a human hand first made her feel 'very queerish . . . somehow the cutting at a hand so like one's own'.[59] Studying anatomy was not something she could publicly discuss; she kept this information from Mariana, and when she told Vere Hobart, a prospective lover, Vere remarked 'what pleasure you will have some time in dissecting me I merely said oh no even if I felt it a duty to have her opened I should not could not be there to see no one dissected those they had loved or had even much known'.[60] In Britain dissections offended the devout, and only murderers could be legally anatomised. As a result, anatomists employed body-snatchers to find corpses to provide material for them,[61] leading to several murders in Edinburgh, the infamous 'burking' of which Anne was well aware.[62] In 1834, she noted that the people of Hull were 'threatening to pull [the museum's public dissecting rooms] down'.[63] In contrast, since the Revolution, French doctors could dissect the bodies of diseased patients in charity hospitals.[64] As Foucault points out, doctors thus exerted power over the bodies of the poor, who had to submit to become 'spectacles' in order to receive treatment.[65]

Anne enjoyed the intellectual and social ferment of early nineteenth-century Paris, where ladies attended scientific and medical lectures, in part to learn, and in part as a form of entertainment. She was omnivorously curious, attending lectures on botany, geology, chemistry, comparative animal anatomy and human anatomy. She was able to meet eminent lecturers such as Geoffrey Saint-Hilaire and Georges Cuvier, and even socialised with Cuvier's wife and daughter. As Outram writes, the household and the natural history museum had porous boundaries. These eminent men often disagreed with each other fundamentally on the way to approach the examination of human and animal bodies, whether to follow form or function, similarities or differences on the surface or deep in the body.[66] Anne was interested in much more than her own body, but she certainly mentioned lectures that touched on 'generation' or reproduction, even among molluscs.[67]

Studying anatomy in Paris exposed Anne even more to new approaches to anatomy and physiology.[68] The older anatomy was interested in surveying and categorising all the organs of the body in a taxonomy, but the Paris School of Medicine focused on the functions of the tissues of the body.[69] Bichat, who pioneered this approach, identified the different types of tissues that could be found across the body in various organs, so he would look beyond the individual organ to see its components. He also focused on the function of these tissues in terms of 'contractability and sensibility' that tied together the functions of the system of the body; furthermore, he organised his anatomy in terms of a 'hierarchy' of these systems.[70] Paris anatomists did mention the clitoris, but these new ways of thinking about the body meant they sometimes downplayed it. Bichat describes the clitoris and notes the similarity in the tissue between the clitoris and the penis, with its *corpus caverneaux*, but in this he is echoing longstanding anatomical tradition. He noted that unlike the male genitals, which could be analysed 'according to the principal phenomena of the function which they exercise; those of the woman do not lend themselves to this distribution'.[71] Although Anne took out Bichat's book from the circulating library and returned it, she does not mention any findings from it.[72] She did read the works of his associates Pierre-Hubert Nysten, Pierre Béclard, and the brothers Hippolyte and Jules Cloquet.[73]

Even when she read these advanced anatomists, the necessary information was hard to find and decipher: it took a year and a half. Today, we can just look in the index or Google search a term, as I have done in this research. But French books had their tables of contents at the back and did not index them. Anne tended to read through books systematically, noting which pages she read each day, so it took some time to get to the end of the book – and to find information about female sexual organs, which even then was not entirely clear.

First, Anne found Nysten's dictionary of medicine to be useful – and stimulating. In February 1830 she wrote in code, 'Reading anatomy from 12 to 1 50/60. Chiefly dictionary, clitoris, etc., & at last, in trying if I had much of one, incurred a cross on my chair.'[74] Nysten described the clitoris as something which is often touched, 'titiller', at the 'partie superiore de la vulve', composed of erectile tissue and analogous to the penis. However, this meant the 'top' or upper part of the vulva, so that Anne might have confused it with the top of the vagina.[75]

She then read Béclard, who followed Bichat's discipline in emphasising function; instead of presenting his book as a visual tour through anatomy, he organised it by tracing the function of bodily fluids: 'The human body, like all organised bodies, is composed of solid parts and of fluids, which have a similar composition, and continually change into each other.' Furthermore, he also delineated sensations such as irritability that produce motion. Generation was another function produced by irritability: 'the sensations and voluntary motions which accompany it, the motions of irritation, the phenomena of the secretion of the spermatic fluid and the formation of the ovula, those of the nutrition and grow the fecundated egg, are all seen to be more or less directly subject to the nervous action'. Béclard mentioned the clitoris, but it is buried in the text of a chapter on 'Erectile tissue' and its function and sensation are not described.[76]

Anne finally made the discovery in reading the works of the Cloquet brothers, but it took from June 1829, when she bought Hippolyte

Cloquet's *Traité d'anatomie*, to February 1831.[77] Hippolyte Cloquet's book was all text, and to identify the organs Anne had to purchase or obtain the very expensive plates of his brother Jules's anatomy books. First, she had to plough through Hippolyte Cloquet's dry prose about the heart and the brain; on 6 March 1830 she read on the urinary tract, and on 13 March 1830, she started reading a bit on the organs of generation, but soon nodded off.[78] Hippolyte Cloquet, as usual, described the clitoris as resembling the penis because they were both composed of erectile tissue; he also noted that, like the penis, the *corpus cavernus* behind the clitoris had 'an extraordinary number of blood vessels and nerves'. But these lists of anatomical parts did not help Anne conceptualise the location of the clitoris. She did borrow and eventually buy Jules Cloquet's expensive book of plates, but it put her to sleep when she started to read it on 8 May 1830.[79]

It took another year for Anne to make the final discovery. On 25 January and 1 February, the comparative anatomist Cuvier lectured on the process of reproduction, including 'the hymen uterus menstrual discharge and penis', and she noted that half a dozen ladies, plus Cuvier's wife and daughter, attended, undeterred by the topic.[80] In his later published lectures, Cuvier described the vagina as analogous to the penis only in that it was made to receive the liquor of 'fecundation'. However, like the anatomists, he mentions the clitoris briefly and as an afterthought. He states that it has 'erectile tissue' somewhat analogous to the penis, and that it was exquisitely 'sensible', but this is not related directly to sexual pleasure, unlike earlier anatomical descriptions.[81]

Anne decided to buy Jules Cloquet's book for herself on 27 January. At the same time, she bought Sarlandière's anatomy book.[82] Finally, on 17 February 1831, she wrote that she fell asleep reading Cloquet, and then incurred a cross, noting, 'it was from studying the female [parts of] generation and finding out distinctly for the first time in my life the clitoris'. [83] Anne must have put together the description in Hippolyte Cloquet's written text with the plates in Jules Cloquet's *Anatomy*.[84] To figure it out, she would have to look at each plate, and go back to the description of the plates to find out which organ each number corresponded to. Since the clitoris was so small, not all the plates made this very obvious. But one side view did make it quite clear; the clitoris appears as a little protrusion from the nymphae, but it is quite distinct. The same day, she also read more in Sarlandière, who described the clitoris and the external organs as 'organe de l'appétit vénérien de la femme', separately categorising the vagina and the uterus. A plate on the previous page clearly labelled them. The organs of digestion are on the same page.

PL. 312.

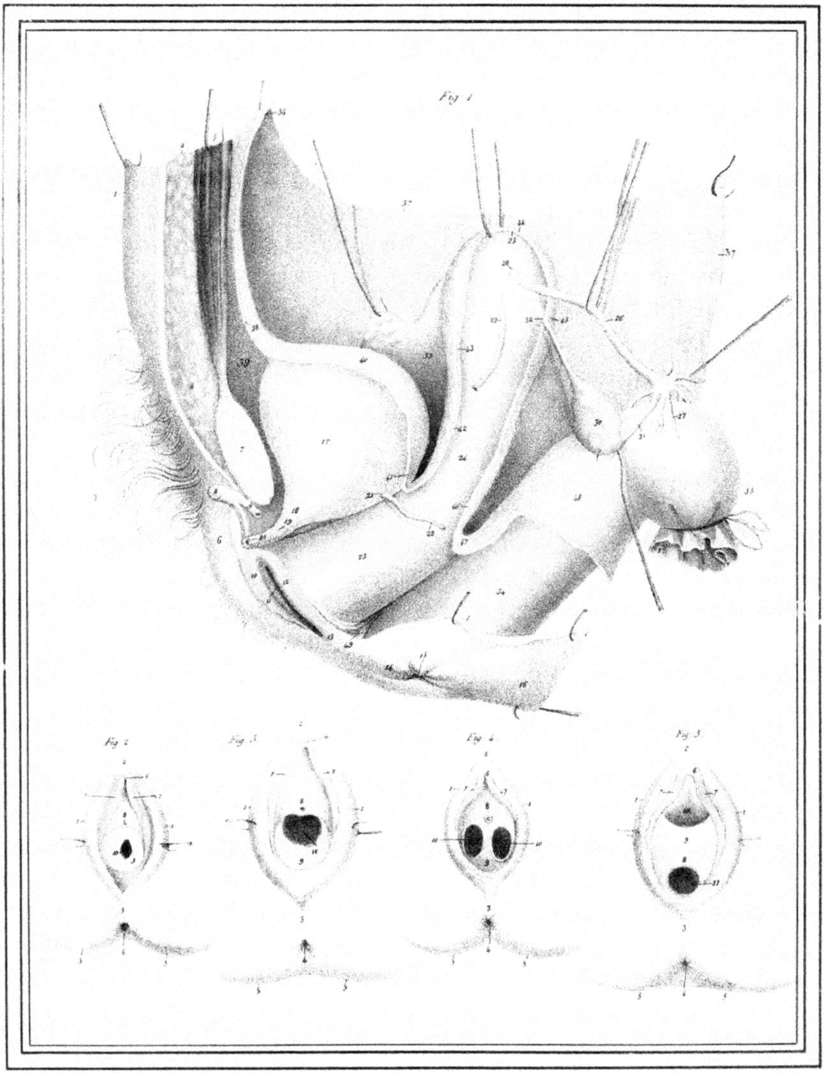

Figure 3 *Manuel d'anatomie descriptive du corps humain: représentée en planches lithographiées* by Jules Cloquet. Public domain.

In reading these texts, Anne also had to contend with the fact that Parisian sources tended to link the clitoris negatively with sex between women. Bichat began his discussion of the clitoris by disapprovingly mentioning the problem of women with enlarged clitorises who engage in 'vicious' practices and become too masculine and lascivious.[85] In his dictionary, Nysten noted that a M. Fournier had invented the word 'clitorisme' to diagnose those women with enlarged clitorises who 'abused' other women with them.[86] If Anne had investigated this definition further, she could have found an entry in the *Dictionnaire des sciences médicales* (1813) that presented titillation of the clitoris in highly negative terms as leading to 'bizarre tastes' for relations between women, such as that indulged by Sappho, which would distract from the natural relations between women and lead to 'bitter feelings'; it also led to excessive masturbation.[87] Anne had to read such texts with all the tools of queer reading to take the information she needed without feeling as if she were tainted by such perversity.

Anne also read cultural and anthropological works that took a negative approach to women's anatomy. For example, she read J.-J. Virey's *Histoire naturelle du genre humain* and *De la femme*.[88] Virey stressed that men and women were different in every way, and women were suited to the softer domestic world owing to their physiology. Anne did not take on Virey's ideas about women's soft and submissive nature; in fact, around the same time, she planned to write a book arguing that women of property deserved the vote. Virey mentioned the clitoris only in the context of puberty, and in more detail, in exotic and racialised tales of the so-called Hottentot Venus as well as oriental women with supposedly large clitorises.[89] On 20 April, Anne read the very pages in which Virey mentioned the Hottentot Venus and the necessity in oriental countries of female circumcision for enlarged clitorises, and then spent half an hour in the closet touching her clitoris; the next day she tried to titillate it in order to enlarge it.[90] Although Virey clearly meant accounts of enlarged clitorises to indicate racial difference and pathology, Anne found these accounts instead to be inspiring.

Virey probably learned of the Hottentot Venus from the pre-eminent anatomist Georges Cuvier. She was actually Sara Bartmann, a woman of KhoeKhoe heritage from South Africa, who had been taken first to London, then to Paris, to be exhibited on the stage as exotic. When she died, Cuvier obtained her body and dissected her, and then wrote a great deal about her supposedly elongated labia and clitoris, repeating these mentions in his book on anatomy that Anne read.[91] He and other anatomists were pioneers of racist interpretations of human physiology.[92] Anne also visited Johann Blumenbach in Germany, another scientist well-known for his racial theories.[93] However, Anne seems to have simply ignored the racist implications of the anatomical works she was studying (although further transcriptions may reveal more of her opinions).[94]

What can Anne's search for the clitoris tell us? This is a very unusual example of how a nineteenth-century person studied anatomy to understand her own body, and how it took so long for her, a well-educated and sexually experienced woman, to figure it out. On the one hand, she was so shaped by *Aristotle's Masterpiece* and dominant phallic discourses that she was searching for the clitoris deep within her own and her lover's vaginas. On the other hand, she used her tools of queer reading in searching for the clitoris, taking on negative depictions and turning them around – and getting turned on by them. At first, she thought she would find something about her own anatomy that was different, such as an enlarged clitoris, and that would explain why she was so attracted to women. But as she searched for the clitoris, she was also trying to find her lovers' clitorises to give them pleasure, and to give herself pleasure; she saw herself as different from them, as masculine and usually not wanting to be touched, but also as similar, in sharing the same anatomy. For Anne, the search for the clitoris was part of her general tendency to study, document and control; she sought to explore her own body and those of her lovers in the same way as she mapped and controlled her land and her destiny, but the surrounding culture mapped sexual anatomy in a way that sometimes took her in a false direction.

Notes

1 Anne Lister, *Extracts from Books Read, Anne Lister Papers* [hereafter *Lister Papers*], West Yorkshire Archive Service, Calderdale, SH:7/ML/EX/6, ff. 26–7, quoted in A. Clark, 'Anne Lister's Construction of Lesbian Identity', *Journal of the History of Sexuality* 7.1 (1996), 32. S. Turton has published this sexual vocabulary from these extracts in 'The Lexicographical Lesbian: Remaking the Body in Anne Lister's Erotic Glossary', *Review of English Studies* (2022), advanced online publication.

2 A. Choma, *Gentleman Jack: the Real Anne Lister* (London: Penguin 2017), p. 15.

3 T. Laqueur, *Making Sex: Body and Gender from the Greeks to Freud* (Cambridge, MA: Harvard University Press, 1992), p. 129. For a critique of this model, see H. King, *The One-Sex Body on Trial: the Classical and Early Modern Evidence* (London: Taylor and Francis, 2016), pp. 12, 35.

4 S. Chaperon, 'Le Trône des plaisirs et des voluptés: anatomie politique du clitoris, de l'antiquité à la fin du Xème siècle', *Cahiers d'histoire. Revue d'histoire critique* 118 (2012), 41–60; A. M. Moore, 'Victorian Medicine Was Not Responsible for Repressing the Clitoris: Rethinking Homology in the Long History of Women's Genital Anatomy', *Signs: Journal of Women in Culture and Society* 44.1 (2018), 61.

5 D. Margócsy, M. Somos and S. N. Joffe, 'Sex, Religion and a Towering Treatise on Anatomy', *Nature* 560.7718 (2018), 304–5.

6 S. Pilloud and M. Louis-Courvoisier, 'The Intimate Experience of the Body in the Eighteenth Century: Between Interiority and Exteriority', *Medical History* 47.4 (2003), 451–72; D. Porter and R. Porter, *Patient's Progress: Doctors and Doctoring in Eighteenth-Century England* (Stanford: Stanford University Press, 1989); S. Boon, *Telling the Flesh: Life Writing, Citizenship, and the Body in the Letters to Samuel Auguste Tissot* (Montreal: McGill-Queen's University Press, 2015); M. Stolberg, *Experiencing Illness and the Sick Body in Early Modern Europe* (New York: Palgrave Macmillan, 2011).

7 S. Pilloud, 'Mettre les maux en mots, médiations dans la consultation épistolaire au XVIIIe siècle: les malades du Dr Tissot (1728–1797)' ['The Sick Patients of Dr Tissot (1728–1797)'], *Canadian Bulletin of Medical History* 16.2 (1999), 215–45; M. E. Fissell, *Patients, Power, and the Poor in Eighteenth-Century Bristol* (Cambridge: Cambridge University Press, 1991).

8 The website 'Packed with Potential', put together by volunteer transcribers, contains an invaluable list of 'Anne Lister's Bookshelf', noting all the books mentioned in the transcribed diaries; www.packedwithpotential.org/projects/anne-lister-bookshelf.

9 A. Clark, *Alternative Histories of the Self: a Cultural History of Sexuality and Secrets* (London: Bloomsbury, 2017), p. 5.

10 Clark, 'Anne Lister's Construction of Lesbian Identity', 23–50; A. Clark, *Alternative Histories of the Self* (London: Bloomsbury, 2017), pp. 60–7.

11 4 March 1822, *Lister Papers*, SH:7/ML/E/5. For a wider consideration of masturbation in diaries, see L. Vermeer, 'Tiny Symbols Tell Big Stories: Naming and Concealing Masturbation in Diaries (1660–1940)', *European Journal of Life Writing* 6 (2017), 101–34.

12 S. Gallaway and L. Labate, 'Incurred a Cross', 'Anne's Sex Guide', in 'Packed with Potential' website, www.packedwithpotential.org/projects/anne-lister-sex-guide; 5 December 1819, SH:7/ML/E/4/0010; 29 June 1820, SH:7/ML/E/4/0066; for use of the term 'masturbation', see 15 January 1823, SH:7/ML/E/6/0084.

13 S. Tissot, *Onania, or the Heinous Sin of Self-Pollution* (London, 1760), p. 188.

14 15 October 1824, *Lister Papers*, SH:7/ML/E/8/0059; https://whatdoesshedotothem.tumblr.com/post/665081008918609920/1824-october-Friday-15.

15 S. Gallaway and L. Labate, 'Anne's Sex Guide', in 'Packed with Potential' website, www.packedwithpotential.org/projects/anne-lister-sex-guide.

16 Patricia Hughes speculates this means sex, in her pathbreaking transcriptions; see her *Gentleman Jack: the Early Life of Miss Anne Lister and the Curious Tale*

of Miss Eliza Raine (n.p.: Lulu.com, 2019), p. 36. It might also mean masturbation: see 15 August 1808, *Lister Papers*, SH:7/ML/E/26/1/0011.

17 14 August 1816, *Lister Papers*, SH:7/ML/E/26/2.

18 Thanks to Laura Gowing for this suggestion.

19 28 December 1817, *Lister Papers*, SH:7/ML/E/1.

20 19 October 1821, *Lister Papers*, SH:7/ML/E/5.

21 3 July 1819, *Lister Papers*, SH:7/ML/E/3.

22 20 and 25 October 1818, *Lister Papers*, SH:7/ML/E/2; for quim, see F. Grose, *Dictionary of Vulgar Tongue* (London, 1811).

23 For a discussion of Lister's vocabulary, see D. Orr, 'A Sojourn in Paris, 1824–1825: Sex and Sociability in the Manuscript Writings of Anne Lister (1791–1840)', unpublished PhD thesis, Murdoch University, Sydney (2006), p. 69.

24 29 June 1820, *Lister Papers*, SH:7/ML/E/4.

25 Apparently, her aunt confiscated it from a maid, and then it came into Anne's possession. She showed it to Mariana Belcombe's mother, 20 November 1819, *Lister Papers*, SH:7/ML/E/3/0115; 23 February 1817, *Lister Papers*, SH:7/ML/E/26/3. On 28 August 1820, *Lister Papers*, SH:7/ML/E/4/0078 (*Lister Papers*, 1819–21), she wrote that reading *Aristotle's Masterpiece* put her in a 'high state of excitation'. She also read it on the 'parts of generation', 11 August 1821, *Lister Papers*, SH:7/ML/E/4/0075.

26 M. E Fissell, 'Hairy Women and Naked Truths: Gender and the Politics of Knowledge in *Aristotle's Masterpiece*', *William and Mary Quarterly* 60.1 (2003), 48.

27 *Aristotle's Master-Piece: Compleated, in Two Parts. The First Containing the Secrets of Generation, in All the Parts Thereof ... The Second Part, Being a Private Looking Glass for the Femalei* [sic] *Sex* (1717), pp. 70–1, 7, 85, 95.

28 6 November 1818, *Lister Papers*, SH:7/ML/E/2/0080. *Yorick's Jests: Being a New Collection of Jokes* (London, 1774), p. 144. Lister also read Colman's letters, which she found 'capital' but 'indecent'; 31 January 1821, *Lister Papers*, SH:7/ML/E/4/0123. George Colman, *Posthumous Letters, from Various Celebrated Men* (London, 1820), p. 2.

29 22 December 1820, *Lister Papers*, SH:7/ML/E/5/0089.

30 'Of the Descending or Falling of the Mother, The falling down of the womb is a relaxation of the ligatures, whereby the matrix is carried backward, and in some hangs out in the bigness of an egg'; *Aristotle's Master-Piece*, p. 126.

31 11 October 1820, *Lister Papers*, SH:7/ML/E/4/0089.

32 10 August 1821, *Lister Papers*, SH:7/ML/E/5/005.1.

33 14 January 1825, my transcription, *Lister Papers*, SH:7/ML/E/8/0116; see also http://xldev.co.uk/listeria/Default.aspx?page=61#1825Jan13. Anne Lister used the word 'cross' as a coded term for 'orgasm'.

34 10 August 1821, *Lister Papers*, SH:7/ML/E/5/0051.

35 Laqueur, *Making Sex*, p. 129. For the most recent refutation of the popular understanding of early modern sex as fluid, see B. Holmes, 'Let Go of Laqueur: Towards New Histories of the Sexed Body', *Eugesta* 9 (2019), 136–75.

36 *Aristotle's Master-Piece*, pp. 70–1.
37 Ibid.
38 13 November 1824, *Lister Papers*, SH:7/ML/E/8/0078; https://whatdoesshedotothem.tumblr.com/post/634663863599661056/saturday-13-november-1824.
39 J. F. Blumenbach and J. Elliotson, *The Institutions of Physiology* (London: Bensley, 1817), p. 275.
40 18 January 1825, my transcription, *Lister Papers*, SH:7/ML/E/8/0117.
41 9 May 1825, *Lister Papers*, SH:7/ML/E/8/0154; https://skgway.tumblr.com/tagged/Shibden+Hall+1825/page/2.
42 H. Whitbread (ed.), *The Secret Diaries of Miss Anne Lister*, vol. II (New York: Little, Brown Book Group, 2020), pp. 256–7.
43 18 August 1821, *Lister Papers*, SH:7/ML/E/5/0054; W. Cheselden, *Anatomy of the Human Body* (London, 1768 (1713)), p. 272. Cheselden was an expert on bones; the rest of his anatomy was somewhat outdated; see W. F. Bynum, *Science and the Practice of Medicine in the Nineteenth Century* (Cambridge: Cambridge University Press, 1994), pp. 13, 32.
44 See Lister's entry from 8 September 1825, *Lister Papers*, SH:7/ML/E/9/0015; https://whatdoesshedotothem.tumblr.com/post/661740000705150976/Thursday-8-september-1825.
45 8 December 1826, *Lister Papers*, SH:7/ML/E/10/0027 and SH:7/ML/E/10/0028; https://magnesiaandlemonjuice.tumblr.com/post/625999401748398080/Friday-8-december-1826.
46 30 January 1825, *Lister Papers*, SH:7/ML/E/8/0122; https://whatdoesshedotothem.tumblr.com/post/674778533707563009/sunday-30-january-1825.
47 2 December 1826, *Lister Papers*, SH:7/ML/E/10/0025; https://magnesiaandlemonjuice.tumblr.com/post/624461512825864193/Saturday-2-december-1826.
48 Thanks to Steph Galloway for these references and interesting suggestions along these lines. S. Galloway and L. Labate, 'Anne's Sex Guide', www.packedwithpotential.org/projects/anne-lister-sex-guide. For example, see 30 June 1834, SH:7/ML/E/17/0048; https://woollyslisterblog.tumblr.com/post/190460356540/1834-june-Monday-30th-part-33.
49 F. Vienne, 'Eggs and Sperm as Germ Cells', in L. Kassell, N. Hopwood and R. Flemming (eds.), *Reproduction: Antiquity to the Present Day* (Cambridge: Cambridge University Press, 2018), p. 415.
50 18 January 1819, *Lister Papers*, SH:7/ML/E/2/0100.
51 17 August 1824, *Lister Papers*, SH:7/ML/E/8/0032; https://oeillade.tumblr.com/post/635587716976869376/oh-lord-luke-green wood-from-the-cunnery-was. By September, Anne was in Paris and talking with a doctor, Mr Brande, about the *cabinet d'anatomie* at the Jardin des Plantes; 5 September 1824, *Lister Papers*, SH:7/ML/E/8/0040; https://awhilesince.tumblr.com/post/648201745864048640/Sunday-5-september-1824.

52 Medical experts could entertain the two models in the same text. For instance, Blumenbach writes both 'As the male organs are fitted for affording, so the female organs are fitted for receiving, and are correspondently opposite to the former. In some parts, the organs of each sex are very analogous to each other in structure.' Additionally he discusses how the uterine 'orgasm' is excited by the sperm and stimulates ovulation, while he also claims to prove that the egg can be released in virgins. Blumenbach and Elliotson, *The Institutions of Physiology*, pp. 298, 313.

53 A. Fyfe, *A Compendium of the Anatomy of the Human Body: Intended Principally for the Use of Students*, vol. II (London: Pillans and Sons, 1810), pp. 314–17.

54 A. Monro, *Outlines of the Anatomy of the Human Body: In Its Sound and Diseased State* (1813), p. 71. Anne noted it in the booksellers on 24 January 1824; *Lister Papers*, SH:7/ML/E/7/0100.

55 M. Ramachandran and J. K. Aronson, 'John Bostock's First Description of Hayfever', *Journal of the Royal Society of Medicine* 104.6 (2011), 237–40, 237–8.

56 J. Bostock, *An Elementary System of Physiology* (Wells and Lilly, 1828), pp. 25–45. Anne did not read him until 6 March 1830; *Lister Papers*, SH:7/ML/E/13/0008; https://agreeableizing.blogspot.com/2021/01/saturday-march-6-1830.html.

57 16 February 1830, *Lister Papers*, SH:7/ML/E/12/0165–6; https://awhilesince.tumblr.com/post/625057086586437632/Tuesday-16-february-1830.

58 2 May 1829, *Lister Papers*, SH:7/ML/E/12/0013. SH:7/ML/E/12/0013; https://veryfineday.tumblr.com/post/623591913307635712/Saturday-2-may-1829.

59 13 February 1830, *Lister Papers*, SH:7/ML/E/12/0165; https://awhilesince.tumblr.com/post/624789431554064384/Saturday-13-february-1830.

60 14 November 1831, *Lister Papers*, SH:7/ML/E/14/0150; https://veryfineday.tumblr.com/post/627851465305800704/Monday-14-november-1831.

61 R. Richardson, *Death, Dissection, and the Destitute* (Chicago: University of Chicago Press, 2000), pp. 143, 273.

62 Burking refers to the murder of people to provide bodies for anatomists, the term derived from the practices of Edinburgh murderers Burke and Hare; 3 December 1831, *Lister Papers*, SH:7/ML/E/14/0158; https://veryfineday.tumblr.com/post/628679671343726592/Saturday-3-december-1831.

63 This may have been in response to the 1832 Anatomy attack that allowed dissection of unclaimed bodies in workhouses, and/or to a cholera epidemic; 17 January 1834, *Lister Papers*, SH:7/ML/E/16/0159; https://awhilesince.tumblr.com/post/641026817290010624/Wednesday-22-january-1834.

64 D. B. Weiner and M. J. Sauter, 'The City of Paris and the Rise of Clinical Medicine', *Osiris* 18 (2003), 23–42, 25.

65 M. Foucault, *The Birth of the Clinic* (London: Taylor and Francis, 2012), p. 84.

66 D. Outram, *Georges Cuvier: Vocation, Science and Authority in Post-Revolutionary France* (Manchester: Manchester University Press, 1984), p. 181.

67 Apparently, it was 'not proper' for Mrs Barlow's young daughter Jane to hear a lecture on generation even among animals; 19 June 1829, *Lister Papers*, SH:7/ML/E/12/0045; https://accountformiscellany.tumblr.com/.

68 K. E. Rothschuh, *History of Physiology*, trans. Guenther E. Risse (Huntington, NY: Krieger, 1973), p. xviii.

69 J. V. Pickstone, 'Bureaucracy, Liberalism and the Body in Post-Revolutionary France: Bichat's Physiology and the Paris School of Medicine', *History of Science* 19.2 (1981), 115–42, 117–18; Rothschuh, *History of Physiology*, p. 116; R. S. Tubbs et al., *History of Anatomy: an International Perspective* (Hoboken, NJ: John Wiley and Sons, 2019), p. 107.

70 E. A. Williams, *The Physical and the Moral: Anthropology, Physiology, and Philosophical Medicine in France, 1750–1850* (Cambridge: Cambridge University Press, 2002), p. 95.

71 'Nous avons divisé les organes génitaux de l'homme d'après les principaux phénomènes de la fonction qu'ils exercent; ceux de la femme ne se prêtent point à cette distribution'; X. Bichat, *Oeuvres complètes de Bichat*, vol. XI (Paris: J.-S. Chaudé, 1832), p. 280.

72 30 March 1830, *Lister Papers*, SH:7/ML/E/13/0015; https://agreeableizing.blogspot.com/2021/01/saturday-march-20-1830.html.

73 C. Régnier, 'Body Painting: Five Centuries of French Anatomical Illustrations', *Medicographia* 34.1 (2012), 106–15, 111; Tubbs et al., *History of Anatomy*, p. 116.

74 Catherine Euler first discovered this quotation; see C. A. Euler, 'Moving between Worlds: Gender, Class, Politics, Sexuality and Women's Networks in the Diaries of Anne of Shibden Hall, Halifax, Yorkshire, 1830–1840', unpublished PhD, University of York (1995), p. 322; 23 February 1830, *Lister Papers*, SH:7/ML/E/12/0169; https://awhilesince.tumblr.com/post/625683664082239488/tuesday-23-february-1830.

75 P. H. Nysten, *Dictionnaire de médicine de chirurgie de pharmacie*. . ., 4th ed. (Paris: J. A. Brosson, 1824), p. 188. Anne bought Nysten on 19 February 1830, *Lister Papers*, SH:7/ML/E/12/0167; https://awhilesince.tumblr.com/post/625330553139363840/Friday-19-february-1830

76 P. A. Béclard, *Eléments d'anatomie général ou description de tous les genres d'organes qui composent le corps humain* (Paris: Béchet Jeune, 1827), pp. 333–4, 35, 68. This resembles the theory of Broussais, the controversial anatomist who believed that anatomy was explained by irritation or stimulations that caused contractions or at worst inflammation in the body. E. H. Ackerknecht, 'Broussais or a Forgotten Medical Revolution', *Bulletin of the History of Medicine* 27 (1953), 320–43, 330.

77 18 July 1829, Lister Papers, SH:7/ML/E/12/0058; https://annelister-wellwellwell.tumblr.com/post/627456169161654272/saturday-july-18-1829.

78 Hippolyte Cloquet, *Traité d'anatomie descriptive*, 2 vols. (Paris: Clochard, 1816), vol. II, p. 172; 13 March 1830, *Lister Papers*, SH:7/ML/E/13/0011; https://agreeableizing.blogspot.com/2021/01/1830-march-saturday13-710.html.

79 8 May 1830, Lister Papers, SH:7/ML/E/13/0036; https://wasalwaysagreatpickle.tumblr.com/post/624178122589437952/Saturday-8-may-1830. Anne had to borrow Cloquet from M. Audoin but obtained another copy later. 1 June 1830, Lister Papers, SH:7/ML/E/13/0047; https://wasalwaysagreatpickle.tumblr.com/post/625626868903723009/Tuesday-1-june-1830.

80 25 January 1831, Lister Papers, SH:7/ML/E/14/0017; https://wrotetheaboveoftoday.tumblr.com/post/632783000736808960/1831-tues-25-january. For Cuvier's lectures, and the attendance of women at lectures, see Outram, *Georges Cuvier*, p. 181.

81 G. Cuvier and G. Duvernoy, *Leçons d'anatomie comparée*, vol. VIII (Paris, 1846), p. 249.

82 On 1 February 1831, she had bought the anatomy book of J. B Sarlandière, *Anatomie méthodique* (Paris, 1829). *Lister Papers*, SH:7/ML/E/14/0020; https://wrotetheaboveoftoday.tumblr.com/post/633417235211386881/1831-tues-1-february.

83 17 February 1831, *Lister Papers*, SH:7/ML/E/12/0169, my transcription. The same day she read about female anatomy in Sarlandière, *Anatomie méthodique*, p. 43. I am attributing the source for her discovery somewhat differently to Anne Choma, in her excellent *Gentleman Jack* (London: Penguin 2017), p. 15. While Choma is correct on the date of this discovery, she attributes this to reading Virey, but in fact, Lister read Virey later, in April 1831.

84 J. Cloquet, *Manuel d'anatomie descriptive du corps humain: représentée en planches lithographiées*, 3 vols. (Paris: Bechet, 1825), vol. I, p. 177.

85 Bichat, *Oeuvres*, p. 284.

86 Nysten, *Dictionnaire de médicine*, pp. 187–8.

87 'Clitorisme', in *Dictionaire des sciences médicales* (Paris: Panckoucke, 1813), p. 380.

88 11 April 1831, '[B]ought both books of Virey and started reading them'; *Lister Papers*, SH:7/ML/E/14/0048; https://veryfineday.tumblr.com/post/626777122383462401/Monday-11-april-1831; J.-J. Virey, *Histoire naturelle du genre humain*, vol. II (Paris: Louis Hauman, 1834), and *De la femme, sous ses rapports physiologique, moral et littéraire* (Paris: Crochard, 1825).

89 For Virey, see S. Quinlan, 'Writing the Natural History of Women: Medicine, Social Thought and Genre in Post-Revolutionary France', in A. K. Doig and F. B. Sturzer (eds.), *Women, Gender and Disease in Eighteenth-Century England and France* (Newcastle upon Tyne: Cambridge Scholars, 2014), p. 33.

90 Virey, *Histoire naturelle*, vol. II, pp. 246; 20 April 1831, *Lister Papers*, SH:7/ML/E/14/0051; https://veryfineday.tumblr.com/post/627139642625490944/Wednesday-20-april-1831; 21 April 1831, *Lister Papers*, SH:7/ML/E/14/0051; https://veryfineday.tumblr.com/post/627230142593400832/Thursday-21-april-1831.

91 P. Scully and C. Crais, *Sara Baartman and the Hottentot Venus: a Ghost Story and a Biography* (Princeton: Princeton University Press, 2009), p. 133; Cuvier and Duvernoy, Leçons d'anatomie comparée, vol. VIII, p. 249. For Anne reading his book: Tuesday 25 May 1830, *Lister Papers*, SH:7/ML/E/13/0045; https://veryfineday.tumblr.com/post/624874521778847744/tuesday-25-may-1830. However, we do not know if she read that volume; this refers to vol. I.

92 U. Kistner, 'Georges Cuvier: Founder of Modern Biology (Foucault), or Scientific Racist (Cultural Studies)?', *Configurations* 7.2 (1999), 175–90, 180, 189; Williams, *The Physical and the Moral*, p. 207.

93 N. Rupke and G. Lauer, *Johann Friedrich Blumenbach: Race and Natural History, 1750–1850* (Abingdon: Taylor and Francis, 2018), pp. 1–8.

94 Eliza Raine, Anne's first lover, of half-Indian birth, faced racism from their friends. P. Hughes, *The Early Life of Miss Anne Lister and the Curious Tale of Miss Eliza Raine*, 2nd ed. (Ebook: Hues Books, 2015), p. 157.

PART II

'My spirit's oil': Lister Reading, Lister Writing

CHAPTER 4

'My Use of the Word Love': Lister, Language and the Dictionary

Stephen Turton

If the history of lesbianism has often been cast as one of invisibility and erasure,[1] then the history of lesbians using dictionaries could just as easily be described in terms of absence. In 1938, Virginia Woolf started writing a 'Supplement to the Dictionary of the English Language' and stopped after three entries. Her last definition was 'A word for those who put living people into books', but what that word should have been was left as a question mark.[2] When, in the 1970s, Judy Grahn began researching the etymologies of words for gay women and men, she 'spent more than one evening in complete frustration sitting banging a dictionary against [her] knees screaming, "I know you're in there!" after months of chasing the word *bulldike*'.[3] Monique Wittig and Sande Zeig chose to redress the gaps in mainstream dictionaries by compiling their own lexicon, *Lesbian Peoples: Material for a Dictionary* (1980, original French edition 1976), in which they imagine a forgotten lesbian past and a utopian lesbian future. However, as they note in their entry for *dictionary* itself, their work is 'only a rough draft', and its 'arrangement could be called lacunary'.[4] The most famous lacuna occurs at the entry for *Sappho*, which is a blank page.

Although absences like these may feel disheartening, I want to consider how they can also open up a space for creativity. Woolf's question mark solicits an answer. When Grahn did not find a definition of *bulldike*, she wrote her own – 'In slang, a strong, warriorlike Lesbian, assertive-looking Gay woman' – and fancifully carried its origins back to the Iceni queen Boudica.[5] The blank space Wittig and Zeig left under *Sappho* could be a testament to how little is known for certain about Sappho's life, or it could be an invitation to the dictionary's users to fill in what they imagine about the poet for themselves. And why not? After all, we routinely speak of 'using' a dictionary rather than simply 'reading' it. 'Use' is mutable and multifunctional. Using a dictionary might mean accepting what one finds in it, but it might also mean arguing with it, reinterpreting it, or even rewriting it to serve some alternative purpose.

In her own style, Anne Lister did all these things. Her interest in classical and modern languages made her a habitual user of dictionaries and grammars of Greek, Latin, French, Italian, German and Russian, as well as English. When she was twelve, she asked her aunt to get her the best dictionary that her savings (five guineas) could buy.[6] In her twenties, she compiled a short, private glossary of erotic and anatomical words she had gleaned from several reference works, starting with *fuck* and ending with *tribas*.[7] When the library she built up at Shibden Hall was auctioned after her death in 1840, a partial catalogue of its contents included thirty-nine dictionaries, ranging from Johann Scapula's *Lexicon Graeco-Latinum* to Pierre-Hubert Nysten's *Dictionnaire de médecine*.[8] It goes without saying that not all these titles (or terms) would have been expected to appear in a gentlewoman's library (or in her vocabulary). Then again, Lister was never averse to what Sara Ahmed has called 'queer uses'. *Queer* in this context refers not only to uses that are sexually subversive, but to any occasions when 'things [are] used in ways other than for which they were intended or by those other than for whom they were intended'. Importantly, Ahmed proposes that spaces as well as things can be turned to queer use, if they are occupied for functions unforeseen by the people who left them open.[9]

This chapter will trace the spaces and passages between Lister, language and dictionaries. Some of this ground has already been covered, of course. Scholars have addressed Lister's 'crypt hand', her codewords and her classical philology.[10] At the meta-critical level, there has been robust debate over the validity of applying to Lister labels such as *queer* and *lesbian*, with all the contemporary baggage that comes attached to them (see Gonda, this volume). Although I have already used both labels in proximity to Lister, this chapter will focus on the erotic words to which Lister did have access in the early nineteenth century, and the ways in which she found and refitted them to suit her personal needs. For modern readers, lexicography offers one window into Lister's verbal innovations. It also gives us a view of how she manoeuvred around certain patriarchal language attitudes inherited from the eighteenth century, which derided novelties in women's speech and writing as signs of ignorance rather than ingenuity.

In what follows, I will survey some of Lister's unconventional uses of dictionaries, as well as her inventive usage of language to express ideas that went unrecognised by dictionaries in her time. I will close with a comment on her use *by* dictionaries in our own time, when her life is chronicled in the *Dictionary of National Biography* and her diaries are quoted in the

Oxford English Dictionary. Throughout, it will be apparent that writing a lexicon is no more an impassive activity than using one. Samuel Johnson may have claimed in his landmark dictionary of 1755 that he did 'not form, but register[ed] the language ... [did] not teach men how they should think, but relate[d] how they have hitherto expressed their thoughts',[11] yet even the largest reference work can only provide a selective view of a living language. That the words, meanings and illustrative quotations selected by standard dictionaries have tended to favour the thoughts of men was a problem that Lister had to overcome, and one that still hampers lexicographers' treatment of her writing today.

Lister's Lookups

Admittedly, Lister often did use dictionaries in ways that their writers had intended: as guides to general knowledge and self-improvement. As a child, she had asked her aunt to ensure that the dictionary she bought her would 'not only instruct [her] in Spelling, but in the ... fashionable way of pronounciation [*sic*]'.[12] Years later, her high-society aspirations still made her sensitive to anything in her speech that might mark her out as parochial. When she was told by Isabella Norcliffe that her pronunciation of *iron* as it was spelled was a 'Yorkshirism', Lister initially 'resist[e]d' but then 'turn[in]g to Sheridan's pronounc[in]g dict[ionary]' was vexed to 'find she [was] right'.[13] Thomas Sheridan's dictionary – which aimed at 'fix[ing] a general standard' of English pronunciation throughout Britain – did not actually proscribe the northern form of *iron*, but the only pronunciation it registered was the southern 'i′-urn'.[14] As Lister's anxiety makes plain, exclusions such as this were (and are) socially meaningful. When a dictionary is intended to provide a model of 'standard' English, then whatever it omits is positioned as illegitimate – and delegitimising certain words can in turn stigmatise the people who use them.[15] At the same time, words may be delegitimised in the first place *because* of the people who use them, or who are thought to use them.

This illegitimation is not always effected by omission. Johnson's dictionary, for example, included several headwords that he nonetheless disparaged as 'women's cant', though the quotations with which he illustrated them were all drawn from male authors. *Flirtation* ('A cant word among women') and *horrid* (sense 2, 'in womens cant' [*sic*]) were supported by extracts from Alexander Pope, *frightfully* (sense 2, 'A woman's word') by one from Jonathan Swift, and so on.[16] Swift's own unflattering remark on women's speech is quoted in the dictionary under *fluency* (sense 2): 'The common *fluency* of speech in many men, and most women, is owing to a scarcity of matter, and a scarcity of words; for whoever is a master of language, and hath a mind full of ideas, will be apt, in speaking, to hesitate upon the choice of both.' In a similar vein, the Earl of Chesterfield – Johnson's ineffectual patron – wrote sardonically just before the dictionary's publication that he hoped Johnson would not 'proscribe any of those happy redundancies and luxuriancies of expression' with which the language had been 'enriched' by his 'fair countrywomen, whose natural turn [was] more to the copiousness, than to the correctness of diction'.[17]

Lister was thus linguistically marginalised by her gender as well as her provincialism. Yet, while she was willing to defer to a southern standard of pronunciation, her navigation of sexist language norms was more complex. Ironically, though the above male writers dismissed female innovations as misuses, their own writing would be exploited by the innovative Lister, who turned their words to her own ends. She found Swift's *fluency* quotation in Johnson and copied it into her diary – but only to apply it to a man, the 'slow, & tedious, & tiresome' Dr Scudamore.[18] Given her erudition, Lister doubtless saw herself as the exception to Swift's rule. More subversively, she took Dr Johnson's famed rejection of Chesterfield's belated show of interest in his dictionary – 'The notice . . . had it been early, had been kind' – and reworked it into a defence of her decision to visit, at last, the home of the attractive but unpedigreed Miss Elizabeth Browne. 'S[ai]d ye D[octo]r', she reminded herself, 'H[a]d it been earl[ie]r it h[a]d been kind[e]r. . .'[19]

As other scholars have observed, Lister's social conservatism was engaged in an intricate dance with her gender nonconformity.[20] This sometimes led her to object to improprieties in other women that she privately allowed in herself. While she criticised Isabella for being '*too fond of gross language*',[21] Lister made a point of looking up obscene words in the *Universal Etymological English Dictionary* of Nathan Bailey. She gathered her findings into an encrypted glossary in one of her commonplace books, which included:

> *Fuck . . . fœminam subagitare* [to handle a woman sexually]
> *Cunt . . . pudendum muliebre* [the genitals of a woman]
> *Prick . . . a mans yard*[22]

In this case, Lister's was surely not a use of the dictionary that its compiler had anticipated. Bailey's screening of the first two definitions behind Latin – a language known to few Englishmen and fewer Englishwomen – exemplifies how elite male stereotypes about women's discourse existed alongside attempts to control the discourses to which women did have access. Yet, while classical tongues were obstacles to many readers, to Lister they were stepping-stones to knowledge she could obtain in few other places. Her exceptional learning and relative wealth allowed her not only to interpret definitions but to consult dictionaries (as well as other books) that were not addressed to her.

When she was twenty-eight, she learnt from Scapula's Greek–Latin lexicon that *τριβάδες* (*tribades*) were 'dicuntur fœminæ, perditæ libidinis ac nefariæ lasciviæ: quæ *ὀλίσβῳ* sese *τρίβουσιν* mutuo' (said to be women of depraved lustfulness and vile lasciviousness who mutually *rub* themselves with an *olisbos* [i.e. a dildo]).[23] Lister may have been prompted to look up the word after reading a 'ver[y] interest[in]g' article on Sappho in the *Historical and Critical Dictionary* of Pierre Bayle: written for an audience of male scholars, the dictionary candidly described Sappho as 'a Famous *Tribas*' whose poetic fragments included 'an Ode to one of her Mistresses'.[24] Around the same time, Lister was intrigued by allusions she found in Suetonius's *De Vita Caesarum* and Martial's epigrams to the lost erotic works of another female poet, Elephantis.[25] Bayle's dictionary had no entry for Elephantis, but Lister walked down to Halifax's subscription library to consult the *Bibliotheca Classica* of John Lemprière. Unfortunately, all she learnt from Lemprière's dictionary was that Elephantis was 'a poetess who wrote lascivious verses'.[26]

Such was the unpredictability of tracing the sexual bi(bli)ographies of ancient women through books written by and for men.[27] Still, Lister must have drawn her own conclusions about what Martial had meant when he told of the 'Veneris novae figurae' (novel erotic postures) once unfolded by Elephantis.[28] Her imagination would certainly be fired up a few months later, when she came across the word *crisantis* in Juvenal's satires and looked it up in Adam Littleton's *Latin Dictionary*. There, the translation of the lemma *crisso* as '*to wag the tail* (de muliere dic. *in actu copulationis*)' (said of a woman in the act of copulation) so excited Lister that she gave herself an orgasm.[29] Though *crisso* was conventionally applied to cross-sex intercourse, the dictionary entry did not actually make the presence of a man explicit – and this gap was enough for Lister to use as a way in.

Studying anatomy would prove equally stimulating. Among the French medical books Lister bought in Paris in 1830 was Nysten's *Dictionnaire de médecine*; while perusing its definition of '*clitoris* &c. &c'., she decided to '*tr*[y] *if* [she] *had much of one*' and ended up masturbating in her seat.[30] Nysten's description of the *clitoris* as possessing a structure 'analogue à celle du pénis' (analogous to that of the penis) would have appealed to Lister, given her daydreams about having a phallus, but perhaps she was more enticed by the adjacent entry for *clitorisme*, 'l'abus que les femmes font quelquefois de leur sexe lorsqu'elles ont un clitoris volumineux' (the abuse that women sometimes make of their sex when they have an enlarged clitoris; see Clark, this volume).[31] Even if Lister found her body to be of ordinary proportions, her extraordinary use of the dictionary shows that intellectual self-improvement can lie on a continuum with self-discovery, and even with '*self pollution*' – the definition she gave to *masturbation* in her personal glossary.[32] Although she often regretted the physical consequences of her imagination, she betrayed no shame in the imagination itself, or in its ability to find channels for her desire through hostile scholarly terrain.

Novel Denominations

In conversation with other women, Lister's learning became a means both of flirting and of showing off, and these performances were sometimes accompanied by language play. To Anne 'Nantz' Belcombe she related '*the anecdote of the ancients using lead plates to prevent pain in their knees the expression which I use & which she understands to mean desire*'. Having laid this groundwork, Lister could later seductively tell Nantz about the '*pain* [she felt] *in* [her own] *knees*'.[33] To Nantz's sister, Mariana Lawton, Lister revealed that the emperor Tiberius was said to have owned a '*picture by Parrhasius of Meleager & Atalanta sucking his queer*'.[34] *Queer* (or *quere*) is well known to researchers as Lister's euphemism for the vulva, though she applied it to the penis too. Of course, here and elsewhere in the diaries, it is not clear whether Lister actually used *queer* in speech or if she just inserted it into her write-up afterwards. A similar question hangs over some of the terms Lister attributes to her conversational partners. When Lister reports that Isabella '*said she was well of her cousin*' – *cousin* being Lister's customary word for menstruation – was it Isabella's word too or has she been paraphrased on the page?[35] *Cousin*, at least, was probably not limited to Lister – or indeed to her social network – but the status of certain other 'Listerisms' is harder to appraise.[36] Although evidence of use beyond Lister's diary can sometimes be gleaned from the letters and journals of her friends and lovers, at present it is difficult to be sure which terms were idiolectal (restricted to Lister), duolectal (shared between Lister and one partner) or sociolectal (common to multiple members of Lister's circle); in the latter cases, Lister might not have been the originator of every term.

Whatever their range of circulation, Lister did not use her codewords for want of a knowledge of their more common – or more esoteric – synonyms. Her private glossary shows that she knew the vulva could be called a '*cunt*' or '*pudendum*' and the penis a '*prick … yard peni*[s] *veratrum* [or] *verenda*' as well as a *queer*, and that menstruation could be called '*catamen*[i]*a the menses monthly courses or flowers*' as well as *cousin*.[37] The Earl of Chesterfield may have scoffed at women who took existing words and gave them new meanings – as he said, changing them 'like a guinea into shillings for pocket money, to be employed in the several occasional purposes of the day'[38] – but Lister's coinages served vital personal and relational functions.

First, creating a private vocabulary and orthography was a way of fostering intimacy with other women and of protecting that intimacy from suspicious eavesdroppers and snooping readers. While Lister lived with Maria Barlow, for instance, the two used the phrase *going to Italy* to signal Lister's '*acknowledg*[ing Mrs Barlow] *as* [her] *own & giv*[ing] *her* [her] *promise for life*'.[39] Years before, Lister had devised her crypt hand at least partly so that she and her first love, Eliza Raine, could record the details of their relationship in secret; later, the code allowed Lister and Mariana to shield their correspondence from the latter's jealous husband.[40] Lister was understandably annoyed when Isabella divulged to a group of acquaintances that she '[kept] a journ[al], & [set] d[o]wn ev[ery]one's conversat[io]n in [her] peculiar handwrit[in]g'. Nonetheless, it is hard not to detect a note of pride in Lister's retort that the code was 'alm[o]st imposs[ible]' to decipher.[41]

Crypt hand began as a simple Greek letter cipher (*a* = **α**, *b* = **β**, etc.) but grew to incorporate Latin letters, Arabic numerals and mathematical signs as well. Inventing this labyrinth of glyphs was not just a defensive strategy but an intellectual game – one that allowed Lister to play with the relations between symbols and entire words or names. By 1818, she was placing the mark + or × in the margins of diary entries on days when she masturbated. *Cross* in turn became her name for the mark and, metonymically, for the act it signified.

September 1818: *thinking of Miss B*[elcombe] *& only just escaped* +[42]
December 1819: *observe the cross at the head of today*['s entry] *oh I wish I could get off this vile habit*[43]
August 1820: *got to Martial & read him till near five when it ended in a cross astride of the bed post*[44]

As early as 1817, Lister began using another symbol to mark days on which she had sex with a woman, or what she called *kisses* (the word is returned to below). This symbol, 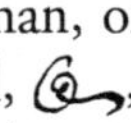, resembled a ligature of the Greek letters *ος* (i.e. *os*) – perhaps an abbreviation of Latin *osculum* 'kiss'.[45] (In the first of the following quotations, **Π** stands for Mariana.)

January 1817:  **Π** *gave me two very good kisses last night*[46]
November 1820: *I have had nothing to do with Tib* [i.e. Isabella] *when there is not this mark made* [47]

Beyond intimacy, secrecy and creativity, the resignification of words afforded Lister's desires and relationships a legitimacy that the standard language would have denied them. At times, this was as simple as laying claim to the word *love*, as Lister did when she tried to persuade Mary

Vallance of the ardour of her feelings during their brief affair at Langton Hall in 1820: '*I made her understand my use of the word love & still she said she did not wish me not to love her.*'[48] Even one of Lister's now most familiar declarations – '*I love & only love the fairer sex ... my heart revolts from any other love than theirs*' – becomes radical again when placed beside the limited definitions of *love*, noun and verb, offered by contemporary lexicography.[49] For Johnson, the primary meanings of *love* and *to love* were 'The passion between the sexes' and 'To regard with passionate affection, as that of one sex to the other'. Usages like Lister's, had his dictionary acknowledged them at all, would probably have been degraded to sense 7 of the noun, 'Lewdness'.[50]

Nor would Lister's more serious romantic unions be intelligible under Johnson's definition of *marriage*, 'The act of uniting a man and woman for life'.[51] Chris Roulston has written in detail about Lister's and her partners' reappropriation of marital discourse.[52] Some of their marriage talk was simply optative – with Mrs Barlow: '*said again & again I wished I could marry her*' – or similative – with Ann Walker: '*it is to be as a marriage between us*' – but the lovers also referred to each other unequivocally in (cross-sex) spousal terms.[53] Eliza Raine called Lister her 'husband', as did Mariana, who further promised to be Lister's 'faithful wife'.[54] Privately, Lister referred to Mariana and Mrs Barlow as her '*wife & mistress*' respectively.[55] In these partnerships, the language of marriage carried emotional weight even if it had no legal recognition. At the same time, Roulston points out that the more outwardly legible a same-sex union became as a marriage, the more it risked attracting unfriendly notice.[56] The desire for validation did not trump the need for discretion.

Still, the subtle and the sentimental were not always opposed. Lister managed to combine the two in her preferred word for sex between women (or an orgasm resulting from it), *kiss*. This was a well-established literary euphemism for penovaginal sex, but Lister's usage suggests a further play on the standard meaning of the word – as Johnson had put it, a 'Salute given by joining lips'.[57] Lister resignified both the verb and the noun.

> November 1816: [Nantz] *said I wanted to make a fool of her & if she had more resolution she would not kiss me again*[58]
>
> October 1820: [Isabella] *wanted a kiss ... however grubbling seemed to satisfy her*[59]
>
> November 1834: *a tolerable kiss* [with Ann Walker] *last night*[60]

Kiss was a word that Lister appears to have shared with at least one of her lovers: the November 1834 quotation has a corresponding entry in Ann Walker's own journal, which concludes, 'went to bed – K –'.[61] The October 1820 quotation is also perhaps Lister's earliest recorded use of *grubbling* to denote fingering a woman. This may have been another literary borrowing. In general use, *grubble* simply meant 'to grope' without a sexual connotation. Johnson defined it as 'To feel in the dark', supported by one quotation from John Dryden's *Don Sebastian*, 'Now let me rowl and *grubble* thee', in reference to drawing lots.[62] But Dryden had given the word a sexual spin elsewhere, in his translation of one of the elegies from the *Amores* of Ovid. The elegy depicts a man who hopes to meet his mistress at a crowded feast that is also attended by her husband: 'There I will be, and there we cannot miss, / Perhaps to grubble, or at least to kiss.'[63] Dannielle Orr proposes that Lister may have derived her use of *grubble* from this passage.[64] While direct evidence is wanting, Lister did own a copy of Dryden's *Miscellanies*, and by January 1820 she had acquired an English translation of Ovid's *Ars Amatoria*, which often came bound with the *Amores*.[65] If she came across Dryden's version of the elegy, then she could well have sympathised with its lament for forbidden love.

Crucially, although Lister drew from the language of cross-sex intimacy, she rearranged what she took into a personal taxonomy of sexual ethics. While a medical lexicographer such as Nysten might condemn all kinds of *masturbation* as 'vice honteux' (shameful vice),[66] for Lister it was imperative to maintain a distinction between manually gratifying oneself (*crosses*) and others (*grubbling*). Whereas the former was a sin that had '*no mutual affection to excuse it*', the latter was a valid expression of '*natural & undeviating feeling*'.[67] This naturalness did not, however, extend to the use of a dildo between women. As Lister declared to Mrs Barlow, that was '*artifice*': '*it was very different from mine* [and] *would be no pleasure to me . . . I know she understands all about the use of a olisbos* [*sic*]'.[68] Curiously, while Lister was aware of *Sapphic* as a general label for sexuality between women, she seems to have used the phrases '*Saφic regard*' and '*Sapphic love*' to refer to sex with a dildo in particular.[69] How she formed this association is unclear, but it may have been influenced by what she had read about Sappho's status as a tribas, and the tribades' preference for olisboi, in Bayle's and Scapula's dictionaries. At any rate, these acts of stimulation – with hands or with toys, of the self or of another – were ethically discrete, and so they needed to be lexically separate. I have referred to Lister's novel linguistic uses as forms of 'play', but it should be clear that this was play with a serious intent. Lister was not just changing guineas into shillings: she was casting her own currency of desire.

A Legacy in Words

In the present day, dictionary users can find information on Lister's erotic writings more easily than she could track down those of Sappho or Elephantis. Her entry in the *Oxford Dictionary of National Biography*, in addition to discussing her studies, politics and travels, is explicit about 'her first lesbian experiences' with Eliza Raine, her love affair with Mariana Lawton and her domestic partnership with Ann Walker.[70] This entry, first published in the revised *DNB* in 2004, is one instance of the revisers' attempts to combat the androcentrism of the dictionary's first edition (1885–1900) and its supplements, in which entries about women made up 5 per cent of the total. In the 2004 edition, that number rose to 10 per cent.[71]

Gendered exclusions have likewise marked the pages of another historical reference work, the *Oxford English Dictionary*. As had been the case in Johnson's dictionary more than a century before, the quotation banks of the *OED*'s first edition (1884–1928) were dominated by the writings of male authors from the traditional literary canon.[72] Its compilers were also more reticent in print than Lister had been in her private glossary: they included an entry for *cock* but balked at *cunt*. In 1933, the sexual sense of *lesbian* was left out of the *OED*'s first *Supplement* because the editor in charge of *L* objected to it. *Lesbian* and *cunt* at last appeared in the more permissive second *Supplement* (1972–86), along with *fuck*, after its chief editor consulted several scholars about the propriety of admitting words such as these.[73] Notably, one Oxford professor protested that the draft definition of *fuck* should be altered to specify that in its transitive sense 'the word is used only of males'. 'You may not think this worth pointing out,' he warned, 'but I incline to think it is; otherwise lady novelists not themselves brought up on the word, and looking for something new, might misapply it!'[74] Male anxieties about women's linguistic and erotic agency clearly did not evaporate after the nineteenth century.

There was little change in the *OED*'s second edition (1989), which was mostly an amalgam of the first edition and its supplements into one alphabetical sequence. However, since the *OED* was put online in 2000 – at which point work began on fully revising the dictionary for its third edition (*OED3*) – its editorial team have affirmed their commitment to improving the coverage of 'women's writing and non-literary texts', including diaries.[75] Lister's journals have so far played a very small part in this. As of December 2021, Lister is quoted eight times in the online *OED*, all in entries that have been updated or created for the third edition: see Table 1. Three of the quotations, marked by asterisks, provide the earliest evidence that the *OED* has been able to find for the senses they illustrate. None of the quotations is for a nonce-use (that is, a word or sense for which Lister is the only author cited). All but one of the extracts were sourced from Helena Whitbread's second edited volume of Lister's diaries, *No Priest but Love*. The last quotation, for *potheration*, was copied from the now-defunct website www.herstoryuntold.org.uk.

Table 1 *Quotations from Lister in* OED3

Headword	Quotation
Bakewell, n. 1	1825 A. LISTER *Diary* 13 Sept. in *No Priest but Love* (1992) 128 Dessert of Bakewell cheesecake, something like a raspberry puff.*
beaucoup, n.	1824 A. LISTER *Diary* 13 Dec. in *No Priest but Love* (1992) 64 I ought to drink beaucoup of my barley water nitre.
daybook, n. 2	1826 A. LISTER *Diary* 9 July in *No Priest but Love* (1992) 181 He explained the nature of account by a treble entry – day book, cash book, ledger.
fell, v. 3	1826 A. LISTER *Diary* 10 Jan. in H. Whitbread *No Priest but Love* (1992) 154 The Keighleys felling a large willow by the brookside.
leaf tin (s.v. *leaf*, n.[1])	1826 A. LISTER *Diary* 29 June in *No Priest but Love* (1992) 178 About ½ hour undergoing the operation of having the tooth filled with leaf tin.
motto, n. 2c	1824 A. LISTER *Diary* 4 Sept. in *No Priest but Love* (1992) 14 We had..as we always have at dinner, those little bonbons wrapt up in mottos.*
patisserie, n. 2	1824 A. LISTER *Diary* 25 Oct. in *No Priest but Love* (1992) 36 I set off to..the best patissérie in Paris.*
potheration (s.v. *pother*, v.)	1839 A. LISTER *Diary* Oct. in *www.herstoryuntold.org.uk* (OED Archive) The man must have been a little beside himself this morning; for nothing called for such a potheration.

The small number of quotations from *Priest*, not to mention the inconsistent citing of Whitbread as its editor, suggests that the book was consulted *ad hoc* for particular words by different contributors, rather than being systematically combed through by one reader. Overall, the words for which Lister is cited – culinary, social, domestic – belong to the same semantic fields that Charlotte Brewer has identified as predominant in the *OED*'s treatment (on a larger scale) of one of Lister's near-contemporaries, Jane Austen.[76] Brewer wonders how much the *OED*'s favouring of quotations for 'ordinary' words from Austen reflects the general diction of her novels, and how much it is inflected by the 'assumption, that it [is] appropriate to source household, family and domestic terms' – rather than, say, 'moral vocabulary' – 'from texts written by women'.[77] Lister was writing a diary, not a novel, and her prose is understandably rich in the language of domesticity and sociability. If *Priest* had been read methodically for the *OED*, it could have provided other usages from this sphere that antedate the earliest evidence at present in the dictionary. For example, *OED3* traces *passé* in the sense of 'No longer fashionable; out of date; superseded' back to 1844; Lister had employed this sense – 'I loved her once, but this last was passé' – in 1824.[78] Also overlooked is Lister's use of *napkin* to mean a menstrual cloth – 'she considers me too much as a woman . . . I have aired napkins before her' (1825) – a sense that *OED3* dates only to 1873.[79]

But Lister's vocabulary encompassed more than ordinary words. The non-standard words used by her or her circle, such as *cousin* for menstruation and *queer* for genitals, have not been registered in *OED3*'s entries for those words. The entries for *cross*, *grubble* and *kiss* have yet to be updated for the third edition, and it remains to be seen whether Lister's resignifications of them will fare any better. Of course, there are limits to the number of nonce-uses that a dictionary can include, no matter its size. Yet, even if *OED3* did not attempt to tease out the precise shades of meaning in, for instance, Lister's usage of *Sapphic*, that usage is surely still worth quoting under the dictionary's current definition of *Sapphic* (adj. sense 2), 'Of, relating to, engaging in, or characterized by sexual activity between women or female same-sex desire; = LESBIAN *adj.* 2'. This definition was revised in 2018. It is followed by seven quotations taken from texts written between 1761 and 2006 – none of which is attributed to a woman.[80]

Male writers likewise supply all eight of the quotations (from 1602 to 2004) under *OED3*'s definition of *husband* (n. sense 2b), updated in 2016: 'In other (esp. same-sex) relationships in which the two partners are regarded as occupying roles analogous to those in a traditional mixed-sex marriage: the person assuming the role regarded as more stereotypically masculine, i.e. as being equivalent to that of the husband'.[81] All but one of the quotations describe male same-sex relationships. The exception, from the *American Journal of Sociology* (1931) – 'These "honies" refer to each other as "my man" and "my woman", "my wife" and "my husband"' – does not make the gender of its subjects clear, and users must unearth the original article to learn that it concerns the 'problem of homosexuality' at an institution for 'delinquent girls'.[82] Even here, the voices of women are mediated by an unsympathetic male ventriloquist. How strikingly different is Mariana's use of *wife* in her heartfelt pledge to Lister in *Priest*: 'so long as life shall last, I will be your lover, friend & your faithful wife'.[83]

A similar note of dissent could be added to *OED3*'s entry for *olisbos*, 'A dildo', revised in 2004. Its earliest quotation comes from an 1887 translation of the *Manual of Classical Erotology* by Friedrich Karl Forberg, commenting on the tribadic figure of Bassa in Martial's epigrams: 'There are expounders..who..have imagined that Bassa misused women by introducing into their vagina a leathern contrivance, an olisbos, a godemiche' (original ellipses). Lister was familiar with this view. As noted earlier, she had read about women rubbing each other with olisboi in the entry for τριβάδες in Scapula's Greek–Latin lexicon. However, perhaps because of her own dislike of dildos, she was sceptical of their universality among classical tribades. Her own interpretation of Bassa was that '*it does not appear that she made use of olisbos a leather penis as Scapula says some of them did*' – a remark that not only argues against that in *Classical Erotology* but antedates its use of *olisbos* to 1820.[84] Of course, this comment appears in one of Lister's as-yet undigitised papers, and given the limited interest *OED* contributors have so far shown in her published diaries, it seems doubtful they will read the manuscripts.

The gender bias in these entries is not exceptional.[85] As a historical dictionary, the *OED* is bound to document centuries of English in which works by men have been produced more frequently, distributed more widely and valued more highly than those by women. Nonetheless, at any point in time, there is never just one side to the linguistic guinea. As Ahmed reminds us, 'A history of use is also a history of that which is not deemed useful enough to be preserved or retained.'[86] The history of a word is a history not only of what it has been used to mean but whom it has been used by. When a dictionary fails to preserve the usage of the marginalised, it reinforces that marginalisation.

There will always be gaps in the record, it is true. Woolf couldn't think of a term for 'those who put living people into books'; nor is there a term for those who put living languages into books. Lexicographers cannot capture everything a word has ever meant. Then again, they also cannot constrain everything a word may yet mean. Silence in the lexicon, rather than being an end-point, might only be the start of a conversation. So it was for Lister and Ann Walker one morning in 1834, when the two were travelling in France. As Walker's journal records, 'd[ea]r[es]t slept till 8 – & I then went to her – at 9$^{\underline{15}}$ we got up, explained to me all [the] words I had written down that I c[oul]d not find in [the] Diction[ar]y'.[87] A century and a half before Wittig and Zeig, Lister and Walker showed that moving beyond the dictionary can be an act of intimacy between women. In her own writings, Lister's linguistic innovations may not have been publicly political in the manner of *Lesbian Peoples*, but they were equally a means of laying claim to a language whose standard histories were devoid of words that affirmed her emotions and relationships.[88] Happily, as she discovered, empty spaces provided some of the most fertile ground for self-articulation.

Notes

1 For a recent discussion, see V. Traub, *Thinking Sex with the Early Moderns* (Philadelphia: University of Pennsylvania Press, 2016), pp. 283–8. Parts of this chapter were presented at the April 2022 meeting of the Anne Lister Society in Halifax, Yorkshire, and have been greatly improved by the insights of other participants.

2 R. Fowler, 'Virginia Woolf: Lexicographer', *English Language Notes* 29 (2002), 54–70.

3 J. Grahn, *Another Mother Tongue: Gay Words, Gay Worlds* (Boston: Beacon Press, 1984), pp. xii–xiii.

4 M. Wittig and S. Zeig, *Lesbian Peoples: Material for a Dictionary*, trans. M. Wittig and S. Zeig (London: Virago, 1980), s.v. *dictionary*.

5 Grahn, *Another Mother Tongue*, p. 305.

6 Anne Lister to Anne Lister (senior), 3 February 1803, *Anne Lister Papers*, West Yorkshire Archive Service, Calderdale, SH:7/ML/3 [hereafter *Lister Papers*]. This letter, like several journal passages cited in this chapter, appears in Helena Whitbread's indispensable editions of Lister's diaries, but I have quoted directly from the manuscripts where possible.

7 See S. Turton, 'The Lexicographical Lesbian: Remaking the Body in Anne Lister's Erotic Glossary', *Review of English Studies* 73.310 (2022), 537–51, from which this chapter incorporates several findings.

8 *Catalogue of the Valuable Library of Books, Maps, &c. (Formerly the Property of the Late Mrs Lister, of Shibden Hall,) to Be Sold by Auction, without Reserve* (Halifax: W. Birtwhistle, 1846).

9 S. Ahmed, *What's the Use? On the Uses of Use* (Durham, NC: Duke University Press, 2019), pp. 199–200.

10 All three are discussed by A. Rowanchild, '"Peeping behind the curtain": the Significance of Classical Texts in the Sexual Self-Construction of Anne Lister', in R. Pearson (ed.), *The Victorians and the Ancient World: Archaeology and Classicism in Nineteenth-Century Culture* (Newcastle upon Tyne: Cambridge Scholars, 2006), pp. 139–51. The evolution of crypt hand is traced in greater detail by J. Liddington, 'Anne Lister of Shibden Hall, Halifax (1791–1840): Her Diaries and the Historians', *History Workshop Journal* 35 (1993), 45–77. There are several commentaries on codewords in H. Whitbread (ed.), *The Secret Diaries of Anne Lister: No Priest but Love* (London: Virago, 2015, originally published in 1992), pp. 91, 92, 201. Lister's classical learning is further explored by A. Clark, 'Anne Lister's Construction of Lesbian Identity', *Journal of the History of Sexuality*, 7 (1996), 23–50, and C. Roulston, 'Sexuality in Translation: Anne Lister and the Ancients', *Journal of the History of Sexuality* 30 (2021), 112–35.

11 S. Johnson, *A Dictionary of the English Language*, 2 vols. (London: J. Knapton et al., 1755), vol. 1, sig. C1^{v}.

12 Anne Lister to Anne Lister (senior), 3 February 1803, *Lister Papers*, SH:7/ML/3.

13 31 August 1819, *Lister Papers*, SH:7/ML/E/3/0088.
14 T. Sheridan, *A General Dictionary of the English Language* (London: J. Dodsley, C. Dilly and J. Wilkie, 1780), sig. B1^{v}, s.v. *iron*.
15 See S. Turton, '"Improper words": Silencing Same-Sex Desire in Eighteenth-Century General English Dictionaries', *Oxford Research in English*, 8 (2019), 9–36.
16 Quoted in C. Brewer, '"A Goose-Quill or a Gander's?": Female Writers in Johnson's Dictionary', in F. Johnston and L. Mugglestone (eds.), *Samuel Johnson: the Arc of the Pendulum* (Oxford: Oxford University Press, 2012), pp. 120–39. Brewer finds that barely any works by women were quoted in Johnson's dictionary.
17 [P. D. Stanhope], *The World*, 100 (1754), 603.
18 21 September 1825, *Lister Papers*, SH:7/ML/E/9/0019.
19 S. Johnson. *The Celebrated Letter from Samuel Johnson, LLD, to Philip Dormer Stanhope, Earl of Chesterfield; Now First Published, with Notes*, ed. J. Boswell (London: C. Dilly, 1790), p. 4; 2 March 1819, *Anne Lister Papers*, SH:7/ML/E/2/0114.
20 S. Lanser, 'Tory Lesbians: Economies of Intimacy and the Status of Desire', in J. C. Beynon and C. Gonda (eds.), *Lesbian Dames: Sapphism in the Long Eighteenth Century* (Farnham: Ashgate, 2010), pp. 173–89; Roulston, 'Sexuality in Translation', p. 115.
21 21 September 1818, *Lister Papers*, SH:7/ML/E/2/0069. I have followed the convention of transcribing passages decoded from Lister's crypt hand in italics.
22 May(?) 1820, Extracts from Books Read, *Lister Papers*, SH:7/ML/EX/6, f. 26.
23 May(?) 1820, Extracts from Books Read, SH:7/ML/EX/6, f. 27; J. Scapula, *Lexicon Graeco-Latinum*, new ed., 2 vols. (Glasgow: J. Cuthell et al., 1816), vol. II, s.v. τριβάδες.
24 16 March 1820, *Lister Papers*, SH:7/ML/E/4/0038; P. Bayle, *An Historical and Critical Dictionary*, trans., 4 vols. (London: C. Harper et al., 1710), vol. IV, s. v. *Sappho*.
25 May(?) 1820, Extracts from Books Read, SH:7/ML/EX/6, f. 27.
26 11 January 1820, *Lister Papers*, SH:7/ML/E/4/0022; J. Lemprière, *Bibliotheca Classica; or, a Classical Dictionary*, 3rd ed. (London: T. Cadell, Jr., and W. Davies, 1797), s.v. *Elephantis*.
27 Later, when Lemprière's dictionary was adapted 'for the use of both sexes in Public Schools and Private Academies', the entry for Elephantis was omitted (J. Lemprière and E. H. Barker, *Lempriere's Classical Dictionary* (London: printed by A. J. Valpy, 1833), pp. vii–viii).
28 Martial, *Epigrams*, ed. and trans. D. R. Shackleton Bailey, 3 vols. (Cambridge, MA: Harvard University Press, 1993), vol. III, pp. 124–5.
29 A. Littleton, *Dr Adam Littleton's Latin Dictionary*, 6th ed. (London: J. Walthoe et al., 1735), s.v. *crisso*; 29 June 1820, *Lister Papers*, SH:7/ML/E/4/0066.
30 18 February 1830, *Lister Papers*, SH:7/ML/E/12/0166; 23 February 1830, *Lister Papers*, SH:7/ML/E/12/0169.

31 P.-H. Nysten, *Dictionnaire de médecine*, 3rd ed. (Paris: J.-A. Brosson et J.-S. Chaudé, 1814), s.v. *clitoris*, *clitorisme*; for Lister's interest in phallic terminology, see Turton, 'The Lexicographical Lesbian'.
32 May(?) 1820, Extracts from Books Read, SH:7/ML/EX/6, f. 27.
33 14 November 1816, *Anne Lister Papers*, SH:7/ML/E/26/3/0005; 20 December 1820, *Anne Lister Papers*, SH:7/ML/E/4/0113.
34 7 February 1820, *Lister Papers*, SH:7/ML/E/4/0030.
35 18 October 1820, *Lister Papers*, SH:7/ML/E/4/0092.
36 *Country cousin* has been documented as a regional term for menstruation in the USA since at least 1908 (F. G. Cassidy et al., *Dictionary of American Regional English*, 6 vols. (Cambridge, MA: Harvard University Press, 1985), vol. I), and *cousin red* remains in use with the same meaning; a link between these and an earlier, wider distribution of *cousin* in England seems plausible.
37 May(?) 1820, Extracts from Books Read, SH:7/ML/EX/6, f. 26.
38 [P. D. Stanhope], *The World*, 101 (1754), 607.
39 26 January 1825, *Lister Papers*, SH:7/ML/E/8/0121. For a detailed discussion of *going to Italy*, see D. Orr, 'A Sojourn in Paris 1824–25: Sex and Sociability in the Manuscript Writings of Anne Lister (1791–1840)', unpublished PhD thesis, Murdoch University (2006), pp. 221–51.
40 Liddington, 'Anne Lister of Shibden Hall', pp. 61–2; Whitbread, *No Priest but Love*, p. 25.
41 16 August 1819, *Lister Papers*, SH:7/ML/E/3/0081.
42 12 September 1818, *Lister Papers*, SH:7/ML/E/2/0065. It is hard to determine exactly when + or × started being used for this purpose, as both could also signal references to books Lister was reading that day: the marks' meanings were inconsistent across time.
43 5 December 1819, *Lister Papers*, SH:7/ML/E/4/0010.
44 5 August 1820, *Lister Papers*, SH:7/ML/E/4/0074.
45 Compare the use of Latin *felix* 'happy' in both Lister's and Eliza Raine's diaries to mark days on which they were intimate in 1808 (Liddington, 'Anne Lister of Shibden Hall', p. 75, n. 64), and Lister's signalling with Greek ξ the occasions on which she used a syringe to treat her venereal infection (from 25 August 1821, *Anne Lister Papers*, SH:7/ML/E/5/0056). I am indebted to Marc D. Schachter for observing the similarity between Lister's kiss mark and the *oς* ligature.
46 30 January 1817, *Lister Papers*, SH:7/ML/E/26/3/0018.
47 2 November 1820, *Lister Papers*, SH:7/ML/E/4/0096.
48 25 October 1820, *Lister Papers*, SH:7/ML/E/4/0094.
49 29 January 1821, *Lister Papers*, SH:7/ML/E/4/0122.
50 Johnson, *Dictionary*, vol. II, s.vv. *love*, *to love*.
51 Ibid., s.v. *marriage*.
52 C. Roulston, 'Marriage and Its Queer Identifications in the Anne Lister Diaries', in K. Leydecker and J. DiPlacidi (eds.), *After Marriage in the Long Eighteenth Century: Literature, Law and Society* (Cham: Palgrave Macmillan, 2018), pp. 181–203.

53 22 November 1824, *Lister Papers*, SH:7/ML/E/8/0084; 15 December 1832, *Lister Papers*, SH:7/ML/E/15/0164.
54 Quoted in Roulston, 'Marriage', pp. 183, 189–90.
55 27 August 1825, *Lister Papers*, SH:7/ML/E/9/0013.
56 Roulston, 'Marriage', p. 197.
57 Johnson, *Dictionary*, vol. I, s.v. *kiss*. See G. Williams, *A Dictionary of Sexual Language and Imagery in Shakespearean and Stuart Literature*, 3 vols. (London: Athlone Press, 1994), vol. II, s.v. *kiss*.
58 12 November 1816, *Lister Papers*, SH:7/ML/E/26/3/0004.
59 18 October 1820, *Lister Papers*, SH:7/ML/E/4/0092.
60 29 November 1834, *Lister Papers*, SH:7/ML/E/17/0115.
61 28 November 1834, *Ann Walker Papers*, West Yorkshire Archive Service, Calderdale, WYC:1525/7/1/5/1/34.
62 Johnson, *Dictionary*, vol. I, s.v. *to grubble*.
63 Ovid, *The Art of Love, in Three Books. The Remedy of Love, the Art of Beauty, and Amours*, trans. J. Dryden et al. (London: B. Crosby and Co., 1804), p. 151.
64 Orr, 'A Sojourn in Paris', p. 129.
65 *Catalogue of the Valuable Library of Books, Maps, &c.*, p. 14; 10 January 1820, *Anne Lister Papers*, SH:7/ML/E/4/0022.
66 Nysten, *Dictionnaire de médecine*, s.v. *masturbation*.
67 5 August 1823, *Lister Papers*, SH:7/ML/E/7/0049; 27 November 1832, *Lister Papers*, SH:7/ML/E/15/0155, where Lister tries to assuage Ann Walker's sense of guilt after Lister has grubbled her.
68 13 November 1824, *Lister Papers*, SH:7/ML/E/8/0077.
69 13–14 November 1824, *Lister Papers*, SH:7/ML/E/8/0077–0078. Whitbread's edition (*No Priest but Love*, p. 82) transcribes the former as 'Saffic regard', reading the Greek letter φ as Lister's crypt character for *ff*, which is ψ. Earlier, while Lister was still wary of giving too much of herself away to Mrs Barlow, she had assured her, '*I was not the person she thought me I thought a Sapphic attachment must be stupid work*', where the reference is seemingly to same-sex desire rather than a specific physical act (1 November 1824, *Lister Papers*, SH:7/ML/E/8/0069).
70 E. Baigent, 'Lister, Anne', *Oxford Dictionary of National Biography* (2019, originally published in 2004), retrieved from doi.org/10.1093/ref:odnb/37678 on 21 December 2021.
71 E. Baigent, C. Brewer and V. Larminie, 'Gender in the Archive: Women in the *Oxford Dictionary of National Biography* and the *Oxford English Dictionary*', *Archives* 30 (2005), 13–35.
72 Ibid., pp. 23–31.
73 C. Brewer, *Treasure-House of the Language: the Living OED* (New Haven: Yale University Press, 2007), pp. 49, 122, 203–4.
74 19 January 1968, letter to R. W. Burchfield, Oxford University Press Archives, OED/C/2/8/7. The *Supplement* ultimately defined *fuck* (v. 1) as '*intr.* To copulate. *trans.* (Rarely used with female subject.) To copulate with; to have

sexual connection with' (R. W. Burchfield (ed.), *A Supplement to the Oxford English Dictionary*, 4 vols. (Oxford: Clarendon Press, 1972–86), vol. 1, s.v. *fuck*).

75 'Reading Programme', *Oxford English Dictionary* (n.d.), retrieved from public .oed.com/history/reading-programme/ on 21 December 2021.

76 C. Brewer, '"That Reliance on the Ordinary": Jane Austen and the *Oxford English Dictionary*', *Review of English Studies*, new series, 66 (2015), 744–65.

77 Ibid., pp. 756, 764. Brewer notes that Austen has been quoted in every *OED* edition and supplement, though largely for the same 'ordinary' words throughout.

78 Whitbread, *No Priest but Love*, p. 101.

79 Ibid., p. 138. Earlier examples can be found in the manuscripts, e.g. '*she has a napkin on ... her cousin has come probably this evening*' (28 November 1820, *Anne Lister Papers*, SH:7/ML/E/4/0106).

80 They are *The Banquet* (1761) by Floyer Sydenham; *Genuine Memoirs of Miss Maria Brown* (1766), spuriously credited to John Cleland on its title page; an unsigned article in the *Edinburgh Medical and Surgical Journal* (1808); a letter by Alfred Douglas (1895); *Chicago: Confidential* (1950) by Jack Lait and Lee Mortimer; and two articles in *Gay Times* (1991) and the *Telegraph* (2006) by Kris Kirk and Dominic Cavendish. *OED3* typically reduces authors' first names to initials for quotations from books, and omits authors' names entirely for quotations from periodicals, so the extent of the gender asymmetry is not evident unless users look up the sources.

81 *The Lives of Epaminondas* (1602) by Simon Goulart, trans. Thomas North; *Analecta Caesarum Romanorum* (1664) by Edward Leigh; *The History of the Roman Emperors* by Jean-Baptiste Louis Crévier (1761), trans. John Mills; *Sexual Impotence in the Male* by William A. Hammond (1883); three articles in the *American Journal of Sociology* (1931), *Billboard* (1942) and *Transition* (1966) by Lowell S. Selling, Harry Poole and Ralph Tanner; and *Hungochani* (2004) by Marc Epprecht.

82 L. S. Selling, 'The Pseudo-Family', *American Journal of Sociology* 37 (1931), 247–53.

83 Whitbread, *No Priest but Love*, p. 206.

84 May(?) 1820, Extracts from Books Read, *Lister Papers*, SH:7/ML/EX/6, f. 27.

85 At present, among the thousand most-quoted sources on *OED* Online, there are twenty-nine women named (Charlotte Brewer, personal communication, December 2021). The other 971 sources are a mixture of named male authors (e.g. Shakespeare in second place) and anonymously cited works (e.g. *The Times* in first place).

86 Ahmed, *What's the Use?*, 20.

87 17 August 1834, *Walker Papers*, WYC:1525/7/1/5/1/29.

88 Lister's innovations now have their own, expanded history of use on TV and in fandom: see M. H. Sjölin, 'Adapting the queer language of Anne Lister's diaries', in J. Reed and E. B. Hagai (eds.), *Gentleman Jack and the (Re)Discovery of Anne Lister*, special issue of *Journal of Lesbian Studies* 26.4 (2022), 382–99.

CHAPTER 5

Self-Conscious Closeting and Paradoxical Writing in Anne Lister's Diaries

Caroline Baylis-Green

If the publication of Eve Kosofsky Sedgwick's *Epistemology of the Closet* (1990) marks a key and hugely influential moment in the analysis of internal, queer spaces and forms of literary closeting, then the past decade has seen a significant growth in interdisciplinary, scholarly work focusing on closets/closeting located in earlier historical contexts (before 1880 moving backwards into the eighteenth century).[1] This chapter engages with this work, whilst also proposing new ways of reading and analysing Anne Lister's life writing and negotiation of identity. It introduces the concept of the self-conscious closet and the protective diary code-cover, and their links to Lister's paradoxical aesthetics. Lister's code-cover operates as a multifunctional device, serving as a comfort blanket, an exclusionary barrier and an indicator of status and learning. This chapter also reflects on Romantic and classical intertextuality in the journals and asks how this intertextuality contributes to tropes of binary space, as well as foregrounding concerns with thresholds. Finally, it analyses the importance of the recent archival discovery of Ann Walker's diary (1834–5) and how this sheds new light on Lister's diary writing, offering new opportunities for a comparative analysis of identity and its refusal.

Spatial Tropes

Lister's diaries have often been labelled colloquially as the 'Rosetta Stone' of lesbian or queer women's writing and a treasure trove for scholars working on writing, gender and sexuality in the early nineteenth century. From the start of the diaries, Lister is keen to display her erudition as a classical scholar and reader. The first clear reference to classical texts appears in Lister's loose diary notes of 1808: 'Wednesday March 2nd Begun Xenophon's Memorabilum and left off Horace for a while. Monday 7th Begun Tacitus Life of Agricola.'[2] However, I want to propose a different classical source for my initial analysis. The most obvious reference to charged interior spaces in classical mythology is contained in the tale of Pandora's box. In the myth, Pandora is described as the first human woman and instructed not to open the box that she receives as a wedding gift. Pandora disobeys, and by opening the box she unleashes the evils of the world, but leaves hope left inside. Classical scholars are still debating whether the survival of hope is a trope of human resilience, or a reminder to maintain faith in even the darkest times. As Todd Worner notes: 'Too often the myth's focus is on the evil that is let loose, and not the hope that remains. But what an omission! The endurance of hope embodies just what we have left when all else has gone wrong. And it is simply brilliant.'[3]

Pandora was still a source of cultural fascination in later nineteenth-century painting and sculpture; the best-known images are provided by the Pre-Raphaelites, as in John William Waterhouse's *Pandora* (1896). It is likely that Lister would have been familiar with early nineteenth-century versions of this classical tale and the link to Hesiod's *Works and Days*. Pandora is enticed by an ornate and elaborate box (originally a jar) which flamboyantly draws attention to its complex construction and use of ancient shorthand and symbols. Lister is also seduced by classical knowledge and linguistic ornamentation. The diary's cipher key pulls both the writer/s/' and readers' focus in opposite directions, asking to be acknowledged but also obscured in a kind of ambivalent dance. Lister may possibly have developed her code with help from her boarding-school first love, Eliza Raine, given that their early letters are partly encoded, or more likely (given Lister's interest in classical languages and algebra) she invented it on her own and then passed on the key to Raine.[4] In any case, Lister later shared the code with a small number of other confidants.

With its showy outer casing and complex interiority, the structural elements of Pandora's box work as a particularly appropriate analogy for Lister's diary writing. While Lister's diary can contain transgressive material within a safe, private space, as with Pandora's box it is also potentially at risk of discovery and of being 'revealed'. Furthermore, Pandora's box forms an uncanny parallel with Lister's code in the residual hope it offers. The word 'hope' famously provided the key to the cipher for John Lister and Arthur Burrell's code breaking:

> And telling Mr Lister that I was certain of 2 letters, h and e; and I asked him if there was any likelihood that a further clue could be found. We then examined one of the boxes behind the panels and half way down the collection of deeds we found on a scrap of paper these words: 'In God is my . . . . '. We at once saw that the word must be 'hope' and the h and

> e corresponded with my guess. The word 'hope' was in cipher. With these four letters almost certain we began very late at night to find the remaining clues.[5]

It may seem that the word itself is a pure coincidence, in that it could have been any word discovered by Burrell and Lister, yet there are a number of diary entries that reinforce the value Lister placed on stoicism, faith and progress. For example, on 8 September 1835, she notes: 'Would that we could look on the past with satisfaction, on the present with complacency, and to the future with hope.'[6]

Lister's use of the term 'crypt' rather than 'cryptic' in describing her code and coded writing also opens up some intriguing linguistic possibilities. The *Oxford English Dictionary* lists crypt as '[a]n underground room or vault beneath a church, used as a chapel or burial place', whereas the *Cambridge Online Dictionary* offers the following definition: 'A room under the floor of a church where bodies are buried.'[7] Ironically, Lister's 'bodies' are also buried under the crypt space, although Lister imagines their resurrection through the language of anxiety, as in the following entry from 1819:

> Isabel much to my annoyance, mentioned my keeping a journal, & setting down everyone's conversation in my peculiar handwriting (what I call crypt hand). I mentioned the almost impossibility of its being deciphered & the facility with which I wrote and not at all sharing my vexation at Isabella's folly at naming the thing. Never say before her what she may not tell for, as to what she ought to keep or what she ought not to publish, she has the worst judgement in the world.[8]

Isabella's declaration creates danger and threat precisely because it fails to recognise both the crypt and cryptic elements of Lister's diary writing. It also confronts the edge of Lister's social closet and tries to wrest control away from the closet's owner, potentially outing her in the process. This interaction highlights the precarity of Lister's social closeting, in that someone in her inner circle can fail to acknowledge the need for discretion.

Self-Conscious and Unconscious Closets

I argue that Lister's diary cipher acts as a cover and protection from unwanted attention in the same vein as a physically locked journal. Despite the huge volume of research on the history of diaries, there is a surprising gap or silence regarding diary locks and their use in life writing. The diary's internal space acts as a room of requirement, or a specially

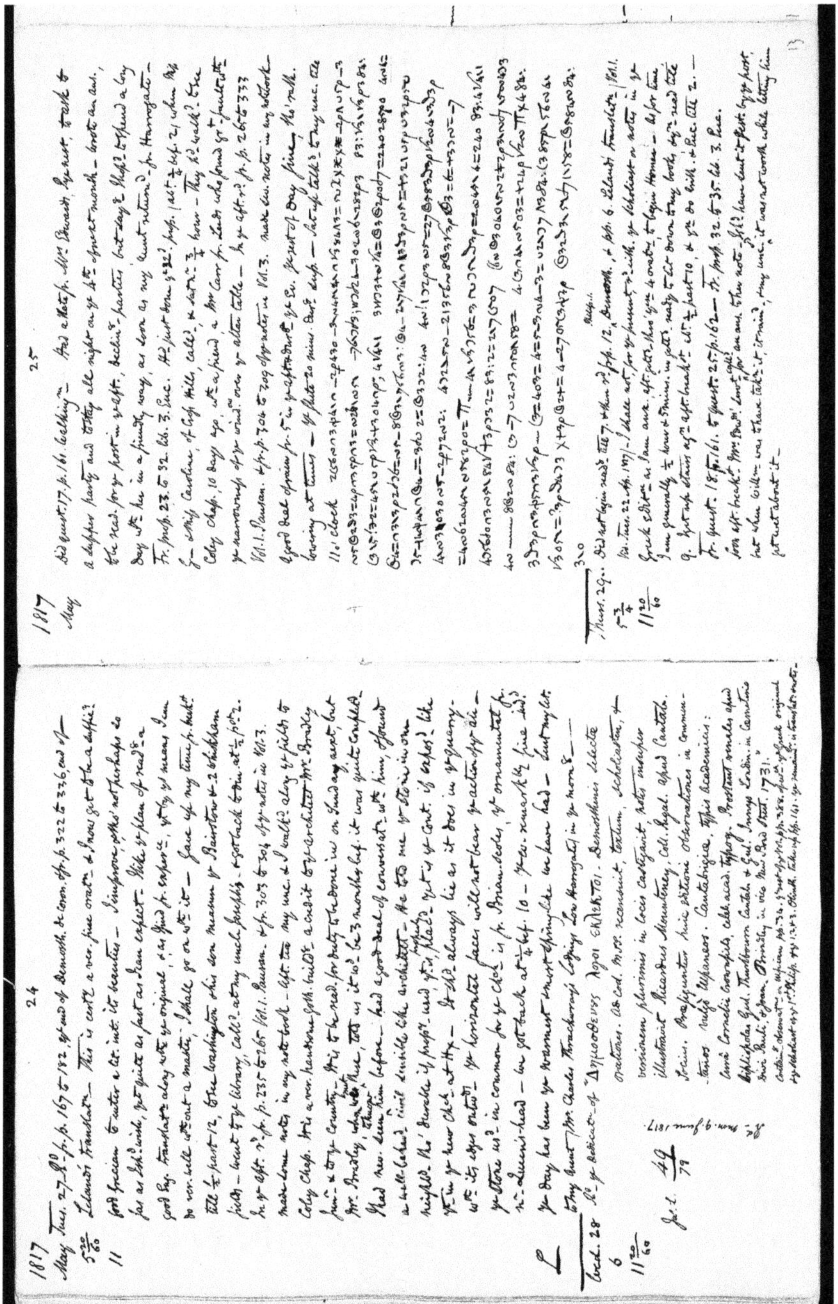

Figure 4 Anne Lister diary entry (28 May 1817). West Yorkshire Archive Service, Calderdale, SH:7/ML/E/1/0014.

reserved space akin to architectural and domestic closets used by the aristocratic classes in the eighteenth and early nineteenth century. Dominic Janes's and Danielle Bobker's recent publications on links between queer sexuality, intimacy and architectural closets in the eighteenth century have provided a very welcome addition to research on spatial and psychological closets, although their primary focus is on male writers and historical figures.[9]

Bobker's linking of eighteenth-century closets with twentieth- and twenty-first-century coming-out stories is a timely intervention for those who are working on links between literary structures, psychological processing and queer spaces. The closet as the space of identity construction is moving backwards in recent scholarship away from Michel Foucault's late nineteenth-century designation of this phenomenon.[10] Here, I need to clarify the difference between an externally imposed closet and a self-conscious closet, the self-conscious closet being the less dangerous or harmful of the two. In an ideal world, no one should ever need a closet. The paradox is that if you know you are in a closet and you acknowledge your othered identity, then your closet is never fully sealed or closed. However, historically individuals with self-conscious closets remain subject to threats from external readings and judgements, hence the need for protective, linguistic armour.

Furthermore, Lister's peculiar handwriting still represents a challenge for those looking at the diaries and the wider Lister/Shibden Hall archives. Researchers have recently discovered a diary entry previously thought to be part of Lister's diaries that has now been re-attributed to Ann Walker and included within her year-long diary as part of a project to collate and transcribe Walker's writing.[11] The related Twitter account and website now provide researchers with a chance to compare diary entries written by Lister and Walker during 1834 and 1835. The fact that Walker did not use code suggests that she did not invest in a self-conscious textual closet in the same way as Lister. This is extremely valuable information for scholars looking at self-identity and self-processing in Lister's diaries. This dual archive now offers a way to map differences in perception and disclosure in both women's work. Comparing the two would suggest that no explicit sexual content equals no explicit code.

For example, comparing Walker's and Lister's entries for Sunday, 24 August 1834, there is a clear difference in their content. Lister's entry contains a brief coded section describing their intimacy: '*she with me in my bed half hour this morning but quite quitely* [*quietly*]', whereas Walker's entry begins with a reference to breakfast: 'Up at 8.20. breakfast, and gaitner came with gaiters, had them to alter.'[12] Walker's and Lister's entries from the day before (Saturday, 23 August 1834) follow the same pattern. Walker writes: 'Up at 10 to 6 – wrote letter to my aunt Monsieur Perrelet brought watches,' whereas Lister's entry is as follows: '[up at] 8 ¾ [to bed] at 12 ¼ *good kiss last night* – up at 6 ½ a.m. with regular bowel complaint – Perrelet a little before 9'.[13] It is interesting to note that Lister does not code the reference to her bowels after her coded 'kiss'. The omission of sexual details from Walker's diary entries provides an intriguing contrast to Lister's focus on sexual satisfaction and a poignant commentary on the differences between the two women's approaches to recording their activities and their sense of identity. In Walker's diary, the notion of platonic, romantic friendship is inscribed by the omission of any sexual reference, while Lister's diary persona of the same period seems increasingly frustrated.[14]

Domestic and Physical Closets

A direct search of the word 'closet' within the complete diary archives produces seven results: five direct and two indirect. The references are contained in diary entries written between Thursday, 9 April 1818 and Sunday, 15 October 1820. At first glance, these entries seem unremarkable; however, on closer inspection they exhibit an intriguing link between physical and textual closets, offering rare examples of explicit, non-coded content near or within physical closets, such as china, bedroom and water closets.[15]

The following example links Lister's studies to her bedroom closet: '(Could not however, manage to get the right answer to example 4, page 123.) then moved all my things out of my room (the blue room) closet and dawdled away all the morning.'[16] In this entry, the connection between 'the blue room' and the closet is not clear, or even whether they are the same thing. The bracketing of the blue room is also odd and reads as though Lister is providing clarification for those unfamiliar with the layout of Shibden Hall. The next relevant entry is dated Saturday, 18 July 1818, and follows a similar pattern, as Lister summarises her reading progress and notetaking: 'Read from page 403–420 volume 3 Les Leçons de l'Histoire, in the china closet, finding this place not quite suit me, went into the red room, read section 28 librum 1... overcome with the heat slept near an hour.'[17] Once again, we note the strange use of a china closet space and the lack of any accompanying qualification or explanation. The same entry contains a reference to a third type of closet, namely a water closet: 'Just before dressing (Mariana) proposed our going down to the water closet where all over in five minutes she gave me a very good kiss.'[18] This entry creates an explicit link between the physical space of the closet and the recording of sex between women. The final closet entry from 15 October 1820 also includes a mention of potential sexual activity in the water closet:

> Directly on our return from church saw Miss Vallance in the passage took her near the downstairs water closet jammed her against the door and excited both our feelings very came upstairs and leaned on the bed she soon came in and saw the state I was in was bad enough herself and at last promised not to refuse me tonight.[19]

As water closets adjoining bedrooms were being developed as early as the seventeenth century, there is a longstanding link between closets and sanitation: 'In the seventeenth and eighteenth centuries small rooms or closets were introduced that adjoined bedrooms. These areas were outfitted with a comfortable commode, under which a pan would be placed.'[20] In Lister's entry above, the water closet as a sanitary space and as a space for illicit sex between women blurs the boundaries between the proper and the improper, and the clean and the unclean.

Working out what a closet is or is not in the eighteenth and early nineteenth century is still a challenging proposition for historians and literary critics. According to Bobker, 'Closet was the generic term for any lockable room in seventeenth- and eighteenth-century British architecture. As private wealth grew, closets of all kinds were increasingly available across the social spectrum.'[21] A further search of references to 'water closet' on the WYAS catalogue produces two entries including the ones mentioned above and the following note dated 19 February 1820: 'Mr D. [Duffin] and I walked with Mrs A. [Anne Norcliffe] and Miss G. [Gage] – kiss in the water closet.'[22] Both entries include coded references to orgasms (kisses) occurring in a space that can only be entered by invitation. The qualification of the term 'closet' with 'water' is helpful in negotiating the lexical ambiguity of the term, marking it as a room rather than a piece of furniture; the water closet as a lavatory or commode room rather than a pot or toilet. Historically, the water closet has moved from a space of shared, aristocratic intimacy in the enfilade to a space usually associated with individual and private use in middle-class homes.

Thresholds and Risk-Taking

The foregrounding of paradoxical space continues throughout the diaries, with their emphasis on layered discourses, liminal spaces and movements across thresholds, as well as the negotiation of binaries more traditionally associated with diary writing: public/private, inside/outside and so on. In addition, Lister created symbols of protection and invitation in her domestic space by the placing of unusual female carved figures on the main staircase of Shibden Hall. The staircase figures mark the edge of public space, providing not only a form of protective guardianship, but also a possible queer invitation, in a vein similar to Christabel's chamber in Samuel Taylor Coleridge's poem of the same name (1816):

> The chamber carved so curiously,
> Carved with figures strange and sweet,
> All made out of the carver's brain
> For a lady's chamber meet:
> The lamp with twofold silver chain
> Is fastened to an angel's feet.[23]

The time-span of Lister's life and diary writing overlaps with the evolution of the dark Romantic era of the late eighteenth and early nineteenth century. Anira Rowanchild and Alison Oram have explored connections between the gothic and Lister's textual and social aesthetics in their work.[24] Rowanchild's analysis of gothic connections also provides a succinct summary of competing antinomies in Lister's world, by arguing that '[Lister's] interest in the picturesque and Gothic was stimulated by their ability to combine display with concealment.'[25]

I want to suggest a further correspondence between vampiric tropes in Romantic literature and ideas of risk-taking and control in the crossing of Lister's closeted and uncloseted thresholds. The first notebook of Lister's diary (not in loose-leaf form) is dated from August to November 1816, the same year as Coleridge's 'Christabel', although the volumes which constitute this unfinished poem were composed at an earlier date. While not directly mentioned by Lister, this text provides an intriguing contemporary example of problematic, vampiric thresholds:

> They crossed the moat, and Christabel
> Took the key that fitted well;
> A little door she opened straight,
> All in the middle of the gate;
> The gate that was ironed within and without,
> Where an army in battle array had marched out.
> The lady sank, belike through pain,
> And Christabel with might and main
> Lifted her up, a weary weight,
> Over the threshold of the gate:
> Then the lady rose again,
> And moved, as she were not in pain.[26]

The topos of invitation runs through vampiric literature throughout the nineteenth century, as in, for example, Sheridan LeFanu's *Carmilla* (1872), in which Carmilla is invited into Laura's home after a carriage accident. In the same way, Lister issues invitations to her private spaces – both linguistic and physical – to select members of her inner circle but keeps unwanted guests in her wider social circle at bay by using the cipher as a gate. This is not to suggest a literal correspondence between Lister and the vampiric, but rather that her diary writing shares certain characteristics with gothic literature, including a focus on inclusion and exclusion, entry, permission and consent, all of which designate sites of anxiety and erotic charge in early nineteenth-century texts.

While Lister's code-cover system of crypt hand, secure containment and limited circulation of diary writing is undoubtedly robust and comforting, there are occasions in the diary when she appears confused in her understanding of public/private boundaries and the differences between protected and non-protected spaces. There is one notable instance where Lister's desire to make a romantic and Romantic gesture undermines the stability of her social and textual closet. In the famous 'Blackstone Edge' or 'three steps' entry of 19 August 1823, there is an odd inconsistency in the use of the code cipher, with content that would seem to be ripe for coding remaining uncoded. This, in turn, mirrors the emotional and psychological trauma being experienced in the moment and in later references to the incident. In this episode, Lister walks briskly across open countryside beyond the boundaries of the Shibden estate, with the goal of surprising her lover, Mariana Lawton, who is traveling by coach from York towards Halifax. Upon reaching the coach, Lister describes 'in too hastily taking each step of the carriage & stretching over the pile of dressing-boxes etc., that should have stopped such eager ingress, I unluckily seemed to M – to have taken 3 steps at once'.[27] Mariana, in turn, is 'horror struck' at Lister's sudden appearance, which signals a complete lack of proper decorum.

Although Lister thinks she is safe in wanting to surprise her lover, on reflection she records in her diary having breached a prohibited boundary, both physically and symbolically. This entry contains a rare instance of shame being internalised or breaking through Lister's protective mechanisms and provoking a split subjectivity: 'I scarce knew what my feelings were. They were in tumult. "Shame, shame," said I to myself, "to be so overcome."'[28] This long entry moves between coded and uncoded sections, although the same emotional tone is maintained throughout. While the following line is coded, 'I felt more easily under my own control,' the entry then slips into plain hand: 'Alas I had not forgotten. The heart has a memory of its own, but I had ceased to appear to remember save in occasional joking allusions to "the three steps".'[29] The odd humour relating to 'the three steps' suggests Lister's need to deflect her extreme discomfort while remaining haunted by the incident. The three steps not only designate a reference to the coach, but also serve as an indicator of Lister having overstepped the mark. The tension between risk and control is outlined here, as is the difference between Lister's reading of her wider social context and Mariana's understanding of acceptable levels of intimacy and their public display. While the following coded entry of 20 August 1823 begins with Lister recording the resumption of sexual activity with her lover at Shibden Hall, the residual trauma is still in evidence. Mariana's fear of potential exposure requires firm assurances from Lister, as she seeks to regain control of their narrative:

> The fear of discovery is strong. It rather increases, I think, but her conscience seems seared as long as concealment is secure . . . Told her she need not fear my conduct letting out our secret. I could deceive anyone. Then told her how completely I had deceived Miss Pickford & that the success of such deceit almost smote me.[30]

Lister's reference to deception here is clearly not self-deception, as she displays an acute understanding of her need for self-determination and control, and for the ways in which she is being forced back into a closet imposed by Mariana's refusal of her oddity. As Lister poignantly and intriguingly reflects in long hand: 'It was a coward love that dared not brave the storm &, in desperate despair, my proud, indignant spirit watched it sculk [*sic*] away.'[31] While Mariana is happy to have sex with Anne, she feels no need to label herself as other or distinctive in the way that Lister does: Mariana is attached to behaviour rather than to identity; in other words she is closeted but not in the same strategic, self-conscious way that Lister is. The exchange between the two lovers foreshadows the difference between behaviour and identity fifty years before this paradigm shift that Foucault records as happening in the 1870s.[32] Lister is both ahead of her time and of her time, dissident but also highly conservative.

In constructing her own crypt (hand), Lister knows where the threats are located and, as mentioned, where the bodies are buried. At the same time, she is aware of her own oddity and repeatedly 'asserts the naturalness of her position'.[33] One of the challenges for scholars working on the Lister diaries is the sheer scale of the entries, which provide an endless supply of variation but also, inevitably, an endless supply of contradictions. For example, the vexation noted above is undercut by instances of Lister's diary persona brandishing her secret code as a seductive tool, or conversely as a weapon. As Rowanchild suggests, Lister is not above using her code as a means of flirtation when it suits her; on 7 January 1821, Lister writes that she gave a new love interest, Miss Vallance, 'the crypt hand alphabet'.[34] One of the diaries' central enigmas concerns the choice of topics that Lister chooses to encrypt, which include financial matters, legal discussions, medical concerns, estate management and certain political issues, as well as sex and desire.[35] Lister's choice of coded 'areas' offers an apposite and eerie foreshadowing of the connections between sexuality and, increasingly, the pathologising institutional discourses discussed by Foucault in his *History of Sexuality*.[36] Coded diary passages often alternate between descriptions of sexual activity and these broader social concerns. For example, diary transcripts for 1816 include coded mentions of kisses (orgasms) and coded passages discussing business and inheritance issues. On 15 August 1816, Lister writes in code: 'L had a kiss', and on 5 November she also records in code:

> I advised my uncle to entail Shibden and at his death should my aunt Anne survive let her come into all as it stands for her life I said I wished him to prevent my aunt Lister or my mother having thirds and mentioned my fathers having once said/namely 3, July 1814/he would leave Marian and me joint heirs to which I objected as it might lead to the place being sold.[37]

There are also numerous mixed diary entries that combine plain hand and crypt hand and others which are coded but do not seem to relate directly to sex or business. For instance, the diary entry for 14 September 1814 mentions a gap in diary writing and the copying of previous notes (the whole entry was originally written in code): 'Wrote out this part of my journal from notes after my return here from Lawton which accounts for the date of my getting this book, Saturday, the fourteenth of September one thousand eight hundred and sixteen.'[38] This fully coded entry reads as an apology for lateness to the diary project itself and as a note on accountability. In this entry, the diary persona appears to role-play or to be rehearsing the role of professional author as a way of establishing a form of regular creative practice. Lister's diary persona at times displays concerns regarding the temporal disjunction or gap between the original experience and its recording in diary form. New research presented by Jenna Beyer and Dannielle Orr at the recent Anne Lister Research Summit has also focused on issues raised by the diaries' indexing and ordering.[39] Lister's reticence is understandable given the enduring social judgement levelled at female writers and ideas of 'creative femininity' in the early nineteenth century. As Gillian Paku suggests:

> Some stigma also adhered to female writers, for whom writing did not fall within the usual sanctioned circle of female accomplishments at the start of the [nineteenth] century and in whose case the public articulation of texts could be portrayed as immodest and improper. Derisory terms such as 'female quill-driver,' 'half man,' or 'scribbling Dame,' persisted well into the nineteenth century.[40]

This may also partly explain the diaries' lack of references to female writers, with the exception of Lady Caroline Lamb and her novel *Glenarvon*, which is discussed by Lister and Mariana.[41] Upon its publication in 1816, the same year as Coleridge's 'Christabel', *Glenarvon* caused a sensation as a transgressive novel, famously offering an early example of a cross-dressing character in a nineteenth-century novel. According to Bill Hughes: '*Glenarvon* was seen by critics as transgressing gender by its clashing of genres ... genre and gender become confused like the "doubtful gender" of Lamb herself with her notorious cross-dressing.'[42] The diary section pertaining to *Glenarvon* codes only the novel's title, although its presence offers a pointed and painful reminder of discussions between Lister and Mariana earlier in the day concerning Lister's masculine appearance and failure to pass as a feminine woman. As the entry notes, it is an example of a 'scandalous' text: 'Agreed that Lady Caroline Lamb's novel, Glenarvon, is a very talented but a very dangerous sort of book.'[43] Lister's reference to *Glenarvon* is both provocative and ironic.

While the desire to claim Lister as a dissident, queer icon for contemporary LGBTQIA readers and researchers is understandable, failure to acknowledge Lister as a product of her own time is also problematic. As Chris Roulston argues:

> [T]here is a risk in seeing Lister as a figure who defied her historical moment rather than being defined by it. With the diaries' groundbreaking status as a record of early lesbian sexuality, it is important to remember the degree to which Lister continued to reflect and embody the values of her social and economic class, particularly in terms of her unswerving Tory politics.[44]

Lister's self-consciousness in the diaries is also double-edged; she displays, on the one hand, self-knowledge and awareness and, on the other, forms of social discomfort and non-belonging. Despite her sense of class superiority in her Halifax social circle, there are entries that express awkwardness and insecurity, as in this entry from 29 April 1832: 'I felt, myself in reality gauche, and besides in false position. I have difficulty enough in the usage of high society and feeling unknown, but have ten times ... I will eventually hide my head somewhere or other ... The mortification of feeling my gaucherie is wholesome.'[45]

Diary Code as Split Paratext?

In *Paratexts; Thresholds of Interpretation* (1997), Gérard Genette suggests that '[m]ore than a boundary or a sealed border, the paratext is rather a threshold.'[46] Genette uses the term to recognise framing devices employed by writers and publishers, such as indexes, dates and dedications. I want to argue that Lister's diary crypt hand works equally as paratext and text. Discussions of paratexts and marginalia are still on the margins of the history of literary scholarship, perhaps in an ironically appropriate way. The critical terrain that exists between literary theory, and textual and autobiographical criticism is underexplored. Discussions of codes in life writing are still seen as niche, specialist or as an offshoot of corpus linguistics.[47] There is a need for new conceptual life writing frameworks that would allow us to work with explicitly coded texts, Lister's diaries being a prime example.

Lister's code occupies an unusual position by being both inside and outside the text, as both cover and content. With the exception of additional cipher and loose-leaf pages which pre-date the start of the journal notebooks, there are no formal paratexts outside of code use in Lister's diaries. At this point, it is helpful to consider other diaries that use code. Parts of Samuel Pepys's diaries, written in the 1660s and first published in 1825, offer a similar use of code to cover explicit sexual content, albeit from a hetero-normative perspective. The publication of the first decoded edition of Pepys's diaries was within Lister's lifetime. As with Lister's diaries, Pepys's diaries were hidden for a period of one hundred and fifty years, with the explicitly coded diary sections only deciphered in 1819.[48] Given that, as far as we know, Lister started to develop a form of code from 1808 onwards, it is unlikely that she would have been influenced by knowledge of Pepys's code use.[49] Nor do Lister's diaries contain any indexed reference to Pepys's work. There are later examples of coded diaries by queer public figures, such as Ludwig Wittgenstein, but as someone who was highly ambivalent about his sexual identity, Wittgenstein's use of code more likely designates a form of internalised homophobia.[50]

While the use of code in diaries produces a binary between the coded and the uncoded, the levels and layers within the written space are more nuanced and non-binary, providing an interlocking structure similar to Eve Sedgwick's 'mesh of queer possibilities':

> Queer is a continuing moment, movement, motive – recurrent, eddying, *troublant* ... It is the open mesh of possibilities, gaps, overlaps, dissonances and resonances, lapses and excesses of meaning when the constituent

> element of anyone's gender, of anyone's sexuality are not made (or cannot be made to signify monolithically... Queer is relational. It is strange. To think, read, or act queerly is to think across boundaries, beyond what is deemed to be normal, to jump at the possibilities opened up by celebrating marginality, which in itself serves to destabilize the mainstream.[51]

It is the protection afforded by the code-cover that allows Lister to explore the wider parameters of her gender and sexuality and to reject contemporary socially closeted romantic friendship models. As Leonieke Vermeer argues, '[t]he study of disguising strategies in diaries can provide us with information on a subject for which source material is rare: bodily and sexual experiences.'[52] Vermeer highlights one of the key contradictions in the work of coded diary writers, including Lister, in that 'a code draws attention to the secrets it supposedly conceals'.[53] In the process of code-covering, Lister tantalises potential readers and highlights taboo elements. While her code is an oxymoronic, obvious disguise, there are also elements within the diaries that offer other kinds of obscure writing or silences: missing dates, blank sections, crammed marginalia and, for the modern reader, illegible handwriting. Lister's use of crypt hand and code produces a strange anomaly, in which the diary subject speaks both in, and through, the code-cover as a form of ventriloquism. It also gestures towards forms of historical biofiction, which focus on the expression and recovery of posthumous voices.[54]

Lister's diary persona and voice are still being recovered through ongoing diary transcriptions. With the development of twenty-first-century computer software, large, historical diaries are now being made available on and in different platforms. These new resources are extremely helpful for researchers, but also have the effect of producing the journal in a multiplicity of sequences, patterns and datings, depending on areas of particular interest. The Lister diaries will continue to evolve through the completion of transcription and sequencing online; these diaries are still in the process of being written and remain unfixed and open to further interpretation.

The link between diary writing and psychological processing is often featured in studies of life writing. The volume of life writing produced by queer writers in the nineteenth century suggests a clear link between the processing of sexuality, gender and other consciously closeted states. Another example is *Works and Days* by the Michael Fields (Katherine Bradley and Edith Cooper), a diary covering the years 1888–1913, made up of multiple volumes still in the process of being transcribed.[55] *Works and Days* offers another example of a multifunctional text that negotiates professional and personal terrain in relation to queer lives, intimacy and the question of identity.

It is useful here to make a distinction between code-cover and additional or accidental opacity. The relationship between historical diary writing and potential audiences (including chosen audiences and the author-as-audience) continues to provoke debate, as do discussions on diary writing as form/genre within potential life writing canons. Some researchers, such as Rebecca Hogan, argue that diaries are more subversive in their openness, as a 'plurality of voices and perspectives', and as 'a form which preserves "otherness within the text" and within the self'.[56] Conversely, many researchers stress that diary writing personas are as performative as fictional characters.

Lister's diary shows her life writing persona trying on different hats, outfits, languages and alternative signifiers, with voices that refuse to accept easy labelling or classification. We cannot, of course, know the level of censorship that Lister imposed upon herself and her writing, and the extent to which topics and extremities of feeling were omitted or considered to be off-limits. Meta-commentaries on diary writing are unusual before the twentieth century and even rarer for unpublished life writing. Ironically, producers of diary notebooks, for example, Letts the stationer, founded in 1796, were keen to promote the idea of diaries as private or confessional works. In one advertisement, they instructed writers to 'Use your diary with the utmost familiarity and confidence, conceal nothing from its pages nor suffer any other eye than your own to scan them.'[57]

Treating Lister as a life writer and placing her writing alongside other substantial diaries published in the nineteenth and twentieth centuries would undoubtedly shed further light on the connections between form and identity, as in, for example, those of John Evelyn (1640–1706, first published in 1818), Samuel Pepys (1660–9, first published in abridged form in 1825), and later nineteenth-century queer life writers such as the Michael Fields.

Conclusion

In this chapter, I have shown the ways in which Lister's diary code supports the negotiation of her self-conscious closet, as both shield and psychological comfort blanket. There are multiple references to comfort in the diaries as well as references to Lister's robust code-cover, as in, for example: 'What a comfort my journal is. How I can write in crypt all as it really is . . . and console myself.'[58]

I have reflected on existing conceptual frameworks and definitions of the closet derived from contemporary queer theory and proposed new readings based on the differences between self-conscious and unconscious closeted writing. There continue to be difficult questions concerning the links between explicitly coded texts and the closet, for example, when is a closet not a closet? As a diarist, Lister uses her code to combine competing elements of her diary persona into a form of paradoxical writing that both attracts and repels potential readership. The tension between code as cover and code as content would undoubtedly also benefit from readings provided by newer conceptual areas such as surface studies.[59] Using the Lister diaries, I propose a case for the reclamation of 'missing' closets in queer women's writing from the eighteenth and nineteenth centuries, and to argue for their inclusion in interdisciplinary studies of psychological, social and physical spaces.

Notes

I do not use the term lesbian as an identity label for Anne Lister. I concur with A.-M. Jagose's view that it is possible to offer a more nuanced reading of Lister's subjectivity without making her queerness invisible: 'I suggest that the rich context of the diaries and the sex/gender system they articulate provide an interpretive frame for reading the indisputable articulations of Lister's sexual subjectivity without pressganging them into the modern category of "lesbian".' *Inconsequence, Lesbian Representation and the Logic of Sexual Sequence* (Ithaca: Cornell University Press, 2002), p. 16.

1 See D. Bobker, *The Closet: the Eighteenth-Century Architecture of Intimacy* (Princeton, NJ: Princeton University Press, 2021); D. Janes, *Picturing the Closet: Male Secrecy and Homosexual Visibility in Britain* (Oxford: Oxford University Press, 2015).

2 1808, *Anne Lister Papers (Loose Diary Notes)*, West Yorkshire Archive Service (WYAS), Calderdale, SH:7/ML/E-26; www.wyjs.org.uk/archive-service/our-collections/search-our-catalogue/.

3 T. Worner, 'The Hope at the Bottom of Pandora's Box', 1 February 2022, Word on Fire, www.wordonfire.org/articles/fellows/the-hope-at-the-bottom-of-pandoras-box/, accessed 26 May 2022. See also V. Geoghegan, 'Pandora's Box: Reflections on a Myth', *Critical Horizons* 9.1 (2008), 24–41.

4 According to A. Steidele, Lister's relationship with Raine provided the impetus for her code creation. See online extract from *Gentleman Jack: a Biography of Anne Lister. Regency Landowner, Seducer and Secret Diarist* (London: Serpent's Tail, 2019), https://serpentstail.com/2018/06/28/gentleman-jack-extract/, accessed 26 May 2022.

5 12 December 1936, Letter from Arthur Burrell to the Halifax Borough librarian, WYAS, SH:7/JN/B/74?6.

6 8 September 1835, quoted by Anne Choma [@AnneChoma], https://twitter.com/AnneChoma/status/1272803028718874624; *Lister Papers*, SH:7/ML/E/18/0094.

7 *Cambridge Online Dictionary*, second entry as follows, 'For a subject who harbors a crypt, the prospect of it being opened brings on a fear of death, usually figurative, rather than literal'; https://dictionary.cambridge.org/ accessed 15 November 2021.

8 H. Whitbread (ed.), *The Secret Diaries of Miss Anne Lister* (London: Virago, 2010), p. 111.

9 Janes, *Picturing the Closet*; Bobker, *The Closet.*

10 See M. Foucault, *The History of Sexuality: Introduction* (London: Penguin, 1979).

11 See the following: 'The group's (In Search of Ann Walker) find has now been verified by archivists who say that this exciting discovery will allow the same-sex relationship between Anne Lister and Ann Walker to be studied from the perspective of both women'; www//forreadingaddicts.co.uk, accessed 29 December 2021, or via @SearchingForAnn Twitter account (insearchofannwalker.com). See Ann Walker's diary, WYC:1525/7/1/5/1 (within Rawson Papers, WYAS catalogue).

12 24 August 1834, *Lister Papers*, SH:7/ML/E/17?0079; 24 August 1834, Anne Walker, *Diary Notes*, WYC:1525/7/1/5/1/31.

13 23 August 1834, *Lister Papers*, SH:7/E/17/0078; 23 August 1834, Walker, *Diary Notes*, WYC:1525/7/1/5/1/21.

14 This sense of isolation is particularly pronounced in Lister's diary entry for Friday 22 August 1834: '*she above half hour with me in my bed last night but tried in vain could (not) give her a right kiss*'; SH:7/ML/E/17/0078. Again, Walker's diary includes no mention of intimacy.

15 Note that none of the entries about closets is included in the published diary volumes.

16 9 April 1818, *Lister Papers*, SH:7/ML/E/2/0021.

17 18 July 1818, *Lister Papers*, SH:7/ML/E/0046.

18 18 July 1818, *Lister Papers*, SH:7/ML/E/0046.

19 15 October 1820, *Lister Papers*, SH:7/ML/E/0090.

20 D. J. Eveleigh, 'Review of *Privies and Water Closets*', *Jane Austen's World* (3 August 2010), www.janeaustensworld.com, accessed 15 December 2021.

21 See D. Bobker, interview on 'The Closet: Eighteenth-Century Architecture of Intimacy', www.notchesblog.com/2021/05/13/the-closet-the-eighteenth-century-architecture-of-intimacy/, accessed 1 December 2021;
also in 'The Literature and Culture of the Closet in the Eighteenth Century', *Digital Defoe: Studies in Defoe and His Contemporaries* 16 (Fall 2014), 70–94, Bobker writes, 'merging with the bath or privy, closets into bathing closets, closets of ease, outdoor privies known as earth closets and eventually water closets' (p. 70), www.english.illinoisstate.edu/digitaldefoe/teaching/bobker/, accessed 1 December 2021.

22 19 February 1820, *Lister Papers*, SH:7/ML/E/4/0134.

23 S. T. Coleridge, *Christabel, etc.* (Whitefish, MT: Kessinger Publishing, 2010), ll. 76–81.

24 A. Rowanchild, '"Everything Done for Effect": Georgic, Gothic and Picturesque in Anne Lister's Self-Production', *Women's Writing* 7.1 (2000), 89–104; A. Oram, 'Going on an Outing: the Historic House and Queer Public History', *Rethinking History: the Journal of Theory and Practice* 15.2 (2011), 189–207.

25 Rowanchild, 'Everything Done for Effect', article abstract.

26 Coleridge, *Christabel*, ll. 115–27.

27 Whitbread, *Secret Diaries*, p. 301.

28 Ibid., p. 302.

29 Ibid., p. 303.

30 Ibid., p. 305.

31 Ibid., pp. 305–6.

32 See Foucault, *History of Sexuality*.

33 C. Baylis-Green, 'Queer Subjectivities, Closeting and Non-Normative Desire in Nineteenth-Century Women's Poetry and Life Writing', unpublished PhD thesis, Manchester Metropolitan University (2016), pp. 45–79, 53, www.e-space.mmu.ac.uk, accessed 30 November 2021. In terms of Lister's 'oddity', see Whitbread, *Secret Diaries*, entry for Saturday, 19 June 1824 [Halifax]: 'Speaking of my oddity, Mrs Priestley said that she always told people I was natural, but she thought nature was in an odd freak when she made me' (p. 374).

34 7 January 1821, Whitbread, *Secret Diaries*, p. 158.

35 This paradox is further complicated by the difference between the diary page summaries online and the published coded entries; the WYAS transcribed pages do not italicise the coded diary sections, making it much harder to differentiate between Lister's crypt and long hand. The WYAS archives do provide copied versions of the original pages, but these are notoriously difficult to read.

36 See Foucault, *History of Sexuality*, p. 101. A. Clark also argues that the existence of Lister's diaries calls for a reassessment of Foucault's work: 'The theory that individuals could only acquire "homosexual identity" when it was invented by sexologists – that they are inserted into discourses – does not hold water historically'; 'Anne Lister's Construction of Lesbian Identity', *Journal of the History of Sexuality* 7.1 (July 1996), 25.

37 5 November 1816, *Lister Papers*, SH:7/ML/E/26/2/0007.

38 14 September 1814, *Lister Papers*, SH:7/ML/E-25-2.

39 D. Orr and J. Meyer, 'Wrote the Above of Today: Anne Lister's Writings', 19 October 2021, https://youtu.be/s9qY3ap5T74, accessed 23 July 2022.

40 G. Paku, 'Anonymity in the Eighteenth Century', *Oxford Online Handbook, Literature, Literary Studies, 1701 to 1800*, para. 7, Online Publication Date: August 2015, DOI: 10.1093/oxfordhb/9780199935338.013.37, accessed 10 December 2021.

41 Whitbread provides a useful note concerning the novel's context: '*Glenarvon* is Lady Caroline Lamb's first novel. When it appeared in May 1816 it created

a scandal because it appeared to be a kiss-and-tell (or as Byron crudely put it, a "F- and-publish") account of her affair with him in 1812'; *Secret Diaries* (p. 411, n. 15).

42 B. Hughes, 'Rebellion, Treachery, and Glamour: Lady Caroline Lamb's *Glenarvon* and Progress of the Byronic Vampire', Conference paper, p. 2, www.opengravesopenminds.com, accessed 5 December 2021.

43 16 September 1823, Whitbread, *Secret Diaries*, p. 319.

44 C. Roulston, 'Sexuality in Translation: Anne Lister and the Ancients', *Journal of the History of Sexuality* 30.1 (January 2021), 112–35, 113.

45 29 April 1832, *Lister Papers*, SH:7/ML/E/0046.

46 G. Genette, *Paratexts: Thresholds of Interpretation* (Cambridge: Cambridge University Press, 1997), pp. 1–2.

47 Corpus linguistics is a form of data retrieval applied to the analysis of language use in large online bodies of writing.

48 See the following from the *Encyclopedia Britannica*'s entry on Pepys' Diary: 'Pepys did his part to make sure that prying eyes could not read his work during his lifetime. He wrote *The Diary of Samuel Pepys* in a cryptic code, which was his variation on an existing form of shorthand. The first edition was edited by Lord Braybrooke and released in an abridged form in 1825 in two volumes'; www.encyclopedia.com, accessed 5 November 2021.

49 See D. Swift, 'A Goodbye to Pepys's Diary' (31 May 2019), for more on Pepys's code shorthand: 'Pepys began his entries on New Year's Day in 1660 using Thomas Shelton's shorthand, a method he probably used in his work life for speed. The diary at first looks like impenetrable code – all squiggles and dots with only the occasional recognisable word. Pepys also used this "code" for privacy; for he certainly would not have wanted his wife to read about his extra-marital affairs'; www.historiamag.com, accessed 30 November 2021.

50 As D. L. Gorlee suggests, 'The metafictional diversity of Wittgenstein's literary and scientific works inspired and influenced the secrecy of his life, in which the philosopher formed and shaped the "private" identity of his "public" works written in a strange code'; *Wittgenstein's Secret Diaries: Semiotic Writing in Cryptography* (London: Bloomsbury, 2020), p. 1.

51 E. K. Sedgwick, *Tendencies* (London: Routledge, 1994), p. xii.

52 L. Vermeer, 'Tiny Symbols Tell Big Stories: Naming and Concealing Masturbation in Diaries (1650–1840)', *European Journal of Life Writing* 6 (2017), 101–34, 103.

53 Ibid., 114.

54 See C. Padmore, 'The Paradox of Writing the Dead: Voice, Empathy and Authenticity in Historical Biofictions', National Association of Writers in Education *(NAWE): Writing in Practice* 3 (2017), www.nawe.co.uk/DB/wip-editions/articles/the-paradox-of-writing-the-dead-voice-empathy-and-authenticity-in-historical-biofictions.html, accessed 27 May 2022.

55 M. Thain and A. P. Vadillo (eds.), *Michael Field: the Poet* (Peterborough: Broadview Press, 2009).

56 R. Hogan, 'Diary Audiences: a Paradox', *MLA Conference Report in* a/b:Auto/ Biography Studies, 2.2 (1986), 24, www://doi.org/10.1080/08989575.1986.10815401, accessed 20 November 2021.

57 Letts of London, 'The History of Letts of London', https://UK.lettsoflondon.com.

58 29 April 1832, *Lister Papers*, SH:7/ML/E/15/0059.

59 Surface studies is a relatively new area of research which has been developed by researchers working in literature, film, fine art, geography and philosophy. Its focus is on the examination of surfaces, such as skin, cloth/clothing, landscape and film/celluloid. The Surface Studies website is run by two UK-based academics, L. Oakley-Brown, Lancaster University, and S. Colling, Manchester Metropolitan University. See the Surface Studies website: www.surfacestudies.org.

PART III

'Born at Halifax': Lister's Politics, Local and Global

CHAPTER 6

Anne Lister's Politics

Susan S. Lanser

Anne Lister lived in tumultuous times. Born during the less sanguinary phase of the French Revolution, she grew up in an England riven by political dissent and embroiled in relentless war with France. When she was sixteen, Britain abolished the slave trade under the leadership of Yorkshire MP William Wilberforce. She came of age during the Regency and saw the accession of the controversial Prince of Wales, of the 'Sailor King' William and of the unlikely Victoria. She learned within a day about the infamous Peterloo Massacre on 16 August 1819, in not-so-distant Manchester. She saw Irish rebellion, annexation and mass immigration. Her mature years encompassed the removal of disabilities against Roman Catholics in 1829, the dramatic expansion of the franchise through the Great Reform Act of 1832 and the government-subsidised emancipation of enslaved Africans in 1833. She read her way through the literary transformations wrought by two generations of Romantic poets. She crossed the English Channel in one of the earliest steamships, rode a train from Manchester to Liverpool in the first year of its operation and explored innovations in agriculture, shipping and coal manufacture. She was in Europe, though not in Paris, when a new Revolution broke out in July 1830. By 1834 her Halifax had become a hotbed of Whig politics and soon thereafter of Chartist activity. And her life coincided with the emergence of an empire on which the sun proverbially never set.

How did Anne Lister respond to this national and global tumult while negotiating her own tumultuous love life, her complicated social relationships, her ambitious travels and her relentless pursuit of an improved estate? Which issues preoccupied her and which did she ignore? Did her views change over time? What did it mean to her to be English? In raising such questions, I also confront the partiality – in both senses – of my research. I rely gratefully for this project on the letters, diaries and diary excerpts that have already been transcribed. I draw too on the superb scholarship that already grapples with Lister's politics, most fully the work of Jill Liddington and Catherine Euler. But I have not braved the facsimiles. And, of course, even textual resources as voluminous as Lister's diaries and letters cannot capture the conversations and actions that often provide the most reliable key to political practice. My opening litany is thus somewhat proleptic: Lister's perspectives on some or even most of the events I have outlined are unknown and may be unknowable.

In one crucial sense, of course, the phrase 'Anne Lister's politics' leaves little doubt: Lister was a lifelong Tory who campaigned for Tory members of Parliament and vocally supported Tory values, which emphasised the preservation of order and inherited traditions, the rights of country landowners, patriotic loyalty to the Protestant crown and adherence to the Anglican establishment. I had no trouble including Lister in a 2010 essay anchored by the term 'Tory Lesbians' or in arguing in 1998 that Lister's conservatism, like that of the 'Ladies of Llangollen', Lady Eleanor Butler and Sarah Ponsonby, may have been a compensatory assertion of class and caste conformity that Lister's gender, sexuality, her singleness and her singularity could not confer.

In this chapter, however, I want to complicate these claims not only by looking more broadly and more fully at Anne Lister's politics, but also by asking what the phrase 'Anne Lister's politics' might mean. Which concerns most motivated Lister? How did she position herself when the Tory party was itself riven into more liberal and conservative poles? Are there gaps or contradictions between her public and private professions? Do her exceptional life practices themselves constitute a 'politics'? And is it possible that Lister's conservatism was not so much compensatory as *constitutive*, parcel to her self-fashioning in ways that merit a deeper exploration than the ameliorative notion of 'compensation' affords?

I organise my exploration of these questions around three conceptions of 'politics': first, and most obviously, of politics as 'activities or policies associated with government', a definition I draw from the *Oxford English Dictionary*; second, as 'actions concerned with the acquisition or exercise of power, status, or authority' (also taken from the *OED*); and third, politics as a disturbance in the field of authorised bodies that inserts a new part or party of humanity, a concept I take from the philosopher Jacques Rancière. As I address Anne Lister's politics through these definitions, I will propose that her responses to national concerns (definition 1) underwrote her quest for status (definition 2), which in turn sustained a self-insertion into public life on innovative terms (definition 3). Methodologically, I take up this inquiry through a reading of the letters and diaries that focuses especially on words and phrases that Lister repeats across entries and for topics about which she writes at length. I find particularly illuminating the occasions when she repeats, for the sake of her journal, what she has said or written to someone else, narrating herself back to herself in a form that resembles free indirect discourse. Occasions when the letters and diaries conflict overtly or even subtly also seem to me to offer important insights.

Throughout her adult life, Anne Lister was passionately Protestant and passionately English, identities that were effectively co-constitutive: as Linda Colley reminds us, in the late eighteenth century 'Protestantism lay at the core of British national identity.'[1] To be patriotic in Lister's lifetime was to define oneself against continental and colonial others, and especially against Catholicism, the entrenched signifier of the enemy without and within. For Lister as for most Britons, 'Protestant' meant Church of England, and if her religious investments were more formal than deeply spiritual, that is also typical for her generation and her class.

Patriotism was especially intense during Lister's formative years, when Britain and France were at war almost non-stop and when French threats of invasion and conquest were far from idle. Lister's reading list for the late 1810s and early 1820s shows a copious interest in the Napoleonic wars and in Napoleon himself. In 1810 she records attending a performance of 'Rule Britannia' and notes that 'the company consisted of about 60 of our most respectable people'.[2] In 1816 she gloats that Britain has 'humbled La Grande Nation, and some of them will owe us a grudge for it, for some time to come'.[3] It is perhaps her eagerness to celebrate the restoration of the Bourbon throne that leads her to misread Helen Maria Williams, one of the firmest English adherents of the French Revolution, as 'a staunch friend to Louis 18';[4] in fact, Williams hated Napoleon (who hated her) and only hoped that the restored king would respect the 'rights of man' as the French emperor had not. There are also intimations that, during this period at least, Lister was fascinated by Napoleon,[5] a quality that she would have shared with quite a few Britons, including her stealthily admired Lord Byron, a locus of interesting contradictions in Lister's politics to which I will return.

We might rightly ask what it means politically that Lister, for all her professed love of England, chose to spend so much of her time outside it. It is touching to see a fifteen-year-old Anne writing in her journal that a trip to the small town of Bacup in August 1806 was 'the first time I ever Was out of Yorkshire',[6] and then to absorb the voluminous list of her adult travels: Scotland, Wales, Ireland, France, Belgium, Switzerland, Holland, Denmark, Prussia, Italy, Finland and Russia, with Paris a familiar point of return. In the early years, Lister's writings are filled with encomiums to

England, which becomes the ground of comparison next to which every elsewhere falls short: writing to the Duffins, she extols 'this favoured island, the admiration of every enlightened and impartial mind' is 'where the wise man sees abundant reason to be satisfied and happy'.[7] On her first trip to Paris in 1819, she finds the French capital a 'shabby' disappointment at first compared wth London.[8] But she thinks Dieppe 'might almost pass for English'.[9] Rouen reminds her of Manchester, and in 1822, she identifies London's Regent's Crescent as 'now, surely, the finest street' in all of Europe, though this would be a Europe she has at that point hardly seen.[10]

As Lister becomes a habitual traveller, England does cease to be the measure of all things beautiful, but it remains the measure of all things right. In the 1820s and perhaps beyond, Lister seems to show a certain guilty pleasure in loving the continent. She writes on 31 March 1825, in one of her self-reflexive passages,

> I leave Paris, said I to myself, with sentiments how different from those with which I arrived. My eye was accustomed to all it saw – it was no longer a stranger nor found fault as before with all that differed from what it left at home. Imperfectly as I speak the language, I felt almost at home in Paris & seemed to feel so in France.[11]

As soon as she is home, however, she seems to need to prove her patriotism: just two weeks later, she writes a letter affirming that 'French manners & habits of thinking [are] very different from ours', and then, even more dismissively in another recounting of her own words, 'My being in Paris was a mere nothing. Scarce deserved the name of being abroad. Like a dream which I had already forgotten'; indeed, she 'told them all I was more than ever English at heart'.[12] On another occasion, after thinking wistfully about France, she writes, 'But don't mistake me. Ours is the land of righteous law & liberty; & I would not change my birthplace for all the loveliest spots that smile upon the god of day. But we may migrate now & then, & yet be patriot still.'[13] In a society where the Grand Tour is not only a commonplace for upper-class men, but in some circles even an expectation for men and a possibility for women, this level of protest is interestingly intense.

I have not found the same defensiveness regarding Lister's later travels, perhaps because they enabled her to meet continental royalty while also advancing her relationships with the English elite. She does still enjoy marking English – and Yorkshire – superiority; in summer 1831, returning from travels in Holland, Belgium and several English cathedral towns, she pronounces that 'up to this moment, no ecclesiastical building I have ever seen equals York cathedral', while more equivocally attributing to Norwich 'the best bread and butter I have ever tasted, *save* in Lombardy'.[14] And by the time she reaches Moscow in 1840, she can call the city's beauty 'indescribable' and the Kremlin 'unrivalled', aesthetically leaving England behind. Yet even then her justification is English, and poignantly so when we remember that she never returned to England: evoking Samuel Johnson, she extols the 'enlarging' benefits of travel and her hopes 'to be richer in these by and by; and then it will be more flattering to this fair city [Moscow] to repeat, that I still think it the most beautiful town I have ever seen'.[15]

Given her prolific patriotic protestations, it is significant but not surprising that Lister's travels were not necessarily 'enlarging' of her views at home. A common gesture in the diaries is to recognise and record the opinions, problems and sometimes the sufferings of local people, but then to affirm viewpoints that I propose to call kingly – and this at a time when challenges to absolutism pervaded the European continent. We see often in Lister's writings support for kings whom others of her class and political leanings are unwilling to defend. For example, although she acknowledged the legitimacy of French frustrations with the ultra-right French king Charles X, whom Isabella Norcliffe's mother, Ann, was more typical in naming a 'despot',[16] Lister takes the trouble to praise Charles's philanthropy toward his servants. Ann Norcliffe also professes herself glad when the time comes in England that 'William 4th reigns instead of George 4th!',[17] while Lister seems to have been among a distinct minority of women to support the wildly unpopular George. The Prince Regent's behaviour towards his estranged wife, Caroline, so outraged English women that (despite Caroline's own clear transgressions) tens of thousands of them, including some 3,700 'ladies' from Halifax, signed petitions supporting the queen when some members of Parliament wanted to try Caroline for adultery rather than allow her to take part in George IV's coronation.[18] But Lister used a trip to Italy in 1827 to visit Caroline's villa and affirm that 'unfortunately, we heard quite enough to persuade us, our King was quite right not to suffer such a queen to be the crowned queen of England'.[19]

No surprise either, then, that it was with the crown that Lister had also sided on the occasion of the Peterloo Massacre of 16 August 1819, when some sixty thousand peacefully assembled petitioners, a majority of them women and children, were charged by cavalry, killing dozens of unarmed demonstrators and slashing and trampling another three to five hundred.

In her diary two days later, Lister records the 'sad work at Manchester – a crowded meeting of these radical reformers', misrepresenting the crowd as a 'mob armed with pistols' while making no mention of royal sabres; for her, the 'reports are so vague and monstrous' that she 'scarce knows what to believe'.[20] Lister's scepticism is understandable, for 'monstrous' indeed became the judgement of history; the poet Percy Shelley spoke for the majority of Britons when he memorialised this senseless rampage of 'Rulers who neither see nor feel nor know'.[21] But Lister was explicit in her worry over the 'grievous . . . unsettled state of peoples and governments' and in declaring 'liberty and equality' to be both an 'absurdity' and an 'impracticability'.[22]

This belief in the impossibility – and, for all we know, the undesirability – of 'liberty and equality' probably also extends to Lister's views about enslavement and abolition. The public record gives no evidence of any holdings that implicate Shibden during Anne Lister's lifetime or the lifetimes of her uncle and aunt. Profits from enslavement do appear in the Lister family record: as Liddington notes, two of Anne's great-uncles, Thomas and William, 'emigrated to Virginia in the 1730s, pinning their hopes on the tobacco trade' and enslaving some fifteen Africans.[23] The greatest beneficiary of slavery in Lister's family, however, was the Lister who inherited Shibden after Ann Walker's death: Thomas's grandson John, whose wife, Louisa Grant, owned a sizeable St Vincent plantation. In the 1830s England imperilled its fiscal stability to award 20 million pounds to British enslavers – and nothing to the enslaved; Louisa Grant Lister received a whopping £12,765 13s. 8d. for the mandatory emancipation of 485 enslaved persons.[24] The website of the Centre for the Study of the Legacies of British Slavery shows several other Listers receiving more modest compensation for one or more emancipated persons. Ann Walker's brother-in-law George Sutherland also held persons in bondage in St Vincent and received a significant sum.

Slavery and abolition were hot topics in Yorkshire during Lister's life. On the one hand, the region's economy and many of its landowners were implicated beneficiaries of what S. D. Smith calls 'gentry capitalism': the efforts of 'landed and respectable' gentry 'to increase their wealth and influence through colonial trade'.[25] On the other hand, Yorkshire was also a site of intense abolitionist activity, not least among women and not least because William Wilberforce, Parliament's prime mover for abolition, was a long-time Yorkshire MP, and ultimately it was anti-slavery sentiment that won county support. At this juncture we do not know Anne Lister's views on this critical issue of her times, and she would certainly have lacked the means to become a 'gentry capitalist'. When Lister (slightly mis)quotes from William Cowper's *The Task* in 1825 to say that 'we all agree with Cowper, "England! My country! With all thy faults I love thee still"', she may or may not have recognised that for Cowper slavery was first among those faults.[26]

As far as I have read, slavery comes up only once in the transcribed diaries, but that entry, at more than 1,200 words, comprises one of Lister's longest records of a single conversation. The entry reports the experiences of a John Robinson, who visited Shibden on 22 January 1818 to contract for repairs. Robinson had spent two years on a Liverpool slave ship and 'gave us an amusing account of what he had seen'. He describes the brutal capture and transport of some six hundred Africans, 'chained by tens together', four of whom jumped overboard in their shared chains rather than accept captivity. Without critical comment, Lister recounts the treatment and the suffering of these Africans and dwells on the details of their sale in Jamaica: 'men bought at about £13 a piece – women £2 less, tho if pregnant only £1 less, and, if with a fine child at the breast, the same price as the men'.[27] The entry also records Robinson's account of African customs, an account that dehumanises the captives and implies that they mistreat their own children such that many of them die. If Lister supported abolition or even amelioration, one would expect a report like this one, written a decade after the slave trade was banned, to have included at least a word of critical comment. But we have only her silence here, and it is challenging to imagine that this silence does not speak complicity.

Lister was not silent about Catholicism, however, and eventually her views took an ultra-conservative and minoritarian stance. As I have noted, in Lister's day anti-Catholicism was parcel to Englishness: triumph over the Gunpowder Plot engineered in 1605 by the Catholic Guy Fawkes engendered a decreed national holiday and a prescribed liturgy in the Book of Common Prayer that officially lasted until 1859; the 1701 Act of Settlement set forth an order of appointment to the English throne that would guarantee perpetual Protestant accession; and the anti-Catholic Gordon Riots that terrorised London in 1780 remained a recent reminder of English hysteria over Parliament's efforts to remove minor restrictions against Roman Catholics put in place by the Anti-Popery Act of 1698. Nonetheless, new efforts for fair treatment began percolating in Parliament by 1805 in the wake of Great Britain's 1801 Act of Union with Ireland. These efforts culminated in the passage of the Roman Catholic Relief Act of 1829, which allowed Catholics to hold parliamentary office though not yet to enter the universities of Oxford and Cambridge.

The Tory party and its public were deeply divided over the 1829 bill. If Lister occasionally maintains that she has 'always been for the Roman Catholics', as Catherine Euler reports, the diaries had also expressed anti-Catholic views.[28] In 1817 Lister comments that 'the order of Jesuits is the most dangerous and insidious enemy we can possibly suffer to set itself up against the protestant religion'; that diary entry also cites at some length concerns about an increase in Catholics in Lancashire where, she claims, 'almost all the neighbouring population has been brought over to the popish Faith'.[29] While she delights in the majestic cathedrals of the continent, she laments that 'there are now a thousand Roman Catholic chapels in England'.[30] By 1825 she is calling upon 'all Protestants to stand firm in support of their religion'.[31] And echoing longstanding British ideology, she warns that the 'foreign influence' of Catholics 'will not go down with Englishmen'.[32]

But what almost surely solidified Lister's opposition to the Catholic Relief Act of 1829 was her new friendship with Lady Louisa Stuart, granddaughter of the Earl of Bute and of the renowned writer and traveller Lady Mary Wortley Montagu. I propose this friendship as a key to understanding Anne Lister's politics in all three of the respects that I take up here. For most Tories, the Catholic Relief Act was a compromise for the sake of the union; in Lister's resistance to that compromise, we see not only the conventional insistence on Britain as an exclusively Protestant state, but Lister's thrall to Lady Stuart, a relationship that, as Jill Liddington has observed, 'hardened [Lister's] conservative politics'.[33] Importantly, this relationship emerged in Lister's life at a time when Britain itself was on the cusp of changing in ways that Lister would find disturbing.

Lister was doubtless among the many who were surprised in 1830 by the collapse of a Tory hegemony that had lasted for the better part of seven decades. The Whig takeover also ousted Lady Stuart's nephew Charles from his position as ambassador to France and coincided with the 'July Days' in France that led to the abdication of Charles X, days that Lister marks with the language of 'horror' and 'carnage'. Lady Stuart, ever the arch-conservative, worried in a letter to Lister that 'the terrible state of this country . . . seems fast verging to that of France'.[34] Britain's new and more liberal government was solidified by the Reform Bill of 1832, which expanded the male franchise to include many of Lister's own tenants. An interest in electoral politics turns up in Lister's journal as early as 1807, when she mentions that 'Mr R went to York to vote'[35] – and one wishes she had said more about what is now called the Great Yorkshire Election that returned William Wilberforce and gave a second seat to the Whig Lord Milton, supporter of electoral reform and workers' rights, over the Tory enslaver and plantation magnate Henry Lascelles, who, incidentally, as Carol Adlam and San Ní Ríocáin have discovered, turns out to be a distant relation of Eliza Raine.[36]

Lister brings up electoral politics more fully in 1817 when her diary for four days running is focused almost wholly on the local contest between Scott and Hawksworth, with copious detail and passionate commentary about the poll,[37] and in 1823 she is musing about Tory candidates who might be recruited to run for Halifax. But her political investments heat up most intensely after the collapse of the Tory government in 1830, when the question of electoral reform becomes paramount. Lister wrote on 5 March 1831 that she was

> not committed on the reform question as yet. I have always lately and to the Stuarts and people here *professed myself* a friend of the Duke of Wellington. In my heart I scarce know whether to wish for the reform or not. I think I rather incline towards it but I shall wait for circumstances before I declare myself. Not even my aunt as yet know[s] what I wish about it.[38]

Here we see a private Lister uncertain of her position, unwilling to be open about that uncertainty, perhaps waiting to see what Lady Stuart will do. For as Liddington discusses more deeply in *Female Fortune*, the friendship with Lady Stuart and the high-level connections that it conferred on Lister seem to have won out when she was undecided. And in the next three parliamentary elections – 1832, 1835 and 1837 – when Lady Stuart's own nephew James Stuart Wortley was a candidate for West Yorkshire, Lister found herself even more firmly on what Liddington calls 'the uncompromising diehard wing of the Tories' where her opposition to the Catholic Relief Act already placed her in 1829.[39]

The Reform Bill brought politics literally home: even as it explicitly disenfranchised women, who had only rarely dared to vote, it gave Lister the landowner a new influence. As Euler and Liddington have documented more fully, Lister openly strong-armed her eligible tenants to vote (Tory) blue and publicised her vow to 'not take a new tenant who would not give me a vote':[40] 'I had made up my mind to take none but blue tenants.'[41] She probably did help Wortley squeak into a one-vote victory in 1835 – he had come in at the bottom of four candidates in 1832 – but after that second election, she insists that she will 'give up talking politics – no hope of gaining people over, such is the spirit abroad for innovation'.[42] Indeed, Halifax became a Whig and then radical stronghold in spite of

Lister and her fellow landowners, and Wortley's humiliating defeat in 1837, when (though incumbent) he came in again at the bottom, also showed Lister the limits of her influence. Already with Wortley's 1832 loss, however, she was expressing dismay and ambivalence about her involvement in politics. 'I hardly thought myself capable of such strong political excitement and mortification,' she wrote thereafter. 'I am completely sick of public events.'[43]

In moving towards the second conception of 'Anne Lister's politics', I want to dwell on that word 'mortification' and on what that sentiment might have meant for Lister as a precarious member of her class. I have agreed with Jill Liddington that Lady Stuart was a catalyst for some of Lister's more conservative positions. In Lister's letters to Lady Stuart we can find many a performance of conservative lament; she tells us in a diary entry, for example, that she began one letter to Lady Stuart by saying that 'The political mind of the people is sadly warped ... The registration [of new voters] has not gained us much, if anything.'[44] But I would argue that the real catalyst for Anne Lister's politics lay in the preservation – or enhancement – of her rank. I see Lister's adulation of Lady Stuart as less about politics as national governance than about politics as 'actions concerned with the acquisition or exercise of power, status, or authority'.[45] I propose, in short, that the quest for status drove Lister's Tory politics rather than the other way around. For, if we look at the diaries across time, what mattered most to Lister was to secure her identity as a member of the landowning elite. And it seems to me too that it is in the diary entries about status that we find a particular intensity of hyperbolic and redundant prose.

The signs of Lister's status insecurity are manifold and, given the precarity of her family's finances especially before she went to live at Shibden, that insecurity is, of course, founded in fact. In her most overblown prose, the twenty-one-year-old Anne exhorts her brother, Sam, as 'the last remaining hope and stay of an old, but lately drooping family', to 'seize it in its fall. Renovate its languid energies; rear it with a tender hand, and let it once more bloom upon the spray. Ah! let the well-ascended blood that trickles in your veins stimulate the generous enthusiasm of your soul, and prove it is not degenerated from the spirit of your ancestors.'[46] She is thrilled in 1817 to have the official copy of her family's pedigree 'entered in the college' and will 'make it a rule to have the pedigree brought down & read aloud the 21st day of every June and December'.[47] She admits to her diary in 1825 that 'I always doubt my own importance & if people are not civil in calling, etc., fancy they mean to cut, or not to know, me. I shall never feel right on this point till I am evidently in good society & rank, with a good establishment.'[48] She believes that 'one can hardly carry oneself too high or keep people at too great a distance'.[49] She fears that 'without some intellectual superiority over the common mass of those I meet with, what am I? *Pejus quam nihil* [worse than nothing].'[50] She acknowledges her awe of Lady Stuart's elevated rank and contemplates a strategy for recruiting a Tory candidate for Halifax that will bring her renown, even as she recognises her own wine-induced foolishness: 'Began building castles about the result of my success, the notoriety it would gain me. An introduction to court. Perhaps a Barony, etc . . . I thought to myself, how slight the partition between sanity & not.'[51] Ironically, however, Lister has come of age at a time when the status of status is itself becoming precarious; as Clara Tuite puts it, 'in the 1820s, in the wake of the French Revolution, Waterloo and Peterloo, and the consolidation of English radical culture into the parliamentary reform movement, the aristocracy's supposedly natural claims to rule are not self-evident'.[52] Lister is chasing the end of a curve.

It is poignant, then, that the political theme that runs most through the diaries is Lister's insistence on her status, along with an oft-articulated contempt for anyone she deems lower either by birth or by manners. The word 'vulgar' appears copiously in the diaries, as she dismisses people as 'a vulgar set', 'a sad vulgar set'. [53] She avows in 1825 that 'Vulgarity gravifies & sickens me more than ever.'[54] She suddenly sees Emma Saltmarshe as 'sadly vulgar', and her 'heart sighed after some better & higher bred companion that it could love'.[55] Ann Walker also gets the label 'vulgar' at one early moment in their acquaintance.[56] Even Lister's venereal disease must be pronounced high-class, as she assures Mrs Barlow that it did not come 'from anyone in low life. I never associated with people below myself.'[57] And vulgarity, it seems, begins at home, for Lister's own parents fall under that label: they 'were both grown 10 times more vulgar than ever', she writes in her diary in 1817; tellingly, she conceals that admission in code.[58]

People in trade also, of course, fall within the low-class label, despite or because of the Lister family's own history; Lister derides Maria Barlow's beau as 'a thorough tradesman . . . clean & neat but thoroughly a tradesman',[59] and resists attending a fair on a Sunday, the 'vulgar day' with 'all the common people there'.[60] Closer to home, she opposes her sister Marian's marriage to a wool stapler and sets Marian a rule that she not invite to Shibden 'people she knew I did not wish to have anything to do with'.[61] English 'blood' is also a status marker for Lister. The simple recognition that she is attracted to a French woman unleashes this sermon against intermarriage: if she were a man, she

> would only have married an Englishwoman. Would not mix the blood ... I was proud of my country. Loved the little spot where my ancestors had lived for centuries. Should inherit from them with pure English blood for five or six centuries and my children should not say I had mixed it. I loved my king & country & compatriots & would not take more fortune away from them. I should be head of my family & it should remain English still.[62]

When Lister writes to Lady Stuart that 'The spirit of the times is hard to manage',[63] it is tempting to weigh the word 'manage' as a sign of her aspiration to control her world. It is ironic, of course, that her unconventionality – her refusal to marry, her insistence on singular and genderqueer fashion, and the open secret of her love of women – undermined the very status she sought to secure, doubtless also intensifying her elitist discourse.

Yet Lister's views departed dramatically from those of her more conservative friends on at least one subject (apart from her obvious but secret views about sex between women): her passion for that most controversial – and most high-born – of Romantic poets, Lord Byron, whose writings she cherished along with Rousseau's *Confessions* and whose death in 1824 shocked and saddened her. Byron was both a political radical and a scribe of what were deemed obscenities; many of his initial upper-class admirers abandoned him after the publication of *Childe Harold*, and most of the remaining fans after the publication of *Don Juan*, to which even Byron's own publisher, John Murray, would not affix his name. Friedrich Engels probably did not exaggerate much when he wrote in 1843 that 'Byron and Shelley are read almost exclusively by the lower classes.'[64] In terms of both politics and propriety, one could have expected Lister to prefer Wordsworth, but she acknowledges, in reporting a conversation with the Belcombes in July 1821 about 'the merits of modern poets', that while Steph preferred 'Southey, Hope, and Wordsworth to Lord Byron', 'not so Mariana and I'.[65] The diaries suggest that Lister fancied herself a Rousseauvian individualist and something of a Byronic hero in ways that sit uneasily with her need for social belonging, as does her cathexis to Byron, whose politics could not have been more unlike her own.

No wonder, then, that Lister tended to keep her love of Byron, and especially of the castigated *Don Juan*, secret. She reports in 1820, for example, that 'Mrs Waterhouse asked me afterwards if I had *read Don Juan*. I would not own it.'[66] Byron's poetry does become code in her courting of Miss Brown: '*do you like Lord Byrons poetry*', Anne asks, to be answered, '*yes perhaps too well*'.[67] Lister alludes in her journal to reviews that condemn *Don Juan* 'of course', but is glad that they also 'do justice to the genius shown in the work'.[68] On 19 May 1824, when she records the death of 'his lordship', she asks, 'Who admired him as a man?' 'Yet "he is gone & forever!" The greatest poet of the age! And I am sorry.'[69] Lister later acknowledges admiring not just the poems but the poet: in 1827 she visits Clarens and 'sat an hour where Lord Byron would be taken and spent two or three days. A young lady who went the other day, kissed his bed twenty times . . . Lord B – seems to have been much liked by the people around here – the old woman told us, she had cried like a child when she heard of his death.'[70] Tuite has argued that despite their differences, 'in gender, rank, sexual practice, party-political identification, religion and region', Lister's 'sociable performance is paradigmatically Byronic';[71] certainly Lister's passion for Byron suggests that his aristocratic entitlement and Romantic self-fashioning outweighed his politics. It seems, however, that she mostly kept this to herself.

Lister's passion for a poet of high rank but low morals, along with her renowned self-understanding as a Romantic individualist 'different from any others who exist' in the Rousseauvian sense,[72] suggests a person whose politics were not so simply conservative as I have implied. This leads me to the third and most innovative way of approaching 'Anne Lister's politics': what Majid Yar describes as the attempt 'to introduce new, heretofore 'non-political' issues, into the realm of legitimate political concern'.[73] Yar's concept derives from the philosophical approach of Jacques Rancière, who argues that politics 'happens' when a group 'with no firmly determined place in the hierarchical social edifice' inserts itself as a part or party of humanity entitled to its full rights and benefits.[74] In Slavoj Žižek's rephrasing, politics happens when the members of a particular constituency 'not only demand that their voice be heard' but 'present themselves as the representatives, the stand-ins, for the Whole of Society'.[75] In our own time, both LGBTQ rights and Black Lives Matter have operated in this way: by inserting a new polity and insisting that it stands for humanity itself.

I would suggest that Anne Lister, though usually acting on her own rather than claiming a shared identity, was bent on propelling just such a redistribution. If she was simply following her 'nature', as she often claimed, she also made no attempt to conform to the standards of femininity current in her day: at the age of eighteen she reports a second-hand comment of 'pity that she doesn't pay more attention to her appearance', and yet within the week is purchasing 'gentlemen's braces' that would make her even more conspicuously 'singular'.[76] She believed, and may have been right, that marriage could give her 'rank, fortune and talent, a title and several thousand a year', yet she 'refused from principle' to take that heteronormative path.[77] She wilfully inserted herself into all-male social, political and commercial spheres as an unmarried female landowner and entrepreneur, effectively claiming the rights of rank against the disabilities of gender. She was elected to the Halifax Literary and Philosophical Society during its first year of operation in 1830–1 and was the only female member during her lifetime. Anira Rowanchild, noting that there were at least two other unmarried female landowners in the area – both of whom had been at school with Lister – observes a 'relative flexibility of social discourse in relation to class and gender in this rapidly expanding provincial town';[78] I wonder whether Lister helped to make that flexibility possible. Lister also, of course, inserted what could readily be recognised as a same-sex partnership into Halifax society when she brought Ann Walker to live at Shibden, and both women paid with slurs that included a fake marriage announcement for 'Captain Tom Lister' and Miss Ann Walker in the Yorkshire press;[79] after all, Walker had a perfectly good (or even better) home of her own nearby. Cassandra Ulph makes an astute comment when she evokes the question that Lenore Davidoff and Catherine Hall raise in their iconic *Family Fortunes*: 'Men built, men planned, men organized, men acted. Meanwhile, what did women do?'[80] To which Ulph wryly answers, 'Anne Lister would not recognize the question.'[81] It is this insistence on taking her unconventional place in the world that I would argue constitutes 'Anne Lister's politics' in a different way.

One dramatic sign of Lister's investment in this practice of politics as a 'disturbance in the field' occurs in an incident involving that icon of Lister's aristocratic imagination, Lady Stuart. Lister was apparently insistent that her relationship with Ann Walker be accepted in even the highest of her social spheres. In 1836, when Lady Stuart neglected to invite Walker to accompany Lister on a visit to Richmond, Lister wrote insisting that she would not visit without Ann. As Anira Rowanchild tells it, she received a 'surprisingly ingratiating' reply from Lady Stuart: 'My house *is now entirely at your service* for yourself and Miss Walker . . . I have had my own Bedroom pulled to piece[s] to have it *washed & glazed* . . . [I will sleep] in the Dressing room. Your friend can occupy what was . . . [my niece] *Vere's room*.'[82] Here Lister stands up to that same ultra-Tory Lady Stuart, daughter of an earl and granddaughter of the famed Lady Mary Wortley Montagu, the woman she has for a decade been effectively fashioning and refashioning herself to please – by insisting on having Ann Walker recognised as her essential companion. This is a fine example of Lister enacting a politics not of reaction but of reform – a word that she herself, of course, might have been loath to use.

What enabled Anne Lister, lesser gentry and relatively impoverished landowner that she was, to press Lady Stuart in this way? Lister was aware that Lady Stuart's fortunes were declining; a diary entry of 10 June 1834 recognises that '*there is a sad want of money and she is not in her splendour now – but all kindness to me and I will behave with tact I think I shall get on in high life and carry on with me Miss Walker by and by*'.[83] But this is also the point at which I would revise my thinking about what I have called Lister's *compensatory* conservatism. When I introduced the term in 1998, I argued that in eighteenth-century England, same-sex friendship was coded as a high-status phenomenon and that 'women whose erotic orientation might be seen as directed toward other women', or what I called 'gentry sapphists' like Elizabeth Carter, Sarah Scott, the 'Ladies of Llangollen' Eleanor Butler and Sarah Ponsonby, and the Dutch couple Aagje Deken and Betje Wolff, could 'exploit the symbols of class status to sustain an image of sexual innocence. Rather than mere passive beneficiaries of a class-based bifurcation, in other words, these women were sometimes active agents in cultivating their class status as a screen.'[84] I took Lister as a prime example, though I noted that her appearance 'attracted more familiar treatment than a respectable gentrywoman had reason to expect'.[85] In my 2010 essay 'Tory Lesbians', I argued again that Lister's 'self-fashioning threatened her social status', which she attempted to 'shore up ... through an aggressively conservative class politics'.[86]

It is possible that both Lister's conservatism and her assertions of status began as compensation. But the word 'constitutive' carries a more positive agency that seems to me appropriate in her case. Conservative politics placed Lister so squarely in the right wing of the landed gentry as to provide some reassurance that she was not a sexual threat. Conservative politics authorised her to do what single women didn't do – both in the board room and in bed. Rather than seeing her as someone who effectively *became* conservative by virtue of her difference, I would now say that her conservatism emboldened her to embrace that difference.

Lister's conscious cultivation of status, which enabled her self-fashioning as visibly and remarkably queer, thus constitutes a claim of privilege as powerful in its way as Byron's, and one that arguably gave her the best of both worlds. For as Chris Roulston reminds us, 'Lister simultaneously sought conformity and nonconformity, belonging and difference, community and radical individualism.'[87] We see that uneasy mix in a politics that is conformist by dictionary definitions but insistently nonconformist, even anti-conformist, by understandings of politics like Jacques Rancière's. As Amanda Vickery puts it in *The Gentleman's Daughter*, most women of Lister's class wore propriety like a 'tight-fitting suit' in order to achieve freedoms of other kinds.[88] But Lister engaged in literal self-fashioning. Certainly Lister's spirit was also entrepreneurial; she craved knowledge and experience, was fascinated by how things work and took pleasure in new inventions, scientific discoveries and technological improvements. Had her means been more opulent, her status more secure, her patrons differently positioned in national politics, she might well have engaged differently in the politics of both status and governance. But we can say that it was with boldness, brilliance and remarkable self-invention that Anne Lister of Shibden Hall confronted her tumultuous times.

Notes

1 L. Colley, *Britons: Forging the Nation, 1707–1837* (New Haven: Yale University Press, 1999), p. 369.
2 26 June 1810, *Anne Lister Papers*, West Yorkshire Archive Service, Calderdale [hereafter *Lister Papers*], SH:7/ML/E/26/1. Lister often abbreviated common words; I have chosen to write them out in full.
3 25 October 1816, *Lister Papers*, SH:7/ML/E/26/2.
4 Ibid.
5 The intensity of Lister's reading about Napoleon may be evidence in itself. But see also, for example, her diary entry for 8 November 1816, when she names the *Secret Memoirs of Napoleon* 'the most interesting work I have read for long' (*Lister Papers*, SH:7/ML/E/26/3).
6 25 August 1806, *Lister Papers*, SH:7/ML/E/26/1.
7 M. Green (ed.), *Miss Lister of Shibden Hall: Selected Letters, 1800–1840* (Lewes: Book Guild, 1992), 22 December 1819, p. 54.
8 15 May 1819, *Anne Lister Papers*, West Yorkshire Archive Service (WYAS), Calderdale, SH:7/ML/E/3.
9 Ibid., 22 December 1819, p. 53.
10 Ibid., 7 September 1822, p. 61.
11 H. Whitbread (ed.), *No Priest but Love: the Journals of Anne Lister from 1824–1826* (New York: New York University Press, 1992), 31 March 1825, p. 88.
12 Whitbread, *No Priest but Love*, 17 April 1825, pp. 98–9.
13 Ibid., 15 December 1825, p. 143.
14 Green, *Miss Lister*, 20 August 1831, pp. 157–8.
15 Ibid., 13 January 1840, p. 196.
16 Ibid., p. 130. In this letter Ann Norcliffe asks Lister *not* to be 'so horribly diplomatic as you were in a letter written some time since in answer to a

remark I made upon the detestable Polignac ministry, and the despotism of the ex-King [Charles X]'. Lister may have been silently dissenting from that charge of despotism.

17 Ibid., p. 131.

18 Colley, *Britons*, p. 265.

19 Green, *Miss Lister*, p. 110.

20 18 August 1819, *Lister Papers*, SH:7/ML/E/3.

21 P. B. Shelley, 'England in 1819', in Z. Leader and M. O'Neill (eds.), *Percy Bysshe Shelley: the Major Works* (Oxford: Oxford University Press, 2003), p. 446.

22 Green, *Miss Lister*, pp. 131, 47.

23 J. Liddington, *Female Fortune: Land, Gender and Authority: the Anne Lister Diaries and Other Writings, 1833–36* (London: Rivers Oram, 1998), p. 6.

24 See Centre for the Study of the Legacies of British Slavery, www.ucl.ac.uk/lbs/search/.

25 S. D. Smith, *Slavery, Family, and Gentry Capitalism in the British Atlantic: the World of the Lascelles, 1648–1834* (Cambridge: Cambridge University Press, 2006), p. 9.

26 Whitbread, *No Priest but Love*, 15 December 1825, p. 143. The passage from *The Task* (Book II) actually reads as follows: 'England, with all thy faults, I love thee still— / My country!'

27 22 January 1818, *Lister Papers*, SH:7/ML/E/1.

28 C. A. Euler, 'Moving between Worlds: Gender, Class, Sexuality, Politics, and Women's Networks in the Diaries of Anne Lister of Shibden Hall, Halifax, Yorkshire, 1830–1840', unpublished PhD thesis, University of York (1995). Lister's confounding language even in that letter belies her claim: she says here that she 'would do them a kindness handsomely, not reluctantly grant what I dare not withhold' (ibid., p. 113).

29 17 June 1817, *Lister Papers*, SH:7/ML/E/1.

30 Ibid.

31 Whitbread, *No Priest but Love*, 25 November 1825, p. 141

32 Ibid.

33 Liddington, *Female Fortune*, p. 23.

34 Green, *Miss Lister*, p. 142.

35 27 May 1807, *Lister Papers*, SH:7/ML/E/26/1.

36 C. Adlam, pers. comm.

37 See entries for 11–17 May 1817, *Lister Papers*, SH:7/ML/E/1.

38 Euler, *Moving between Worlds*, p. 242.

39 Liddington, *Female Fortune*, p. 128.

40 Ibid., 4 November 1835, p. 197.

41 Ibid., 6 January 1835, p. 140.

42 Ibid., p. 162.

43 Green, *Miss Lister*, 2 September 1835, p. 175.

44 Liddington, *Female Fortune*, 10 November 1835, p. 197.

45 'Politics, n.', *Oxford English Dictionary* online.

46 Green, *Miss Lister*, February 1813, p. 38.
47 26 April 1817, *Lister Papers*, SH:7/ML/E/1.
48 Whitbread, *No Priest but Love*, 3 October 1825, p. 24.
49 H. Whitbread (ed.), *I Know My Own Heart: the Diaries of Anne Lister, 1791–1840* (London: Virago, 1988), 5 May 1820, p. 124.
50 Whitbread, *No Priest but Love*, 23 September 1825, p. 133.
51 Whitbread, *I Know My Own Heart*, 18 July 1823, p. 264.
52 C. Tuite, 'The Byronic Woman: Anne Lister's Style, Sociability and Sexuality', in G. Russell and C. Tuite (eds.), *Romantic Sociability: Social Networks and Literary Culture in Britain, 1770–1840* (Cambridge: Cambridge University Press, 2006), pp. 186–210, p. 195.
53 7 May and 14 July 1817, *Lister Papers*, SH:7/ML/E/1.
54 Whitbread, *No Priest but Love*, 18 April 1825, p. 99.
55 Whitbread, *I Know My Own Heart*, 31 May 1824, p. 344.
56 Whitbread, *I Know My Own Heart*, 18 June 1822, p. 189.
57 Whitbread, *No Priest but Love*, 28 November 1824, p. 58.
58 30 January 1817, *Lister Papers*, SH:7/ML/E/26/3.
59 Whitbread, *No Priest but Love*, 5 April 1825, p. 91.
60 Ibid., 6 September 1824, p. 15.
61 Liddington, *Female Fortune*, 10 December 1834, p. 134.
62 Whitbread, *No Priest but Love*, 29 October 1824, p. 39.
63 Liddington, *Female Fortune*, p. 153.
64 F. Engels, 'Letter to the *Swiss Republican* (1843)', in K. Marx and F. Engels, *On Literature and Art* (Moscow: Progress, 1976), p. 162.
65 27 July 1821, *Lister Papers*, SH:7/ML/E/5.
66 Whitbread, *I Know My Own Heart*, 25 July 1820, p. 131.
67 29 April 1818, *Lister Papers*, SH:7/ML/E/2.
68 13 September1820, *Lister Papers*, SH:7/ML/E/4.
69 Whitbread, *I Know My Own Heart*, 30 May 1824, p. 344.
70 Green, *Miss Lister*, 27 August 1827, p. 10.
71 Tuite, 'The Byronic Woman', pp. 189–90.
72 See the first words of Jean-Jacques Rousseau's *Confessions*.
73 M. Yar, 'Hannah Arendt', *Encyclopedia of Philosophy*, https://iep.utm.edu/arendt/, accessed 3 May 2022.
74 J. Rancière, *Disagreement: Politics and Philosophy*, trans. Julie Rose (Minneapolis: University of Minnesota Press, 1999), p. 22.
75 S. Žižek, *The Ticklish Subject: the Absent Centre of Political Ontology* (London: Verso, 1999), p. 188.
76 21 and 27 March 1809, *Lister Papers*, SH:7/ML/E/26/1.
77 Liddington, *Female Fortune*, p. 18.
78 A. Rowanchild, 'Skirting the Margins: Anne Lister, Self-Representation, and Lesbian Identity in Early Nineteenth-Century Yorkshire', in R. Phillips et al. (eds.), *De-Centering Sexualities: Politics and Representations beyond the Metropolis* (London: Taylor and Francis, 2000), pp. 145–58, p. 148.
79 Liddington, *Female Fortune*, 10 January 1835, p. 143.

80 L. Davidoff and C. Hall, *Family Fortunes: Men and Women of the English Middle Class, 1780–1850* (London: Hutchinson, 1987), p. 416.
81 C. Ulph, '"Under the Existing Rules": Anne Lister and the Halifax Literary and Philosophical Society', *Nineteenth-Century Literature* 73.4 (2019), 462–85, 484.
82 Rowanchild, 'Skirting the Margins', 151–2 (original emphasis).
83 Lister diary entry, 10 June 1834, 'In Search of Ann Walker', https://insearchofannwalker.com/Tuesday-10th-june-1834/, accessed 24 July 2022.
84 S. S. Lanser, 'Befriending the Body: Female Intimacies as Class Acts', *Eighteenth-Century Studies* 32.2 (1998–9), 179–98.
85 Ibid., 190.
86 S. S. Lanser, 'Tory Lesbians: Economies of Intimacy and the Status of Desire', in J. C. Beynon and C. Gonda (eds.), *Lesbian Dames: Sapphism in the Long Eighteenth Century* (Farnham: Ashgate, 2010), pp. 173–89, p. 186.
87 C. Roulston, 'Sexuality in Translation: Anne Lister and the Ancients', *Journal of the History of Sexuality* 30 (2021), 112–35, 120.
88 A. Vickery, *The Gentleman's Daughter: Women's Lives in Georgian England* (New Haven: Yale University Press, 1998), p. 294.

CHAPTER 7

'Building Castles in the Air': Anne Lister and Associational Life

Cassandra Ulph

In recent years the explosion of interest in Anne Lister, accelerated in no small measure by Sally Wainwright's television series *Gentleman Jack* (2019), has seen her become one of the most famous daughters of the Yorkshire cloth town of Halifax. When I first began researching Lister and her association with the Halifax Literary and Philosophical Society in 2012, her story was known by local historians and many scholars of queer literature and history, women's writing and intellectual history, but in the intervening ten years popular interest in her life has grown exponentially and internationally. The impact of Wainwright's re-telling of Lister's story, which builds on years of research by Jill Liddington, Helena Whitbread and others, can be seen in Halifax in material and economic terms, with a boom in 'Lister Tourism' to Shibden Hall. In September 2021, a public sculpture in her memory, 'Contemplation' by Diane Lawrenson, was unveiled in the town's Grade I listed Piece Hall, where it is now on permanent display.

Lister's new cultural prominence seems in keeping with the recent history of the town, and in particular alongside the renovation of the eighteenth-century Piece Hall, which reopened in 2017 following a multi-million-pound renovation and conservation project. As the only remaining Georgian cloth hall (a purpose-built marketplace for the trade of 'pieces' of cloth) in Britain, the Piece Hall is central to Halifax's secular history as a key point on the transpennine route of the cloth trade, and to its development as a civic centre. Lister played a significant role in the economic and civic development of Halifax during her own lifetime, through her management of the Shibden Hall estate and the development of buildings in the town centre, as well as through political campaigning. This chapter connects what is known of Lister's economic and political participation in Halifax life to her intellectual and social identity, by exploring her involvement in the associational life of the town and, in particular, the Halifax Literary and Philosophical Society, of which she was famously the first female member.

Under Existing Rules: Women in the Lit. and Phil.

Lister's membership of the Halifax Literary and Philosophical Society (or the Lit. and Phil.) is relatively well known, but her active participation has tended to be assumed rather than comprehensively proved. The society was inaugurated in 1830 and, within a year, had elected Lister as an ordinary member. The society's Centenary Handbook in 1930 relates its history, and records simply that 'at the first Annual Meeting ... it being the opinion of the council that Ladies were eligible as members Miss Anne Lister, of Shibden Hall, was duly elected'.[1] Similarly, the original minutes of that meeting, held in the Calderdale Archive in Halifax, emphasised that, as far as the committee were concerned, no positive change to the society's constitution needed to be made. In some senses, the resolution passed on 3 October 1831, 'that it is the Opinion of the Meeting under the existing Rules Ladies are eligible as Members', could hardly be called a resolution at all.[2] This clarification of the rules – one which was clearly deemed necessary – was prompted by the more concerted voice of the ordinary members at the monthly general meeting in September, at which 'it was Resolved, that it is the Opinion of the present meeting that the Attendance of Ladies at the monthly meetings is very desirable and that the same be submitted for consideration and adoption at the ensuing annual meeting'.[3] Lister was duly elected on 7 October 1831.

Despite the apparent enthusiasm for female members at the monthly meeting, where their attendance was deemed not merely permissible but 'desirable', as far as can be established through the society's own records, Lister remained the only one elected in her lifetime (she died in 1840), and the extent of her active engagement with the society is unclear. Helena Whitbread states that Lister 'became the first woman to be elected to the Committee of the Halifax Branch of the Literary and Philosophical Society because of her academic contributions to that society', but there is no evidence that Lister was ever more than an ordinary member, and evidence of her attendance at meetings is elusive.[4] During her nine years of membership, Lister was often travelling, abroad and in the UK, so her regular attendance was unlikely.[5] What is known is that she contributed significantly to the building of a new museum, a total of £150 in the space of little more than a year. When a subscription for the museum was raised,

Lister's name was first on the list.[6] In Lister's correspondence, the Lit. and Phil. is most frequently mentioned where a financial transaction, such as the payment of membership fees or a contribution to the museum fund, takes place; her involvement (or not) in the associational activities of the society is less well documented.

The Halifax Lit. and Phil.'s establishment, and Lister's election to it, took place at a relatively late stage of the 'Lit. and Phil.' movement of the late eighteenth and early nineteenth century. Literary and philosophical societies in this period have been seen, generally speaking, to operate within a masculine model of civic sociability. Davidoff and Hall, for example, observe that 'this public world was consistently organized in gendered ways and had little space for women'.[7] Although Peter Clark (in his study of British clubs and societies before 1800) identifies an increase in female participation in associational life in the late eighteenth century, he notes that this is limited to particular areas: 'during George III's reign, women began to make more of an impact particularly with the appearance of new subscription associations and philanthropic societies, but the great majority of societies remained exclusively male'.[8] There is some evidence to suggest that this exclusion was, in the case of the literary and philosophical societies, by default rather than by design. Just as Halifax Lit. and Phil. would later confirm that women were allowed as members 'under existing rules', the Newcastle Lit. and Phil. claimed that it had *theoretically* allowed female members since its inception in 1793, but it wasn't until 1798 that the question of female participation was seriously considered, when a query from John Clennell about female membership prompted the proposal of a category of 'reading members'.[9] Reading members would be allowed to attend lectures, but not the monthly meetings that ordinary members attended. This new category would allow for the 'delicacy' of female members; by implication, the kind of membership that had previously been available to women in theory would have been considered 'indelicate' and therefore unlikely to be adopted in practice.

Similarly, women seem to have been admitted to public lectures of the Manchester Lit. and Phil., but not to its meetings. A letter by a female correspondent to the *Leeds Mercury* in 1819 claims that 'at the celebrated societies of Liverpool and Manchester, ladies are admitted', and proposes the same measure be adopted at the Leeds Phil. and Lit. Another correspondent, a week later, 'seconds her motion' by citing the example of Birmingham Philosophical Society, 'in which is to be seen every Monday night, (in the Winter season,) an assemblage of the most respected *Ladies* of that town and neighbourhood. And why not?'[10] It seemed, then, that by this point women were being admitted to several major societies, but (Birmingham apparently excepted) this was usually a kind of auxiliary membership that did not penetrate the concentric inner circles of ordinary and committee membership. The pattern that emerges here is one of distinction between theory and practice: while the rules did not theoretically exclude women, the practices of such societies remained discursively gendered.

The Late 'Lit. and Phil.' Movement and Shifting Modes of Participation

The practices of the Halifax Lit. and Phil. are best understood as consciously modelled on antecedent societies, as demonstrated by the records of committee meetings from 1830 and 1831. These reveal the extent of borrowing from established nearby societies – those of Leeds, Manchester, Liverpool, Newcastle and York, in particular – in terms of both organisational and physical structure. For example, the Halifax membership certificate was copied from the Society of Antiquaries of Newcastle-upon-Tyne, the museum's cabinet maker (and the plans to which he worked) borrowed from the Yorkshire Philosophical Society, and envoys were dispatched to all corners of the north: 'Mr Smith and Mr Leyland having undertaken to examine the Museums at Manchester and Liverpool, and Mr E Alexander those at York and Scarborough'.[11] The committee's intention was to replicate the success of neighbouring societies by abiding by an established set of practices. It seems reasonable, then, that in the matter of female participation, Halifax would take its cues from these older, more established societies. However, a gradual shift in focus of literary and philosophical societies towards civic improvement meant that attendance at monthly meetings and public lectures did not necessarily remain the dominant modes of participation.

The Halifax Lit. and Phil. was established, first and foremost, with a view to tangible civic improvement, which would be expressed in the concrete form of a museum. As David Livingstone has argued, 'the museum voiced the values of its curators and disclosed their mental geographies'.[12] The immediacy with which the Halifax society set about establishing an architectural manifestation of those values anticipates the Victorian preoccupation with the spatial and material nature of public culture that Livingstone identifies: 'While its architecture was intervening in the cultural struggles of late Victorian society, the museum as an institution did much to promote what has been called an 'object-based' approach to knowing in the decades around 1900.'[13] The material manifestation of knowledge, and the need to house that knowledge, is thus one of the driving principles behind the establishment not only of the museum, but of the society itself. Furthermore, the gendering of scientific space required the founders to consider, in its admission practices, the mediation of such supposedly 'masculine' knowledge for an unregulated (possibly female) audience, in accordance with the paternalistic values the museum embodied. The minutes of the inaugural meeting of the Halifax Lit. and Phil., on 30 August 1830, launch immediately into the details of trusteeship of the proposed institution, and its projected status in the Halifax community. The meeting resolved as follows:

> [W]ith a view to extend more generally the great Advantages and Information to be derived from the Establishment of the Museum, Individuals, not being Members of the Society, be allowed to become Subscribers to the Museum, on payment of the annual sum of One Pound, and that in Consideration of such payment they, together with the Members of their Families actually resident with them, shall have the Privilege of visiting the museum at all times during the Hours of Attendance to be fixed by the Society's Rules, and also of introducing personally or by Ticket, Friends and Strangers resident upwards of Five Miles from Halifax, but such subscribers are not to have any Control whatever over or interest in the Museum, nor to be considered in any way Members of the Society.[14]

This resolution outlines the complex relationship between the society and the museum, which were intricately connected whilst remaining separable. The society was to curate the museum, the trustees of which would 'consist of Depositors of Collections to the actual value of fifty pounds and upwards, and of Contributors in Money or Specimens to the Amount of Twenty pounds'.[15] Trustees, then, did not necessarily have to be members, and it was possible to subscribe to the museum, thus receiving the tickets, without joining the society. As Catherine Euler notes, being a subscriber to the museum meant Lister had tickets such as these in her gift, which she could bestow on her servants. Euler points out that 'these gifts, which were not gifts, were a display of gentry paternalism which was not really paternalism. It reflected self-interest more than philanthropy.'[16] Yet, as Davidoff and Hall have argued, 'philanthropy came to occupy the status of a profession for some women', thus Lister's philanthropy could also be means of cementing her social status along appropriately feminine lines.[17]

Regardless, philanthropy and self-interest in this case were highly compatible. In contrast to the Machiavellian function of the museum as symbolic of princely power, Tony Bennett has argued that 'nineteenth-century reformers . . . typically sought to enlist high cultural practices for a diversity of ends: as an antidote to drunkenness; an alternative to riot; or an instrument for civilizing the morals and manners of the population'.[18] Established before the governmentalisation of cultural spaces that gathered pace in the late Victorian period, the Halifax Museum's system of ticketed access would seem to fulfil all these functions, allowing Lister to reinforce her construction of dynastic status, whilst offering a practical mechanism for the regulation of the behaviour of her dependants.

The complex relationship between the society, the museum and its subscribers underscores the committee's assumption that visitors to the museum would extend to the friends, neighbours and families of their membership, and subscription would reach beyond the society's membership, the core of which was Halifax's wealthy elite. The paternalist dissemination of knowledge embodied in this model of access, filtered through traditional family networks or patronage relationships, does not necessarily extend to inclusion or proprietorship. It is this same paternalism that Euler identifies in Lister's bestowal of tickets on her servants. From its inception in 1831, then, the society reinforced the existing hierarchy of Halifax's wealthy and established industrialist families. Arnold Thackray has noted an important generational shift in his study of the Manchester Lit. and Phil., one of the several major societies either side of the Pennines from which the Halifax one borrowed:

> By the 1830s and 1840s the descendants of Manchester manufacturers were active in the consolidation of science within the central value system of English life and, in response to the challenges they now faced from a new urban lower class, in finding deeper conservative meanings in the very structure of natural knowledge.[19]

Just as Thackray here identifies the movement of the descendants of manufacturers into a bourgeois respectability, so the founders of the Halifax society were overwhelmingly drawn from wealthy and powerful families such as the Waterhouses and Rawsons, who had made their money, a generation back, in woollen and worsted manufacturing.[20] Many of those listed as 'founders' in the society's 1930 centenary handbook also appear as part of a committee formed for the support of those affected by the Luddite uprisings of 1811–16 (which had particularly targeted wealthy industrialists). The membership of this committee is detailed in a notice in the *Leeds Intelligencer*, which records:

> a numerous and highly respectable Public Meeting of Inhabitants of the Town and Parish of Halifax, called by the Constables of Halifax, to take into Consideration the Services of those Gentleman who so meritoriously exerted themselves during the late Disturbances in the West Riding of the County of York, and held on Wednesday, the 12th of May, 1813, at the White Lion Inn.[21]

These 'Gentlemen' included several founder members including the society's first two presidents, Christopher Rawson (banker, and later chairman of Halifax and Huddersfield Union Banking Co., 1836–43) and John Waterhouse Jr, son of woollen merchant John Waterhouse Sr.[22] The exertions in question had taken the form of financial assistance to William Cartwright, whose factory had been one of the targets of the uprising, and of keeping the 'public peace'. The interests of the cloth trade that had built Halifax's merchant elite were protected and the social status quo maintained.

That such prominent local 'Gentlemen' were also some of the key proponents in establishing the society at Halifax suggests a change in the nature of the Literary and Philosophical Society as an institution by 1830. Underlining the role that the Manchester Lit. and Phil. had formerly played in 'the social legitimation of marginal men', Thackray argues that 'when political power finally arrived it was members of the "Lit. & Phil." who, as the local elite, naturally exercised it'.[23] The Halifax Lit. and Phil. was established at precisely this crucial political moment; following the death of George IV in June 1830, electoral reform began to look like a serious prospect, with the first Reform Bill being brought before the House of Commons in March 1831 and its final iteration being passed by the House of Lords in June 1832. It is this political moment to which Thackray refers, when the members of the Lit. and Phil. constituted the 'social elite', and it is in this context that the Halifax society was inaugurated. The founding membership of the society itself represented the next generation of literary and philosophical societies in a literal sense. Edward Nelson Alexander was probably a descendent of William Alexander MD, Halifax, who is listed as an honorary member at Manchester in 1798 and early subscriber to the Halifax Circulating Library in 1768; the Rev. William Turner, minister of Northgate End Unitarian Chapel, Halifax, was the son of another William Turner, an honorary member of Manchester Lit. and Phil. and founder of the Newcastle Lit. and Phil.[24] Many of those early members had also been members of other, smaller societies such as the Halifax Convivial Society (formerly the Conversational Society), at which Lit. and Phil. founder member John

Stott, engraver, gave at least two lectures; the society also had strong links with the Mechanics' Institute (founded in 1825), of which John Waterhouse Jr. was chair, and of which the Rev. William Turner would become president.[25] Furthermore, the prominent Halifax families that established the Halifax Literary and Philosophical Society echoed the names that appeared on the first committee of the Halifax Circulating Library in 1768: Alexanders, Waterhouses, Rawsons and Briggses dominated, and a Miss Lister (possibly Lister's aunt Anne) is also amongst the names in the first subscription book.[26] All this positioned Halifax Lit. and Phil. as a natural inheritor of the modes and mores of these earlier societies, and the result of an evolution those societies had already undergone.

'This my Native Town': Anne Lister's Investment in Halifax

In some ways, a shift in core membership of the literary and philosophical societies from marginality to centrality, as posited by Thackray, might preclude Anne Lister's membership of such a society. Her 'masculinity' had long been the subject of Halifax gossip, and by 1831 she was living in what she considered a 'married' state with her partner, neighbouring heiress Ann Walker. Lister's homosexuality continues to attract more popular and academic attention than any other aspect of her life, and her relationship with Walker is repeatedly cited as an important early example of same-sex marriage, as other chapters in this volume explore in more detail. In the context of her role in Halifax civic life, what is crucial is that Lister was doubly marginalised, through her sex and her sexuality, and that discourses of gender and sexuality necessarily inflected those of politics, power and social status. While the first literary and philosophical societies may have offered a route to respectability for 'marginal *men*', the Halifax Lit. and Phil. belonged to the later generation of more conservative institutions that Thackray describes, so should have been unlikely to welcome this unconventional woman as a member; the fact that they did admit her is therefore highly significant.

There is an understandable impulse to equate Lister's unconventional personal life with unconventional politics, but this would be an oversimplification. As a local landowner from an established family, Lister was part of the conservative, Anglican elite of Halifax. Euler observes that Lister was 'not "ahead of her time" in any obvious way', calling her a 'snobbish but untitled member of the lesser gentry, and an enthusiastic Tory'.[27] Lister had many tenants, and under the reformed system anyone renting a property for £50 per year or more was eligible to vote in local elections;

Jill Liddington describes how in one case Lister increased a tenant's rent to £50 temporarily during the election year of 1833, but then made them a 'gift' equal to the increase (on the understanding, of course, that they voted 'blue').[28] As outlined by Euler and Liddington, Lister's election-rigging activities ranged from bribery to intimidation, and she was not above threatening to turn tenants off her property should they support the Whig cause. Lister's political ambition is manifest in her diary as early in 1823 – prior to inheriting Shibden – following a discussion with the Waterhouses of the prospect of a new MP for Halifax. She imagined writing to the Chancellor of the Exchequer for advice on who this should be, and then 'began building castles about the result of my success, the notoriety it would gain me. An introduction to court. Perhaps a Barony, etc.' Although Lister immediately dismisses her fantasy as the result of 'too much negus', observing 'how slight the partition between sanity & not', this episode exemplifies her desire for an aristocratic model of success, aptly figured as 'building castles', that was remote for many men of her class, and nigh-impossible for a woman.[29]

Aware of the social reality, nevertheless Lister did not let her gender limit her ambition. As Euler outlines, political influence was something Lister actively courted:

> Anne Lister knew exactly where the blue political power in the borough lay: with those old gentry families with whom she had been on visiting terms since her youth. She made a point of visiting the men who would consistently play their part for the next decade: James Edward Norris, Christopher Rawson and John Waterhouse.[30]

Lister was part of a powerful network by birth and rank, and her willingness (and ability) to champion the Tory cause cemented her position within that group of 'old gentry families', who sought her support in the political campaigns of the 1830s. The same group who sought to determine the political future of Halifax were arguably more successful in directing its civic development: as noted above, Christopher Rawson and John Waterhouse were the first two presidents of the Literary and Philosophical Society, and between them held the office for thirty-three years.[31]

The evidence that remains of Lister's involvement in the Literary and Philosophical Society is mostly limited to her financial contributions. Although by the time of the society's inception Lister's financial circumstances were materially improved, her investment of £150 in the building of the museum in 1833–4 is significant at a time when she was often required to draw on her partner, Ann Walker, for money to make improvements to her estate.[32] As Lister's editors have frequently observed, her attention to financial details is minute and shrewd; her accounts and journals take sedulous note of her income and outgoings, and she is reluctant to involve herself in unnecessary expense. Indeed, such prudence was necessary; Liddington notes that by 1832, 'her aristocratic ambitions already outstripped her modest estate income'.[33] However, when Lister did invest, there was a pattern to that investment. Euler's analysis of the Shibden Hall records demonstrates that Lister was often driven by dynastic motives over and above the financial, noting, for example, that 'when she planted trees on the estate, she planted oaks and hollies in their thousands, with less regard to profit and loss than in almost any other area of activity'.[34] Short of 'building castles', long-term plantation was an 'improvement' that smacked more of dynastic pride than Lister's usual shrewd financial calculations. Not content with a metaphorical castle, she ultimately erected a huge property in the centre of Halifax, the Northgate Inn, and her address at the ground-breaking ceremony in 1835 conveys characteristic ambition: 'I am very anxious that this ... should be an accommodation to the public at large, but more especially to this my native town in whose prosperity I ever have felt, and ever shall feel, deeply interested.'[35] Lister's speech here is intended to cement her status as part of the civic elite, constructing an 'accommodation' not only for the people of Halifax, but for the increasing traffic of the rapidly industrialising town; it was also a financial speculation, giving her a landlord's interest in the centre of town. Her subscription to the Lit. and Phil.'s new museum represents a similar speculation, reinforcing the civic status of the ancient family of the Listers alongside the rich industrialists who were expanding the town. Lister Lane, in the centre of modern-day Halifax, seems testament to her success in this regard. Whether her personal standing in the Lit. and Phil. itself reflected her investment is less certain.

Lister's decision to focus her investments locally is prefigured in 1821, in an episode that also casts light on her associational activity. Lister was an honorary member of the York Female Friendly Society, with which she had been associated through the family of her lover, Mariana Belcombe. According to Jane Rendall, Mariana was active on the committee until around 1815. Lister's name appears on two lists of Honorary Members of the York Female Friendly Society, one begun in 1796 but updated later, and another begun in 1811. In both cases Mariana Belcombe's name appears a few entries above Lister's. Also present are the names of Ann and Charlotte Norcliffe, mother and sister respectively of another of Lister's lovers, Isabella.[36] In 1821, however, Lister gave up her membership:

> Letter . . . from York about the Friendly Society there, of which I have been an honorary member (12s. a year) ever since 1810 or 1811 but, during my last stay at York, I asked Miss Marsh to withdraw my name from their books. Whatever I can give in charity, my uncle & aunt have long said should be given here [i.e. in Halifax], to which Miss Marsh readily agreed.[37]

Lister remained in contact with the Belcombes and Norcliffes throughout her life, despite Mariana's marriage to Charles Lawton in 1816 – in fact their affair continued[38] – so her withdrawal from the York society in 1821 seems to have been motivated by financial expediency rather than estrangement from that circle.

Lister's membership of the York Friendly Society is evidence of just one institution with which she had links before the Lit. and Phil., and one of several examples of how selectively she participated in associational activity. Within a week of withdrawing from this society in York, Lister declined an invitation to another: she records being asked by Mr Edward Priestley,

> if I would be a subscriber to a book society they wished to establish. About 12 subscribers at one guinea per annum each, the books to be disposed of every year to the highest bidder of the subscribers, but if none wished to purchase, the recommender of the work should take it at half-price. I said should be sorry their plan fell through for want of one subscriber but that such a thing was quite out of my way who went so often to the Halifax library & had there as much reading as I had time for. The thing originated with the young ladies at Crownest, tho Mr Edward Priestly [*sic*] had long ago thought of it, it was so long before they could get popular new works from the Halifax library, but I have no difficulty of this sort.[39]

The Halifax library mentioned here is almost certainly the above-mentioned Halifax Circulating Library founded in 1768 which, despite its name, was in fact a subscription library.[40] While Priestley complained of the long wait for 'popular new works', Lister's claim that she had 'no difficulty of this sort' is explained by a private arrangement with the librarian, detailed in her diary a year earlier: 'Gave the librarian five shillings as I said, last September, I would do every half-year on condition of his managing to let me have as many books at a time as I wanted. Not, however, that I think of exceeding the regulated allowance by more than two.'[41] Lister's status as a member of the Shibden Hall family, as much as her judicious application of five shillings, probably explains her ability to circumvent the library's rules in a way that the Priestleys and the Walker family at Crow Nest – wealthier than but socially inferior to the Listers – would not have been able to do.[42] It also demonstrates Lister's rather individualistic approach to the mutual basis of the subscription library, as she has no qualms about exceeding the 'regulated allowance' for members, if only by two books.[43] What this reveals is Lister's sense of her own exceptionality within the Halifax community, in both social and intellectual status.

Castles in the Air: Imagining Female Participation

The Halifax Circulating Library was one of several avenues of self-improvement open to residents (including women) before the inauguration of the Lit. and Phil., and not the only one in which Lister participated. According to her diary, for example, Lister attended lectures in the Halifax area by prominent natural philosophers: in August 1817, she records attending at least two lectures by 'Dalton', presumably John Dalton of the Manchester Lit. and Phil.; in March 1819 she attends a lecture by the renowned geologist Thomas Webster at the Assembly Rooms; and in 1823 she refers to attending a further lecture by a 'Mr W', possibly also Webster. She remarks in particular her surprise on finding 'his oratory ... disfigured by frequent instances of bad grammar': 'I have read Mr Webster's book on chemical & natural philosophy & not remembering or observing in it any heinous sins against grammar, I did not expect that his oral language would be so thickly strewn with the misuse of the person of his verbs.'[44]

Lister's attendance at these lectures is part of a wider round of entertainments in which she is a regular participant. In late 1819 and early 1820, she records attending Oratoria in Southowram, an officer's ball in York and a display of Madame Tussaud's waxworks in Halifax; in 1824 she attends an exhibition of two 'Esquimaux Indians' and a balloon launch.[45] For Lister, Webster's lectures in particular held the promise of social and possibly even sexual contact with other women. Clara Tuite has observed of Lister's diaries, 'how different spaces of sociability, such as the circles of Halifax society, work to tolerate and enable different degrees of gender and sexual deviance'.[46] Indeed, Lister exploited those tolerant spaces in order to pursue her flirtations. She relates telling her aunt 'of my fancy for Miss Browne. Told her I had gone to the lectures for no other purpose than to see her.'[47] Anne Lister senior seems to have been aware of her niece's interest in women (although she may have refrained from enquiring too closely into the details), and Lister's journal records her occasionally 'testing' her aunt's knowledge, so this statement is probably a deliberate exaggeration. After all, Lister's claim that she had 'no other purpose' in attending Webster's lectures sounds disingenuous given that she has in fact read his work on natural chemistry. Neither her interest in chemistry, nor her romantic interest in Miss Browne, conforms to contemporary ideals of genteel femininity, which she seems to take pleasure in confounding.

Lister's use of intellectual sociability as a means of meeting or pursuing potential sexual partners is well established. As Stephen Colclough observes, Lister used the 'shared act of reading, the shared intimacy of the page' to enact 'the transition from "friendship" to "romance"'. She gave gifts of particular texts as a coded sexual overture, and used shared literary tastes as a barometer of sexual affinity; in Miss Browne's case, Lister interpreted her taste for Byron as evidence of her attraction.[48] Similarly, I would argue, she reinforced homosexual and homosocial relationships with more structured networks and social encounters such as her membership, along with Mariana, of the York Female Friendly Society, or her attendance of lectures with Miss Browne and later Miss Pickford, who Lister describes, rather disparagingly, as a '*bas bleu*'.[49] Lister's attitude to intellectual community with her female networks was rather contradictory, however. Of Miss Pickford, she remarks that 'she is better informed than some ladies & a godsend of a companion in my present scarcity, but I am not an admirer of learned ladies. They are not the sweet, interesting creatures I should love.'[50] On the one hand, she suggests that Miss Pickford's company is a poor substitute for the preferred 'sweet, interesting creature' who is by implication 'not learned'. On the other, she expresses her frustration with one of her lovers, Isabella Norcliffe, for retarding her 'improvement': 'I am never much good at study when she is with me, and I am wary of this long stoppage I have had to all improvement.' While Lister had entertained hopes that Isabella might prove the long-term companion she wanted, she gradually became convinced of both her intellectual and social inadequacy to the task, concluding that 'she [would] by no means relish the sort of elegant society I covet to acquire'.[51] Lister's idea of 'improvement' was doubly intellectual and material, particularly prior to inheriting the Shibden Hall estate: 'I must ... study only to improve myself in the hope of the possibility of making something by writing.'[52] The 'improvement' Lister seeks, to enable her to 'make something', prefigures the political 'castles' she builds. Her determination to 'make something' is realised in her development of the Northgate Inn and her significant investment in the Halifax Museum.

Lister's acceptance in Halifax society depended, in many ways, on her exceptionality. There was no public language with which to talk about lesbian sexuality; in a landed culture dominated by primogeniture, female landowners were the exception rather than the rule. Her admission to the Literary and Philosophical Society, according to the rules, was not an exception, yet in practice this did not open the floodgates to female membership, and Lister herself seems to have attended rarely. Women, particularly the wives and daughters of members, participated in other ways, particularly through the disseminated access to the museum through families, and contributions made to the collections.[53] The museum was an interface between the scientific community and the public, and women's bodily presence as a constituent part of that audience was therefore mediated in a variety of ways. As David Livingstone notes, 'for all the rhetorical claims to the disembodied character of scientific knowing, there was a long-standing "understanding" that female corporeality rendered women unsuitable for intellectual pursuits in general and for science in particular. Scientific space, by and large, was masculine space.'[54]

Livingstone's observations in relation to spaces of science, from the laboratory to the museum, are applicable by extension to the Literary and Philosophical Society as an institution, which had bodily presence of its ordinary members at the heart of its associational model. (Corresponding members, of course, complicated, but were not an adequate substitute for, this physical presence.) Indeed, Lister could have elided some of this troubling corporeality by becoming a subscriber to the museum without joining the society, and for less money. However, the Halifax Lit. and Phil. presented another opportunity to make her mark on the local community, just as she hoped to do in politics and in 'making something'. In a partially coded diary entry of 27 February 1831, excerpted (and deciphered) by Liddington, she writes:

> Thinking as I dressed of the Literary & philosophical society just established at Halifax. I have thought of it repeatedly since hearing of it – *building castles in the air about the* part I *myself may take in furthering it – about its becoming celebrated* – etc etc. Think of rules that might be for the good of the Society – ladies should be admitted as fellows . . . To prevent overflow of useless members let everyone be elected on the doing some benefit to the society by mind or money.[55]

Once more, we find Lister building 'castles', with her thoughts turning to the society being 'celebrated', just as she had fantasised in 1823 about political 'notoriety'. Again, Lister has identified a pre-existing structure to which she might contribute, establishing her local importance 'through mind or money', but with the emphasis on the money. It is revealing, I think, that 'the 'castles in the air' she builds 'about the part I myself may take' are recorded in code, concealed from prying eyes or (she may have supposed) her future editors. In concealing her ambition of making a public contribution to civic life, using a cipher more frequently employed to record her emotional and sexual encounters with other women, Lister tacitly discloses the potential impropriety of that ambition as equivalent to sexual transgression. The diary entry of 27 February 1831 as quoted by Liddington is incomplete, however. The complete entry in the original diary includes the following passage, and reveals Lister's concern with the more prosaic problems that the female body, in the case of 'ladies admitted as fellows', would present in a civic space:

> It strikes me it would be well in such a case to have a sort of sumptuary law so that there could be no tendency to any inconvenience about dress, & what more incommodious than a large bonnet over which nobody can see & which too often prevents the unfortunate wearer from either seeing or hearing clearly – let there be a costume – black, with a small brimmed hat that could incommode nobody.[56]

Lister recapitulates the problem of conspicuousness for women participating in public life, as a matter both originating in, and solvable through, sartorial choices. The potential of fashion, such as that for 'large bonnets', to 'incommode' both its wearer and other audience members can be overcome by 'costume', which can similarly prevent 'inconvenience about dress'. The 'inconvenience' Lister identifies might be one of cost, but it seems likely that she has in mind the problem of knowing what to wear as much as being able to afford it. On 2 September 1817 she recorded that 'I have entered upon my plan of always wearing black,' and Whitbread notes her 'secretive attitude towards discussing or writing about her clothes. She obviously felt reticent about her dress and appearance and was constantly the subject of criticism for her shabby and unfashionable wardrobe.'[57] In imagining a place for women in public institutions, she also imagines a place in which her own singular appearance is rendered unremarkable, or even becomes the sartorial model for female intellectualism.

In many ways, Anne Lister's motivations in joining the Literary and Philosophical Society – civic improvement, the reputation of the town and of her family, and political consolidation – were the same reasons motivating its founders. Lister's financial contribution suggests a strong reason for them to welcome her as a member, but evidence that she regularly attended the associational forum that was the monthly meetings is not forthcoming in the minutes. In fact, Liddington suggests that Lister, despite being a member of the society, may have been excluded from events, such as members' dinners, because of her sex.[58] However, it was Lister's desire to construct an edifice, 'to build something', that, at least imaginatively, united her with the men of the Halifax Lit. and Phil. In this, both were partially successful. Although its collections were absorbed into the new Bankfield Museum in 1897, the society's lecture theatre and museum in Harrison Road, Halifax, still stands, albeit in private hands.[59] The Northgate Hotel, the foundations of which Lister laid in 1835, became the Theatre De Luxe, which finally closed in 1938 and was demolished after the Second World War to make way for a shopping plaza, but her mark remains on the town through the buildings and streets that bear her name. Ultimately, though, while Lister harnessed the conventional channels of wealth and landed status to 'make something', it is her unconventional life, and the remarkable writing she left behind, that have brought her the notoriety she dreamt of, and proved her greatest legacy to her native town.

Notes

1 *Halifax Literary and Philosophical Society, 1830–1930: Centenary Handbook* (Halifax: Stott Brothers, Lister Lane, 1930), p. 19.
2 *Council Minute Book of the Halifax Literary and Philosophical Society, 1831–39*, West Yorkshire Archive Service, Calderdale, MISC 49/7, 3 October 1831.
3 *Transactions of the Halifax Literary and Philosophical Society, 1831–39*, West Yorkshire Archive Service, Calderdale, mm. MISC 49/14, 2 September 1831.
4 H. Whitbread (ed.), *I Know My Own Heart: the Diaries of Anne Lister, 1791–1840* (London: Virago, 1988), p. xxvii. Unless otherwise indicated, references to Lister's diary are taken from this edition. The Halifax Literary and Philosophical Society (like others in Britain) was an autonomous institution, rather than a "branch" of any national association (albeit with links to other similar institutions through kinship, shared membership and friendly correspondence).
5 For a rough guide to Lister's movements during this period, see 'Chronology', in M. Green (ed.), *Miss Lister of Shibden Hall: Selected Letters, 1600–1840* (Lewes: Book Guild, 1992), pp. 7–13.
6 *Council Minute Book*, 11 March 1833.
7 L. Davidoff and C. Hall, *Family Fortunes: Men and Women of the English Middle Class, 1780–1850* (London: Hutchinson, 1987), p. 416.
8 P. Clark, *British Clubs and Societies, 1580–1800: the Origins of an Associational World* (Oxford: Clarendon Press, 2000), pp. 130–1.
9 According to Jon Mee and Jennifer Wilkes, 'Ladies ... were allowed tickets for the lectures at half price, although they were not allowed to be full members of the parent society. Although the committee responded to an enquiry from John Clennell by claiming "ladies are & always have been admissible as members by the rules of the Society", in 1799 it had introduced the idea of "reading members" as a "mode [of membership] less revolting to

their delicacy"'; Mee and Wilkes, 'Transpennine Enlightenment: the Literary and Philosophical Societies and Knowledge Networks in the North, 1781–1830', *Journal for Eighteenth-Century Studies* 38.4 (2015), 599–612, 606. As Mee notes, 'Clennell … did encourage women members in his various associational ventures in Hackney early in the nineteenth century'; J. Mee, 'Introduction', *Networks of Improvement: Literature, Bodies and Machines in the Industrial Revolution* (Chicago: University of Chicago Press, forthcoming), pp. 475–82, p. 477.

10 *Leeds Mercury*, 20 and 27 February 1819. Thanks to Jon Mee and Jenny Wilkes for information about female membership (or lack thereof) at Newcastle Literary and Philosophical Society and Leeds Philosophical and Literary Society.

11 *Council Minute Book*, 6 December and 30 August 1830.

12 D. Livingstone, *Putting Science in Its Place: Geographies of Scientific Knowledge* (Chicago: University of Chicago Press, 2003), pp. 33, 57.

13 Ibid., p. 38.

14 *Council Minute Book*, 30 August 1830.

15 *Council Minute Book*, p. 2.

16 C. Euler, 'Moving between Worlds: Gender, Class, Politics, Sexuality and Women's Networks in the Diaries of Anne Lister of Shibden Hall, Halifax, Yorkshire, 1830 to 1840', unpublished PhD thesis, thesis, University of York (1995), p. 210.

17 Davidoff and Hall, *Family Fortunes*, p. 431.

18 T. Bennett, *The Birth of the Museum* (London: Routledge, 1995), p. 22.

19 A. Thackray, 'Natural Knowledge in Cultural Context: the Manchester Mode', *American Historical Review* 79.3 (1974), 678–9.

20 The composition of the list of 'founders' makes interesting reading, particularly for the occupations of its members. Of the fifty-five 'founders' listed, six were bankers (mostly with links to cloth-merchant families such as the Rawsons), eight were legal professionals (i.e. solicitors, barristers or attorneys), eight were doctors and nine were woollen and/or worsted manufacturers or merchants. There were also three clergymen (from the Anglican, Unitarian and Methodist churches), a schoolmaster, a drawing master and a handful of artisans or small tradesmen, including the bookseller Roberts Leyland. Thus, the demographic of the Halifax Lit. and Phil. at its inception was largely, if not exclusively, the wealthy and socially influential. *Centenary Handbook*, pp. 6–15. The Waterhouses were particularly prominent in Halifax and are listed amongst the 'Testamentary Burials' detailed in the Rev. J. Watson's *Biographia Halifaxiensis*, in which the family merits numerous entries (pp. 174–5 and *passim*).

21 *Leeds Intelligencer*, 24 May 1813.

22 Other members of the committee featuring on the society's list of 'founders' included: George Pollard JP, of John Pollard and Co. wool merchants, lieutenant-colonel of the 2nd West York Yeoman Cavalry and chairman of the Halifax Commercial Banking Co., 1859–66; William Henry Rawson,

chairman of Halifax and Huddersfield Union Banking Co., 1856–64; and Christopher Saltmarshe of the firm of Rawdon and Saltmarshe, stuff and woollen cloth merchants. *Centenary Handbook*, pp. 6–15.

23 Thackray, 'Natural Knowledge', pp. 678, 680.

24 *Memoirs of the Manchester Literary and Philosophical Society*, vol. v (1798). Thanks to Jon Mee for this reference. William Turner of Halifax (1788–1853) was the son of William Turner (1761–1859), the minister of Hanover Square Unitarian Chapel in Newcastle and former student at Warrington Academy, and the grandson of yet another William Turner (1714–94), minister at Westgate Unitarian Chapel, Wakefield. The founding membership of the Halifax Literary and Philosophical Society also included Methodist and Anglican clergymen, so appears to have been non-denominational in this sense.

25 See A. Porritt, '18th and 19th Century Clubs and Societies in Halifax', *Transactions of the Halifax Antiquarian Society* (1963–5), pp. 65–93.

26 E. P. Rouse, 'Old Halifax Circulating Library, 1768–1866', *Papers, Reports, &c., Read before the Halifax Antiquarian Society* (1911), p. 47.

27 Euler, 'Moving between Two Worlds', p. 393.

28 J. Liddington, *Female Fortune: Land, Gender and Authority. The Anne Lister Diaries and Other Writings, 1833–36* (London: Rivers Oram, 1998), p. 51.

29 Whitbread, *I Know My Own Heart*, 18 July 1823, p. 264.

30 Euler, 'Moving between Two Worlds', p. 245.

31 Rawson was president from 1830 to 1842, with Waterhouse succeeding him, remaining in post until 1863. *Centenary Handbook*, pp. 33–6.

32 See Liddington, *Female Fortune*, p. 135 and *passim*.

33 J. Liddington, *Presenting the Past: Anne Lister of Halifax, 1791–1840* (Halifax: Pennine Pens, 1994) p. 39.

34 Euler, 'Moving between Two Worlds', p. 173.

35 Lister, diary for 26 September 1835, cited in Liddington, *Female Fortune*, p. 191.

36 'Private Funds: Resolutions and Memoranda. Book completed at both ends. The Cash Book belonging to the Honorary Members of the York Female Friendly Society Instituted August 1st 1788', York City Library, MS Acc 50/24. I owe this information to Jane Rendall.

37 Whitbread, *I Know My Own Heart*, 19 January 1821, p. 143.

38 Diary entries relating to Lister's relationship with Mariana Lawton are collected in H. Whitbread, *No Priest but Love: the Journals of Anne Lister from 1824–1826* (Otley: Smith Settle, 1992).

39 Whitbread, *I Know My Own Heart*, 25 January 1821, pp. 143–4.

40 Like the Lit. and Phil. more than sixty years later, the founding of this library was influenced heavily by similar institutions in Liverpool and Manchester. See Rouse, 'Old Halifax Circulating Library', p. 47.

41 Lister, diary for 4 January 1820, cited in Liddington, *Female Fortune*, p. 113.

42 'The young ladies at Crownest' included Ann Walker, Lister's future partner.

43 Conversely, the library committee viewed such transgressions starkly, instituting a rule in 1786 that 'If any subscriber take out from the library any more

books than are allowed by Rule 9, or shall take out any book without having it entered to his account, he shall forfeit for every book so taken the sum of 2s. 6d.' As of 1790, the librarian was liable to a fine of half a guinea should he be found to have delivered a book to any subscriber except at the regular hours. According to Rouse, the committee 'enforced their own rules vigorously'; 'Old Halifax Circulating Library', pp. 53–7. This penalty (10s. 6d.) was significantly more than the 5s. bribe Lister was offering for a comparable infraction, reinforcing the argument that she was exercising primarily social rather than financial influence over the librarian.

44 Whitbread, *I Know My Own Heart*, 18 and 27 August 1817, pp. 12–13; 27 March 1819, p. 84; 19 February 1823, p. 235.

45 See ibid., pp. 101–20, 337–40.

46 C. Tuite, 'The Byronic Woman: Anne Lister's Style, Sociability and Sexuality', in G. Russell and C. Tuite (eds.), *Romantic Sociability: Social Networks and Literary Culture in Britain, 1770–1840* (Cambridge: Cambridge University Press, 2002), p. 206.

47 Whitbread, *I Know My Own Heart*, 3 March 1819, p. 82.

48 S. Colclough, *Consuming Texts: Readers and Reading Communities, 1695–1870* (Basingstoke: Palgrave, 2007), p. 139.

49 Whitbread, *I Know My Own Heart*, 30 November 1819, p. 106.

50 Ibid., 1 March 1823, p. 237.

51 Ibid., 17 September 1819, p. 99.

52 Ibid., 30 October 1819, p. 102.

53 For instance, one set of minutes records 'the Thanks of the Society . . . to Miss Walkinson for Present of a Young Crocodile'; *Council Minute Book*, 25 October 1830.

54 Livingstone, *Putting Science in Its Place*, p. 78.

55 Liddington, *Female Fortune*, 27 February 1831, p. 45.

56 27 February 1831, *Anne Lister Papers*, West Yorkshire Archive Service, Calderdale, SH:7/M/E/14 (my transcription).

57 Whitbread, *I Know My Own Heart*, 2 September 1817, p. 14.

58 See Liddington, *Female Fortune*, 11 May 1834, pp. 103–4.

59 Harrison House (10 Harrison Road, Halifax) is a Grade II listed building with Historic England; www.historicengland.org.uk/listing/the-list/list-entry/1133909, accessed 15 March 2016. In 2017 it was acquired by Malik House Business Centres.

CHAPTER 8

Anne Lister's Home

Angela Clare

Introduction

The story of Anne Lister (1791–1840) is now interpreted primarily through three main sources. First, through her five-million-word diaries, currently being transcribed and available online. Second, through Sally Wainwright's television character, 'Gentleman Jack', embodied by actor Suranne Jones. And third, through her home, Shibden Hall, in Halifax, West Yorkshire. It is the relationship between Anne Lister and her home that I shall explore in this chapter.

Shibden Hall used to be a 'hidden gem' of a council-funded historic estate with around twenty thousand visitors per year. It is now internationally known as 'the Home of Anne Lister', the lesbian icon and prolific diarist, traveller, mountaineer and businesswoman, and is a place of pilgrimage for the LGBTQ+ community. Since the *Gentleman Jack* television series aired in May 2019, my role as Collections Manager for Calderdale Museum Service has changed from giving talks and tours, which started by having to explain who Anne Lister was, to welcoming international visitors, researchers and 'Lister Sister' fans, with far more knowledge than previous visitors and often more than me! Shibden Hall is also now seen as a 'literary house', esteemed alongside the Brontë Parsonage in nearby Haworth, a status I could barely have imagined when I arrived to work there in 2014.

The Calderdale Museum Service is part of Calderdale Metropolitan Borough Council, which manages both Shibden Hall and Bankfield Museum in Halifax, and the Smith Art Gallery in the nearby town of Brighouse, as well as two large collections stores. My responsibilities are for the preservation of the museum's objects and sharing their stories through displays, exhibitions and events across our three sites, and online through our website and social media. Our collections number around seventy thousand objects, from fine art, costumes and textiles to everyday objects and toys. Our Museum Service team (half the size it was ten years ago) also includes a Museums Manager, a Front of House Manager, two curators, an education officer, a museums assistant, several Front of House staff and volunteers.

On arriving at Shibden Hall in 2014, despite my Masters in Gender Studies and prior work in the heritage sector sharing women's stories, I had not heard of Anne Lister. I wondered, and worried, given the small staff and low budget, about how to share her fascinating story with the world. The most recent guidebook, from 2014, contained limited information about Lister and her legacy.[1] By 2015 we had incorporated new information in the Hall thanks to an Arts Council grant; this included more about Anne Lister, and an audio-visual unit with pages of Lister's diaries and information by biographer Helena Whitbread. In 2015 Shibden Hall was selected by Historic England as one of the nation's historic sites for their 'Pride of Place' Project,[2] showcasing sites with LGBTQ+ heritage links. In 2016, I produced a longer interview with Helena Whitbread, 'The Anne Lister Story',[3] to be played at the Hall and shared online (now viewed more than 400,000 times online) and a marketing film, 'Shibden Hall: 500 Years of History'[4] (with more than 90,000 views to date).

The year 2018 saw television presenter Mary Portas meeting Whitbread at Shibden Hall to share Anne Lister's story for the Channel 4 documentary *Britain's Great Gay Buildings*,[5] hosted by Stephen Fry, bringing Lister's story and the site of Shibden Hall to yet more new audiences. Growing interest in Lister, and lack of a clear overview of her legacy in the form of the Hall and museum collections, spurred me to produce a new book, *Anne Lister of Shibden Hall*, in 2018 (reprinted in 2019, with an updated version of the Hall's' guidebook).[6] Thanks primarily to the exposure provided by Sally Wainwright's *Gentleman Jack* television series (April–July 2019), Shibden Hall entered 2020 as the busiest and most internationally known it had ever been. That year I also organised a conference at Bankfield Museum, in conjunction with the nearby Brontë Parsonage Museum, entitled 'Interpreting Anne Lister and the Brontës', discussing museum, television and film adaptations of their stories and the Brontë novel adaptations. During the Covid-19 closures of 2020–1, the few remaining staff focused on sharing content about Anne Lister and our museums on our website and across our main online channels, Twitter and Facebook, and used the time to create a new 3D virtual tour of the Hall,[7] several 'behind the scenes' films,[8] and a new 600-year timeline of the Hall's history,[9] created with researchers from the group 'Packed with Potential'.[10]

I will examine how Shibden Hall and its landscape defined and was shaped by Anne Lister's remarkable character and life, and how it can still be experienced today. I show that the physical Hall and landscape can bring people even closer to the 'real' Anne Lister than her extensive diaries and now-iconic, top-hatted 'Gentleman Jack' character. I will also explain the challenges faced by a small museum service in meeting expectations, the physical difficulties in representing historic stories within a museum setting, and the complexities of constructing interpretations of history and people.

Shibden Hall's History

Shibden Hall has been a public museum since 1934. The estate is a historic landmark within a public park attracting thousands of visitors a year and is also a place for weddings, talks and tours, craft fairs, school education, family trails and arts activities. The earliest reference to the Hall is in a document in the West Yorkshire Archives dated 1420–1 and it was a residence until 1933, inhabited by various families including the Otes, Saviles, Waterhouses and Listers.

Figure 5 Shibden Hall. Photography Chris Roulston, 2022.

Shibden Hall first came into the Lister family in the seventeenth century, and they would own the Hall for more than three hundred years, during which time the family's fortunes varied. It is from the Lister period that most records of the estate survive, including the first inventory of contents of the house from 1677 and the first complete plan of the estate from 1791. The accounts of information on the Hall and estate's history are now rather dated and subsequent work has largely been based on these earlier accounts. John Lister (who first shared Lister's diaries in the 1880s) was a historian and keen to document his family heritage. He published several accounts in the *Transactions of the Halifax Antiquarian Society* in the early 1900s,[11] and T. W. Hanson's book and article on Shibden are also from this period.[12]

Anne Lister's uncle, James Lister (1748–1826), inherited Shibden after his father's death in 1788, living there with his sister Anne (1765–1836) and various servants and house guests. Their brother Joseph (1750–1817) lived at Northgate House in the centre of Halifax, later demolished in 1961. Their younger brother, Jeremy (1752–1836), Anne Lister's father, was commissioned into the 10th Regiment of Foot (the Lincolnshire Regiment) on Christmas Day, 1770, and saw active service in the American War of Independence. He was injured at the Battle of Concord in 1775 and on his return to England was appointed recruiting officer at Gainsborough. Jeremy married Rebecca Battle of Welton Hall in 1788 and they settled on her estate at Market Weighton in the East Riding of Yorkshire. The couple had six children, four sons and two daughters. Two sons died in infancy, a third died aged fourteen and the fourth, Samuel, died in 1813, at the age of twenty, whilst serving with the army in Ireland. Rebecca died in 1817, the same month as Joseph Lister of Northgate.

Anne Lister's Inheritance

Anne Lister moved in with her Uncle James and Aunt Anne in 1815, and in 1826, when her uncle died, she inherited a third of the estate, her aunt and father also receiving a third each, and she seems to have taken over the running of Shibden Hall. Her father, Jeremy, and younger sister, Marian (1798–1882), had also moved into Shibden by 1832. In 1836 her father and aunt both died, leaving Lister to fully inherit the whole estate. Her sister, Marian, returned to live in Market Weighton. Marian long survived her family members and died in 1882, aged eighty-four. It is not thought she ever returned to Shibden to live, but interestingly there is a photograph recorded as being of her, seated outside Shibden, possibly on a visit to the

Hall at a later date. There are currently no known photographs of Anne Lister.

Anne Lister's full ownership and control of Shibden Hall and estate was for just four years from 1836 until her death in 1840. However, having lived there from 1815, and taking majority control of the estate in 1826, this extends her involvement to twenty-five years. This is still a short time in the three hundred years of Lister ownership, which adds to how remarkable her changes and physical legacy at Shibden are.

Under the terms of Lister's will, her partner, Ann Walker (1803–54), inherited Shibden Hall on her death in 1840. There are few records of this time, but it is known that Ann Walker was removed from Shibden Hall in 1843. She was taken to York Asylum and her brother-in-law, Captain George MacKay Sutherland (1798–1847), later moved into Shibden Hall. Walker never returned to Shibden and died at Cliffe Hill in 1854. Whilst she was still alive, several different families lived at Shibden. Anne Lister had mortgaged the estate in 1837, and to pay off the debt, some of Shibden's contents, including Lister's library, were sold in 1846. Some of the estate's land was then sold in 1847 for the new railway line, opened in 1850. On Walker's death the property reverted to Lister family ownership as the estate was inherited by Dr John Lister (1802–67), the great-grandson of Anne Lister's grandfather's brother, Thomas Lister (1708–40) of Virginia, a doctor by profession with a practice in Sandown on the Isle of Wight, and his wife, Louisa Grant (1815–1892).

Anne Lister's Alterations to Shibden Hall

By 1836 the Lister family had been in residence for two hundred years. All around them, stone houses were being built by the wealthy yeoman clothiers, but the family seemed relatively happy with their home. Their principal architectural achievement before 1836 was building the barn on the north side of the house in the mid-seventeenth century, and the south front of the house had been rendered and sash windows installed. The Shibden estate produced income from agriculture, coal mining, stone quarrying and brick making. The Listers also had some income from canal shares, turnpike road trusts and pew rents. It was the stable income of rents from the farms and cottages on the estate that gave Anne Lister a firm base from which she could branch out into riskier investments.

From first moving in with her aunt and uncle in 1815, Lister had ambitions for Shibden Hall and estate and proved herself a capable manager of it. Muriel Green neatly summarises her skill and interest:

> Anne helped with the management of her uncle's estate. The early Tudor house and grounds were very dear to her, and she encouraged her uncle to buy old farms and property in the neighbourhood which had formerly belonged to Shibden Hall estate. She was an astute businesswoman, capable of drawing up legal documents, negotiating purchases and sales. She superintended repairs to the farm and cottages, the planting and pruning of trees, the making of paths and roads on the estate, and the working of the coalmines which, in the nineteenth century, were at the height of their prosperity.[13]

Since her uncle remained the owner, Lister also faced issues persuading him to agree to her point of view. She notes in January 1824 that her uncle 'Listens more patiently than ever to my little plans about a few improvements at home & appears to have confidence in my being able to manage things.'[14]

By 1825 Lister was starting to take control, and her uncle had clearly started to concede to her judgement: 'Paid for the trees we had had – 2500 oaks at 30 shillings a thousand & 300 beeches at 35 shillings a thousand. Then ordered & paid for 300 more beeches myself without saying a word to my uncle who likes not so much expense';[15] 'Talked about planting, walling, alterations & improvements. My uncle took it more patiently.'[16]

On his death in 1826, her uncle left Anne in charge of the Hall and estate, with income shared with her father and aunt. 'I have much to think of, and to do. My uncle's confidence and affection have placed me in a very responsible and by no means unoccupying [*sic*] situation. The executorship is left solely to me.'[17] From 1826, Anne and her aunt spent eighteen months based in France. Lister continued to travel widely through Europe between 1828 and 1839, with just a three-year gap around 1836 when she was particularly focused on Shibden Hall alterations, coal mines, local elections and her relationship with neighbouring landowner Ann Walker. Lister's business endeavours and management of Shibden Hall are closely examined by Catherine Euler, who explains that 'by 1837 [Anne] was involved in very complex and interrelated works regarding coal pits, strata, the angles of inclines, drainage, ventilation, water pressure, the construction of a water-wheel, and calculations about the part a steam engine would play in all of this. She was practically obsessed with questions of water drainage and the use the drained or pumped water could be put to.'[18]

In 1836, after the deaths of her aunt and father, Lister had sole ownership of the Hall and estate, and commissioned John Harper

(1809–42), an architect from York. She initially asked him for plans for Northgate House, another Lister property in the centre of Halifax, which she wanted to convert into a hotel and casino. She was impressed with his work and turned her attention to Shibden Hall. Lister wanted a far grander and more imposing property. At the beginning of the nineteenth century there was a trend for medieval and Jacobean styles; Walter Scott's novels and Byron's poetry were bestsellers. Anne Lister travelled through England finding inspiration for her alterations in cathedrals, castles and ruined abbeys.

The initial plans by Harper were costly and together he and Lister reworked them.[19] Rendering was stripped off the south front, half-timbering restored and new timber bay windows installed. They settled on a new three-storey gothic tower with a library and modern water closets on the west side, and an east wing with new kitchen, servants' quarters and dressing rooms. Lister made changes to improve the look and size of the Hall and to increase the grandeur of the estate, but clearly questioned how far she should go with her plans, as reflected in her comment in 1836: 'only afraid of making the house too large-looking and important'.[20] Anira Rowanchild has explored Lister's alterations to the Hall and writes that 'at a time when it was rare for women to control their physical environment', Anne Lister needed to show tradition and convention: 'Shibden Hall embodied the delicate balance of [Anne Lister's] self-production.'[21]

The front parlour is now known as the Savile room after Robert Savile, who made alterations to the room in 1525 when he added bosses to the new ceiling, with an owl, an initial 'I' for his wife and Tudor roses. The room was repanelled by Anne Lister in about 1834 and she reduced the size of the large fireplace and installed bigger windows. On 12 May 1836, she cleared out the upper rooms prior to taking out the floor and opening the housebody (the central large room downstairs) to the rafters. A new fireplace was copied from the one at The Grange, a house near Shibden, and part of the buttery built during the residency of the Waterhouse family in the 1500s was removed to accommodate the staircase and gallery above. According to archives, the work on the new staircase by John Wolstenholme of York included forty-two double twist balusters costing twenty-nine pounds and eight shillings, fifty-three plainer ones costing six pounds, twelve shillings and six pence, four figures in Norwegian oak, including the Lister lion set upright holding the family coat of arms, costing a further eighteen pounds, and the Lister family motto, *Justus Propositi Tenax* ('Just and True of Purpose'),[22] costing two pounds and six shillings. The expense totalled about fifty-five-pounds, which would be about £50,000 in today's money. Lister also added her initials on either side.

To keep servants out of sight, Lister commissioned the digging of cellars beneath the Hall to link the buttery, kitchen and her new tower. By 1839 the initial alterations were complete, and indentations can be seen today on the tower's exterior where there would have been more additions to the building work if Lister had lived to return from her travels in 1840. Shibden Hall would have ended up as a castle-like building, alluding to Lister's love of Norman and early medieval architecture. Architect John Harper then died in 1842 from malaria in Italy, aged just thirty-three, and no further plans were completed.

Subsequent residents made some changes to Shibden Hall too, but none on the scale of Anne Lister's. This may well have been because coal mining gave Lister her main income, but once that was exhausted, later residents only had farm and cottage rents, and over time the farms were sold off one by one. Nearly all Anne Lister's alterations to the Hall can still be seen today.

Anne Lister's Landscape

Surrounding Shibden, the landscape also reveals Lister's grand plans and ambitions for the Hall and estate, which continue to bear her mark, this time in a grand gatehouse (sometimes known as The Lodge), high walls, trees, ponds, walkways and the lake at the bottom of the valley. Standing outside the Hall, it is possible to walk in Lister's footsteps and see her vision of Shibden, just ignoring the newer houses now peering from the horizon into the previously private Shibden grounds. Originally, the Listers had 400 acres of farmland stretching from Shibden Mill beyond Salterlee, down the valley, and Cunnery Wood above the Hall on the hill. By the time of Anne Lister's ownership, the size was much reduced, and she sought to reclaim the land surrounding the Hall from farmland into a landscaped park – in a way, pushing other people further away and out of sight, much like the servants' tunnels inside the Hall.

Never one to do things by halves or delegate, as Liddington describes it:

> [Lister] was soon filling her diary pages with dense agricultural details, as she commanded a small army of men to heave and dig, plant and cart soil for her, as she began to shape nature to her desire by disciplining one of Red Beck's boggier curves, and by rooting up the ancient agricultural hedges spoiling the leisured view from Shibden.[23]

The terrace was raised using John Harper's designs to provide Shibden with an elevated platform, and at the east end tunnels were created for gardeners to use so that they would not be seen from the garden. When recently renovated, it seems there may have been future plans for another tunnel leading to the house. To the west of the Hall is a series of terraces created as an orchard. Lister added fishponds and large rockwork to create a cascade between them, in addition to a walled garden and a garden cottage. The 'wilderness garden' that Lister created, with its cascade and pools, leads to the tunnel under Shibden Hall Road and on through to Cunnery Wood, where there was a kitchen garden and ponds providing water for domestic supply.

Lister maximised the potential for coal mining on her land. Halfway between the lake and the Hall, there is a small group of trees, underplanted with daffodils, which marks the entrance to one of the old mines. Halifax had notoriously shallow coal seams that were very difficult to work. Lister's work managing the coal mines is explored further by Liddington, John Lister, Catherine Euler and W. B. Trigg.[24]

Landscape gardener Mr Gray suggested Anne Lister widen Red Beck, named after the polluting red oxides from the coal mines. In February 1836, work began creating the Meer, a lake at the bottom of the valley using Red Beck. The lake is dammed with an ornamental balustrade of sandstone, again designed by John Harper, and had an added attraction for Lister in that she could harness its waterpower. As Euler explains:

> These operations took up by far the majority of her time and the majority of the journal space for 1835 and 1837 is primarily devoted to her estate concerns, especially those having to do with coal ... Based on the information they provided she used her own mathematical knowledge to calculate that 1,512½ cubic feet of water would be needed to work the wheel for one hour. She designed the meer, or lake, which still lies below Shibden Hall, with this calculation in mind.[25]

From the lake it is difficult to see the Hall on its terrace, screened by trees and a high wall. Lister also created a small private place away from her family and servants on the lower slopes of Shibden. Her initial plans grew to become a 'chaumière', a small, thatched cottage, later referred to as the moss-house.[26] The fate and exact location of the moss-house are currently unknown.

Lister also had the 'Lister's Lane' carriage drive built to join the Hall to the main road to Halifax and Leeds, now the A58, with the addition of a grand gatehouse. It is a copy of the one at Kirkham Priory, North

Yorkshire, supporting a gothic arch, once again designed by John Harper. She first used the drive on 27 June 1837, when she visited Halifax to hear Victoria proclaimed queen. A few days later, when the gatehouse was finished, she celebrated by buying the masons a drink at the Stump Cross Inn. The Shibden Park that the public can walk around and enjoy for free today is largely thanks to Anne Lister, who may never have anticipated public access to her land and private spaces.

Anne Lister's Collections

Very few of Anne Lister's personal possessions survive today and the few remaining items are always displayed for visitors to see. As her vast library was sold at auction in 1846, just a handful of books remain at Shibden with her signature in them, and none has her book plate. A list of Anne Lister's reading and books is being compiled from her diaries and it is hoped some of her collection may one day be discovered now the name Anne Lister is more recognised.[27] Two large bound volumes of music remain at Shibden, both believed to be hers, one with 'Miss Lister' embossed on red leather on the front and both are signed inside 'A. Lister'. A wooden travel case, with a writing slope inside and a gold plate reading 'Miss Lister, Shibden Hall', was purchased by Calderdale Museums from France and returned to Shibden Hall. The date and style of it make it most likely to be our Anne Lister's. A Halifax slip-ware planter is also inscribed 'Anne Lister, Shibden Hall', but this most likely belonged to the last Anne Lister of Shibden (1852–1929).

Another object relating to our Anne Lister is her painted funeral hatchment, which would have cost about five pounds at the time and was probably purchased by Ann Walker. The custom was to hang it outside the house for a year after a person's death, before removing it to their church, in this case, Halifax Parish Church, now Halifax Minster. The last resident of Shibden, John Lister, rescued three Lister hatchments from the church and returned them to Shibden. The other two are likely to be those of Lister's father and aunt, but they were already in disrepair, so they are kept in store as they cannot be displayed.

There are three portraits reputedly of Anne Lister, all displayed at the Hall. The oil painting attributed to Joshua Horner (1811–81) was completed posthumously and hangs in the main housebody at Shibden between those of her aunt (painted in 1833 by Thomas Binns) and uncle (also painted posthumously by Joshua Horner). There is reference in Lister's diaries to both her and Ann Walker being sketched by Horner, and Ann Walker may have commissioned the portrait on her return to Shibden after Lister's death. We await further discoveries from the diaries of another mention of the final oil painting being completed in her lifetime, hopefully with a note of what she thought of it! The other two portraits, one watercolour on paper and the other a small oil painting in an elaborate frame, have similarities, but their provenance is uncertain. None of the portraits has any signature or note on them, and it is interesting that the watercolour on paper has two copies, one held by the Museum Service and one in the Archives; they are slightly different from each other but feature clothes similar to those in the final portrait by Joshua Horner.

The Archives also hold more personal items than just the diaries and travel notes, including Lister's passport to Russia from 1839 and a map of the Pyrenees. In addition, there are approximately 1,800 letters between Lister and her family, friends and business contacts, including her Aunt Anne, Eliza Raine, Mariana Lawton, Maria Barlow, Lady Stuart de Rothsay, Lady Gordon, Sibbella Maclean, Ann Walker and members of the Norcliffe family, all written between 1800 and 1840. There are also notebooks comprising approximately 500 draft business letters to people including Robert Parker, her Halifax solicitor, David Booth, her last steward, John Harper, her architect, and Grays, her solicitors. In addition, there are thirty-two volumes of account and day books covering household, estate and travelling expenses, eleven volumes of schoolbooks and notebooks, eleven volumes of extracts of books read by Lister, lecture notes and miscellaneous notes. These are not yet digitised or online and require in-person viewing.

We know some of the furniture at Shibden Hall would have been present in Anne Lister's time, including the large table in the housebody, made in Yorkshire around 1595 and assembled inside Shibden. Built of oak and made with hand tools, the table extends on draw-leaves to about sixteen feet/five metres in length. The bench alongside the table may have always been at Shibden too, while the settle (a wooden bench with a back) dated 1690 and the carved wooden court cupboard, used to store and display crockery, have certainly been on site since before 1845. The richly carved bed in the Red Room made in about 1630 is also likely to have always been at Shibden.

Nearly all the oil paintings in the Hall have also been *in situ* since before Anne Lister's time, although they may, of course, have been in different positions. H. Brothers has shared references from Lister's diaries about getting three portraits of her ancestors – James Lister (1705–67), Samuel Lister (1706–66) and Reverend John Lister (1703–59) – restored by local artist John Horner (1784–1867), reframed in 1833 and ordered from Millbourne and Sons, London.[28] Lister commissioned the portrait of her Aunt Anne by Thomas Binns, and, as her sister Marian did not want a portrait, Lister commissioned a painting for her of Shibden Valley by John Horner, known as *Marian's View*.

Another surviving object from Lister's time is the Lister Chaise. Built around 1725, it is one of the oldest surviving carriages in the world. It was used by the Lister family for many years and has the Lister coat of arms painted on each door. The current green and gold colours appear to be the original ones, although at some point it was painted grey, before being restored and returned to its original colours in the 1950s. It is a travelling carriage with broad windows, drawn by two horses driven by a rider, called a 'postilion', who sat on one of the horses. The carriage remains on display in the aisled barn where it has been housed for nearly three hundred years. The barn itself was first recorded in 1677 and would have been used by Lister and her staff.

Interpreting Anne Lister at Shibden

Shibden's role when it opened in the 1930s was as a museum. There was no focus on Anne Lister and the curators aimed to present the Hall itself as a point of interest, with a wide range of historical collections on display. To explain to visitors all the changes made by the numerous residents and owners of Shibden Hall over six hundred years is not an easy task. Whilst guidebooks allow space to include finer details, they are not purchased by the majority of visitors. Within the Hall itself there are restrictions on space to display information, with requirements for text to be of a legible size as well as being interesting and accessible to all ages. This often results in a room's entire six-hundred-year history being condensed into two hundred words. There is also no ideal space for individual object labels and no museum cases to securely display vulnerable or valuable objects within the room spaces. Care is taken to display objects off limits, but they are still on open display, therefore vulnerable to children swinging under ropes, enthusiastic selfie fans, dust, dirt, insects, and an occasional bat or bird.[29]

There are also physical issues about which parts of the Hall can be accessed by visitors. There is often now a demand to see Anne Lister's library at the top of the tower. This is up a narrow, low-ceilinged, spiral staircase, with just one entrance, and so is restricted to only a handful of visitors at a time, and when staff are not too busy to facilitate this.

Similarly, the servants' tunnel running under the buttery to the dining room is down a steep staircase with low-hanging pipes and, again, has only one entrance. Other rooms that unfortunately remain off limits are the servants' quarters, up a staircase again and currently containing a staff room, toilet, office and shop store, which are needed until a separate visitor centre is created to house them. Even if these spaces did become accessible, there would be the challenge of how to re-dress the rooms with no records of what they looked like, nor with any of the original furniture. We are unable to re-dress the whole Hall as it would have been in Anne Lister's time as there is not enough pre-1840 furniture in our collections. Most of the smaller collection items at Shibden have no provenance and John Lister, the last resident, was an avid and eclectic collector of items, even including a small stuffed crocodile. During Anne Lister's twenty-five years there, the Hall would have no doubt seen regular changes in decoration, furnishings and paintings. Trying to capture a specific time-period, which has been further explored by Alison Oram, would also mean the removal of many other furniture items and collections and, in turn, ignoring any subsequent residents.[30]

An example of the difficulty in choosing a time-period or theme for a room is the upstairs guest bedroom. Previously dressed as a nursery, this then gave the confusing idea of a family home with young children, when it was really being used as a space for education workshops on old toys, rather than representing a connection to the Hall's history. The tradition in presenting historic houses to the public was often to create the idea of a 'family home', and, in turn, a heterosexual space.[31] Whilst the Listers were certainly all part of the same family, there were very few young children ever living at Shibden. Since 2018, the room has been a mixed-period space, displaying oil paintings, a piano, a table, chairs, a large dresser and, randomly, a narwhal horn with no provenance.[32] During Anne Lister's occupation, the room was decorated with yards of fabric hung like a tent and it was known as the 'tented room'. To display it as such – drawing from a few diary references – especially when we consider the cost of acquiring period furnishings while not knowing exactly what it looked like, does not seem viable. Instead, we say it was referred to by Lister as the 'tented room' and allow visitors to imagine it for themselves.

In trying to focus on Anne Lister, we are restricted by the lack of collections directly related to Lister herself, as outlined above. Her personal possessions are few, which makes representing her and her story within the Hall even harder. Whilst we can see her changes to the physical building and accept that some of the furniture was there in her time, how do we really get close to her without personal effects, clothing, or being able to display on site her diaries and letters? The physical changes to Shibden made by Anne Lister are a representation of herself to others, her public face, in stark contrast to the diaries, especially the coded sections, which were never meant to be seen by anyone. I wonder what Lister would think of us walking in her home, let alone reading the coded sections of her diaries. I think she might like the narwhal horn, though.

The interpretation of the Hall as Anne Lister's home is further complicated by *Gentleman Jack* and the wonderful filming sets created within Shibden, designed without the limits we have of keeping them clean and far enough away from visitors not to be touched. The production designer and team had lorry-loads of furniture and props at their disposal, which we were rather envious of, but everything was taken down and removed after use. Some visitors have expected to see the film sets still *in situ* or have assumed Shibden was filmed exactly as-is. Anne Lister's bedroom was later used by Dr John Lister's family and became the bedroom of John Lister, the last resident. None of the original furniture remains from Anne Lister's time in this room, the fireplace is blocked off and the ceiling and walls long since redecorated. Only the floorboards are original. The small Porch Chamber room next door, where Lister probably wrote her diaries, is off limits to visitors behind a glass door, as the original flooring beams are uneven and the ceiling is very low.

The bedroom and Porch Chamber were too small for the film crew to enter, so these rooms were re-created in a studio in Leeds, with both rooms noticeably larger in the television series than at Shibden. On visiting the set, we realised there would be expectations for the rooms to look similar at Shibden and found ourselves in the strange position of re-creating a historic room based on a television series. We decided the bedroom was the most personal space in the house for Anne Lister, the place where visitors would possibly feel closest to her. We purchased a replica bed of the period style, as they did for the bedroom set in *Gentleman Jack*. We had new bedding made and copied the television series' style and colour. We kept the room open for access by visitors as there were no historic collections in there, which led to some interesting reactions. Many visitors believed the room and bed to be 'real', belonging to and used by Anne Lister, even with our interpretation in place explaining it was based on the film set and what we thought was obviously a replica bed and new bedding. For a photo opportunity we placed a modern replica top hat on the bed, innocently thinking it would make a fun shot, only to find people distraught that we had allowed the public to try on Anne Lister's top hat![33]

We found our staff dealing with a new type of visitor following the television series, ones often more interested in the film sets and taking a selfie with the *Gentleman Jack* poster that we displayed in the entranceway, showcasing Suranne Jones, than with the portrait of the real Anne Lister. There were more incidents of people breaching the traditional rope barriers, taking selfies, touching off-limits collections and even daring each other on social media to do things in the Hall.

To summarise, the advantages of Shibden Hall featuring so prominently in *Gentleman Jack* have included the enormous benefit of new audiences, income from filming, increased visitors and ticket sales, and increased awareness of both Anne Lister and the Hall. All of which is priceless in sustaining the Hall's future. The disadvantages and complexities include loss of income and access for the public when closed for filming, exposure of the house and collections to potential damage from filming and increased visitor numbers, increased wear and tear, higher costs for extra staffing and cleaning, and increased expectations to deliver events and magically make the house larger to fit more people.

Conclusion

The Museum Service's focus has always been to ensure the long-term survival of our historic sites and collections, along with sharing the stories they contain. The 2019 television series, and the international exposure it afforded Anne Lister and her legacy of Shibden Hall, have certainly improved the future security of the Hall compared with just ten years ago, when it had little income and recognition outside West Yorkshire. However, we still face struggles to ride the wave of Anne Lister interest and to preserve some income for a site which is expensive to maintain. With potentially more series of *Gentleman Jack* and other new fictional interpretations in novels, poetry, art and theatre, amongst other media, along with new studies and hopefully more biographies, Anne Lister's story is no longer tied just to her diaries and to Shibden Hall.[34] But I believe it remains important to be able to walk in her footsteps in order to truly connect: to see, smell, hear, touch and experience first-hand the world of Shibden which Anne Lister created around her.

Notes

1 *Shibden Hall Guidebook* (Calderdale Museum Service, 2010).
2 Historic England's 'Pride of Place Project', historicengland.org.uk/research/inclusive-heritage/lgbtq-heritage-project/, accessed 3 March 2022.

3 'The Anne Lister Story', YouTube, www.youtube.com/watch?v=HWMMdnzojbY&t=3s, accessed 3 March 2022.
4 'Shibden Hall: 500 Years of History', YouTube, www.youtube.com/watch?v=kIB-oRh8gYU.
5 *Britain's Great Gay Buildings*, Channel 4 documentary (June 2017).
6 A. Clare, *Anne Lister of Shibden Hall* (Halifax: Calderdale Museum Service 2018).
7 Shibden Hall 3D tour, museums.calderdale.gov.uk/visit/shibden-hall/virtual-tour.
8 See @ShibdenHall on Twitter for previous media shares.
9 Shibden Hall timeline with 'Packed with Potential', cdn.knightlab.com/libs/timeline3/latest/embed/index.html?source=1qt4nz8k4iowStcIIq33aux6IaUCV1tdlGTgATouViu8&font=OpenSansGentiumBook&lang=en&hash_bookmark=true&initial_zoom=2&height=750#event-the-history-of-shibden-hall.
10 'Packed with Potential', www.packedwithpotential.org/home, accessed 3 March 2022.
11 J. Lister, 'Shibden Hall History', *Transactions of the Halifax Antiquarian Society*, (1907, 1910, 1915–17, 1921, 1926).
12 T. W. Hanson, *The Story of Old Halifax* (Halifax: F. King & Sons, 1920); 'A Short History of Shibden Hall', *Bankfield Museum Notes*, County Borough of Halifax, 1934.
13 M. Green (ed.), *Miss Lister of Shibden Hall: Selected Letters, 1600–1840* (Lewes: Book Guild, 1992).
14 H. Whitbread (ed.), *The Secret Diaries of Miss Anne Lister, 1791–1840* (New York: New York University Press, 2010), 6 January 1824, p. 346.
15 H. Whitbread (ed.), *No Priest but Love: the Journals of Anne Lister from 1824–1826* (Otley: Smith Settle, 1992), 17 November 1825, p. 140.
16 Ibid., 27 November 1825, pp. 141–2.
17 Green, *Miss Lister of Shibden Hall*, 21 February 1826, p. 93.
18 C. Euler, 'Moving between Worlds: Gender, Class, Politics, Sexuality and Women's Networks in the Diaries of Anne Lister of Shibden Hall, Halifax, West Yorkshire, 1830–1840', unpublished PhD thesis, University of York (1995), p. 109.
19 John Harper's drawings of plans are in the *Anne Lister Papers*, West Yorkshire Archive Service, Calderdale, SH:2/M/2/1, and are also in J. Liddington, *Female Fortune: Land, Gender and Authority. The Anne Lister Diaries and Other Writings, 1833–36* (London: Rivers Oram, 1998; 2018 edition), p. 194.
20 Diary extract 16 April 1836; Liddington, *Female Fortune*, p. 230.
21 A. Rowanchild, '"Everything Done for Effect": Georgic, Gothic and Picturesque in Anne Lister's Self-Production', *Women's Writing* 7.1 (2000), 89–104, 89, 101.
22 Taken from the *Odes of Horace*.
23 J. Liddington, *Nature's Domain: Anne Lister and the Landscape of Desire* (Hebden Bridge: Pennine Pens, 2003), p. 11.

24 J. Lister, 'Coal Mining in Halifax', *Old Yorkshire* (1885); Euler, 'Moving between Worlds'; W. B. Trigg, 'The Shibden Hall Pits', *Transactions of the Halifax Antiquarian Society* (1930).
25 Euler, 'Moving between Worlds', pp. 180, 199.
26 Liddington, *Nature's Domain*, p. 51.
27 'Packed with Potential' are working on a full list of books recorded in Lister's diaries.
28 H. Brothers, 'Framing the Shibden Hall Portraits: a Commission Fulfilled by Anne Lister during an Awkward Stay in London, 1833', *Transactions of Halifax Antiquarian Society* 4 (1996).
29 The main portrait of Anne Lister in the housebody was damaged by a bird that pooed on Anne Lister's face and shoulder (possibly a good luck omen!); it had to be cleaned and conserved in 2014. Luckily this was covered by insurance, as the costs ran into thousands of pounds. With visitors coming and going it is easy for birds, rodents and insects to enter, and during filming of *Gentleman Jack* doors were propped open for hours on end, leaving the Hall in need of continuous cleaning, although most of the paintings and collections were removed to other rooms or sites for safe keeping.
30 A. Oram, 'Sexuality in Heterotopia: Time, Space and Love between Women in the Historic House', *Women's History Review* 21.4 (2012), 533–51.
31 Ibid., 533.
32 The joys of having an eclectic collection to manage! (The tusk of the male narwhal is in fact a large sensitive tooth.)
33 A. Clare, 'Dressing Gentleman Jack', *Somewhere Magazine* 5–6 (October 2021 and February 2022). Costume designer Tom Pye explains the creation of the top hat and how iconic it has become.
34 Such as my own version of the Anne Lister story in the novel *The Moss House* (2019), published under the pen name Clara Barley.

PART IV

'Curious scenes': Lister's Travels

CHAPTER 9

'The Art of Travelling Requires an Apprenticeship': Anne Lister's Diaries and Travel

Kirsty McHugh

Travel is key to Anne Lister's story: it shaped her experience of the world and her sense of self. It has also played an important part in shaping her posthumous reputation: famously, she was the first amateur to climb the Vignemale in the French Pyrenees in 1838, and she died on one of her most ambitious journeys, to Russia, in 1840. Yet her travels, and her approach to undertaking and writing about her journeys at home and abroad, deserve more scholarly attention than they have hitherto attracted. This chapter highlights the potential of the large amount of unpublished material in her diaries relating to travel (now becoming more accessible through transcription and digital resources). Citing examples from Lister's home tours in the 1820s, I argue that a distinctive female voice such as Lister's is an important, but until now neglected, element in the recovery of female travel writing, which has been a recent focus for scholars. While her importance to LGBTQ+ history cannot be underestimated, changing social attitudes which made possible the publication of decoded passages of Lister's diaries since the 1980s have shifted focus away from other interesting aspects of her life. To understand her life fully we need, I suggest, to investigate more closely how her diaries can be read as life writing and travel writing. Whilst in many ways extraordinary texts, Lister's writing about travel can be understood in the context of other contemporary travelogues where the boundaries of class and gender are revealed through the writer's interaction with place. Anne Lister's travels through Britain helped her explore her own character as well as gain practical experience; as she noted in July 1822: 'The art of travelling requires an apprenticeship.'[1]

Travel Writing Studies

Travel writing studies are a vibrant area of scholarly research which has attracted increased interest in recent years. Often dismissed in the past as unworthy of academic study and used primarily by local and social historians, travel writing has been rehabilitated over the past few decades. The subject's potential was brought into focus by postcolonial theory and feminism, and today it is usually recognised as a source for exploring self-identity, rather than being treated as a reliable description of places and people.[2] That travel writing not only records 'temporal and spatial progress' but also 'throws light on how we define ourselves and on how we identify others' is implicit throughout much contemporary study of the genre.[3] The recovery of marginalised voices, including women's travel writing, has been ongoing since the 1970s. Projects like the British Women's Travel Writing bibliographical database have sought to quantify and identify publications by women in the period 1780–1840. The under-representation of women's travel writing in print is largely due to the limited opportunities for women to publish in the eighteenth and nineteenth centuries, and this has shaped subsequent research.[4] For example, it has required scholars to look increasingly to manuscript material, because publishing could be a socially transgressive act for a woman, and to approach female-authored works in a way which is sensitive to the context of their creation. Series like the Chawton House Library editions are important contributions to making women's travel writing available.[5] While travel writing scholarship has explored twentieth-century gay travel writing, as Carl Thompson points out, travel writing has 'traditionally had a strong heteronormative aspect' and historically gay writers, as in other areas of literature, have had to hide their sexuality.[6] Lister's diaries are therefore a rare and valuable account which records her experience of travel in the nineteenth century alongside her life as a lesbian.

Described memorably by Amanda Gilroy as a 'capacious cultural hold-all', travel writing is a complex mix of literary genres such as natural history, archaeology, topography, autobiography, aesthetics and anthropology.[7] Travel writing in its eighteenth- and nineteenth-century form may share common features with travel literature today, but it is not equivalent to the genre of 'voyages and travels'. 'Voyages and travels', Charles L. Batten has suggested, was second in popularity only to the novel in the eighteenth century, and Shef Rogers asserts it was 'probably the most self-consciously print-informed genre of the period'. Travel was traditionally regarded as part of elite young men's education, and books of 'travels and voyages' were seen as particularly suited to young people.[8] Many accounts of travel undertaken for leisure, education and health survive in print and manuscript in libraries and archives and offer important evidence about the demographics of those engaged in travel. The rise of picturesque tourism and the popularity of 'home tours' of beauty spots such as North Wales, the Scottish Highlands and the English Lakes from the latter part of the eighteenth century made tourism increasingly accessible to men and women from the middle ranks of society. In the classic work on picturesque tourism, Malcolm Andrews described domestic tours as a form of 'cultural self-definition' and demonstrated how picturesque tourism was part of a wider rejection of the classical and an embracing of native British traditions. By the late eighteenth century socially sanctioned itineraries and conventions for writing about tourist sites had been established, and the ability to talk and write about the places, people and landscapes of these regions was an important social skill.[9] Travel writing conventions were often gendered, with women expected to leave topics like politics and economics to male writers.

Nineteenth-century travel is often characterised by increased range and mobility, with improved transport and communication, industrialisation and imperial expansion revolutionising travel patterns. An important change in terms of tourist behaviour, from 1815 onwards, was an influx of British tourists to the continent. The end of the Napoleonic wars, James Buzard has asserted, saw Britons taking part in European tourism 'in greater numbers than ever before'.[10] These tourists were often drawn from the middle ranks of British society, which included the professional and new industrialist class. In literary studies, the Romantic period (covering roughly 1789–1832) is often associated with what Margaret Drabble has described as a 'shift in sensibility': a move towards valuing self-expression and individual experience that can be seen, in part, as a reaction against eighteenth-century Enlightenment rationality.[11] These developments might be identified with an 'inward turn', which emerged in travelogues from the late eighteenth century, although travel writing primarily remained a 'knowledge genre' until perhaps the mid-nineteenth century.[12]

Anne Lister's Travels and her Diaries

In her early life Lister travelled locally: perhaps her first significant experience of domestic tourism was her visit to Bath in 1813, which she described in a letter to her brother and in a fragmentary early diary entry.[13] Her first overseas visit, to Paris, took place in 1819 when she was aged twenty-eight, and the city would continue to be important to her throughout her life.[14] Her diary entries and the seventy-one-page letter that she sent to the Duffins might be considered Lister's first substantial piece of travel writing.[15] From the 1820s to her death in 1840, she travelled extensively at home (including the Yorkshire Dales, Oxford, Buxton, Bath, London, Wales, Scotland, the English Lakes, Hastings, Dublin) and in Europe (including France, Switzerland, Belgium, Germany, Denmark, Norway, Sweden, Finland, Russia, Georgia and Azerbaijan). Travel appealed to an inquisitive, intelligent and active woman such as Lister, and the genre seems particularly suited to someone who was interested in many branches of literature and science. Spending time abroad also appears to have fulfilled a need to escape the limits of local Halifax society and to socialise in (what she saw as) more elevated, cosmopolitan and cultured circles.

Lister's ability to travel, however, was constrained by funds and her role in managing the Shibden Hall estate. The responsibilities usually associated with male heirs to an estate were compounded by the financial precarity of her gender. In the period up to 1826 (when her uncle James Lister died), she spent time in Paris, but many of her travels were domestic tours undertaken for her aunt's health. Lister was reliant on her father, aunt and uncle to pay for her living expenses, but in 1822 her financial independence increased with a twice-yearly payment of £25 and her appointment as her uncle's heir. In December 1821 Lister had purchased a gig for Shibden Hall for £65, and after James Lister's death a large travelling carriage was acquired at a cost of £220.[16] As Lister's opportunities for travel increased, she commented in her diary on her approach to recording her journeys. For example, she noted in 1822, before travelling to Paris, that she intended to record her impressions straight away: 'I shall always be sure as I travel along that my observations, when made at the instant, are correct, at least as far as they can be so.'[17] In 1827, before setting out on a tour of Switzerland and northern Italy, she wrote of keeping separate notebooks for her travels, so that 'all that is more strictly private' might be kept back for her 'private journal'.[18] Lister's first travel journal covering France, Italy and Switzerland was commenced in the summer of 1827; however, some travel, including her 1828 Scottish tour, continued to be recorded within her daily diaries, using code, as she regularly did, as a mechanism for concealing personal content. She also kept notes of her travelling expenses in separate notebooks.[19] Throughout her diaries Lister expressed literary aspirations, and in 1832 contemplated writing an account of her travels in the Pyrenees ('a sort of sensible, popular travels') under the pen name 'Viator', but no evidence has yet come to light to suggest she produced anything for publication.[20]

Scholarly and Popular Interest in Anne Lister's Travels

Anne Lister's enthusiasm for travel is well known, but it has received little detailed study owing to the limited sections of her diaries available in print and (until recently) lack of remote access to her original diaries and travel journals. Vivien Ingham, who studied Lister's mountaineering in the Pyrenees in the 1960s, recognised her writing as valuable for its detailed and scholarly descriptions of the places she visited. She praised Lister for being 'never content to keep solely to the routes and sights recommended by the guide-books'.[21] A good overview of Lister's travels at home and abroad is given in Muriel Green's *Miss Lister of Shibden Hall* (1992). But this edition of her letters is limited to what Lister chose to share with her correspondents and, because Green's research was undertaken in the 1930s, it does not discuss Lister's sexuality. In the past couple of years many transcriptions of Lister's tours have been made by 'codebreakers', volunteers contributing to West Yorkshire Archive Services' diary transcription project, from the digital images of Lister's diaries available on their website. At the time of writing, journal transcriptions up to May 1822 are available on their online catalogue, but other extracts have been published elsewhere online, and transcribers have discussed their transcriptions of Lister's travel accounts in the Anne Lister Research Summit conferences.[22]

Renewed interest in Lister's travels has emerged since 2018, in part prompted by the BBC/HBO drama *Gentleman Jack*. Lister, for example, was one of four female travellers featured in Bankfield Museum's 2018/19 exhibition.[23] Recent publications that contain information on Lister's travels include Angela Steidele's *Gentleman Jack: a Biography of Anne Lister, Regency Landowner, Seducer and Secret Diarist* (2018), which draws on the work of previous scholars such as Helena Whitbread, Muriel M. Green, Jill Liddington, Vivien Ingham and Phyllis Ramsden to offer a survey of her life.[24] Building on Whitbread's edited extracts covering 1816–26, Anne Choma's *Gentleman Jack: the Real Anne Lister* (2019) makes available passages from Lister's diaries and travel journals from 1831 to 1834. Lister's tour of France, Germany, Switzerland and Denmark in the summer of 1833 is also the focus of Adeline Lim's *In the Footsteps of Anne Lister* (2021). Lim suggests Lister's travels were 'extensive and intensive', and Choma characterises Lister as 'an adrenaline-fuelled thrill seeker' whose 'powers of observation meant that she went beyond the predictable descriptions of rolling hills or a pretty church'.[25]

Much previous writing on Lister's travels has therefore emphasised its extraordinary aspects, but her travel accounts are equally fascinating because they engage with contemporary discourses. Her writing reflects changes in tourist patterns in the first half of the nineteenth century and is valuable evidence for studying manuscript travelogues. In this chapter, through Lister's home tour travels in the 1820s, I demonstrate why her diaries are a rich resource for the history of tourism, and also highlight how an understanding of nineteenth-century travel can enrich the study of Lister's life.[26]

Anne Lister's Diaries as Evidence for Travel Planning

In a letter of 24 June 1822 Anne explained to her sister, Marian, that their aunt 'wants a little change of air and scene' and 'we talk of taking a little tour in Wales'.[27] She had already planned a Welsh itinerary the previous month as a result of seven hours poring over Cary's *New Itinerary* and Burlington's *The Modern Universal British Traveller* (and possibly one of Daniel Paterson's roadbooks). Between May and July 1822 the Listers changed their initial plans: 'Before breakfast, writing out a rather altered & shorter Welsh tour, finding my aunt & I cannot be absent more than 14 or 15 days,' Lister recorded on 5 July.[28] In gathering information about Wales to inform their tour, she also looked for Mariana Lawton's '2 letters descriptive' about her tour of Wales in 1817, intending to 'take these with us when we go'. She also wrote to Lawton and Isabel Dalton about visiting the Ladies of Llangollen and received information from her Halifax neighbours the Rawsons about Welsh roads and inns. The Rawsons' advice, preserved in the Shibden Hall Archive, includes recommendations such as: 'Bangor to Bettws – one of the finest rides in Wales – see the slate quarries of Lord Penrhyn'; 'Caernarvon, ascend the hill behind the hotel for a beautiful view. Don't ascend Snowdon from Llanberis lakes at Llanberis not worth seeing'; and 'At Corwen, Blind Edward the Harper, if alive and sober, said to be the most classical harper in Wales.'[29]

Lister's records of her reading offer an important historical source for understanding the consumption of travel texts and their use in tour planning, and what is particularly valuable are references in her diaries to printed items, perused, seen and borrowed, as well as actually read. The kinds of titles she consulted prior to commencing her Welsh tour were in many cases learned and information-dense, and show the enduring influence of eighteenth-century figures like Thomas Pennant: they were not the treatises on the picturesque which scholars have often assumed that

Romantic-era travellers read.[30] In the weeks preceding her Welsh tour, Lister looked up information about the salt mines at Northwich (noted as worth a visit by William Henry Rawson) in Robert Bakewell's *Introduction to Geology* (1813), and researched information about Welsh scenery and history. In May she recorded in her diary: 'looking over the Halifax library catalogue, & made minutes of the works there are respecting Wales'. 'I shall', she noted, 'get Pennant, Aikin, Warner, & Bingley.'[31] We know she first read 'Bingley's Tours in North Wales' in 1810, and reread his *A Tour Round North Wales* in 1822.[32] Although much of this detail is omitted from Whitbread's extracts, returning to the original diary reveals that Lister read volume II of Thomas Pennant's *Tour in Wales* (1781), Arthur Aikin's *Journal of a Tour through North Wales and Part of Shropshire with Observations in Mineralogy and Other Branches of Natural History* (1797), the article 'Conquest of Wales' in the *Retrospective Review* (1822), William Warrington's *History of Wales* (1786) and Samuel Parke's *The Chemical Catechism* (1806), which she noted said asbestos was found on Anglesey.[33]

The only book we know that Lister bought specially for her Welsh tour was George Nicholson's *The Cambrian Traveller's Guide*, which she purchased for eighteen shillings from her landlord at the Cernioge Inn near Betws-y-coed.[34] The *Guide* written by Nicholson (1760–1825) was first published in 1808, with the second enlarged edition, used by Lister, coming out in 1813. The book aimed to collect, in one volume, information required by travellers currently contained in multiple books, and included proto-guidebook elements such as a fold-out map, notes on Welsh pronunciation and descriptions of the routes of published tours. Lister's references to *The Cambrian Traveller's Guide* suggest that she read it mainly at their inn: this would have provided entertainment and the chance to review what she had seen that day and plan what she intended to do next. Like many tourists, she used it to check the names of places and other facts when writing up her journal.

More information about Lister's use of early guidebooks is provided in her account of the three-month tour of Scotland she took in 1828 with Sibbella Maclean. As with many contemporary tourist texts, Lister's diary reflects an experience of Scotland which was heavily influenced by improving transport infrastructures, but also interest in Scotland's past stimulated by the popular historical novels and poems of Sir Walter Scott. It is testament to Scott's influence that even though Lister was not particularly an admirer of his works ('stupid enough' was her opinion of Scott's *The Monastery*), she made the fashionable literary pilgrimage to Loch Katrine.[35]

The guide which Lister and Maclean consulted, *The Scottish Tourist and Itinerary; or a Guide to the Scenery and Antiquities of Scotland and the Western Islands. With a description of the Principal Steam-boat Tours*, was first published in 1825 with a second edition appearing two years later, and at least a further seven editions or reprints in the next twenty years. The book was dedicated to Scott and in the preface set itself up as meeting the needs of the modern tourist:

> such a work as the present must be useful, since the formation of new roads, and other important changes, have created new facilities for travelling, opened new communications, and rendered many places accessible by carriages and steamboats, that formerly could only be approached by the pedestrian.[36]

A comparison of the guide's suggested routes with Lister and Maclean's itinerary demonstrates that the independently minded traveller in this period was not entirely reliant on their guidebook, but Lister's tour demonstrates that she embraced the modern transport links with which guidebooks were keen to align themselves. The compact format of *The Scottish Tourist* with its fold-out map means that it is likely Lister carried it with her on journeys, such as on their steamboat passage along Loch Long from Arrochar to Glasgow; however, evidence of her reading the book at tourist sites is scarce. Her diary shows that she consulted the book at the top of Ben Nevis, but tantalizingly, she has little to say, probably due to her sickness on the climb.[37] Lister's diary contains frequent references (nearly eighty) to specific pages of *The Scottish Tourist*, but these supplement her personal narrative rather than providing a substitute for her own impressions. Why Lister provides such frequent and precise citations is unclear, but two practical purposes suggest themselves: avoiding copying out long passages from the book and facilitating location of particular passages in the future. The latter would have allowed her to plan future tours of Scotland or make recommendations to others going there. As noted above, Lister was part of a social group making home tours, and in the context of her relationship with Sibbella Maclean, and the Scottish aristocratic circles this might open up to her, having such information could have proved particularly useful.

Lister's diaries are an important new source for the history of tourism and book history, containing detailed insights which are rare within more conventional travelogues. While her voracious reading might not surprise Lister scholars, it highlights the way in which her travel experiences were filtered through accounts of the same tourist sites by previous visitors. Her undertaking of, and writing about, domestic tours also shows her to be engaging in contemporary tourist practices such as travel for health and the appreciation of picturesque scenery. But because her diaries include personal details, and perhaps attempt to reconcile the complicated and contradictory elements of her life, they offer insights into the interplay of public and private in her life, and in manuscript travelogues more generally.

Public and Private Narratives in Anne Lister's Home Tours

Commencing and concluding her 1822 Welsh tour at Llangollen allowed Anne Lister to make enquiries about the 'Ladies of Llangollen', Eleanor Butler (1739–1829) and Sarah Ponsonby (1755–1831), and to call on them. The two women were well known, having fled from unhappy lives in Ireland and set up home at Llangollen in 1778. The Ladies and their cottage at Plas Newydd, which they moved to in 1780, quickly became an object of curiosity for visitors on the North Wales tour. Tourists recorded descriptions of the cottage and its residents in their journals and sketchbooks. The 1790 article entitled 'Extraordinary Female Affection' which appeared in several newspapers, Fiona Brideoake points out, presented Eleanor Butler and Sarah Ponsonby 'within a sexualized model of gender difference' describing Butler as 'tall and masculine' and Ponsonby as 'polite and effeminate, fair and beautiful' and their clothing as 'somewhat peculiar, dark cloth pelisses or habits, of rather masculine shape'.[38] Lister read of their story in an article in the 1791 volume of *La Belle Assemblée*, and in her opinion, Ponsonby (she did not meet Butler) was 'certainly not masculine, & yet there was a je-ne-sais-quoi striking'.[39]

Lister's visit to Llangollen is well known, but it is a good example of how it is only through her diaries and letters that we can understand the significance of this place to her (and other nineteenth-century women who loved women). The unique perspective that Anne Lister's diaries offer is thrown into relief when compared with other contemporary tourist accounts. Anne Choma and Caroline L. Eisner have both investigated the ways in which Lister maintained two selves, with Eisner suggesting that through the use of code she could divide, at least on paper, 'her deviant self from her public self'.[40] The crypt-hand passages in Lister's 1822 diary allow us to understand that the Ladies offered Lister a model of two women living together, something she wanted for herself and Mariana Lawton. However, reading only the plain-hand narrative presents a travelogue suitable for public consumption.

Christopher Rawson, one of Lister's Halifax neighbours, made a tour of Wales in 1817 with his brother. He wrote in his travel journal of their visit to Llangollen: 'We saw the fair inmates, but could not tell till we neared them close, which sex they belonged to & even then it was a doubtful case from their exterior appearance.' The Ladies, he noted, 'may justly be entitled to the honor of admiral Hood's boys as every hair on their chins could make a toothpick & quire if they share not like the hottentot a leather guard-du-costa got? A sort of lid to a tin pot.' These latter comments quote from the 1815 satirical naval poem *Paddy Hew*. In doing so, Rawson could be suggesting that the Ladies were not only masculine but also unnatural, perhaps even exotic, as the hottentot reference occurs in a section of the poem in which two sailors discuss unusual and unbelievable things said to take place in foreign lands. The line following the one quoted by Rawson reads as follows: 'An't this unnatural and queer? And yet 'tis no less true, my dear.'[41]

Lister records her conversation with Rawson's sister, Emma Saltmarshe (who visited Wales in 1820), about the Ladies of Llangollen during a social call in August 1822. Saltmarshe's remarks, as related in Lister's journals, were that 'they must be 2 romantic girls' and she records that as she walked with Saltmarshe to see her off, 'she said she had thought it a pity that they were not married; it would do them a great deal of good'.[42] The reference to marriage hints at the debate about whether the ladies' relationship was purely platonic. Choma reads this entry as Saltmarshe making the 'contemporary distinction between romantic friendship and marriage', but perhaps there was a more knowing undercurrent to her comment directed at Lister because of local gossip surrounding Lister's own relationships with women and her 'unfeminine' dress.[43]

Lister's first tour with a female partner was a week spent with Isabella Norcliffe apart from the rest of the tour party after leaving Bath in 1813. As Steidele has pointed out, 'such excursions not only satisfied her inquisitive mind, but provided privacy for pursuing relationships with women'.[44] Lister's tour with Sibbella Maclean (*c.*1784–1830), until recently largely unknown, provides an example of how Lister used travel (traditionally used to cement heterosexual unions or nuclear family units) to provide opportunities for pursuing relationships with women. During the tour, Anne and Sibbella were able not only to spend time getting to know each other, and for Lister to initiate sexual contact, but also to visit Maclean's family on Mull and to discuss arrangements for Sibbella to go to Paris with Anne. Again, Lister's narrative hides private content using code, but the plain-hand passages, because they describe travels, might be seen in some way as semi-public.

There has been little scholarship on travel narratives recorded within diaries, but recent research on manuscript culture suggests that accounts of journeys in the forms of reminiscences, journals or letters were often circulated amongst literary coteries or networks of family and friends. Lister's diary opens up interesting questions about the public/private nature of manuscript texts in the early nineteenth century. Her approach contrasts with that of a writer like Ellen Weeton (1776–1850) whose account of her 1825 excursion to Wales does not engage in many of the usual tourist discourses. Weeton prioritises the recording of her life story above the need to create a piece of travel writing which responds to the expected sites and tropes.[45] Betty Hagglund, in her study of the 1822 diary kept by Sarah Hazlitt (1774–1843), has suggested that passages relating to Scottish tourist sites are less 'truly private' than other sections of her diary because writing a travel diary differed from the writing of a domestic diary.[46] Lister's diary perhaps also reflects this distinction, but further investigation is needed. We know that Lister shared passages from her diary with her friends and lovers, and she records listening to Sibbella Maclean read her an entry from her own journal in 1828 (which she thought 'nicely done').[47] So, while the diaries themselves might not be shared without Lister's mediation, the content in them might be written with a wider audience in mind. What is clear is that Lister's detailed writing style and minute observations made her a natural travel writer. Her journals contain comments on topics of specific interest to herself, but many of the observations she makes on her journeys, on topics such as geology, manufactures, historical sites, architecture, agriculture, language and landscape features, are also features of contemporary travelogues.

What sets Lister's descriptions apart from those by other contemporary travellers is the level of detail in her diary travel accounts: not only of new and unfamiliar places, but of everyday aspects of her life. Many of the interesting conversations she records align with the aims of travel writing in collecting useful information and learning about other cultures. Being a tourist allowed her to question the locals she met, request entry to factories and institutions, and (as a woman from the landowning classes) to go into the homes of the working classes. Studies of published travel writing have emphasised the importance authors placed on creating an impression of a reliable and accurate narrative for their readers. Carl Thompson, for example, describes how the 'protocols of epistemological decorum' established in the context of scientific discovery in the seventeenth century had, by the eighteenth century, become 'a rhetorical necessity for travel writers who wished to be believed'. However, the rise of the guidebook, he has argued, resulted in increased 'subjectivism' in travel accounts from the 1840s.[48] Eighteenth- and nineteenth-century travelogues were also influenced by the Grand Tour model of travel for developing taste and cultural awareness, and this, as noted above, manifested itself in the appreciation of British landscape. This vogue for picturesque landscapes required tourists to develop an aesthetic vocabulary, and also encouraged Britons to undertake home tour travel as an expression of British patriotism. Therefore, the expectations of travel writing in the 1800s included the 'on the spot' observations which originated in a scientific context, with a personal and emotional response, influenced by aesthetic and cultural discourses of the period, to sites such as lakes, waterfalls and mountains.

Comparison of Lister's descriptions of travel within her daily diary, her discrete travel journals and her letters is a potentially rich area of research. Letters are explicitly communicative forms, intended often for circulation and reading aloud. The quotation of outgoing letters in her journal suggests Lister was interested in developing or rehearsing her public voice. Extracts of an 1822 letter to Mariana Lawton might be seen as reflecting the patriotic aspects of travel writing, when Lister writes of the Menai Bridge that: 'I am delighted with it & think it so far the germ of the finest thing I ever saw.' She also demonstrates her abilities to write lyrically about landscape when she describes

> The winding down the chasm before Penman Mawr; the 1st view of the sea bounded by Anglesea & Puffin Island; the sun setting most gloriously; the road cut out of the rock about 50 yards from the foot of Penman Mawr, the waves or rather water smooth as glass just murmuring below, formed altogether so fine, so sublimely beautiful a scene as I shall not hastily forget – the shades of evening ushered us into Aber, where we slept & breakfasted the next morning comfortably.[49]

Writing in a format which ensured privacy allowed Anne Lister to record both socially acceptable and private aspects of her life on tour. The dialogue between the personal and the performative aspects of touring, found in many travel journals of the period written for a limited (or imagined) audience, is thrown into relief in Lister's extraordinarily frank and detailed diaries. Below I further explore this topic by discussing the public and private in relation to Lister's sense of her social and gender identity as expressed in her diaries.

Class and Gender in Anne Lister's Home Tours

Lister's account of her excursion to the English Lakes with her aunt in 1824 is notable for the description of her walk of more than twenty miles. The plan to walk to Scale Hill and meet up with her aunt (travelling there by gig) was a spur of the moment decision, she writes, which the local tourist guide tried to persuade her not to undertake. Lister, a keen walker, was not dissuaded, but she found the road over the mountains tough, and described her state on arriving at Gosforth: 'Not a dry thread upon me from fatigue, or rather exertion & anxiety at the thought of our being so lost at night when we could not possibly see to set ourselves right, & the people were gone or going to bed.' At the end of her entry for the day, she reflects: 'we had walked very fast up the mountains & averaged 3 miles an hour the whole way... left to myself I should not have got lost myself – I said repeatedly we must be wrong, but that my guide must know better than I did'.[50] Lister had been accompanied on her walk by a local man, son of the landlady of the inn at Rosthwaite. Although independently minded, Lister, like other contemporary tourists, used local guides with knowledge of the area. Pedestrian travel was traditionally associated with the working classes, and Robin Jarvis has suggested that it was only after the turn of the nineteenth century that pedestrian tours began to be regarded as less unusual, losing their earlier negative connotations of poverty and radicalism, and being seen as healthy, certainly for men.[51] But Sarah Hazlitt, a contemporary of Lister, commented in her journal on her conspicuousness as a lone woman walking through the Scottish countryside in 1822, and records that some assumed she must be a lady's maid seeking work.[52] Kerri Andrews, in her history of women walking, quotes Thomas De Quincey on Dorothy Wordsworth, to draw attention to the way in which walking was seen as an unbecoming habit in her (in contrast to her brother William Wordsworth). De Quincey suggested that 'the quickness of her motions, and other circumstances in her deportment ... gave an ungraceful, and even unsexual character to her appearance when out-of-doors'.[53] Walking, therefore, was an activity with the potential to transgress the boundaries of class and gender.

In a letter to her brother, Anne Lister senior described her niece climbing Snowdon in 1822: 'Anne clamber'd up with the activity of a goat, and quite astonish'd the guide who said he had never seen anyone go up like her.'[54] In making mountain ascents, women also had to negotiate a complicated set of gender boundaries. In his recent study Simon

Bainbridge has suggested that 'women played an active part in the Romantic-period development of mountaineering and its literature' and in some cases 'offered a strong challenge to prevailing social expectations of gender roles'.[55] The examples Bainbridge cites suggest that by 1810 mixed male and female groups were taking part in mountain and hill climbing, but that even in the later Romantic period, when it became more socially acceptable for women to climb mountains, the methods of their ascents were expected to fit within gendered models. As Thompson has pointed out, 'most female travellers and travel writers historically have sought to negotiate the gender norms of their day, rather than confront them head on', but 'travel and travel writing constituted an important route to self-empowerment and cultural authority in the eighteenth and nineteenth centuries'.[56] Lister was perhaps able to exploit the persona of a traveller to publicly display traits which reinforced her own sense of her gender identity. Characteristics of successful travellers, such as physical ability, planning and decision-making, and a capacity for observation, aspects of Lister's personality which she valued, might be expressed on tour because the social implications were not so conspicuous outside a domestic setting.

Devoney Looser draws attention to social status and conservative political views as means by which women might protect themselves against criticism when writing travel narratives for publication, and these strategies may also have influenced Lister in presenting herself to the world in a way which never overstepped too far the boundaries of acceptable, polite, behaviour.[57] Interestingly, one of the female travel writers who seems to have largely avoided censure was Sarah Murray. Her *A Companion and Useful Guide to the Beauties of Scotland, to the Lakes of Westmoreland, Cumberland and Lancashire…*, first published in 1799, was read and praised by Lister on her 1824 tour of the Lakes.[58] Hagglund suggests that social standing and her previous travel experience were key to Murray's authorial persona, and asserts that within her guide she does not depict herself as having attracted disapproval.[59] She played an important role in establishing natural scenery as a key attraction for domestic tourism, and Nigel Leask has asserted that 'Murray assertively unites the sensibility of a socially privileged female tourist with the rhetoric of the picturesque' and 'both for the performative quality of her travelling, as for her writing style, Murray is the "diva" of the Highland Tour'.[60]

But that being a good walker and traveller are not always compatible with being ladylike is suggested by Lister's description of climbing Arthur's Seat in Edinburgh in 1828. While Maclean's friend Miss Riddell ('a nice ladylike sort of person') waits for her, she records:

> [I] got to the top in 10 minutes as fast as I could – wind very high – dared not stand, but sat a while on the topmost crag admiring the fine views all around me – well worth the trouble – amply repaid – no traveller should miss it – the city as a map at my feet – the Firth of Forth very fine – descended in 10 minutes right down in a straight line down the crag never dreaming of its being so bad – ladies should not attempt it, but go round.[61]

The way in which Lister's pedestrian travel is often counterpointed by the activity (or inactivity) of her companions is intriguing, and perhaps suggests it functions as a type of self-fashioning. At the Falls of Clyde, for example, she records leaving Sibbella Maclean at Corra Linn viewing station whilst she walked 'quickish' for ten minutes to reach the fall of Bonnington Linn.[62] Her diary entry for 18 June 1828 contains two descriptions which present Maclean in a domestic role: mending Lister's stays and on their journey up Mount Stronachlachar, where the Scotswoman was on horseback with Lister walking by her side. Interestingly, the latter activity fits with advice identified by Bainbridge from the early decades of the nineteenth century, which recommended that women should ascend mountains on horseback rather than on foot.[63] But it can also perhaps be read as Lister representing herself as taking the lead in their relationship. Lister scholars have identified a number of novelistic devices which Lister adopted in her journals for the purposes of self-representation, and Choma has suggested that she sought to establish a power dynamic between herself and her female circle, using 'feminine ideologies' to create 'a new world in which gender non-conformity and sexual liberation could take place, whilst at the same time reinforcing the proper virtues that these ideologies espoused'.[64]

In travel narratives a tourist often contrasts their behaviour with that of others. The characterisation of fellow 'tourists' as ignorant, frivolous or unobservant in order to present the author as a well-informed, adventurous, proper and serious 'traveller' is a widely acknowledged travel writing trope which is not confined to published travelogues. Lister's diary account of the ascent of Snowdon she and her aunt made on foot in 1822 expresses her irritation at their male companions, who have forced themselves into the party:

> As we went along in the gig we had perceived 2 men on horseback after us – they rode to the pass of Llanberis, sent their horses to the village & we soon found them at our heels going up the mountain – They contrived to join us for the benefit of our guide to which I should have objected but one of them was the son of our innkeeper & the other's (a Mr Reid, an attorney) arm was taken by my aunt.[65]

But she also expresses doubts about her and her aunt's conduct, and that their appearance and behaviour might not reflect their social status. In Wales and the Lakes her comments on tipping guides reflect her concerns around etiquette. In a coded passage she reflected that 'The art of travelling requires an apprenticeship' and lamented:

> We do not cut a figure in travelling equal to our expenses. My aunt is shabbily dressed & does not quite understand the thorough manners of a gentlewoman – for instance, taking the man's arm so readily to Snowdon &c &c. Indescribable. George too is a clown of a servant – simple in the manners of the world. But we are not known. I will try to learn & improve in travelling matters &, by thought & observation, may turn all this to future advantage.[66]

Examples like these show a preoccupation with appearance and an understanding of the performative nature of tourism, and are rare insights into inner thoughts and feelings about travel. Such comments might be confided in a private diary but are less suited to the more public tone of a travelogue. Touring in the nineteenth century, because it was largely restricted to an elite who possessed the resources to undertake leisure travel, was a signifier of social rank. Lister's sense of her social identity as a member of the landed classes was linked both to her roots in Halifax and to mobility. Her tours of Wales, Scotland and the Lake District (and later abroad) therefore had a role in asserting her place in society. Her 1828 tour of Scotland also offered, through Sibbella Maclean, an entry into Scottish aristocratic circles and opportunities for socialising in high society. Therefore, in contrast to her Welsh and Lake District tours, there are comments on socialising in Edinburgh and Glasgow. Through Maclean, Lister made the acquaintance of Lady Stuart and her circle. However, as Steidele has highlighted, travelling in elite circles did not necessarily measure up to Lister's expectations. Not only was it very expensive, but she felt compelled to fit in. Of her 1829 European tour with the dowager Lady Stuart she complained: 'I get no real walking, am getting fatter and all day tortured by dress too tight. Oh that I was unknown and walking and riding about at my ease.'[67]

Conclusion

Lister is a good example of an independently minded woman who skilfully used the structures of tourism and travel texts to give her access to, and information about, places which met her own particular interests as well as access to the usual 'must see' tourist sites. The details her diaries give us about travel are important contributions to the study of tourism, manuscript culture and book history. Her writing offers a valuable record of her walking and climbing activity, but also incorporates more conventional episodes of picturesque tourism and responds to contemporary expectations of travel writing. Lister's attention to detail, including recording precise timings, offers us a new insight into the experience of travel in the 1820s, but as her diaries were also a site of self-fashioning, the sense of objectivity implied by those details may sometimes be misleading. Descriptions of travel within Lister's diaries offer important material for scholars of gender and sexuality, and of nineteenth-century travel writing, and our understanding of Lister's life can be enhanced by drawing on research in both disciplines. This chapter, focusing on Lister's descriptions of travel from her 1820s diaries, has not only sought to develop a new perspective on Lister as a travel writer, but also to insert her invaluable insights into the broader field of women's travel writing from this period.

Notes

1 17 July 1822, *Anne Lister Papers*, West Yorkshire Archive Service, Calderdale, SH:7/ML/E/6/002.
2 For an overview of these developments, see C. Thompson, *Travel Writing* (London: Routledge, 2011) and T. Youngs, *The Cambridge Introduction to Travel Writing* (Cambridge: Cambridge University Press, 2013).
3 Youngs, *Cambridge Introduction*, p. 1.
4 B. Colbert, 'British Women's Travel Writing, 1780–1840: Bibliographical Reflections', *Women's Writing* 24.2 (2017), 151–69; doi.org/10.1080/09699082.2016.1207913.
5 *Women's Travel Writing, 1780–1840*, University of Wolverhampton, www.btw.wlv.ac.uk/. Chawton House Library, www.routledge.com/Chawton-House-Library-Womens-Travel-Writings/book-series/CHLWTW, accessed 12 December 2021.
6 Thompson, *Travel Writing*, p. 179. On gay travel writing, see Youngs, *Cambridge Introduction*, pp. 137–45.
7 A. Gilroy (ed.), *Romantic Geographies: Discourses of Travel, 1775–1844* (Manchester: Manchester University Press, 2000), p. 1.
8 C. L. Batten, *Pleasurable Instruction: Form and Convention in Eighteenth-Century Travel Literature* (Berkeley: University of California Press, 1978), p. 1; S. Rogers, 'Enlarging the Prospect of Happiness: Travel Reading and Travel Writing', in M. F. Suarez and M. L. Turner (eds.), *The Cambridge History of the Book in Britain: 1695–1830*, vol. v (Cambridge: Cambridge University Press, 2009), pp. 781–90, pp. 783–4.

9 M. Andrews, *The Search for the Picturesque: Landscape, Aesthetics and Tourism in Britain, 1760–1800* (London: Scolar Press, 1990), p. 4.

10 C. Thompson, 'Nineteenth-Century Travel Writing', in N. Das and T. Youngs (eds.), *The Cambridge History of Travel Writing* (Cambridge: Cambridge University Press, 2019), pp. 108–24; Buzard, quoted in Youngs, *Cambridge Introduction*, p. 54.

11 Quoted in S. Chaplin, 'Theorizing Romanticism', in D. Higgins and S. Ruston (eds.), *Teaching Romanticism* (London: Palgrave Macmillan, 2010), p. 148.

12 Thompson, *Travel Writing*, pp. 108–18 and 'Nineteenth-Century Travel Writing', p. 111.

13 M. Green (ed.), *Miss Lister of Shibden Hall: Selected Letters, 1800–1840* (Lewes: Book Guild, 1992), pp. 35–9; March 1813, *Lister Papers*, SH:7/ML/E/26/1/0037.

14 On Lister's time in Paris, see H. Whitbread (ed.), *No Priest but Love: the Journals of Anne Lister from 1824–1826*, vol. II (London: Virago, 2020); D. Orr, 'A Sojourn in Paris, 1824–25: Sex and Sociability in the Manuscript Writings of Anne Lister (1791–1840)', unpublished PhD thesis, Murdoch University (2007).

15 10 May–12 June 1819, *Lister Papers*, SH:7/ML/E/3/0015-0062. Green, *Miss Lister*, pp. 40–54.

16 A. Steidele, *Gentleman Jack: a Biography of Anne Lister, Regency Landowner, Seducer and Secret Diarist*, trans. K. Derbyshire (London: Serpent's Tail, 2018), pp. 85, 89–90, 150.

17 2 September 1822, *Lister Papers*, SH:7/ML/E/6/0048.

18 3 May 1827, *Lister Papers*, SH:7/ML/E/10/0088.

19 Lister's travelling accounts can be found within the *Lister Papers*, SH:7/ML/AC.

20 A. Choma, *Gentleman Jack: the Real Anne Lister* (London: BBC Books, 2019), pp. 16–17.

21 V. Ingham, 'Anne Lister in the Pyrenees', *Transactions of the Halifax Antiquarian Society* (1969), 55–70, 56.

22 For a list of available transcripts, see the 'Packed with Potential' website: www.packedwithpotential.org/resources/anne-lister-diary-transcripts; Anne Lister Research Summit, www.annelisterresearchsummit.org/home, accessed 12 December 2021.

23 Calderdale Museums, museums.calderdale.gov.uk/whats-on/exhibitions/women-travellers. West Yorkshire Archive Service, Catablogue, https://wyascatablogue.wordpress.com/exhibitions/anne-lister/anne-lister-the-traveller/, accessed 12 December 2021.

24 Steidele, *Gentleman Jack*, p. xi.

25 A. Lim, *In the Footsteps of Anne Lister: Travels of a Remarkable English Gentlewoman in France, Germany and Denmark in 1833*, vol. I (independently published, 17 February 2021), p. xvii; Choma, *The Real Anne Lister*, pp. xxiii, xxiv.

26 'Anne Lister's Diary, Tour of North Wales, 11–27 July 1822', transcribed with an introduction by K. McHugh and edited by E. Edwards, in *Curious*

Travellers Digital Editions, editions.curioustravellers.ac.uk/doc/0023; K. McHugh, 'Sightseeing, Social Climbing, Steamboats and Sex: Anne Lister's 1828 Tour of Scotland', *Studies in Travel Writing* 22.4 (2018), 420–35; doi.org/10.1080/13645145.2019.1620430.

27 Anne Lister to Marian Lister, 24 June 1822, *Lister Papers*, SH:7/ML/116.

28 20 May 1822, *Lister Papers*, SH:7/ML/E/6/0007; 5 July 1822, *Lister Papers*, SH:7/ML/E/6/0022, Shibden Hall library auction catalogue, SH:3/L/92.

29 28 June 1822, SH:7/ML/E/6/0019; 1 July 1822, SH:7/ML/E/6/0020. Lister probably consulted the Saltmarshe family who spent two months in Wales in 1820; 7 August 1820, *Lister Papers*, SH:7/ML/E/4/0074. William H. Rawson's account of the roads and inns in Wales, 4 July 1822, *Lister Papers*, SH:7/ML/117.

30 E. Edwards, 'Procuring Snakes: Thomas Pennant and Recent Scholarship in Welsh Writing of the Long Eighteenth Century', *Literature Compass* 17.5 (2020), 1–16; 17:e12569 doi.org/10.1111/lic3.12569.

31 20 May 1822, *Lister Papers*, SH:7/ML/E/6/0007; 14 June 1822, *Lister Papers*, SH:7/ML/E/6/0016; 27 June 1822, *Lister Papers*, SH:7/ML/E/6/0019.

32 13 February 1810, *Lister Papers*, SH:7/ML/E/26/1/0036; 21 May 1822, *Lister Papers*, SH:7/ML/E/6/0008. William Bingley wrote *A Tour Round North Wales* (1800) and *North Wales Delineated from Two Excursions* (1804).

33 Literary index, *Lister Papers*, SH:7/ML/E/6/0128; 15 June 1822, *Lister Papers*, SH:7/ML/E/6/0017.

34 15 July 1822, *Lister Papers*, SH:7/ML/E/6/0026; auction catalogue, *Lister Papers*, SH:3/L/92.

35 10 April 1820, *Lister Papers*, SH:7/ML/E/4/0044.

36 *The Scottish Tourist and Itinerary*, 2nd edn. (Edinburgh: Stirling & Kenney; and John Fairbairn, Edinburgh; and James Duncan, London, 1827), p. vii.

37 15 July 1828, *Lister Papers*, SH:7/ML/E/11/0034. For a more detailed analysis, see McHugh, 'Sightseeing, Social Climbing, Steamboats and Sex'.

38 F. Brideoake, '"Extraordinary Female Affection": the Ladies of Llangollen and the Endurance of Queer Community', *Romanticism on the Net* 36–37 (2004). doi.org/10.7202/011141ar.

39 23 July 1822, *Lister Papers*, SH:7/ML/E/6/0031.

40 C. L. Eisner, 'Shifting the Focus: Anne Lister as Pillar of Conservatism', *a/b: Auto/Biography Studies* 17.1 (2001), 28-42, 29; A. Choma, 'Anne Lister and the Split Self (1791–1840): a Critical Study of her Diaries', unpublished Masters dissertation, University of Leeds (1994).

41 'Journal of an inland Voyage through No. Wales AD 1817 & others', by Christopher Rawson, 1817–22, Calderdale, West Yorkshire Archive Service, WYC: 1525/6/5/2. *Paddy Hew: a Poem from the Brain of Timothy Tarpaulin. Whistled by a Sea Lark* (London: Whittingham and Arliss, 1815), p. 84.

42 S. Valladares, 'An Introduction to the "Literary Person(s)" of Anne Lister and the Ladies of Llangollen', *Literature Compass* 10.3 (2013), 353–68, 361; 10 August 1822, *Lister Papers*, SH:7/ML/E/6/0037.

43 Choma, *The Real Anne Lister*, p. 152.

44 Steidele, *Gentleman Jack*, p. 28
45 E. Hall (ed.), *Miss Weeton's Journal of a Governess*, 2 vols. (Newton Abbot: David & Charles, 1969).
46 B. Hagglund, *Tourists and Travellers: Women's Non-Fictional Writing about Scotland, 1770–1830* (Bristol: Channel View, 2010), p. 127.
47 28 June 1828, *Lister Papers*, SH:7/ML/E/11/0026.
48 Thompson, *Travel Writing*, p. 76 and 'Nineteenth-Century Travel Writing', p. 121.
49 19 July 1822, *Lister Papers*, SH:7/ML/E/6/0028.
50 29 July 1824, *Lister Papers*, SH:7/ML/E/8/0025.
51 R. Jarvis, *Romantic Writing and Pedestrian Travel* (London: Palgrave Macmillan, 1997), p. 13.
52 Hagglund, *Tourists and Travellers*, p. 138.
53 K. Andrews, *Wanderers: a History of Women Walking* (London: Reaktion Books, 2020), pp. 20–1.
54 Anne Lister to James Lister, 17 July 1822, *Lister Papers*, SH:7/LL/389.
55 S. Bainbridge, *Mountaineering and British Romanticism: the Literary Cultures of Climbing, 1770–1836* (Oxford: Oxford University Press, 2020), pp. 199, 202–3, 226–8.
56 Thompson, *Travel Writing*, pp. 181, 189.
57 D. Looser (ed.), *The Cambridge Companion to Women's Writing in the Romantic Period* (Cambridge: Cambridge University Press, 2015), p. 76.
58 28 July 1824, *Lister Papers*, SH:7/ML/E/8/0023.
59 Hagglund, *Tourists and Travellers*, pp. 56, 66.
60 N. Leask, *Stepping Westward: Writing the Scottish Tour, c.1720–1830* (Oxford: Oxford University Press, 2019), pp. 187–95.
61 30 May 1828, *Lister Papers*, SH:7/ML/E/11/0006.
62 9 June 1828, *Lister Papers*, SH:7/ML/E/11/0012.
63 Bainbridge, *Mountaineering*, p. 224; 18 June 1828, *Lister Papers*, SH:7/ML/E/11/0018.
64 A. Rowanchild, '"My Mind on Paper": Anne Lister and Literary Self-Construction in Early-Nineteenth-Century Halifax', unpublished PhD thesis, Open University (1999); L. Moore, '"Something More Tender Still than Friendship": Romantic Friendship in Early-Nineteenth-Century England', *Feminist Studies* 18.3 (1992), 499–520; C. A. Euler, 'Moving Between Worlds: Gender, Class, Politics, Sexuality and Women's Networks in the Diaries of Anne Lister of Shibden Hall, Halifax, Yorkshire, 1830–1840', unpublished PhD thesis, University of York (1995), pp. 306–14; Choma, 'Anne Lister and the Split Self', p. 47.
65 15 July 1822, *Lister Papers*, SH:7/ML/E/6/0026.
66 17 July 1822, *Lister Papers*, SH:7/ML/E/6/0027.
67 Quoted in Steidele, *Gentleman Jack*, p. 173.

CHAPTER 10

Travelling in the Caucasus, Travelling in Time: Decoding Biography as Genre

Angela Steidele, Translated by Katy Derbyshire

Anne Lister's last journey took her and her partner, Ann Walker, to Russia and the Caucasus in 1839–40. While working on my biography of Lister, I followed in their footsteps: from Saint Petersburg via Moscow to Nizhny Novgorod, and then along the Volga to Kazan. On a second trip, I went from the Russian–Georgian border in the Darial Gorge via Tbilisi, Kutaisi and Zugdidi in Georgia, all the way to Baku in Azerbaijan. My findings were often sobering. Not even rivers and mountains have remained the same. Stalin had the Volga dammed into a chain of artificial lakes; the Darial Gorge, which seemed to Anne Lister like the earth on the very first day, now thunders with heavy Soviet-built trucks passing through. Doubts were my constant companion during my biographical research. What can today's places, landscapes and people tell us about Anne Lister?

Anne Lister was enthusiastic about the idea of travelling back to antiquity in Georgia, akin to meeting Medea and the Argonauts in Kutaisi. On her search for the past, however, the present bothered her no less than it did me on my research trip. After my biography, her and my travels gave me reason to reflect on biographical writing itself, in *Zeitreisen. Vier Frauen, zwei Jahrhunderte, ein Weg* (Time Travels: Four Women, Two Centuries, One Journey) (2018). The book describes Anne Lister and Ann Walker's trip through Russia and the Caucasus not only in more detail than the biography, but also refracted in the experiences my wife, Susette, and I had in their wake.[1]

The following extracts from *Zeitreisen* describe Anne Lister and Ann Walker's travels through Georgia from late June to early August 1840.

Books and Reality

Anne and Ann stayed in Gori for three days, climbed up to the old castle and went on two excursions described by Frédéric Dubois de Montpéreux (1798–1850) in his *Voyage autour du Caucase.*[2] Since Moscow, Anne Lister and Ann Walker had been lugging along the newly printed first three volumes by the Swiss travel writer, who had circumnavigated the Caucasus in 1833/4. Both destinations were off the post road, only accessible on horseback. Ann Walker was a good rider; she had a pony stabled in England. Anne Lister had previously kept a horse but actually preferred to walk. Perhaps that was to do with the side saddle, however, which was gradually becoming standard for women in England. On the continent, women rode 'German style', straddling the horse like men. Anne and Ann had previously taken long rides in the Alps and the Pyrenees, so both women were familiar with experiencing nature on horseback. Accompanied by their Russian servant, George, and a Cossack officer, they rode uphill according to Dubois' directions. *Ride through hedges and bushes of jasmin, pomegranate, yellow honeysuckle, sweet gall, privet in flower particularly pretty along the banks of the stream here and there.*[3] They eventually reached the village of Ateni and the ancient Sioni church, picturesquely sited above a river, like many of Georgia's churches. *At present, Sion has neither a spiritual shepherd nor a spiritual flock*, Dubois wrote, but only the animal kind; *the shepherds must remove the tremendous layer of dung that gathers here every year, in order to enter through the doors.*[4]

Although Dubois had written about it in detail, Anne Lister repeated in her journal that the church was *now used merely to house sheep and cattle.*[5] On her previous travels guided by the *Handbook for Travellers in Denmark, Norway, Sweden, and Russia*, she had also drawn great satisfaction from comparing the printed details with reality. In the Caucasus, Anne *had fallen more and more under the spell of a guide book*, as Phyllis Ramsden established. *This last section of her narrative is completely dominated by the Frenchman* (Dubois came from Francophone Switzerland).[6] Anne not only attempted to follow Dubois' exact route; she also commented upon and corrected his assessments everywhere she went, even if she merely agreed with him, as in Sioni. What Dubois had first experienced and written down, she read, re-experienced and wrote anew. The manic diarist thus pulled off the trick of exponentiating her life in writing yet again.

The second destination in the area was and still is the rock-fortress town of Uplistsikhe. Frédéric Dubois was the first Western traveller of the modern period to describe this ancient but long-abandoned town; the *buildings consist of cavities aligned alongside and above one another, hewn into the individual rock masses*, as were the paths, stairways and water channels. In sophisticated houses, the workers – presumably slaves – had managed *to imitate in this solid rock all embellishments and details of meticulous woodwork . . . Cornices, small beams, large cross-beams, which are all hewn with great care like in a dwelling of fir.*[7] Ann sat straight down to draw, and Anne Lister also sketched a few outlines in her journal.

The two ladies from England may have been the third and fourth guests from the West in Uplistsikhe. The second was the German botanist Karl Koch (1809–79), who believed himself to be the first modern Western European to set foot there, in 1836. He could not know that Frédéric Dubois had visited three years before him and was already working, back home in Switzerland, on his six-volume work on the Caucasus, which garnered him great fame partly owing to such 'discoveries' (from a Eurocentric perspective; the locals were, of course, perfectly aware of the ancient town's existence). Only a year after Koch's return, in 1838, Dubois was awarded the Paris Société de Géographie's Grande Médaille d'Or des Explorations for his work. While Koch was still writing his two-volume *Reise durch Rußland nach dem kaukasischen Isthmus* (Journey through Russia to the Caucasian Isthmus) (1842–3), volume after volume of Dubois' *Voyage autour du Caucase* was published. The academic fame Karl Koch had hoped to claim by travelling and writing was reaped by Frédéric Dubois. It must have been particularly humiliating for Koch that the French work was immediately translated into German. Instead of presenting new content, Karl Koch had to structure his own books as a commentary on Dubois – just as Anne Lister had done.

I first read Anne Lister's diaries and letters, and then travelled in her footsteps. Did the books come first, or reality? Do I only grasp those aspects of reality I have previously read about? Does the past only come about in the writing process? Am I cribbing my story from prior narratives? Does the story take place from text to text?

My wife and I too are deeply impressed by what wind, weather and, above all, an earthquake in 1920 have left of Uplistsikhe. I can barely tear my eyes away from the coffered ceilings sculpted out of the rock. Uplistsikhe was the region's capital in the pre-Christian era, before first Mtskheta and later Tbilisi moved up in the world.

'I'm really glad Anne and Ann brought us here,' Susette says.

In several houses we find graffiti on the rock walls, banal messages scribbled in felt pen, but also older remnants, elaborately carved in Georgian, Cyrillic and Latin letters. I find an '1882', and elsewhere I think I can decipher an old-fashioned cursive Latin letter A.

'I could carve "AL + AW 1840" right here. Shall I?'

Kutaisi

Can anything be more picturesque than Kutais and its environs? Frédéric Dubois rhapsodised, igniting Anne Lister's anticipation.[8] *The view from the castle mount is magnificent. On two sides, the greenish Rion rushes along its narrow rock bed, and above it stretches the pretty town with its friendly and prudent houses, almost all of which have a small garden, the town occupying much space. Further in the vicinity this side of and beyond the river, unending forests begin, bordering the Colchis Plain as far as the eye can see, behind which the Black Sea is found. To the north were the icy peaks of the Caucasus … topped with snow, while to the south the equally white pinnacles*[9] of the Lesser Caucasus are visible in Armenia, then as now.

The foot of the mountain range has probably always been inhabited. The residents had superior artistic and cultural skills compared with the people of the Mediterranean, as the ancient Greeks report in their tales of forays into this astonishing land. Anne Lister had a classical education, spoke Latin and Greek. For her, Kutaisi was the capital of ancient Colchis and *le séjour de Medée, de Circe, &c., &c.* [10] According to Greek legend, the place was ruled by King Aeëtes, from whom Jason wanted to steal the Golden Fleece. He and his companions sailed on the *Argo* across the Black Sea to the mouth of the Rioni, known as Phasis at the time (hence the name 'pheasant' for the bird from this region, released around Europe for hunting purposes). The Argonauts rowed up this river to Kutaisi. Aeëtes demanded heroic acts in return for the golden sheepskin, acts Jason could never have performed without the aid of Aeëtes' daughter. Medea fell in love with him and helped him to plough a field with fire-breathing bulls, sow dragons' teeth and defeat the soldiers sprung from the planted fangs. Since Aeëtes still refused to surrender the fleece, Medea eventually stole it and fled with Jason to Corinth, where the drama moved on to the next act. A fascinated Anne read in Dubois that the *most natural explanation for the tale of the Golden Fleece is gold panning, for the rivers … carry gold in them* and a sheepskin, stretched in the water, catches the grains of metal. Products of the extremely fine goldsmithing from the second and third millennia BCE, which attracted the Grecian robbers, are now the pride of the national museum in Tbilisi.

Yet *Medea's city is hidden among so many other ruins that it is impossible to find.* Even Anne and Ann could not read Kutaisi's venerable history from the city's repeatedly destroyed face. *The new Russian city rises upon the old*[11] and the *streets run straight and are broad and the country's national character emerges only here and there.*[12] Slightly fewer than three thousand people lived here, largely Armenians, many Jews and some few Georgians. Pigs wandered the streets. *Homer appreciated their behaviour, for it was here that he had the infamous transformation of Ulysses' companions take place.* Circe too, like her niece Medea, was far superior in terms of knowledge and lifestyle to the rough Greek buccaneers, and thus helped them take form.

These pigs, in Kutais and other towns where they roam in herds, are not to the advantage of street cleanliness.[13]

Anne and Ann were accommodated in a government guesthouse, where Frédéric Dubois and Karl Koch had stayed before them. Its four rooms were empty, however, and had to be furnished on the instruction of the Cossack commander Boujourov on their arrival. Anne and Ann had already met his *very amiable*[14] wife in Tbilisi. They had barely unpacked before there was a knock on the door from the English businessman Mr Marr, who lived near Kutaisi and wanted to inspect his surprisingly arrived compatriots immediately. Anne and Ann hid their sparse breakfast so they would not have to share it with him.

'David Agam–, Agsh–, Agmesh–'.

By Kutaisi at the latest, travellers to Georgia have to practise the name of David Agmashenebeli, who meets them at every turn on arrival in the country. The main roads of all towns are named after him, along with many restaurants and hotels, schools, ships and an airport. David was crowned king in Kutaisi's Bagrati Cathedral in 1089. He united the Georgian principalities and improved their administration, built roads and bridges, founded churches, monasteries and educational institutions. His epithet means 'the Builder'. His granddaughter Tamar continued his work, expanding the country's borders (Georgia would never regain such a large territory) and reforming its legal system. Her finance minister and alleged lover, Shota Rustaveli, wrote the Georgian national epic poem *The Knight in the Panther's Skin* (around 1200). If a place in Georgia has a second and third street, they are named after Tamar Mepe ('Queen Tamar') and Rustaveli. The years from David's ascent to the throne until Tamar's death in 1213 are glorified today as the Georgian Golden Age.

The cathedral where David was crowned must have been magnificent. *The whole hill is strewn over and over with rubble, and among it are also the remains of a wonderful large church, of a type not found anywhere else in Transcaucasia. The most beautiful pillars and sculptures lie scattered around, and bear witness to the builders' craft and taste.*[15] Frédéric Dubois prompted such great expectations that Anne Lister could only be disappointed by reality. What was still standing after the Ottomans had blown up the cathedral in 1692 had to be partially dismantled for safety reasons. Nothing but picturesque ruins were left enthroned above the city until the reconstruction of Georgia's once largest and most important church was decided upon, against UNESCO protests, in 2006. Today, a shiny new Bagrati Cathedral soars above the city, its style a pretence of the old building.

Several kilometres outside Kutaisi, David the Builder founded the Gelati monastery and academy; scholars whose work was banned elsewhere, for instance in Constantinople, taught philosophy, rhetoric, grammar, geometry and arithmetic here. For an excursion to Gelati, Mr Marr hired a local guide, Adam, with four horses; *but Mr Marr talked so incessantly, much about himself and his wife, that it was impossible to pay the attention I wished to the road.*[16] However, the destination was worth the effort. *The view of the monastery is one of the most picturesque you can imagine.*[17] Then, as now, three churches richly decorated with frescoes and mosaics were preserved, as well as the main gate, beneath which David was buried so that anyone visiting the monastery had to step over him. Ann Walker drew delighted sketches; Anne Lister compared reality meticulously with the statements in Dubois' guide.

Unlike Bagrati Cathedral in Kutaisi, Gelati probably still looks roughly the same as it did on Anne and Ann's visit. The grounds seem untouched, the paths overgrown with weeds; we look in vain for a monastery shop or café. Only the academy building has been newly built; old photos show merely its foundation walls. Will it ever be reinvigorated to serve the Builder's purpose? Our new friends from the Heinrich Böll Foundation in Tbilisi had told us it was very difficult to get vocational training in modern-day Georgia. Anyone wanting to work as a doctor must present qualifications from the West; people distrust the quality of university teaching in their own country, or suspect the degree may have been bought.

'Pretty long time ago, that Golden Age.'

'That's nothing. Have you ever read the Georgian founding myth? When God created the earth and divided the land between the peoples, the Georgians arrived too late, as usual. But they were so nice, he gave them the land he'd been saving for himself.'

'Georgia is drunk on itself, like Cologne and nowhere else I know.'

During the Soviet period, Kutaisi was built up as a second industrial hub in Georgia, alongside Tbilisi. Hydroelectric power stations on the Rioni fuelled large tractor and truck factories. Vocational colleges and universities trained local experts. The ancient village of Kutaisi grew into Georgia's second-largest city, with socialist living quarters and magnificent boulevards. On independence in 1991, the Soviet market for the goods manufactured here was lost. All the factories were forced to close and the city descended into agony. Nothing here is worth seeing. The best thing about Kutaisi is the tea room opposite the opera house. There, we sit on armchairs rescued from the local dump, eat the most delicate blinis since

Veliki Novgorod and drink the strongest tea in all of Georgia. Non-tea-drinkers will have to opt for the second-best thing in Kutaisi: Argo-brand dark beer. And then get out of there quick-march, just like the Argonauts.

The Colchic Forest

On 9 July 1840 Anne and Ann rode out from Kutaisi, led and accompanied by Adam, the nameless Cossack from Tbilisi, their servant George from Moscow and the groom Mosche with two packhorses: six people and eight horses in total. They followed the same route one takes today from Kutaisi to Racha. The *decent horse-road* in the bed of the Tskaltsitela was *very picturesque – very beautiful ride all day among wooded combes*. Highway 17 is not much less attractive today. *Centaury in flower all today.*[18] They managed twenty-five kilometres and stayed overnight in the village of Satsire. Thanks to their papers from the military administration, they were entitled to demand accommodation for the night from locals. Thus, whereas Karl Koch and Frédéric Dubois had to make do with barns in Racha, the two English ladies were always invited into the local princes' best houses – though the local nobles rarely possessed much more than their titles. In Satsire, Prince Yorghi Kaidsa opened up his doors to them; *in a common dirty Persian coat, and dirty – I should not have taken him for the owner of the place but for him being evidently above all the rest. The women and children that we caught a glimpse of much below the prince himself in appearance*. The room Anne and Ann were given, however, was a *large lofty room – very comfortable*, and the food even better. *The prince asked what we should like – fowl or mutton or both with soup or what*. They contributed trout bought along the way, and were served a feast towards ten o'clock at night, including two types of wine.[19] Ann Walker had problems with her digestion for a week afterwards, longing for a *log-hut privy (but no such luxury to be found here!)*[20]

On the second day, they had to conquer the first significant incline across the Nakerala Pass (1,217 m), which offers a fantastic view to the south over the Colchis Plain, all the way to the snow-capped peaks of the Lesser Caucasus. The path itself also rewarded all the effort. *Beautiful forest all along the fine gorge, fringed with sweet bay and common laurel – the bright shining green that nothing can exceed – and rhododendrum ponitcum in full flower, patches of it here and there on the rocks like lilac carpets scattered up and down. At the top yellow turn-cap lilies and lower down yellow iris. . . . All the hills covered with rhododendrum, oak, Spanish chestnut, beech, elm, and hornbeam, and some very fine trees of all these kinds.*[21] Anne and Ann had never seen such a forest; and neither had Karl Koch or we. The winters are harsh in western Transcaucasia, and the summers not only scorching hot but rather wet. In this climate, deciduous forests with their familiar trees develop in incredible ways, especially as not only beech, oak and so on thrive; wild *fruit trees, cherry, pear and apple alternated with them and were occasionally joined by the date tree*, that is the date-plum, named for its fruit that resembles a cross between both types. The Colchis Forest is famous among botanists; for nature-lovers, it is worth a trip of its own. *Such a primeval forest has an air of magnificence foreign to all our forests.* However, a lack of paths makes this European jungle almost impossible to roam. We have to stick to the road, for which Karl Koch, Anne and Ann would have been grateful. *The path grew more arduous with every step. We all had to dismount and let the horses down ravines, with great effort. Trees brittle with age or torn down by storm winds had often lain across our path and we were forced to clear a track with our sharp weapons. Creepers such as ivy, brambles and smilax* [prickly ivy] *also contributed not little to laying hurdles in the path of our journey through the jungle.*[22] The creepers also include the European grapevine, which originates from these forests and *loops in unbound freedom from tree to tree.*[23]

In Georgia, grapes were pressed for wine as long as six thousand years ago. The oldest known winepress may have been in Iran, but since the Islamic Republic has no wish to laud this heritage, Georgia is regarded as the undisputed birthplace of wine. Along with its intoxicating effects, the Georgian word *gwino* came to Europe. Saint Nino is said to have converted the Georgians so early and easily to Christianity not least because wine plays such a key role in communion. Her cross was made of the wood of grapevines.

Like Anne Lister, my wife and I enjoy a dry red, very heavy and full-bodied. Ann Walker preferred white wine. As in ancient times, the wine matured in buried and shaded jugs. For transport and serving, it was poured into inverted animal skins. *For this purpose, the skins of buffalo, calves or pigs are used in particular, usually inverted during removal so that they retain their original shape, sewing up all the holes with the exception of one hind leg.* Anne Lister was very enthusiastic about this ancient storage method. The taste, however, was presumably rather unusual. *To avoid the wine souring due to the great heat, the fur on the inside is soaked in naphtha.*[24] This crude oil from the Absheron peninsula was supposed to prevent the wine turning to vinegar. Karl Koch was badly disappointed by his first taste, but like Frédéric Dubois, he found one *grows very quickly accustomed* to the *strange bitter flavour.*[25] Anne and Ann seem to have had similar experiences. On their way to Racha, they paid a special visit to a grotto that Dubois had recommended as a natural curiosity, because it was full of ice even in high summer. *Adam brought away 2 nice pieces of ice which we wrapped in moss and contrived to bring home to ice our wine after dinner.*[26]

Towards Racha

Anne and Ann drank their iced wine in Khotevi, thirty-seven kilometres from Satsire. The best house there was *a very poor little place*; Anne and Ann were shown into an even smaller outbuilding. *Terribly dirty, a man partly sweeping it with a long whisk.*[27] Rain dripped through a roof like a sieve and they were given nothing to eat. The rice they had brought along and nine eggs they had purchased en route had to suffice for them and the four men. They stayed a second night nonetheless, to view the church at Nikortsminda, the most beautiful in Racha and, in our opinion, all of Georgia (constructed 1010–14); *the carvings and mouldings and cornices the richest and best done we have seen.*[28] The interior is decorated with whimsical frescoes. While Anne rode on to a river that disappears into the ground, only to reappear numerous kilometres away, Ann preferred to stay at the church and draw. Oh, if only her album had survived!

On the fourth day, Anne Lister could no longer stand the long midday rest they took every day. Once everyone had eaten, she was eager to continue the journey. However, the men refused to ride in the scorching noon heat. The horses too had to rest and graze, since oats were very difficult to obtain. Ann Walker sided with their companions. After writing her journal, Anne could no longer sit still, and set out alone at one o'clock on the steep uphill path to the partly overgrown fortress at the foot of which the group were resting. Her first attempt ended in a rock crevice: *I had had 50 minutes of toil for nothing.* George and Adam had to join her on her second, successful attempt; *back to the tree at 3:18, soaked through, my mouth quite parched. The 2 men (George and Adam) ½ undressed, smoking with heat. We had full sun upon us the latter part of the way, the heat near our walnut tree at 3:35 was F. 104 ½* (40.3° C).[29] George and Adam had gained a first impression of the exertions awaiting them by the side of this energy-laden woman.

The midday rest continued to plague Anne Lister, making her feel robbed of valuable daylight. Though she did everything else Frédéric Dubois suggested, she had no understanding whatsoever of his advice not to travel during the hot hours of the day, *from ten or eleven in the morning until three in the afternoon in July and August.* The only recommendation of his she did follow was *to be careful what one wears.*[30] Lister records *[Leaving] off my woollen undersleeves this morning.* Despite this, Anne was surprised to find that *Ann bears the heat with much less thirst and much better than I.*[31] Often, Ann Walker was the driving force when it came to riding out early in the morning, at the break of dawn. She would enjoy their picnic lunch and then seek a shady place to draw, following a nap. In the late afternoon, she would ride on with a will for adventure. It seems she took what Frédéric Dubois called the *best way to see the country* more to heart than Anne; *when one arrives at a beautiful spot where the horses may rest, one should stop; one lies down beneath a lime tree or an oak and feels as though one were merely taking a pleasure trip.*[32]

In Ambrolauri that day, they re-encountered the Rioni, which they had left in Kutaisi. Dubois and Koch outdo one another with superlatives in their attempts to describe the beauty of the landscape. *The upper valley of the Rion or Racha resembles nowhere more than the upper Rhine Valley, and were the Racha residents' clothes and language not so unfamiliar, one could easily imagine oneself in the romantic areas of Grisons. The same now broad, now narrow valley of mountains, raising their heads boldly to the skies, surround them, the same number of fortresses and towers . . . the same greenish, wildly foaming and loudly rushing river that descends over large stone blocks . . . If travellers were to return highly satisfied from the Rhine Valley, however, and then visit Racha, they would find everything even greater and more majestic.*[33]

Along the Rioni, Anne Lister and Ann Walker reached Oni (800 m above standard zero) on the fifth day of their tour. The main settlement of Upper Racha *consists largely of a long row of piteous houses inhabited by Jews and Armenians.*[34] Whereas Karl Koch had to put up with two poor rooms at the bazaar and Frédéric Dubois almost found no accommodation, Anne and Ann got the top floor of Prince Gregori Tsereteli's house, called the *palace*; Anne wrote: *blessed be the memory of this prince who has so well provided for the shelter of travellers!*[35]

We too are housed in a palace in Oni; our hotel is the only new building in the place, which was destroyed by an earthquake on 29 April 1991. Since then, Oni has suffered not only from this devastating natural disaster, but also from a sense of powerlessness or apathy or poverty of the state, which has provided no help with reconstruction, or at least none visible to us. Near our hotel, building after building is still nothing but rubble. Only the synagogue has been renovated, although Oni's Jewish community has almost entirely left since the earthquake. My wife and I are alone at dinner, and at breakfast.

Patriarchy

In all the houses they stayed in, Anne and Ann also met the women. *The ladies all well enough dressed à la Georgienne and evidently much pleased at our visit. The wife of Ottea not the handsomest, but the most talkative and intelligent. All wore the white thing that when pulled up covers the mouth, but all came to us uncovered except one, and she uncovered at my request and they all laughed.*[36] Despite her previously extravagant love life, Anne Lister seems not to have sought an opportunity to get close to any women in the Caucasus. *These Georgian Mingrelian ladies sit squat all day on their carpets doing nothing and are queer dowdy-looking figures. Crimson or white chemise under their long trailing gowns. Their breasts wobbling about like a couple of bladders.*[37]

Frédéric Dubois and Karl Koch, being men, never saw anything of Georgian family life. *According to custom, the women were not allowed to receive us,*[38] Karl Koch reports on a family in Racha, whose female members took tea with Anne and Ann. *Domestic life is a very closed life; the women rarely leave the house, rarely show themselves and do not take part in public activities.* Regardless of whether they were Christian or Muslim, *all women wear a scarf, which covers them up to their mouths,*[39] and swathed themselves in *a large cotton cloth of white colour, called a chadri.*[40] Despite this, the two explorers both claimed to be experts on Caucasian womankind. *The Circassian women vie with the Georgians for beauty and one does not know to whom to award the prize.* However, their dyed eyelashes, plucked eyebrows, red-varnished fingernails and henna-red hair were too artificial for Dubois' taste. *There is no country where the ladies take coquetry further than here, although only they ever see each other.*[41] So how did he know?

Karl Koch reported with disappointment that there were no women in the world *with as little fire in love as the Georgian women. No matter how much grace and decorum the Georgian woman displays otherwise, she shows great indifference, one might say gaucherie, in the feeling that has buried itself so deep in man's chest.*[42] Koch may have been judging by prostitutes; in any case, he informs his readers of the precise location of Tbilisi's brothels.

According to Dubois and Koch, the only difference between prostitution and marriage was duration. *In Transcaucasia, the female sex is considered a commodity that exists only for the pleasure of gentlemen, of men*, wrote Karl Koch. *This applies among both Mohammedans and Christians.*[43] *Here, one buys … one's wife for a significant wedding present*, Frédéric Dubois explained to his readers in Europe, who expected the opposite: a dowry from the bride. *It is only a short step from this custom to that of selling one's daughter or niece . . . A brother can sell his sister if their parents are no longer alive.* All the work, not only inside the house, was done by women. *These poor women are slaves to their husbands and have to do everything; they not only perform all housework, weave fabrics, sow the grain, but also work the field and the mill . . . The woman is thus, like in all peoples who seek their glory only in pillage, very subordinate to the man, and is more his maid than his companion.*[44]

Anne Lister and Ann Walker had been allowed to visit a harem back in Kazan on the Volga. *Poor things! So many human beings human animals! Except an asylum for insanes I have never seen any sight so melancholy and so humiliating as this harem. They are not admitted or capable of being admitted into society – how terrible the degradation of one half mankind!*[45] Nine months later, however, they had had a magnificent conversation in a harem in Baku and clapped along to the rhythm of the lesghinka the incarcerated women danced for them. *On leaving, just went up to Hadji and the Commandant and one or 2 more men. They had had sweetmeats, but had probably been less amused than we.*[46]

Utsera

Anne and Ann used their palace in Oni as a base camp for three multi-day excursions to the mountains. As always, they followed Dubois and visited first Tsedisi with its *very curious mine, as nearly as may be in the state of nature.* Anne viewed mines on all her travels, taking inspiration for her own coal mines at home. Although the entrance, a small low hole, was *masked with large masses of fallen rock*, the two women squeezed through with lit torches to a steep ladder, which led downwards. Anne *sent Ann back*. She herself descended some thirty metres and explored a tunnel. *Did not stop much, got down quickly and up quickly was in the mine ¼ hour.*[47] In the evening, the villagers fed them trout and eggs; they had to sleep in a barn.

Their second excursion was to the source of the Rioni, which rises on the main crest of the Greater Caucasus. They set out late and arrived at Utsera (950 m), twelve kilometres from Oni, easily along a pleasant path. Anne and Ann slept in an empty hut, the men in the yard. *Too much bit to sleep comfortably, otherwise pretty well off.*[48] The next morning, they visited the mineral springs for which Utsera was famous. *The water is rich in carbon dioxide, which gushes out of cracks in the rock everywhere. The natives bring their sick here in particular, and have them breathe in the gas.*[49]

As Anne Lister described, they did so by *inhaling it through a hollow stem. They cover the little hole in the ground at which the gas issues with leaves and stick the pipe among the leaves and may thus inhale enough to make them sneeze, or feel a sort of intoxication. Was it something of this sort that was so famous at Delphi?*[50]

The local administrator sent four armed men with them for the continuation of their journey, as their path ran close to the border with Ossetia, which was at war with its neighbour at the time. The same applies today. On the Soviet Union's collapse, South Ossetia broke away from Georgia as early as April 1990 and declared itself a sovereign republic. Once Georgia gained its own independence in 1991, South Ossetia refused to rejoin Georgia. UN peacekeeping troops succeeded in preventing a war like that in Abkhazia, but the situation is nonetheless tense. Georgia continues to assert a claim to the two separatist regions, where those in power are Russia-oriented. It is impossible to travel directly from Georgia to South Ossetia or Abkhazia.

Anne and Ann rode out without breakfast at 5:30 a.m. Karl Koch described the following three hours' journey: *Half an hour after Utsere, the surroundings change character all at once. The valley suddenly narrows and barely permits the Rion to penetrate between the tree-high rocks; the path continues onto hillsides covered in the most beautiful deciduous and partly coniferous timber and allowed me only rarely to follow it on horseback. The grapevine, the fruit and nut trees have all at once vanished, for the air blows colder. The entire valley, up to the place where the western and eastern Rion unite, is one of the most beautiful points in the Caucasus and I cannot recall finding anywhere in Switzerland a valley that might match this one for magnificence.*[51]

Anne and Ann were equally enthusiastic. *How fine this defile! We hear the roaring Rioni but see it only now and then, peep through the thick wood. The mountain mixture of spruce, birch and beech very picturesque and beautiful.*[52]

Crossing this wild, narrow valley called for courage, however, as Dubois implied. *To avoid the enormous vertical rock masses that often hang above the river, one must walk now on the right bank, and now on the other.* Anne counted ten adventurous *bridges*, described by Dubois as *supported by three beams laid from one bank to the other; they are overlaid with thick six-foot planks held together by a slat, and have no handholds. The Phasis foams over the porphyric, granite and protogynous blocks and drowns out the human voice; the bridge sways beneath our feet; frequent signs of decay make us tremble.* Anne saw the remains of each bridge's previous construction in the raging waters below them. Travellers were advised *to dismount and lead* [their] *horse by the reins, so as not to get too confused in the event that the bridge might collapse; one walks across carefully, at a suitable distance from one another.*[53] Anne cursed herself for having skipped breakfast, and took a hard-boiled egg from the picnic basket.

Glacier

Anne and Ann's venture through the valley beyond Utsera ended, as Dubois stated, *on a terrible path up a monstrous wall of slate . . . Once one has descended on the other side, all difficulties are overcome.* Before noon, they reached *the last village on the trip up the Phasis.*[54] Anne Lister considered Ghebi (1,337 m), surrounded by snow-capped mountains, *with its two white towers one of the most picturesque villages in the Caucasus.*[55] Dubois ended his excursion here. Karl Koch did not get even this far, having heard people here apparently *did not like to host strangers.*[56] In Ghebi, Anne and Ann learned that the sources of the Rioni were much further away than they had been told in Oni. They had to allow another night's stay to get there alone, not something they had planned. Anne had thought the high mountains were home to another orderly military post with *an officer commandant and 40 Russians (for George had said 40 soldiers) and supposed there would be women and that we could get milk and be tolerably comfortable and that my horse's loose shoe could be fastened on.* They therefore ventured what Dubois had not, and rode further along the Rioni at 1 p.m., higher and higher into the mountains. In the darkness, they reached not a military village with women and milk, but the provisional camp of the last military outpost before the main crest of the Greater Caucasus. The soldiers could only help the two English ladies to survive the night in the open air at an altitude of at least 2,000 m. *A few long thin poles set up meeting in a point and a few small branches thrown over them to the north and a fire in front – and this our bivouac for the night. I kept my thoughts to myself, set the Cossack to bring 3 pieces of wood and arranged Ann's bed very fairly. No wood convenient for me so spread my burca* [a shepherd's coat] *and saddle cloth on the ground, put on my light cloak and wrapped myself up in my mackintosh for the night. Ann had an egg and I my flat cake from Rebi* [Ghebi] *and a bit of cheese and supped very well.*[57]

At four the next morning, twenty-one armed mountain dwellers were ready to accompany them to the source of the Rioni. *The Ossetes lie hid in the wooded mountains along the right bank of the river, and had fired on the people not so long since.* By six o'clock there was no longer even a path. They had to leave the horses behind, under guard, and their helpers hacked a way though the undergrowth for them. At seven they found *a 'cirque' formed by 2 mountains, having the glacier on the col between them. The source is from under a glacier, and 2 picturesque high falls of water, the one double or more the other.* Ann Walker sat down to sketch, while Anne Lister climbed on with difficulty, until she was really at the source at 7.55 a.m. She had reached the large arch of ice, beneath which the glacier water shot out as a *foaming, considerable stream.* Although the Rioni springs from more than one source, Anne and Ann had achieved what no Western European explorers had done before. Johann Anton von Güldenstädt, exploring the Caucasus at the behest of Catherine the Great, had been the first to try to reach the sources of the Rioni in the summer of 1772. However, he did not get beyond Ghebi. Heinrich Julius Klaproth claimed to have been the first Western European traveller to cross the main crest of the mountains in 1807, from Stur-Digora in the north to Ghebi in the south, during which he must have passed the Rioni's source. However, Frédéric Dubois proved Klaproth was lying. In 1825, Eduard von Eichwald made just as little effort as Karl Koch in 1836 to get so far into the high mountains. Anne Lister and Ann Walker trumped them all.

They could not stay at the glacier for long. They were back at the military base at 10.10 a.m. and bid farewell to their helpers with two silver roubles, *with which they seemed well satisfied ... Good honest mountaineers – I would go all the Caucasus over with them.* They returned along the same path and spent the night in a shed in Ghebi. *A threshing-sledge was Ann's bedsted, and 3 boards laid on shallow kneading-troughs was mine. For some time at first the little court filled with people to look at us.* Then *Ann drank about a pint and a half of boiled milk and fell asleep. The good woman brought me a thick cake and 2 thin ones and ½ a large white cheese. I supped magnificently and lay down at 9 ½.*[58]

Violence

Dubois had not made it to the sources of the Rioni, but he did get to Glola, a village in a side valley of the Rioni with the *most beautiful of the mineral springs of High Racha.*[59] What he had seen, Anne Lister wanted to see too. To take a detour via Glola on the way back to Oni, Anne and Ann had to cross two particularly hair-raising bridges: *2 broad rapidy streams, 3 trees over first, only one over second.* Ann Walker had one of the men carry her. *I myself took Ann's burca and bag and my own, and Ann set off. Frightened, but was carried over the first very well. On the second the man who carried her staggered two-thirds over. Frightful! Another man ran to him and between them Ann was safe over – I stood watching them! Then followed, hold one man whose only fault was going too slowly. Obliged to look at one's feet and the rapid stream made me feel giddyish.*[60]

Their six-man escort took the uphill route along the Rioni tributary, weapons cocked; *looking carefully into the wood on both sides at every step as if expecting a party of Ossetes to pounce out upon us.* The border with South Ossetia was still only a few kilometres away. In the village, they drank from the mineral spring and were glad to have made the trip. *Have not seen in the Caucasus a nicer little village than Glola,* Anne Lister noted.[61] With snow-capped mountains as their backdrop, the square towers built on to the houses looked particularly impressive. *This is the building style of the mountain-dwellers who occupy the high part of the valley. The towers are pierced by arrow slots and one can only enter the houses through a door placed on the first floor.* In Racha, these fortified towers have now all but disappeared; they have been preserved in Svaneti and declared world heritage in Ushguli. As picturesque as they may look, they testify to *a continuous state of war, fear and distrust.*[62] Not only the Ossetians, but also the Circassians and Abkhaz, the Lezgins in Dagestan and the Chechens lived in constant conflict with their neighbours. The towers have recently been used only as defence against the Russians; for countless generations, people here entrenched themselves against anyone not belonging to their own family. *The Ossetian does not think it a sin to rob and pillage his fellow countryman, if no familial relationship prevails between them, just as he himself is also always on the alert to receive his foe in worthy manner.*[63] Thus, women who married in were not trusted either. If they had to enter the keep, they were blindfolded so they could not later betray the secret entrance to their original families.

Dubois complained of the rough morals of Glola's inhabitants. Although the village was small, *not a year passes in which several murders do not take place due to abduction of women* (i.e. rape) *or for other causes.*[64] Karl Koch, who stayed overnight in Glola, received a friendly welcome but had to prevent a neighbour from punching his host's teeth out, because the latter had not provided his guest with enough food for the former's taste: the only cow was still grazing outside his house. Koch knew a first blow would have had fatal consequences. *Blood revenge prevails in all its cruelty and unnaturalness … and every misdemeanour, no matter how minor, becomes subject to it. While only blood was avenged with blood among the Circassians, blood must flow at every insult received by an Ossetian.*[65]

In Glola, Anne Lister and Ann Walker had to fear not only for their money, equipment and horses. Kidnappings were commonplace as a means of extracting ransoms. Abduction and slave trading had been profitable business in the Caucasus since ancient times. As slaves shipped across the Black Sea to Constantinople and the Mediterranean, the Caucasian peoples preferred *Russians, because they notice that they are industrious and hardworking* – and nor were they free at home, as serfs. The word 'slaves' is said to be derived from 'Slavs'. In 1840, *this barbaric custom is still present among the Abkhaz,* and other peoples *would like to follow it, if Russia had not put a stop to this trading through extremely severe measures.*[66] Anne Lister and Ann Walker hurried to leave Glola and return to Oni that evening.

Everything Flows

Anne Lister and Ann Walker's third excursion from Oni took them *into the least-known valleys of the Caucasus,* according to Frédéric Dubois; *no traveller had visited them before me, to my knowledge.*[67] That made the excursion all the more enticing for Anne Lister; they took *only the clothes on our backs, except Dubois.*[68] On a long day's ride south, they crossed a mountain crest and arrived in the bed of the Jruchula at the Jruchi monastery, magnificently located on a mountain spur with the river foaming at its feet. The monks gave them a pleasant guestroom in which Dubois had slept before them. The next day, they reached Sachkhere via a route both breath-taking and adventurous. Here, Prince Tsereteli was pleased to make the ladies' acquaintance at last, having hosted them at his palace in Oni. On the third day, they rode along the bed of the Qvirila, which is hemmed in by high cliffs for many kilometres, to the Ghvimevi monastery, with its church, already more than a thousand years old at the time, *built in the mouth of a large cavern – a little gem.* Several monastery buildings preserved to this day were also housed in caves. By the river were thatched huts, shaded by tall walnut trees. *Perfectly beautiful. So taken with the place I would gladly have stayed all night.* The room for visitors was occupied by a sick guest, however, and they had to make do with refreshments; *one of the monks brought us a bottle of such nice light wine that we drank the whole of it.* They rode back to Jruchi monastery that afternoon, spending the night there again; *crossed today Qvirila 29 times and Djouroudja* [Jruchula] *19 times . . . my boots wet though I held up my feet as high as I could.*[69]

Their ride along the river beds took its toll, with two horses lame the next day. They urgently needed replacements, but in Oni *for a largeish grey horse the man asked 40 R. silver – Nonsense, said I, and walked off.*[70] After a day's rest, they therefore set off for the neighbouring province of Letchkhumi to the west, where they had heard it was easier to buy horses than in Racha. They rode back downstream along the Rioni, its wild valley transforming beyond Ambrolauri into a charming orchard. After a forty-kilometre journey, too long for the human and animal travellers, they did not reach the village of Khvanchkara until after dark. *Arrived at 9.35 at a lighted, comfortable well-galleried wood house and open court. I rode up to the lights to see the house. Some ladies asked us in* to stay the night. *We were taken to a large 1-room cottage across the court, 1 divan (carpeted) for Ann and a long low table for me ... They brought a higher table and eggs and cucumbers and fine filberts and bread and wine and good water for supper.* Their servants were also well treated; *The wine excellent ... had drunk all night.*[71] The Khvanchkara wine cultivated here was well known in the Soviet Union, as Stalin enjoyed it as much as Adam and George had.

Beyond Khvanchkara, the Rioni valley grows dramatically narrow and deep. *I suddenly thought myself transported to the grounds of Saxon Switzerland,* wrote Frédéric Dubois. Cliffs *split from top to bottom into huge blocks with vertical walls, divided by chasms more than 500 feet deep* [170 metres] ... *The Phasis flows in one of these crevasses, and if one does not see it, one at least hears it roaring in the chasm. On the highest block, which, rising like an obelisk, presents only a small platform at its peak,* was the small Sairme monastery. *I could barely believe my eyes.*[72] Anne and Ann were no less impressed. After the previous day, they were glad to have demanded only around fifteen kilometres from their horses. *The good monks received us without even looking at our paper. A good wood house to ourselves with gallery for the servants and a private gallery. Excellent – most comfortable. In our grand salon a good broad divan for me and a little cabinet for Ann's bedroom, and a good steady table under the little window.* The abbot himself showed them around and had them served a dinner of *a fine boiled fowl and bread and wine.*[73] They were happy to stay another day.

When Ann Walker wanted to attend lauds in the church at three in the morning, she found the door locked: she had been locked in for her protection, and that of the chaste monks. At six, she went down to the river valley in the morning air to draw the spectacular ravine dug out by the Rioni over several kilometres. She came back to the monastery for breakfast with Anne, only to return to the ravine until the midday heat hailed her for her usual siesta. Anne Lister spent the whole day writing her journal at her desk. To prompt her memory, she used a notebook, the writing in which she then erased so as to refill the pages. Unlike Ann, she did not go down to the river until the hot late afternoon, with George and Adam. *Returned at 7.50 and back, soaked, at 8.25. Had wine and water, glass after glass – very hot in the thick wood at the bottom.*[74]

Lost

The dramatically located Sairme monastery no longer perches atop its rock. Did it collapse into the Rioni in the 1991 earthquake? The monks now live on a mountain on the other side of the river. Nor does the road run along the bottom of the Rioni ravine any longer, instead being sited 500 metres or more from the escarpment. When its course allows a view of the ravine from a distance, my heart cramps up: it is breath-takingly beautiful here, but sadly we cannot get close enough to the ravine. The road had been transformed into a potholed track that our car can barely navigate. We make as slow progress as Anne and Ann with their lame horses. We don't see any footpaths that might take us to the edge of the ravine.

'Perhaps it's better that way. There probably aren't any warning signs at dangerous spots here.'

Anne and Ann would not have got far with that attitude. What can ever be reconstructed, re-experienced? So much has been irrevocably lost. Anne Lister wrote here all day long, with pen and ink on paper. She took her writing case with all the necessary accoutrements even on this tour. To write, she had to keep removing her hand from the page to dip the pen in the ink every few syllables and begin anew. The eye has to move with the hand, from the page to the inkpot and back. Does a person formulate differently, think differently, when that rhythm dictates their writing?

Anne did not go down to the ravine with Ann in the morning because she wanted to use the good desk during daylight. That dependency on natural light is another thing unfamiliar to me. Even at night, it made a difference whether the moon was shining or the sky was clouded. Two days previously, Anne and Ann had got lost. *At 8 too dusk to see anything clearly. Soon afterwards what with night and thick woods we groped in the dark. Could not see each other ½ dozen yards off and I called every now and then to make sure Ann was close behind me.*[75] Once darkness fell outside, it was barely brighter inside. Candles and tallow lamps – one expensive, the other foul-smelling – cast weak light on a room or a sheet of paper. A smartphone torch grants more illumination today. In our light-polluted cities, we never experience complete darkness. We have to seek out high mountains, or perhaps the Rioni valley, to see the black of night.

Travelling itself has changed fundamentally. Anne Lister and Ann Walker would have been disconcerted: seven weeks for Russia, Georgia and Azerbaijan? That's barely enough time for Yorkshire! The two of them assumed they would be travelling for two years; those who could travel for pleasure often stayed abroad that long. The slower speed of transport only partly explains the long stays. People wanted to spend a while in new countries and towns, make acquaintances and take part in local life. Today, many more can afford to travel, but such a long stay is still reserved for the few. As soon as one has got over the jetlag, one heads back home. All the conversations you've had were with other tourists at the breakfast buffet or the woman on the museum cash desk.

Would Anne and Ann even take us seriously as travellers? Travelling by plane deprives you of the gradual changes to the landscape, architecture, people and languages. You only ever visit a kind of island, with terra incognita between the point of departure and the holiday resort. What is regarded as sights has also altered. Anne and Ann viewed schools and factories, visited orphanages or the Moscow water tower. (Susette: 'I'd have been interested in that. Why didn't we go there?')

What remains unchanged is our longing to travel back in time. Anne Lister and Frédéric Dubois were not unique in that respect. Historical events were reconstructed even in ancient times. European princes had romantic ruins built in the eighteenth century. Nineteenth-century historicism made history into the present. Today, we can do all sorts of time travel, from jousting fairs to medieval markets to experimental archaeology, as science fiction, fantasy or science. Thousands of war fans spend their free time recreating battles where no blood is spilled. They go to great lengths to tailor uniforms, obtain authentic weapons, group into well-researched formations – and despite all historical accuracy, they lack the decisive factor that playing at war can never give them: fearing so much for their lives that they vomit or wet themselves, being mutilated, bleeding to death. And yet followers of the various re-enactment scenes have creative disputes over authenticity and obtain precise historical expertise. Can you use a sewing machine for a jester's costume? Can you make a sixteenth-century monk's habit out of cotton? Or even – can you take part in re-enactments in the first place if you were born by caesarean? If you have fillings in your teeth or have been vaccinated? How genuine is genuine?

Mingrelia

From the Sairme monastery, Anne and Ann rode up to the mountain village of Lailashi, where they were accommodated in the guesthouse of the Mingrelian Dadians' modest summer residence. The princely family was currently staying in Zugdidi, however, to where Ekaterina Dadiani – who had enchanted Anne Lister in Tbilisi – had invited the English ladies. Dashing their hopes, there was only a single horse to be had in the *poor little place*[76] that was Lailashi, at the same price as in Oni. This foiled Anne's plan of continuing on Dubois' tracks. She had wanted to descend, like him, via a mountain ridge into the Tskhenistskali valley, which Dubois counted one of the most beautiful in the Caucasus. However, not only their horses but also their men refused. Only the Cossack was willing to accompany them; all the others wanted to return to Kutaisi via the shortest route. Anne Lister had to give in. On 2 August 1840, they rode back to the Rioni and its densely wooded, hilly banks.

The lame horses meant Anne and Ann made only slow progress. Late at night in heavy rain, they reached a tiny village. In the first house there was *no possibility of staying there – full of people ill in 'the hot fever', the 2 or 3 that came to the door pale as ghosts. Rode further into the village. About 9 ¾ before we got quarters in a good cottage with 6 women and 3 men and 3 or 4 children, boys and girls. The children were roused to give us their corner, and there we spread our burcas and saddle-blankets and made ourselves comfortable, all our baggage around us . . . Fire in the middle. Boiled our kettle and eggs and baked our flat cake in the ashes. The rain pelted hard and thunder rolled and lightning flashed and we were satisfied to be so well housed, our wet cloaks hung on the rails suspended from the roof.*[77] The next day, they had to leave three of their eight horses behind along the way. They eventually reached Kutaisi, from where they had set out for the mountain world twenty-six days previously.

Anne Lister and Ann Walker departed a second time from Kutaisi as soon as possible. Susette and I followed them to Jvari, close to the Enguri river in western Georgia, where Anne Lister wrote in her diary for the last time. The *Indian corn barn (a little wicker place perhaps 4 1/2 by 3 yards)*[78] where they stayed overnight is today hard to imagine in front of Europe's highest dam wall. What do we know at all? What do we involuntarily or even necessarily invent in writing Anne Lister's life? What did *she* invent already while living? Is there any history without narrator? History? Which history? And whose?

Zeitreisen became the second part of my trilogy on biographical writing, which I completed with *Poetik der Biographie* (Poetics of Biography (2019): a triple jump from Biography (*Anne Lister*) – to reflection (*Zeitreisen*) – to theory (*Poetik*).

Notes

Extracts from the journals Anne Lister kept on her last travels were transcribed by Phyllis Ramsden and Vivien Ingham, but not published. The typescripts are held at West Yorkshire Archive Services in Halifax, call number RAM:6–25. Citations from these typescripts are given only with date and archive call number.

Please note that when quoting from a primary source accompanied by my comments, the end note number appears at the end of the passage under discussion.

1 See A. Steidele, *Anne Lister. Eine erotische Biographie* (Berlin: Matthes & Seitz, 2017), trans. K. Derbyshire, *Gentleman Jack: a Biography of Anne Lister: Regency Landowner, Seducer and Secret Diarist* (London: Serpent's Tail, 2018); A. Steidele, *Zeitreisen. Vier Frauen, zwei Jahrhunderte, ein Weg* (Berlin: Matthes & Seitz, 2018). A. Steidele, Poetik der Biographie (Berlin: Matthes & Seitz, 2019). The excerpts from Steidele, *Zeitreisen*, are taken between pages 189 and 240. Translation and inclusion by kind permission of the publisher.

2 F. Dubois de Montpéreux, *Voyage autour du Caucase, chez les Tcherkesses et les Abkhases, en Colchide, en Géorgie, en Arménie et en Crimée. Avec un Atlas géographique, pittoresque, archéologique, géologique etc.*, 6 vols. (Paris: Librairie de Gide, 1839–43).

3 P. Ramsden and V. Ingham, Anne Lister Unpublished Transcriptions, West Yorkshire Archive Service, Calderdale, 25 June 1840, RAM:20, p. 4.

4 *Aujourd'hui Sion n'a plus de berger ni de troupeau spirituel . . . chacque année il faut que les bergers déblaient la couche énorme de fumier qui s'y entasse pour pouvoir entrer par les portes* (Dubois, *Voyage*, vol. III, pp. 217–18).

5 25 June 1840, RAM:20, p. 4.

6 RAM:20, p. 7.

7 *[Le reste des] édifices consiste en excavations groupées et terrassées les unes sur les autres et taillées dans des massifs isolés. // Dans cette roche compacte, d'imiter tous les ornements et tous les détails d'une boiserie soignée . . . Vous y retrouvez corniches, petites poutres, grandes poutres traversières, taillées avec le plus grand soin, comme dans une maison en sapin* (Dubois, *Voyage*, vol. III, pp. 196, 198–9).

8 *Est-il rien de plus pittoresque que Koutaïs et ses alentours?* (Dubois, *Voyage*, vol. I, p. 381).

9 K. Koch, *Reise durch Rußland nach dem kaukasischen Isthmus in den Jahren 1836, 1837 und 1838*, vol. I (Stuttgart and Tübingen: Cotta, 1843), p. 165.

10 Anne Lister to Sophia Radziwill, 11 May 1840, in M. Green (ed.), '*A Spirited Yorkshirewoman: the Letters of Anne Lister of Shibden Hall, b. 1791–d 1840*, Library Associations Honours Diploma (1938), p. 537.
11 *Ici commence l'histoire de la toison d'or . . . De tous les temps les rivières . . . ont passé pour charrier de l'or. // La ville de Médée est ensevelie sous tant d'autres ruines qu'elle est introuvable* (Dubois, *Voyage*, vol. II, p. 18; vol. I, pp. 381–2, 428-9).
12 Koch, *Reise durch Rußland*, p. 163.
13 *Homère avait su apprécier leur bonheur, puisque c'est précisément ici qu'eut lieu la fameuse métamorphose des compagnons d'Ulysses. // Ces porcs, dans les villes, à Koutaïs entre autres, où ils se promènent par troupes, contribuent singulièrement à la propreté des rues* (Dubois, *Voyage*, vol. I, p. 390).
14 Early/mid-June 1840, RAM:18, p. 13.
15 Koch, *Reise durch Rußland*, p. 164.
16 30 June 1840, RAM:20, p. 9.
17 *L'aspect de ce monastère est l'une des plus pittoresque que l'on puisse voir* (Dubois, *Voyage*, vol. II, p. 176).
18 9 July 1940, RAM:22, p. 2.
19 9 July 1840, RAM:24, pp. 8, 6.
20 28 July 1840, RAM:24, p. 13.
21 10 July 1840, RAM:22, p. 2.
22 Koch, *Reise durch Rußland*, pp. 151, 166, 146.
23 K. Koch, *Wanderungen im Oriente während der Jahre 1843 und 1844*, 3 vols. (Weimar: Verlag des Landes-Industrie-Comptoirs, 1847), vol. III: *Reise in Grusien, am kaspischen Meere und im Kaukasus*, p. 175.
24 Koch, *Reise durch Rußland*, pp. 328–9.
25 *Un goût particulier d'amertume, auquel on s'habitue très promptement* (Dubois, *Voyage*, vol. I, p. 389).
26 12 July 1840, RAM:22, p. 5.
27 10 July 1840, RAM:24, p. 9.
28 11 July 1840, RAM:23, p. 4.
29 13 July 1840, RAM:23, pp. 2–3.
30 *De ne pas se mettre en route pendant les heures chaudes de la journée depuis dix et onze heures du matin jusqu'à trois heures de l'après midi, dans les mois de juillet et d'août. // d'être sur leurs gardes par rapport à l'habillement* (Dubois, *Voyage*, vol. I, p. 379).
31 Late July 1840, RAM:24, p. 2.
32 *C'est la meilleure manière de voir le pays. // Trouve-t-on un bel endroit pour reposer des chevaux, on s'y arrête; on s'y couche sous un tilleul ou sous un chêne; il semble qu'on ne fasse qu'une promenade de plaisir* (Dubois, *Voyage*, vol. II, p. 424).
33 Koch, *Reise durch Rußland*, p. 125.
34 Ibid., p. 124.
35 20 July 1840, RAM:24, p. 9.
36 28 July 1840, RAM:24, p. 13.

37 7 August 1840, RAM:24, pp. 8–9.
38 Koch, *Reise durch Rußland*, p. 240.
39 *La vie privée est une vie d'isolement. Les femmes sortent peu, se montrent peu; elle ne remplissent aucune fonction quelconque de la vie publique. // Les femmes ont toutes un mouchoir qui leur passe par-dessus la bouche* (Dubois, *Voyage*, vol. I, p. 394; vol. II, p. 413).
40 Koch *Reise durch Rußland*, p. 289.
41 *Les femmes tcherkesses rivalisent en beauté avec les Georgiennes, sans qu'on puisse se décider pour les unes ou pour les autres. // Il n'y a pas de pays où elles poussent plus loin la coquetterie qu'ici, quoiqu'elles ne se voient qu'entre elles* (Dubois, *Voyage*, vol. I, p. 121; vol. III, p. 174).
42 Koch, *Wanderungen im Oriente*, p. 50.
43 Ibid., pp. 49–50.
44 *On achète ici sa femme en payant une forte dot. // De cet usage à celui de vendre sa fille ou sa nièce à un étranger, il n'y a qu'un pas. . . . Un frère a aussi le droit de vendre sa soeur quand ils n'ont plus de parents. // Ces pauvres femmes sont les esclaves de leurs maris: ce sont elles qui font tout; non seulement elles font tout le travail de la maison, tissent des étoffes, vannent le blé, mais elles vont aux champs, au moulin. // On voit que la femme, comme chez tous les peuples qui mettent leur gloire dans le pillage, est très subordonnée à l'homme, et sa servante plus que sa compagne* (Dubois, *Voyage*, vol. I, pp. 124, 126; vol. II, pp. 413–14; vol. I, p. 124).
45 21 February 1840, RAM:15, p. 3.
46 [May] 1840, RAM:15, p. 4.
47 15 July 1840, RAM:22, p. 7.
48 17 July 1840, RAM:22, p. 9.
49 Koch, *Reise durch Rußland*, p. 130.
50 18 July 1840, RAM:22, p. 9.
51 Koch, *Reise durch Rußland*, p. 131.
52 18 July 1840, RAM:22, p. 10.
53 *Pour éviter les énormes masses de rochers à pic qui surplombent souvent le fleuve, nécessité est de passer tantôt sur une rive, tantôt sur l'autre. // Ponts de bois que supportent trois poutres lancées d'une rive à l'autre; elles sont couvertes de madriers de 6 pieds de long, assujétis par une latte, sans garde-fou. Le Phase écume sur les blocs de porphyre, de granit, de protogyne, et mugit à couvrir la voix humaine; le pont se balance sous nos pas; de nombreuses traces de pourriture nous font frémir. // De mettre pied à terre, et de mener mon cheval par la bride, peur ne pas d'être trop embarrassé en cas qu'il s'écroule; on marche à distance* (Dubois, *Voyage*, vol. II, p. 405).
54 *Pour escalader par un affreux chemin une énorme paroi schisteuse qui barre le passage; on ne se fait pas une idée d'un pareil chemin. Redescendu de l'autre côté, toutes les difficultés sont surmontées. // Le dernier village en remontant le Phase* (Dubois, *Voyage*, vol. II, pp. 406, 409).
55 19 July 1840, RAM:22, p. 13.
56 Koch, *Reise durch Rußland*, p. 135.

57 18 July 1840, RAM:22, p. 11.
58 19 July 1840, RAM:22, pp. 12–13.
59 *La plus belle des sources acidulées du Haut-Ratcha* (Dubois, *Voyage*, vol. II, p. 422).
60 20 July 1840, RAM:22, pp. 13–14.
61 20 July 1840, RAM:22, p. 14.
62 *C'est le style d'architecture des montagnards qui occupent la haute partie de la vallée. Les tours sont percées de meurtrières, et ce n'est que par une porte placée à l'étage dans l'intérieur des maisons, qu'on peut y entrer. // Cet état de guerre continuel, de crainte, de méfiance* (Dubois, *Voyage*, vol. II, pp. 401–2; vol. I, p. 129).
63 Koch, *Reise durch Rußland*, pp. 96, 105.
64 *Il ne passe pas d'année où il n'y ait plusieurs meurtres pour enlèvement de femmes ou autres causes* (Dubois, *Voyage*, vol. II, p. 423).
65 Koch, *Reise durch Rußland*, pp. 61, 107.
66 *On aime les Russes, parce qu'on remarque qu'ils sont industrieux, laborieux. // Cet usage barbare répandu aussi chez les Abkhazes. // le feraient bien encore si la Russie n'y avait mis bon ordre par ses mesures sévères* (Dubois, *Voyage*, vol. I, pp. 126, 127).
67 *Des vallées les moins connues du Caucase // pas un voyageur ne l'avait visitée, à ma connaissance, avant moi* (Dubois, *Voyage*, vol. III, p. 156).
68 22 July 1840, RAM:23, p. 4.
69 24 July 1840, RAM:23, pp. 6–7.
70 17 July 1840, RAM:24, p. 3.
71 27 and 28 July 1840, RAM:24, pp. 12, 14.
72 *Je me crus tout à coup transporté dans les* grunds *de la Suisse saxonne. // Toute la formation crayeuse était pourfendue de haut en bas comme par blocs immenses à parois à pic, que des abîmes de plus de 500 pieds de profondeur séparaient les uns des autres . . . Le Phase coule dans l'une de ces fentes, et si on ne le voit pas, on l'entend au moins mugir dans ce gouffre. Sur le plus grand des blocs, qui, dressé comme un obélisque, ne présente à son sommet qu'une étroite plateforme. // Je n'en pouvais croire mes yeux* (Dubois, *Voyage*, vol. II, pp. 431–2).
73 28 July 1840, RAM:23, pp. 8–9.
74 29 July 1840, RAM:23, p. 9.
75 27 July 1840, RAM:24, p. 12.
76 30 July 1840, RAM:24, p. 3.
77 2 August 1840, RAM:24, p. 5.
78 11 August 1840, RAM:25, p. 10.

PART V

'I beg to be remembered': Lister, Public History and Popular Culture

CHAPTER 11

Labels, Plaques and Identity Categories: Finding the Words for Anne Lister

Caroline Gonda

Prologue: Shibden Hall

It's 6 March 2020, a bright cold day in Halifax, and Shibden Hall is closed to the public. Not because of Covid-19 – the first UK lockdown hasn't happened yet – but because the boiler's not working. Angela Clare from Calderdale Museums is waiting at the gate to show us round: me, my friend Harriet from Manchester and two American fans of *Gentleman Jack* who didn't know the house was closed and happened to turn up at just the right moment. 'Wear lots of layers,' Angela had warned me; 'it'll be freezing.' There's a school visit going on as well, and our paths keep almost crossing with troops of primary school children wearing mob caps and aprons. After the house, we go out into the carriage barn, and Angela gestures through the doorway to the courtyard of the Folk Museum, with its reconstruction of shops and crafts. 'Everything beyond this point is fiction,' she says. I take a photograph on my phone, but when I check it later there's nothing there.

My photograph of the plaque on the wall at Shibden comes out fine. I was there nearly a year ago for the unveiling, on Lister's birthday, 3 April 2019. That was a cold wet day. People huddling under fleece blankets in the unheated carriage barn to hear Helena Whitbread and Jill Liddington give their talks, next to the one electric heater. The mayor, speaking warmly about how Anne Lister had been part of his life as a teenager in Halifax, because Helena was a friend of his mother and had talked about Anne Lister at his mother's kitchen table. The rain, finally stopping just in time for the mayor to unveil the plaque. Lots of people taking photographs of Helena and Jill underneath it.

None of us in the UK or the USA had seen *Gentleman Jack* at that point, though we were all keen to know how it would turn out. We had no idea how much was about to change, how many conversations about Anne Lister would be sparked, in and beyond Halifax and across the globe.

Figure 6 Shibden Hall plaque. Photography Chris Roulston, 2022.

How many people would beat a path to her door, would make the pilgrimage to Halifax and Shibden in search of her.

What was already clear, in that pre-*Gentleman Jack* spring of 2019, was just how powerful a thing a plaque could be, and what fierce emotions it could provoke. By the time the Shibden Hall plaque was unveiled, there had already been not one, but two plaques commemorating Anne Lister's place in LGBTQ+ history, both of them at the same site in York, though not at the same time.

A Tale of Two Plaques

On 24 July 2018, York Civic Trust unveiled the first rainbow plaque in the UK, in recognition of Anne Lister and her union with Ann Walker.[1] The plaque, outside the church of Holy Trinity in Goodramgate, York, where the two women celebrated their union by taking communion together, immediately sparked controversy for its wording: 'ANNE LISTER / 1791–1840 / Gender-nonconforming / entrepreneur. Celebrated marital / commitment, without legal / recognition, to Ann Walker / in this church. / Easter, 1834.'

As Kit Heyam, co-organiser of the Rainbow Plaques project in York, recalls: 'within hours of the plaque unveiling, I was receiving angry and often abusive messages on social media. Within a day, this had escalated: a petition was launched against the plaque and several people had got hold of my work phone number.'[2] The online petition, which accused the organisers of erasing lesbian history and demanded that the plaque be replaced with one that would describe Lister as a lesbian, gained upwards of two thousand signatures in its first week and was widely reported in the news media.[3] On 3 September, York Civic Trust announced its decision to change the plaque's wording.[4] A consultation period was introduced on the proposed new wording from 30 October to 25 November 2018, and on 10 December the Trust announced that 95 per cent of those who had responded to the survey were happy with the revised wording, which was as follows:

> ANNE LISTER / 1791–1840 / of Shibden Hall, Halifax / Lesbian and Diarist; took sacrament here / to seal her union with Ann Walker / Easter 1834.[5]

The new plaque was unveiled on 28 February 2019, to mark the end of LGBT History Month in York; York Civic Trust also took the opportunity at this point to correct the rainbow border of the plaque, which had initially been upside down. A talk by Helena Whitbread followed the unveiling of the new plaque – a significant choice, given Whitbread's pioneering role in presenting Lister's diaries to the world and her unwavering view of Lister as a lesbian.[6]

At the unveiling of the Shibden Hall plaque in April 2019, a representative from the Halifax Civic Trust commented privately that they had

Figure 7 Lister/Walker plaque. Photography Eva Attridge-Hall, 2022.

learned from the York experience, and that the word lesbian would definitely be on this one. Unlike the two versions of the York plaque, the Shibden plaque didn't try to sum Lister up in two words ('gender-nonconforming entrepreneur' versus 'lesbian and diarist'), but offered a more expansive description: 'Anne Lister / 1791–1840 / diarist, business-woman, landowner, / traveller and lesbian who recorded / much of her personal life in / a secret code. / She lived at Shibden Hall / from 1815 to 1840.' In fairness, the Shibden plaque had an easier task than the York one; its matter-of-fact statement about Lister's connection with Shibden Hall left more space to describe her, and no room for controversy.

One of the problems with the York plaque was that the Church of England's continuing refusal to recognise same-sex marriages necessitated careful wording about what exactly had happened between Lister and Walker; the desire to claim the church as the site of one of the first same-sex marriages, or the first lesbian wedding, could not be fully realised.[7] Moreover, as Simon Joyce notes in his article 'The Perverse Presentism of Rainbow Plaques', Lister's diary entries don't fully support this claim: Lister and Walker did not celebrate the anniversary of taking communion together at the church, but instead marked the date when they had agreed to make the commitment to each other.[8] Joyce suggests that there is a parallel between the controversy over the York plaque and how *Gentleman Jack* 'downplays [Lister's] gender nonconformity in order to focus instead on her relationship to Ann Walker as a prototypical example of marriage equality'.[9]

Joyce argues that both sides of the plaque debate were based on pre-suppositions that would have made no sense in Lister's historical context, namely 'that we each have a way of self-identifying in terms of gender and sexuality and that this should be considered an unimpeachable truth about ourselves'.[10] The term 'gender-nonconforming', in his view, was rooted in 'a fantasy of stable identity that was just as anachronistic as the labels that had been rejected'.[11] Discussing Jack Halberstam's reading of Lister in *Female Masculinity* as closest to a 'stone butch' in terms of modern identity, Joyce says that if Halberstam is right, 'the York Civic Trust's first instinct was actually more grounded in Lister's own sense of self than its second' and that the impulse to define Lister as 'a lesbian *avant la lettre*' might be more anachronistic than calling her gender-nonconforming.[12]

Anachronism was only part of the story, however, and not the part that made most noise. As Heyam recalls, 'Some of the angry messages (and all of the abuse) came from anti-trans activists who saw Anne's plaque as a symptom of how, in their eyes, advances in trans rights were eroding the rights of lesbians.'[13] Heyam is at pains to point out that 'the majority of anger and hurt came from lesbians and bi women who were explicitly supportive of trans rights, but still felt Anne was an important part of their historical community', and that respect for these women's concerns prompted the revision of the plaque.[14] Nevertheless, the plaque's wording was widely interpreted as having more to do with contemporary LGBTQ+ politics than with the potential for anachronism in applying modern identity categories to historical figures. York Civic Trust's press statement that the choice of 'gender-nonconforming' rather than 'lesbian' was an attempt to 'future-proof' the plaque's description of Lister did not help matters; a discussion in the comments on a Facebook post sharing York LGBT Forum's announcement about the plaque interpreted the reference to 'future-proofing' as a sinister prediction of further lesbian erasure.[15] A blog post by the linguistics professor Deborah Cameron linked the plaque's wording to a recent Buzzfeed article about evolving attitudes to gender identity, particularly amongst young people, and the implications of those changes for the future of supposedly old-fashioned binary labels such as gay and lesbian; the issue about the plaque's wording, Cameron concluded, was not 'what we can't know about the past, it's what we don't agree on in the present'.[16] Shon Faye, who discusses the controversy in a chapter which begins with the disruption of the 2018 Pride parade in London by the anti-trans group Get The L Out, a couple of weeks before the unveiling of the York plaque, comments: 'This fierce dispute over the precise description of a dead Victorian woman is more about contemporary LGBT politics than it is about history.'[17]

Heyam's account of the Rainbow Plaques project is surprising and at times moving. As they explain, the original impetus for Lister's plaque came from an event Heyam co-organised for York LGBT History Month in 2015, in which people were invited to create cardboard rainbow plaques that marked spaces of significant LGBTQ+ history – personal, local or global – which would be displayed for twenty-four hours across the city. Two of these plaques marked Lister's association with York, one at her school, King's Manor, and one at Holy Trinity Goodramgate. Participants in the project were keen for Lister to have a 'real' plaque at the church, which they saw as 'the site of one of the first lesbian marriages in the UK'.[18] This plan was eventually realised in 2018, through a collaboration between York Civic Trust and York LGBT Forum, in conversation with the Churches Conservation Trust, but something clearly went badly wrong in the shift from that creative, community-led, local and temporary project to a permanent memorial.

As Heyam says, the response to the first York plaque showed 'just how many people Anne Lister was important to, and how few of those people our consultation had managed to reach'. Rather than being a deliberate decision motivated by concerns about anachronism, the omission of the word 'lesbian' from the plaque seems to have been the result of that failure: 'No one had highlighted this word as important in our consultation,' Heyam says, 'and (with what seems in retrospect like enormous naivety) I'd assumed that this was because everybody *knew* Anne Lister was a lesbian.'[19] Such naivety is indeed startling; given the long and painful history of lesbian invisibility, what 'everybody knows' is precisely what can't be taken for granted, and it does seem astonishing that nobody realised this was going to be a problem. Heyam's explanation of 'gender-nonconforming' is perhaps less surprising, though it contrasts strikingly with Joyce's reading of the term as rooted in 'a fantasy of stable identity'. For the decision-making committee, Heyam says, 'this was a description of Anne's *behaviour* ... But to many people, it read as a label for Anne's *identity*: a statement that they weren't a woman, and were therefore not a lesbian either.'[20] (Heyam uses they/them pronouns for the historical figures in their book, for reasons they outline in their Author's Note.)

Heyam expresses sadness that the new plaque 'makes no mention of Anne's gender nonconformity' and that 'we've lost an opportunity to commemorate how Anne represents an overlap between trans history and lesbian history'.[21] They argue that we should 'focus less on the impossible task of identifying which historical figures are "really" trans and which aren't, and more on acknowledging the diversity of creative, non-conforming and fluid approaches to gendered dress in the past, and appreciating both the individuality and the shared experiences they represent'.[22]

When the news about the first York plaque was announced, in the summer of 2018, I was struck – as many people were – by the discrepancy between the BBC news headline, 'Plaque in York Honours "First Modern Lesbian" Anne Lister', and the wording of the plaque itself, which described Lister as 'Gender-nonconforming entrepreneur'.[23] I knew very quickly that I wanted to write something about Lister, labelling and identity categories, but I also had a sinking feeling about what I was letting myself in for. And I felt caught in a difficult in-between space, in my own response to that initial news story and the issues it raised. I was aware that some of the loudest voices in the outcry against lesbian erasure in the original wording of the York plaque were coming from a position of intense and persistent hostility to trans and queer identities, a position that has been increasingly visible in the UK in the past few years.[24] As part of my work for this chapter, I read all the comments on the original online petition, an experience I found deeply disheartening. To be clear: I identify as both queer and lesbian; I want my queer history to be inclusive and nuanced, but I had my own pang about the original wording of the plaque. I wanted the word 'lesbian' to be there, even while knowing that using it would be anachronistic, and probably not what Lister would have wanted. 'Gender-nonconforming entrepreneur' felt like a very unsatisfactory and partial description.

Public perceptions of Anne Lister, including my own, were soon to be influenced by a new factor: *Gentleman Jack* was broadcast from 22 April to 10 June 2019 in the USA and from 19 May to 7 July in the UK, nicely timed to coincide with Pride Month in each case. Shibden Hall rapidly became a site of pilgrimage for fans of the series; visitor numbers to the house trebled, and media interest in Anne Lister soared. Lots of well-meaning straight colleagues started asking me if I'd seen *Gentleman Jack* or heard of Anne Lister.

In the run-up to the UK broadcast of the television series, I was interviewed by a journalist, Rebecca Woods, who was writing a piece about Lister for the BBC website.[25] Our email correspondence about Lister and questions of identity made me think about a conversation earlier in 2019 with Dominique Bouchard from English Heritage, about academia and public engagement on LGBTQ+ topics. Dominique had suggested then that we might have to be less nuanced in presenting queer history for a general audience, if the result of trying to be nuanced is that we end up not saying anything at all or end up obscuring or erasing the queerness of historical subjects. In my discussions with Rebecca Woods, the journalist, I tried to emphasise the importance of Lister's place in lesbian history, but I kept getting caught between wanting to say 'yes, of course she's a lesbian' and being acutely aware of the problems with ascribing modern identity categories to historical subjects, and indeed with ascribing lesbian identity in particular to Anne Lister, the woman so often labelled 'the first modern lesbian'.[26]

The Dead Sea Scrolls of Lesbian History

In 2009 or 2010, the historian Laura Doan was approached by a researcher asking if she would be willing to talk about Anne Lister for a television documentary that would present Lister as the first modern lesbian. Mindful of the problems with identity history, Doan explained that she couldn't talk about Lister as unproblematically an example of lesbian identity. The researcher, a bit flustered, went off to check with the programme-makers and came back saying, 'I'm sorry, we really need her to be a lesbian!'[27]

Doan, not surprisingly, did not take part in the documentary, which was made to accompany James Kent's 2010 film, *The Secret Diaries of Miss Anne Lister.* Capitalising on the release of the film, Virago published a revised version of Helena Whitbread's original 1988 selection from Anne Lister's diaries, *I Know My Own Heart*, retitled *The Secret Diaries of Miss Anne Lister.* Above a still from the film showing Maxine Peake and Anna Madeley as Anne Lister and Mariana Lawton, the front cover bears a quotation from Emma Donoghue: 'The Lister diaries are the Dead Sea Scrolls of lesbian history; they changed everything.'[28]

That was rather how it felt, in 1988; the revelations of an early nineteenth-century woman's sexual desire for and sexual exploits with numerous other women were so astonishing that some people actually thought they must be a hoax. It was just too good to be true.[29] The version of lesbian history which Terry Castle mischievously described as 'no lesbians before 1900' was overturned by Lister's detailed record of her love affairs, flirtations, seductions, 'grubbling' (i.e. groping) and multiple 'kisses' (her term for orgasms).[30] Lister's declaration, 'I love, & only love, the fairer sex', was taken up as a statement of lesbian sexual identity, and her assessment of the Ladies of Llangollen's relationship as 'something more tender still than friendship' offered an exhilarating sense of identification.[31] Lister's use of a personal code – her 'crypt hand' – for passages about her sexual activities provided a wonderful metaphor for what had been hidden from history.

Not everyone accepted this view of Lister or her revolutionary effect on lesbian history. In a 2019 blog post on the representation of butchness in recent television dramas, Jack Halberstam noted disapprovingly that there is 'a tendency now to regard Lister as a "lesbian"'. Criticising *Gentleman Jack* for making 'that same mistake', Halberstam stated that

> no such word would have been used during Lister's life-time and the markers of Lister's difference from other women concerned his/her cultivated masculine appearance and his/her desire for women. S/he did not understand herself to be part of a community of others like herself and s/he considered her partners to be women while s/he was something else, something closer to manhood.[32]

Another queer theorist, Annamarie Jagose, similarly insists that 'Lister's many sexual partners do not understand themselves, any more than she understands them, as sharing with Lister a sexual preference, let alone anything like a sexuality. Without exception, Lister's sexual relations with women are not defined as transacted between subjects of the same gender.'[33] As Chris Roulston suggests, 'For eighteenth-century scholars, Lister has repeatedly created a crisis of classification. Labeled as both "the first modern lesbian" and as an example of female masculinity, Lister appears to inhabit and simultaneously to elude the various categories in which she has been placed.'[34] Caroline Baylis-Green argues that 'Lister's *Diaries* show her inhabiting a number of differently gendered personae and subjectivities, which fit more comfortably within a genderqueer or non-binary framework.'[35] Simon Joyce suggests that one of the difficulties for readers of Lister's diaries is 'the absence of stable identity signifiers' but also Lister's need for them, which means that 'she tacks between a number of sexual registers: same-sex desire, the Romantic language of intimate friendship, a language of gender transitivity, and a masculine discourse of sexual libertinism'.[36]

'I look within myself & doubt': Lister's Self-Construction

Despite all these caveats, the 'first modern lesbian' label has adhered to Lister with remarkable persistence, not always helpfully. Jill Liddington's consciously careful description of Lister's diaries as 'the earliest and most candid first-person experience of living a lesbian life' suggests that what's important is not identity, but experience, and particularly the recording of that experience.[37] One of the drawbacks of the 'first modern lesbian' label is that it obscures Lister's work as a writer, presenting the diaries as a straight-from-the-heart outpouring of authentic lesbian emotion. Lister was a self-conscious writer, who reread, indexed and reflected on her own writing, and who thought about becoming a published author.[38] The record of her life comes to us mediated through her deliberate self-construction – she is our source, and that's as problematic as for any other first-person narrative, memoir, journal or epistolary record. Whoever we think she's performing for, even if it's just herself, the sense of an audience and an effect complicated any attempt to see this as an unmediated, innocent or transparent account of the heart she claimed to know so well. Even that claim, 'I know my own heart', is textually mediated, and quoted in French from the opening page of Rousseau's *Confessions*.[39] As Anna Clark notes, Lister's construction of identity drew on Romantic literature (Rousseau and Byron) as well as Greek and Latin classical texts.[40]

Lister's sense of her own sexual and gender identity is hard to pin down. Here, engaging with one of the available terms from her own time, she rejects the idea of a connection between her own desires and actions and Sapphism: 'Got on the subject of Saffic [*sic*] regard. [I] said there was artifice in it. It was very different from mine & would be no pleasure to me.'[41] Lister repeatedly insists on the naturalness of her desire for the fairer sex, and also on her own exceptionalism. Her quotation of Rousseau's claim to be unlike anyone else has often seemed to be taken too much at face value, so that she ends up bearing the whole evidentiary burden of 'proving' lesbian existence in the early nineteenth century. But she is, I think, looking for women like her, not as sexual partners but as models (like the Ladies of Llangollen) or as kindred spirits (like the masculine bluestocking Miss Pickford).[42] She has a network of women friends, some of whom are let into the secret of her code or 'crypt hand', as Anira Rowanchild notes, and with whom she also shares reading practices and gifts of books, as Stephen Colclough has shown.[43] I think there is more of a community here than Halberstam allows for, and I'm interested in the way it keeps dropping out of the picture, whether in critical accounts or dramatisations. Both *Gentleman Jack* and the 2010 film *The Secret Diaries of Miss Anne Lister* focus mainly on the pair-bond – Lister's unhappy relationship with Mariana Belcombe in *Secret Diaries*, and her courtship of Ann Walker in the first series of *Gentleman Jack*. I also think there is something prescriptive in Halberstam's and Jagose's definitions of Lister as not-lesbian because she doesn't want likeness or sameness in her sexual relations, or because she does not see herself as the same as the woman she's having sex with. As I kept finding myself saying to the BBC journalist, it's complicated.

Lister's use of her reading for self-construction has been charted by Anna Clark, Stephen Colclough, Chris Roulston, Marc Schachter, Laurie Shannon, Amy Solomons and Stephen Turton amongst others; but she also constructs herself through the mirror of other women who 'love, & only love, the fairer sex'.[44] Lister's fascination with the Ladies of Llangollen is a particularly rich site for such self-construction, and the effects of her visit to Plas Newydd continue to shape her visions of the life she longs for, in ways that are both practical (her improvements to Shibden's house and grounds) and imaginative.[45] Lister's assessment of Butler and Ponsonby's relationship, prompted by Mariana's question about whether it could be platonic, has been much quoted and discussed:

> I cannot help thinking that surely it was not platonic. Heaven forgive me, but I look within myself & doubt. I feel the infirmity of our nature & hesitate to pronounce such attachments uncemented by something more tender still than friendship. But much, or all, depends upon the story of

> their former lives, the period passed before they lived together, that feverish dream called youth.[46]

But Mariana is not the only woman with whom Lister discusses Butler and Ponsonby; Emma Saltmarshe, a married friend and former flirt, earns Lister's disfavour with her contemptuous account of the Ladies and their estate:

> Mentioned my having seen Miss Ponsonby . . . Not a little to my surprise, Emma launched forth most fluently in dispraise of the place. A little baby house & baby grounds. Bits of painted glass stuck in all the windows. Beautifully morocco-bound books laid about in all the arbours, etc., evidently for shew, perhaps stiff if you touched them & never opened. Tasso, etc., etc. Everything evidently done for effect. She thought they must be 2 romantic girls &, as I walked with her to see her off, she said she had thought it was a pity they were not married; it would do them a great deal of good.[47]

At the risk of over-reading – always a risk with literary critics – I can't help hearing another layer of meaning in Emma Saltmarshe's contemptuous remarks about the Ladies' beautifully bound and displayed books, 'perhaps stiff if you touched them & never opened'. I'm not saying this is a meaning that Emma intends, though in an earlier journal entry Lister comments on Emma's own tendency to over-interpretation: 'She often thinks I mean ten times more than ever entered my head, & fancies smiles & looks & *double entendres* I never dreamt of.'[48] In the wake of Lister's exchange with Mariana about the non-platonic nature of the Ladies' relationship, Emma's suggestion that the Ladies' female bonding may also be 'done for effect', and that they'd be better off married, is a jarring one.

Emma's attack on the Ladies' books and reading seems particularly ill-judged, given the importance that books and reading have in Lister's own life, her sense of her identity and her relationships with other women. When Lister meets Sarah Ponsonby, she compliments Ponsonby on a beautiful bookcase she has noticed earlier, and they discuss reading, translation and poetry. 'Contrived to ask if they were classical,' Lister notes, to which Miss Ponsonby replies, 'No . . . Thank God from Latin & Greek I am free.' They also talk about Byron, who has sent the Ladies 'several of his works', and Lister asks if Miss Ponsonby has read *Don Juan*: 'She was ashamed to say she had read the 1st canto.' As with the question about being classical, Lister seems to be looking for confirmation of likeness, but with limited success.[49]

Lister's visit to the Ladies is a complex event which opens up a world of identification and desire beyond the pair-bond with Mariana. She imagines the possibility of her own desires for domestic partnership with a woman through the Ladies, a process that is strongly evident in her letter to Sibbella Maclean of 19 October 1825. Lister's attempts to persuade Sibbella to come and spend significant time at Shibden, and get to know her better, are bound up with a painful vignette about Butler and Ponsonby's declining health in old age.

> Do turn to my letter again. Perhaps it is merely in that dry sort of style that you would better understand if you had passed a winter with me at Shibden. I have sometimes, they tell me, a way of saying things peculiarly my own. I smiled to read, that it would not now surprise you 'so much', even if I should marry. Be prepared for all things, for I am persuaded 'joy flies monopolists'; and, if you are '*one*', and I am not another 'made to live alone'. I could be happy in a *garret*, or a cellar with the object of my regard, but, in solitude, a prison or a palace would be all alike to me. 'Did Mrs B(arlow) ask your opinion as to marrying?' No! but knowing the circumstances, I have ventured to give it. I have ventured to urge, that the rational union of two amiable persons must be productive of comfort. Trust me, Sibbella, however much you may fancy you differ with me on this subject, we are at heart agreed. There is no pleasure like that of thought meeting thought 'ere from the lips it part'. Give me a mind in unison with my own, and I'll find the way of happiness – without it, I should feel alone among multitudes, and all the world would seem to me a desert.

The letter circles around ideas of marriage, as Lister works to persuade Sibbella of their compatibility and the pleasure it can bring, her prose joining Sibbella and herself as two beings not 'made to live alone' and insisting that 'we are at heart agreed'. The union of like minds becomes something close to a kiss, 'thought meeting thought "ere from the lips it part"'. Lister's hunger for loving companionship and understanding is palpable here; solitude without love is a prison, and the lack of 'a mind in unison with my own' transforms the world into a desert. When Lister turns to the subject of Butler and Ponsonby, presumably in response to something in Sibbella's letter, her own hopes and fears about the possibility of a long-term relationship with Sibbella (older than Lister, aristocratic, potentially the Eleanor Butler to her Sarah Ponsonby) are never far from the surface:

> I was sorry to find it possible for any party of travellers to give such an account of Lady E. B(utler) and Miss Ponsonby. The latter is several years (ten I think) younger than the former, and must be four or five or more years less than eighty. Her first appearance struck me as much, and perhaps, as unfavorably as possible, but there was a flash of mind that bore down on all, and I shall never forget the enchantment that it threw on all around.

> Lady E. B(utler) I have never seen. She was once clever. What she is, it might be humiliating to inquire, for, in this world, minds, like bodies, do appear to wear out. About the time I was at Llangollen the difficulty of seeing the ladies (any one might see the place) seemed considerable. I regret that it is lessened, but the burden of age may lessen the quantity of self-derived resources and thus aggravate the necessity of picking up amusement wherever it is to be had. Lady E. B(utler) has been quite blind more than a year. She had always high spirits, and was always, in this respect, a contrast to her graver friend whom I can well enough imagine to consenting to admit strangers for her friend's sake, and sitting, scarcely uttering a word, intently and almost unconsciously gazing on the eye that could behold that gaze no more. Changed indeed must she be, if there be not a spirit still within her, that, if one spark had lighted it, could not have beamed with all the light of noonday life and intellect! But no more. Should we decay as these have done, may there at last, remain some proud and haughty feelings of reserve, that bars us from the stare of strangers! ... But do try your utmost to let us have an opportunity of coming to a fair understanding of each other's dispositions, &c. &c., next spring. I shall not dare to think much of it for fear of disappointment, but a fortnight will be infinitely better than nothing; and I would endeavour to return with you if possible. Surely, *I shall know you* some time.[50]

Lister imagines what the emotional impact of Lady Eleanor's blindness must be for Ponsonby, even to the extent of seeing Butler from Ponsonby's point of view. It's a complicated act, in which Lister not only imagines an intrusion into the private space of the female couple (whose domestic idyll she seeks to emulate), but performs such an intrusion, becoming a spectator and (in her identification with Ponsonby) a participant in this domestic scene of fragility and vulnerability set against (and menacing) enduring same-sex love. The scene becomes a projection into her own possible old age with Sibbella or another woman companion, at risk of being exposed to the curious and perhaps mocking, gloating, vulgar or disrespectful 'stare of strangers'.

Plaques and Projections

The first time I went to Shibden, for a study day on Lister in the summer of 2014, there was a screening of *The Secret Diaries of Miss Anne Lister* in the Hall in the evening, and from time to time I would glance sideways and see the film's images of Maxine Peake as Lister and Anna Madeley as Mariana reflected in the glass of the Lister family portraits. (Or that's how I remembered it; when I went back to Shibden, I realised the reflection must have been in the photograph of John Lister and his fellow antiquarians, because that's the only one that has glass!) I'm very aware of how *Gentleman Jack* maps and projects a particular image of Lister on to Shibden, in ways more lasting than those fleeting reflections. (Angela Clare's chapter in this volume discusses some of the more lasting material effects of those projected images).

One of the most poignant things for me about season one of *Gentleman Jack* was seeing Suranne Jones as Lister moving through real places that mattered in Lister's life – Shibden, Holy Trinity Goodramgate. Both of those places are altered now by the record of Lister's presence nailed to the walls; the Shibden plaque, in particular, must have been covered up or edited out or filmed around for the shooting of season two. A plaque fixes something in the past, but it's also a tug along the gathers of fabric that pull together past and present. It links person and place but also separates them, holds them apart. It opens up complicated questions about the fixed and the fleeting, and about identity and time.

In his 2018 preface to the twentieth-anniversary edition of *Female Masculinity*, Halberstam offers the image of the butch as a 'bodily catachresis', something that can't be named, or can only be named by a misnomer because the words don't exist for it yet.[51] Halberstam identifies 'what shall hereafter be known as "the temporal paradox of the butch" – s/he is out of time and ahead of his/her time and behind the times all at once'.[52] There's a parallel here with Chris Roulston's 2013 article about Lister as the first modern lesbian, and the way Lister's identity moves both forwards and backwards.[53] But it also made me think about Fanny Derham, in Mary Shelley's 1835 novel *Lodore* – a character who is not a butch as such, though she is described as 'more made to be loved by her own sex than by the opposite one'.[54] Fanny is both closely associated with the ancient world through her reading of Greek and Latin, and someone whose story cannot yet be told by the novel but must wait for an unspecified future time. Like Alice through the looking-glass, I once suggested, the lesbian character of the 1830s can have jam tomorrow, jam yesterday, but never jam today.[55] Questions of lesbian identity seem to present the difficulty, the impossibility even, of being present/being in the present/being now.

Identity categories are necessary fictions, necessary because as queer people we are still under attack. They are powerful and they're tricksy, whether playing over the surface or affixed as a prosthesis or a monument. I talk on Skype with two friends in Canada about all this. 'The plaque is always late from history, but it becomes history itself,' says Nathalie Dupuis-Désormeaux, historian of eighteenth-century music and twenty-first-century composer. She's right: the plaque promises history, the 'real', in a way that – say – the new statue of Anne Lister at the Piece Hall in Halifax doesn't. It can be harder to see the plaque as just another story, another version of Lister, even if that's all it can be. 'The plaque is almost parasitic, like a copyright sign,' the art historian Cristina Martinez tells me.

Cristina's observation about the plaque as copyright sign raises questions of ownership and durability very much at odds with the literally ephemeral cardboard rainbow plaques of Heyam's 2015 project, conceived as an act of love and affective attachment. Heyam's introduction to *Before We Were Trans* notes that they avoid the term 'reclaiming' in the writing of trans history, because of its links with the language of capitalist ownership; they cite Gabrielle M. W. Bychowski's observation that this sort of language fosters an idea of historical representation as 'a scarce resource we need to fight over'.[56] The language of capitalism and ownership has a particular sharpness in relation to Lister and representation, as we wait to find out what will become of *Gentleman Jack* in the wake of its cancellation by HBO: the #SaveGentlemanJack campaign on social media takes place amidst anxious speculation about who might pick up the rights, who has the money to back the series.

The conversational stakes about Lister and identity are higher now than they were when the television researcher told Laura Doan, 'I'm sorry, we really need her to be a lesbian!' There's so much more noise, including the constant outpouring of mainstream media stories about trans issues, most of them hostile. But there's also the amplification created by the *Gentleman Jack* effect: the numbers who feel a sense of identification with Anne Lister, who feel they know her, who have a sense of ownership, as fans and sometimes as researchers. What does it mean, in this context, to talk about what 'we' need Anne Lister to be?

Thanks to the energy unlocked by the television series, the availability of knowledge and information about Lister has increased too, opening up the world of the diaries through the WYAS transcription project. Research on Lister and her world is alive and well in the work of the Anne Lister Society, the Anne Lister Research Summit, the websites 'Packed with Potential' and 'In Search of Ann Walker', funded PhD projects, a special issue of the *Journal of Lesbian Studies*, and indeed the present volume. In 2014, the audience for the first Anne Lister Study Day fitted (rather tightly) into one small room at Shibden Hall; the idea of a week-long celebration of Lister that could fill Halifax Minster was unimaginable. Whatever happens with *Gentleman Jack*, the future of Lister Studies is something to celebrate, and so is this messy, complicated, expansive conversation about who we think she was, and why and how she matters so much.

Conclusion: No Time like the Present

It's April 2022, and I'm back at Shibden, on the Complete Anne and Ann Coach and Walking Tour, as part of the festivities for the long-awaited Anne Lister Birthday Week. The lawn in front of the house is covered with stalls selling *Gentleman Jack*-themed gin, notebooks, walking sticks, art, postcards, memorabilia, and pin badges of the Shibden plaque and of the revised York plaque. There are people in Victorian costumes; I'm not sure which ones are *Gentleman Jack* fans doing cosplay and which ones are stallholders. A man and a woman in Victorian dress are walking around on stilts. It's snowing, just a little, but the sun comes out while our tour group is going round the house. I'm thinking about all the other times I've been here, about the layers of memory and identity that line these walls. Thinking about the inaugural Anne Lister Society meeting later this week, and how the audience for my work on Lister feels so different in 2022 from the one I imagined when I started it in 2018. I'm thinking about what it means, finding the words for Anne Lister: how and where she found the words for herself; how and where we find the words for her, and how they slip or how they stay. About who 'we' are, too, and what we do: code-breakers, scholars, fans, critics, theorists; Civic Trusts and other affixers of plaques; screenwriters, artists; LGBTQ+ people in search of our own history. About the way these categories, too, layer and overlap. About how it's complicated, it's always complicated, finding the words for identity, and how the pursuit of knowledge is bound up with emotion and desire. This is not neutral territory; it never was.

Shibden in brilliant sunshine; I go out to the carriage barn again and take another picture of the doorway. *Everything beyond this point is fiction.*

Notes

1 'Plaque in York Honours "First Modern Lesbian" Anne Lister', BBC News, 24 July 2018, www.bbc.co.uk/news/uk-england-york-north-yorkshire-44938819, accessed 31 July 2022.
2 K. Heyam, *Before We Were Trans* (London: Basic Books, 2022), pp. 87–8.
3 'Anne Lister was a Lesbian: Don't Let them Erase her Story', Change.org petition, 2018, www.change.org/p/to-york-lgbt-history-month-york-civic-trust-anne-lister-was-a-lesbian-don-t-let-them-erase-her-story, accessed 7 August 2022.

4 'Statement on Anne Lister's Rainbow Plaque', issued September 2018 by York Civic Trust, Churches Conservation Trust, York LGBT Forum and York LGBT History Month, https://gallery.mailchimp.com/d75e42de126fedb389cf4f417/files/0d6bf24a-8d10-4ded-9755-181c32598987/2018_09_01_Consultation_Rainbow_Plaque_Postion_Statement_Final.pdf, accessed 22 February 2023.

5 'Rainbow Plaque Honouring Halifax's Anne Lister to Feature the Word "Lesbian" after Backlash', *Halifax Courier*, 21 December 2018, www.halifaxcourier.co.uk/news/rainbow-plaque-honouring-halifaxs-anne-lister-feature-word-lesbian-after-backlash-182102, accessed 10 August 2022.

6 'Helena Whitbread: Anne Lister Plaque Unveiling in York', YouTube video, https://youtu.be/Jfs297sN7bc, accessed 8 August 2002.

7 '[O]ne of the problems was that trying to say "marriage" without saying "marriage" (which we had to do because other organisations involved in the plaque were concerned about "historical accuracy" and religious sensitivity) took up quite a lot of words!'; K. R. Heyam, comment on York LGBT Forum, 'A Sneak Peek at the First Ever PERMANENT Rainbow Plaque!', Facebook, 21 July 2018, www.facebook.com/yorklgbthistory/posts/pfbidoy8mT4jzrSoDkhzSmwxSzbUJUpmcssWtfrH1h2sPBGzJpjPJNPYn4YTJfFKDjLj21l?comment_id=2033959806678210, accessed 10 August 2022.

8 S. Joyce, 'The Perverse Presentism of Rainbow Plaques: Memorializing Anne Lister', *Nineteenth-Century Contexts* 41.5 (2019), 601–10, 603.

9 Ibid., 601.

10 Ibid., 604.

11 Ibid., 606.

12 Ibid., 608.

13 Heyam, *Before We Were Trans*, p. 88.

14 Ibid.

15 Comments in discussion on Facebook post, 30 July 2018, quoting York LGBT History Month's statement about the controversy, www.facebook.com/nimda.wgrid/posts/pfbidoph4w8k8KoHEW6ra8W4cnUNKpFLJQ1jARcmtp4KQWKydWDYrQxHy1Fp1LqjckhMmPl, accessed 10 August 2022. York Civic Trust's statement about the wording was reported in Lydia Smith, 'Anne Lister: 2,000 People Sign Petition against "Erasure" of "First Modern Lesbian" Plaque', *PinkNews*, 3 August 2018:

'York Civic Trust told *PinkNews* the decision of the plaque wording was the result of a "long-thought-out process" at the request of the LGBT partner groups who "had argued it among themselves". "The wording that we chose was supposed to be – I don't know whether it's going to be successful – but it was supposed to be factual and 'future-proofed' so it's understandable into the future without changes in social connotation," York Civic Trust chief executive Dr David Fraser said. "We are conscious that we may have got it wrong," he added'; www.pinknews.co.uk/2018/08/03/anne-lister-2000-people-sign-petition-against-erasure-of-first-modern-lesbian-plaque/, accessed 10 August 2022.

16 D. Cameron, 'Coming to Terms with the Past: What Should we Call Anne Lister?', www.debuk.wordpress.com/2018/11/08/coming-to-terms-with-the-past-what-should-we-call-anne-lister/, accessed 7 August 2022.
17 S. Faye, *The Transgender Issue* (London: Penguin, 2021), p. 80.
18 Heyam, *Before We Were Trans*, p. 87. Images of the cardboard Rainbow Plaques project can be seen at www.sahgb.org.uk/features/rainbow-plaques-making-queer-history-visible.
19 Heyam, *Before We Were Trans*, p. 88.
20 Ibid.
21 Ibid. p. 89.
22 Ibid., p. 90.
23 'Plaque in York Honours "First Modern Lesbian" Anne Lister', BBC News, 24 July 2018, www.bbc.co.uk/news/uk-england-york-north-yorkshire-44938819, accessed 31 July 2022.
24 R. Pearce, S. Erikainen and B. Vincent, 'TERF Wars: an Introduction', *Sociological Review Monographs* 68.4 (2020), 677–98; GATE, *Mapping Anti-Gender Movements in the UK* (New York: GATE, 2022).
25 Rebecca Woods, 'The Life and Loves of Anne Lister', BBC News, 3 May 2019, www.bbc.co.uk/news/resources/idt-sh/the_life_and_loves_of_anne_lister, accessed 10 August 2022.
26 C. Roulston, 'The Revolting Anne Lister: the UK's First Modern Lesbian', in K. Browne et al. (eds.), *Revolting Bodies: Desiring Lesbians*, special issue of *Journal of Lesbian Studies* 17.3–4 (Spring 2013), 267–78.
27 L. Doan, keynote address, 20th Annual Lesbian Lives Conference, 'The Modern Lesbian', Brighton, 15–16 February 2013.
28 H. Whitbread (ed.), *The Secret Diaries of Miss Anne Lister* (London: Virago, 2010). Virago's subsequent reprinting was titled *The Secret Diaries of Miss Anne Lister, vol. I: I Know My Own Heart*; they also reprinted Whitbread's second volume of selections, *No Priest but Love*, as *The Secret Diaries of Miss Anne Lister, vol. II: No Priest but Love* (London: Virago, 2020).
29 '[A] daily memoir of so extraordinary a candour that it was difficult not to think it a forgery'; E. Mavor, 'Gentleman Jack from Halifax', *London Review of Books* 10.3 (1988), 18–19, quoted in F. Brideoake, *The Ladies of Llangollen* (Lewisburg: Bucknell University Press, 2017), p. 31; 'more than a few readers (myself included) questioned the diary's authenticity'; A. Jagose, *Inconsequence: Lesbian Representation and the Logic of Sexual Sequence* (Ithaca: Cornell University Press, 2002), p. 14.
30 T. Castle, *The Apparitional Lesbian* (New York: Columbia University Press, 1993), p. 9.
31 Monday, 29 January 1821, in Whitbread, *Secret Diaries* (2010), p. 161, and Sunday, 3 August 1822, p. 229.
32 J. Halberstam, 'A (K)night of a Thousand Butches', blog post 21 May 2019, bullybloggers.wordpress.com/2019/05/21/a-knight-of-a-thousand-butches-by-jack-halberstam/, accessed 23 July 2022.
33 Jagose, *Inconsequence*, p. 21

34 C. Roulston, 'Transgender Identifications and the Case of Anne Lister', paper presented to the 2015 Annual Meeting of the American Society for Eighteenth Century Studies, Los Angeles, 19–21 March.

35 C. Baylis-Green, 'Queer Subjectivities, Closeting and Non-Normative Desire in Nineteenth-Century Women's Poetry and Life Writing', PhD thesis, Manchester Metropolitan University (2015), p. 65.

36 Joyce, 'Perverse Presentism', 604–5.

37 J. Liddington, talk given at Anne Lister Birthday Weekend, Halifax Minster, 2 April 2022.

38 On Lister's indexing practices, see J. Beyer and D. Orr, '"Wrote the above of today": Anne Lister's Writings', https://youtu.be/s9qY3ap5T74, accessed 23 July 2022.

39 20 August 1823, in Whitbread, *Secret Diaries*, p. 306.

40 A. Clark, 'Anne Lister's Construction of Lesbian Identity', *Journal of the History of Sexuality* 7.1 (July 1996), 23–50; see also her more recent discussion in *Alternative Histories of the Self* (London: Bloomsbury, 2017).

41 Saturday, 13 November 1824, in H. Whitbread (ed.), *No Priest but Love* (New York: New York University Press, 1992), p. 49. See Turton, this volume, for a discussion of Whitbread's transcription here.

42 The WYAS transcription project shows the complexity of Lister's relationship with Miss Pickford in ways there isn't space to discuss here, including Lister's suspicion that Miss Pickford is becoming emotionally attached to her.

43 A. Rowanchild, '"My Mind on Paper": Anne Lister and the Construction of Lesbian Identity', in A. Donnell and P. Polkey (eds.), *Representing Lives: Women and Auto/Biography* (London: Macmillan, 2000), pp. 199–207; S. Colclough, '"Do You Not Know the Quotation?": Reading Anne Lister, Anne Lister Reading', in J. C. Beynon and C. Gonda (eds.), *Lesbian Dames: Sapphism in the Long Eighteenth Century* (Farnham: Ashgate, 2010), pp. 159–72.

44 Clark, 'Anne Lister's Construction'; Colclough, 'Do You Not Know The Quotation?'; C. Roulston, 'Sexuality in Translation: Anne Lister and the Ancients', *Journal of the History of Sexuality* 30.1 (January 2021), 112–35; M. Schachter, 'Making Sense in the Margins: Anne Lister's Notes on Juvenal', paper presented at the Anne Lister Society inaugural meeting, Halifax, 8 April 2022; L. Shannon, 'Anne Lister Reading Genesis: Apples and Etymologies', paper presented at the Anne Lister Society inaugural meeting, Halifax, 8 April 2022, and Shannon, this volume; A. Solomons, '"I am happy among my books – I am not happy without them": Navigating Anne Lister's Reading', paper presented at the Anne Lister Society inaugural meeting, Halifax, 8 April 2022; Turton, this volume.

45 On Lister's improvements to Shibden as influenced by Plas Newydd, see A. Rowanchild, '"Everything Done for Effect": Georgic, Gothic and Picturesque in Anne Lister's Self-Production', *Women's Writing* 7.1 (2000), 89–104.

46 Sunday, 3 August 1822, in Whitbread, *Secret Diaries*, p. 229.

47 Sunday, 10 August 1822, in ibid., p. 230.

48 Sunday, 24 June 1821, in ibid., p. 171.
49 Tuesday, 23 July 1822, in ibid., p. 221
50 Anne Lister to Sibbella Maclean, 19 October 1825, in M. Green (ed.), *Miss Lister of Shibden Hall: Selected Letters, 1600–1840* (Lewes: Book Guild, 1992), pp. 87–9.
51 J. Halberstam, 'Preface to the Twentieth Anniversary Edition', in *Female Masculinity* (Durham, NC: Duke University Press, 2018), p. xx.
52 Ibid., p. xix.
53 Roulston, 'The Revolting Anne Lister'.
54 M. Shelley, *Lodore*, ed. L. Vargo (Peterborough, Ontario: Broadview Press, 1997), p. 317.
55 C. Gonda, '*Lodore* and Fanny Derham's Story', *Women's Writing* 6.3 (1999), 329–44.
56 Heyam, *Before We Were Trans*, p. 27.

CHAPTER 12

From Anne Lister to Gentleman Jack*: Queer Temporality, Fandom and the Gains and Losses of Adaptation*

Chris Roulston

In 2019, the diaries of Anne Lister exploded on to the screen in the form of *Gentleman Jack*, the BBC/HBO series starring Suranne Jones and Sophie Rundle and directed by the award-winning Sally Wainwright. Season one, which focuses on the period of Lister's relationship with Ann Walker, with whom Lister privately sealed a union in Holy Trinity church in York, attracted six million viewers. Season two aired in April 2022 and a BBC One documentary, *Gentleman Jack Changed My Life*, also aired in May 2022.[1] As the BBC documentary title suggests, *Gentleman Jack* has generated a devoted queer and lesbian fanbase, many of whom have claimed the series has transformed their lives.

Through a queer temporality framework, this chapter analyses the effects of the Lister diaries' transition from scholarly archive to mainstream entertainment culture. *Gentleman Jack* has already given rise to scholarly articles and in *The* Gentleman Jack *Effect: Lessons in Breaking Rules and Living Out Loud* (2021), Janet Lea has gathered testimonies from viewers whose lives have been radically transformed by watching season one.[2] Fans have also responded to the show on Twitter and Tumblr, and in 2019, *Diva* published a detailed article by another of the show's early fans, Rachel Biggs, where she describes how deeply the series affected her.[3] By exploring such responses to *Gentleman Jack*, this chapter asks what gains and losses are involved in terms of our relationship to the queer past by translating the Lister archive into the sphere of popular culture.

In *A Theory of Adaptation*, Linda Hutcheon argues that adaptations have always existed – at least from the classical period onwards – and that they are far from being a 'minor and subsidiary' genre that can never live up to the original.[4] She conceptualises adaptation not as a copy, but rather as an 'oscillation', a 're-mediation' and a form of translation between the source text and its reworking.[5] As with translation, adaptation 'has its own aura' and creates its own resonances;[6] borrowing from Walter Benjamin, Hutcheon argues that adaptation, like translation, 'is an engagement with the original text that makes us see the text in different ways'.[7] In other words, adaptation is less a copy of the original than a reinvention and a reimagining of the source text in an ever-evolving present. While adaptation can range in terms of its political register, it is always responding to its historical moment.

In this sense, adaptation speaks to queer theory's refusal of origins, its challenge to linear temporality and its sense of the performative. Hutcheon continues: 'Despite being temporally second, [adaptation] is both an interpretive and a creative act; it is storytelling as both rereading and rerelating.'[8] Within this paradigm, adaptation is a form of queering, in that queerness has always engaged critically with secondariness, imitation and the hierarchy of origins. How, then, might this frame the encounter between adaptation as an engagement with genre and queer theory as an engagement with gender in relation to the Lister diaries and their televisual adaptation? How does the fan response to the adaptation engage with the nonconforming Lister of the historical archive?

Wainwright has herself resisted the term 'adaptation', which she argues suggests the smooth translation from a coherent, recognisable genre to another equally stable generic form, such as novel to film or theatre to musical. In contrast, the Lister diaries were like 'juggling with mercury' and were constantly slipping through her fingers.[9] In the interview with Emma Donoghue for this volume, Wainwright prefers to call her work on Lister 'a dramatisation of a real life'.[10] Rather than seeing them as a fixed account, Wainwright experienced the diaries as an evolving form with unpredictable narrative threads and dead ends. The Lister diaries tell the story of a life evolving on a day-to-day basis, with no endpoint from which the work can be rendered fully coherent. The diaries simply stop when Anne Lister falls ill on her travels and dies. Therefore, Wainwright has had to engage in her own to and fro between history and story – a process that has led to the inclusion of many of the diaries' events and anecdotes and direct transcriptions of the diaries' language into the show – as well as creating a fictional frame to fit the demands of prime-time television.[11]

Gentleman Jack aligns with what Eve Ng, borrowing from Claire Monk, has termed quality 'post-heritage' drama, as well as with the literary concept of 'neo-historical fiction', coined by Katharine Harris.[12] For these scholars, the more recent iterations of historical drama – both on screen and in novel form – self-consciously incorporate an aspect of the present into representations of the past, often through 'the conspicuous use of anachronisms',[13] or by including previously unrepresented subject positions in terms of race, class, sexuality and gender. According to Harris, the goal is to 'push beyond what we know or think is "true" about the past in order to invent new histories'.[14] Both Ng and Harris invoke Sarah Waters's queer lesbian nineteenth-century novels – several of which have been adapted for television by the BBC – as examples of post-heritage and neo-historical narratives that laid the groundwork for queer historical representation.

In televisual terms, the show that *Gentleman Jack* most resembles is the BBC's production of *Portrait of a Marriage* (1990), a three-part mini-series about Vita Sackville-West's 1920s affair with Violet Trefusis, based on Nigel Nicolson's biographical account of his parents' marriage. It stars Janet McTeer as Vita and Cathryn Harrison as Violet, and as with *Gentleman Jack*, it is a historically grounded lesbian narrative. Further echoing the Lister archive, Sackville-West kept a detailed diary of her affair with Violet, as well as with other lovers. Janet McTeer's performance as Vita also parallels Suranne Jones's as Lister in its gender nonconforming presentation and claiming of lesbian sexuality, to the point where Nigel Nicolson, who sold the rights to *Portrait of a Marriage*, argued that the production 'had too much sex in it' and that '[t]he affair could have been suggested much more delicately; it could be done by gesture and look, not necessarily by performance'.[15]

The historical distance between 1990 and 2019, when *Gentleman Jack* aired on BBC's Sunday evening prime-time slot, can best be summed up by contemporary critics' positive response to the representation of lesbian sex on screen.[16] However, for an adaptation such as *Portrait of a Marriage*, which appeared prior to the advent of social media – Facebook having started in 2004 – it is harder to gauge the emergence of a fanbase. While *Diva*, the UK's most widely circulated lesbian magazine, was founded in 1994 and played a key role in disseminating lesbian subculture, nothing resembles the rhizomatic influence of the internet. Therefore, although *Portrait of a Marriage* can be compared to *Gentleman Jack* in terms of content, it is harder to do so in terms of reception. This is reflected in the fanbase itself, which has responded to *Gentleman Jack* as if such lesbian televisual representation of lives from the past was the first of its kind.

Unpacking the underlying causes that have led fans to become so affectively attached to *Gentleman Jack* can give us certain insights into the gains and losses of adaptation and help us to understand the affective mechanisms of post-heritage drama for a queer and lesbian audience. This attachment also engages with questions of queer temporality, in that the fanbase is finding something entirely new in the old and moving backwards in time as a way of reclaiming a present that is itself saturated with a certain kind of nostalgia. As a source text, the Lister diaries are contesting the gender and sexual norms of nineteenth-century society, and Wainwright's challenge has been to capture their already existing nonconformity for a twenty-first-century audience. How can Lister appear queer both in her time and in ours? And what is it, exactly, that the fans have been responding to with such passionate commitment?

At the same time, as Ng suggests, part of the appeal of *Gentleman Jack* lies as much in what is familiar as in what is ground-breaking. As a more lavish production than the original BBC *Secret Diaries of Miss Anne Lister* (2010), *Gentleman Jack* fulfils the mandate of quality drama with its 'innovations in storytelling', its 'high production values' and its 'distinctive aesthetic qualities'.[17] These elements place *Gentleman Jack* alongside the familiar adaptations of Jane Austen novels and create certain expectations in the viewer, ones that include 'a certain image of England and Englishness'[18] generated through what James Leggott and Julie Taddeo describe as key visual hallmarks, such as English landscaping and the representation of stately homes.[19] In its exploitation of certain visual tropes that connote Englishness, such as the rolling hills of the Yorkshire landscape and scenes set in both Walker's and Lister's manor houses, *Gentleman Jack* participates in a mode of representation which Ng notes continues to depend on 'hierarchies of class, race, and nation that have long structured the narratives of the genre'.[20]

The familiar therefore rubs up against the unfamiliar, in that *Gentleman Jack* subverts the content but not the context of quality historical drama. Indeed, one fan became attracted to the show because it was taking place around Jane Austen's time and she knew she would be treated to the familiar props and landscapes of the Regency and early Victorian eras.[21] While Ng is more critical of *Gentleman Jack*'s adherence to the dramatic conventions that reinforce the norms of a certain nostalgic Englishness, Sarah E. Maier and Rachel M. Friars argue that the show also challenges the conventions of historical drama by including multiple perspectives beyond Lister's own privileged one and 'frequent[ly] abandons Lister in favour of a wider picture of rural English life in the 1830s'.[22] This also distinguishes the *Gentleman Jack* series from the first BBC feature adaptation of the Lister diaries, which was entirely from Lister's perspective.

Gentleman Jack's newness, in this sense, depends on how it takes up quality heritage television conventions as a way of subverting certain, although not all, of our expectations. The show also speaks to what Paula Blank argues is a turning away from queer history as 'alterity' and seeing the past 'in terms of difference', towards an embracing of the non-linear and what Madhavi Menon has called 'homohistory' and Carolyn Dinshaw has framed as 'touching across time'.[23] For Blank, the history of sexuality is less forward-moving than palimpsestic, with different models co-existing over the centuries and producing both a mode of 'self-othering' and a 'queer . . . desire for a provisional reidentification with the past'.[24] Carla Freccero has also argued for thinking about the past as a form of 'queer spectrality', a haunting in which 'the past or the future presses upon us with a kind of insistence or demand, a demand to which we must somehow respond'.[25] For Maier and Friars, *Gentleman Jack* positions Lister as 'the connective tissue' between 'a lost past and present paradigm'.[26] In each of these approaches to the queerly historical and the historically queer, there is a desire for both a recuperation of the queer past – defined as it has been by erasure and invisibility – and a refusal to read it in terms of progression. The queer past, these theorists argue, is a living, tactile thing that engages and simultaneously eludes us in a continuous back and forth. Furthermore, in producing an affective rather than a strictly scholarly engagement with the queer historical past, *Gentleman Jack* has created a fluid mode of identification that lies somewhere between fact and fiction.[27]

In fans' responses, there is an implicit recognition of the precarity of queer history and of the unlikely possibility that a series tied to such an archive could exist in the first place. The diaries not only came close to being burned when their encrypted content was first decoded in the 1890s, but they also languished in various repositories for one hundred and fifty years before extracts of the coded sections were published by Helena Whitbread in 1988 and the modern world was ready to read them. The *Gentleman Jack* adaptation of the Lister diaries therefore parallels and undoes the scholarly project in various ways. While the role of the traditional scholar can be thought of as seeking out the truth of the past through accurate historical contextualisation and reconstruction – the past as fully footnoted – the role of the scriptwriter might be seen as adapting the past for the purposes of the present, and for an audience who may have no particular investment in history per se. In the case of *Gentleman Jack*, many fans will have experienced the adaptation *as the original.*

In this sense, *Gentleman Jack* has created a new kind of originating moment for the diaries themselves. Unlike the Anne Lister BBC film, *Gentleman Jack* covers a relatively small portion of the diaries. It is set in the year 1832, when Lister is forty-one years old and has just been rejected by her Scottish lover, Vere Hobart. At this point, Lister is looking for a more permanent companion, having had, over the past twenty years or so, a series of flirtations and more serious affairs with women from the surrounding area and during her stay in Paris in 1824. The first season's eight episodes follow Lister's encounter with and courtship of Ann Walker, a neighbouring heiress who, like Lister, has inherited her own property but is considerably wealthier. Walker is presented as feminine and relatively fragile, and although she is clearly in love with Lister, we see her turning down Lister's initial proposal of 'marriage', the social anomaly of this being too much for Walker to envisage. The couple undergo several setbacks, including Walker's feelings of anxiety over her attraction to Lister and subsequent breakdown. After a separation of some months, the couple are reunited in the final episode, and this time Walker is the one to bring up the marriage proposal, which both then enthusiastically commit to.

Supplementing the couple's romance narrative, we have scenes of Lister's family life, including her close relationship with her aunt and uncle and her sparring and competitive relationship with her sister, Marian. We see Lister dealing with her tenants, competing with the local coal baron, Mr Rawson, and developing her plans to sink her own pit. We also witness her being harassed and accosted on a country road and, of course, we see her writing her diary. As mentioned, landscape plays a key role and scenes of Yorkshire, Halifax, Shibden Hall and Crow Nest are interspersed with European travel, as in episode seven when Lister is invited to the court of the Queen of Denmark.

Through Jones's portrayal, Lister's gentlemanly cosmopolitanism compellingly combines visual and narrative pleasure and the viewer cannot but fully champion her courtship of Ann Walker. (See Figure 8) Yet this on-screen seduction raises interesting questions about its off-screen effects and the fans' own experience of being seduced. Fans have reacted to the show's familiar romance landmarks as much as to its innovative reworking of the romance trope. This has led to three broad modes of response from the fanbase: a sense of community building that connects past and present, personal narratives of self-transformation, and acute feelings of nostalgia and loss. We will unpack these affective responses in order to analyse the *Gentleman Jack* effect in terms of our twenty-first-century understandings of gender and sexuality.

The fanbase has organised itself in different ways, with one of its most striking characteristics being lesbian community building. This has taken place largely on Facebook, coalescing around a lesbian-identified fanbase through various Facebook groups, such as the 'Lister Sisters' and 'Shibden after Dark'. Fans can, of course, belong to multiple platforms depending on their needs and wants. These groups have in turn generated further

Figure 8 *Gentleman Jack*, season one.
© Lookout Point/HBO. Photography Matt Squire.

adaptive mutations, such as cosplay and fanfiction. The Facebook fandom phenomenon is also what led Janet Lea to collect and publish fans' responses in *The* Gentleman Jack *Effect*. Lea is a native of Texas and full-time writer, and her book of interviews with *Gentleman Jack* fans was published in September 2021, barely two years after the airing of season one. Lea frames her project through a specifically lesbian lens, shaping the connection between Jones's Lister, Rundle's Walker and the fanbase as a lesbian one, even though there are also non-lesbian participants and the term 'lesbian' never appears in the Lister diaries.

Lea's range of participants has an impressive global reach, with fans from Kenya, New Zealand, Singapore and the Philippines, among others, encompassing sixty-nine interviews from sixteen countries, only a small selection of the six hundred responses from forty-four countries Lea received when she sent out her questionnaire on Facebook. The *Gentleman Jack* HBO/BBC Facebook group itself contains 10,000 members 'of all ages from 100 different countries'.[28] The use of Facebook as the interview source also signals a particular demographic, and although some fans are in their twenties, the majority are between thirty and seventy years old, which also potentially speaks to their predominant identification as lesbian rather than more recently available terms, suggesting a generational reclaiming of lesbian identity through the figure of 'Gentleman Jack'.

Within this construction of lesbian community, fans describe moments of self-transformation and experiences of identification across time. This identification, in turn, depends on reading Lister as an authentic subject as well as a post-heritage drama lesbian heroine. Authenticity has many resonances, from designating an original document (as in the authentic Lister diaries), to being based on fact (as in the authentic historical archive), to the existential notion of living responsibly (as in living an authentic life), all of which are reflected in fans' responses to *Gentleman Jack*.[29] Fans talk about feelings of recognition and familiarity – 'I felt like I was going home'[30] – as well as becoming who they were supposed to be: 'It's all about just becoming who I really want to be, really who I have been all along.'[31] One of the most moving interviews is with seventy-one-year-old Inna Clawsette (pseudonym), who had been in a heterosexual marriage for thirty years and who had always felt something was missing. She says that after watching *Gentleman Jack*, 'For the first time in my life, I could just be myself . . . and that changed me.'[32] Jones's Lister externalises and makes visible a desire for authenticity that fans come to recognise in themselves, often for the first time. Fans also oscillate between idealising Lister and idealising the Lister–Walker couple, so that part of the fantasy of authenticity *Gentleman Jack* provides is relational: 'If Anne and Ann could be themselves nearly 200 years ago, surely I could do the same in 2019.'[33]

Another identificatory thread that reappears between Jones's Lister and the fans' responses is Lister's firm sense of self at a time when there was no clear language to support it. Paradoxically, it is Lister's absence of identificatory language that creates a strong identification among the fans. The fact that Lister could *be* herself without having to *name* herself seems to open up opportunities for fans who have also struggled with questions of naming, whether in terms of coming out of the closet, asserting themselves in different realms such as the workplace, or resisting certain labels. In this sense, Wainwright's representation of Lister has produced a psychological openness to new trajectories of selfhood.

This sense of newness has created an unprecedented interest in queer historical representation and in the possibilities the past can offer. Accompanying fans' recognition of Lister's existential authenticity – which arguably could also be applied to the characters in adaptations of Waters's novels – is Lister's historical authenticity. In her preface, Lea acknowledges the significance of *Gentleman Jack*'s tie to the historical Anne Lister:

'Thanks to *Gentleman Jack*, I fell in love with a woman who had been buried for nearly two hundred years.'[34] Older fans such as Kate Brown from the United States, in her mid-sixties, have described a form of temporal identification with Lister: 'Seeing that, on TV this late in life and knowing there was a real person who experienced what we've experienced and she did it 200 years ago, was so validating for me.'[35] In this interview, Kate is identifying her queer Baltimore youth in the 1970s with the experiences of nineteenth-century Lister, collapsing both time and place in ways that invoke Dinshaw's notion of 'touching across time'. The historical is subsumed under the personal as well as expanded to include past and present in a synchronous fashion. In this moment of temporal connectivity, Lister's story simultaneously represents both her own present and Kate's past.

For many fans, there is the added experience of unmediated spontaneity, the coming upon Lister without premeditation or intent, which has generated a feeling of authentic connection. Patience, a queer Kenyan fan who settled in the United States in part to escape the gender-normative social structures of her homeland, writes: 'I caught a snippet of Anne Lister when she adjusts her top hat with her stick, and I remember thinking, "What is that? That looks gay."'[36] Patience is one of many fans who came upon *Gentleman Jack* spontaneously and who describes the effect of the series as having a direct impact on her life, from making her change her wardrobe to feeling 'more comfortable and more self-assured'.[37] Jones's Lister created in Patience a new sense of freedom because the character herself claimed that same freedom. Most surprising in this interview is Patience's cross-race as well as her transhistorical identification with Lister. Already positioned outside the American norm by her race – 'everywhere I go, people see me first and foremost as black'[38] – Patience seems to have found a kindred spirit in Lister's own outlier status that combines race and sexuality. Patience, like Lister, finds herself the object of the gaze, and she admires Lister's refusal to be defined by that normative gaze: 'She wasn't looking to be validated by other people. She just knew – in an environment where the culture didn't even have words to describe who she was.'[39] Here the language of existential authenticity enables both a transhistorical and transracial reading of Lister, allowing Patience to see herself in Lister across time.

The queer temporal effect of the Lister diaries – that of moving backwards in time in order to experience a new sense of the present – has a geographical as well as a historical component. One of the more detailed interviews is with Jen Carter from Maharashtra, India, and as with

Patience, it documents some of the difficulties the LGBTQ+ community faces in countries lacking certain human rights protections. In India, even though homosexuality was officially decriminalised in 2018, 'disapproval . . . remains high'.[40] Jen's response to the show is particularly striking in terms of India's own complex history of British colonisation, which was at its height in Lister's era.[41] Lea explains that when Jen was a child, 'her father had given her Jane Austen novels to read to improve her English'.[42] However, in reading *Pride and Prejudice*, rather than being attracted to the figure of Mr Darcy, Jen wanted to *be* him, so that in this case, the British colonial canon is queered by its postcolonial reader and *Gentleman Jack* ultimately provided the perfect Darcy replacement.

As with Patience, Jen finds herself collapsing her personal history into Lister's narrative: 'When I saw the first episode of *Gentleman Jack* and Anne's problems with Vere Hobart, I thought to myself, "Oh my God, I'm watching this – it's my life!"'[43] Importantly, the nineteenth-century constraints around gender and sexuality in Lister's life potentially resemble those in Jen's life more closely than for a Western viewer. While Jen's father was extremely understanding of Jen's sexuality, her female partner's father threatened to kill himself if she did not go through with her arranged marriage.[44] As a result, both young women attempted suicide and their relationship fell apart, a narrative that contains echoes of Ann Walker's own breakdown in response to the constraints of nineteenth-century norms. Nine years later, Jen discovered *Gentleman Jack*: 'Without *Gentleman Jack* I don't know when I would have had the courage to come out.'[45] Lea explains that Jen took the final step by posting her story, along with a photograph of herself, on the 'Shibden after Dark' website on 3 April 2020, Anne Lister's birthday.

In these accounts, the queer lesbian viewer is rendered authentic through the converging vectors of authenticity, as feelings of familiarity, of 'going home' and of historical connection become part of the viewing experience. Yet the issue of authenticity is far from straightforward, as it begs the question of what is being authenticated. To begin with, fans are engaging with a mediated version of Lister, one that has been inevitably shaped and glamorised in the tradition of costume drama, even if that tradition is being queerly challenged. They are also responding to the strategic anachronisms that Wainwright has put in place. This generates a form of historical desire in which 'the creative space of fiction' is used 'to resist a linear construction of time', allowing us to 'imagine anachronistic queer histories'.[46] As Harris points out, the use of anachronism displaces conventional historical representation by layering the present on to the past and producing an affective desire for a relation across time that challenges linear models of historical authenticity.

In particular, the technique of breaking the fourth wall not only creates a synchronous bond between viewer and actor, collapsing past and present, but also produces an intimacy that echoes the genre of the diary, as if Lister were letting the viewer into her private, intimate world. As Wainwright says in her interview, Lister 'talking to camera . . . was a no-brainer because it's just like the immediacy of reading the journal'.[47] In these anachronistic moments of connection, Jones's Lister quotes directly from the diaries, returning us to the original source at the very moment when Jones in the present is displacing the Lister of the past. The breaking of the fourth wall not only reminds the viewer that they are watching a fictional performance on screen, but also brings attention to the fact of adaptation. In this sense, the figure of Lister becomes more historical – through her original words addressed directly to the viewer – and less so – through Jones's direct gaze into the viewer's sitting room.

Several fans, such as Michaela Dresel from New Zealand, have recorded the breaking of the fourth wall as being a defining moment: 'The fourth wall breaks in the show when Anne Lister looks into the camera and quotes from her diaries got me hooked.'[48] Katherina Oh from Singapore experienced the breaking of the fourth wall as a mode of 'cheeky . . . flirting', saying, 'I loved when Suranne Jones broke the fourth wall. She is very cheeky when she does the raising of her eyebrows and flirting with the camera.'[49] It is also significant that while Dresel refers to Anne Lister, Oh refers to Suranne Jones, so that while Dresel is inside the narrative and sustains the fiction of Lister's presence, Oh steps outside it.

A further paradox of the felt authenticity of Lister and Walker in *Gentleman Jack* lies in Wainwright's exploitation of sartorial seduction, made possible by the show's status as a high-quality drama production. Perhaps the most idealised and fictionalised aspect of the series, and of a quality well beyond what Lister herself would have worn or been able to afford, the *Gentleman Jack* wardrobe adds a visual and tactile glamour to the characters that seduces the viewing public and paradoxically affirms a mode of queer authenticity. While Lister appears in black skirts and a military-inspired greatcoat, Ann Walker's richly textured dresses allude to the eighteenth-century portraiture of a Fragonard or a Boucher. Furthermore, the gender-bending butch–femme contrast of Lister and Walker references the queer tradition of gender performativity and a queer sartorial history that spans the twentieth century, from the aristocratic Radclyffe Hall through to 1950s butch–femme working-class culture.

Wainwright's addition of Lister's top hat – which Lister herself never wore – gives her an added masculinised authority, while also echoing the eighteenth-century drawings and caricatures of the Ladies of Llangollen, a famous female couple who eloped from Ireland to Wales in the 1780s to set up home together, and whom Lister greatly admired.

Yet Jones's Lister also remains remarkably faithful to the descriptions in the diaries. In her diary entries, Lister frequently described both her own sense of her appearance and how others saw her, leaving us with a rich account of her clothing choices – in particular her early decision to wear only black – along with her body language and her nonconforming gender presentation. Lister was acutely aware of the effects of her physical presence and paid attention to gestures large and small, from her energetic walk to how she held her cane and twirled her watch. Jones, in turn, follows Lister's lead, and through her glamorous androgynous wardrobe, her butch walk and her seductive presence, her Lister repeatedly contests the codes of nineteenth-century normative femininity – particularly when placed in the context of mainstream nineteenth-century heritage drama.

In terms of fans' responses, Lister's appeal therefore lies as much in her gender presentation as in her queer sexuality. Importantly, this has fed into Twitter debates that reflect our current struggles over identity politics. In an echo of the controversy concerning the plaques celebrating Lister and Walker's union in Holy Trinity Church, York – where the phrase 'gender-nonconforming' was replaced, after protests, with 'lesbian' – Twitter responses to *Gentleman Jack* have ranged from claiming Lister as a lesbian, to seeing her as 'the Great Butch of History',[50] to insisting she was 'AT THE VERY LEAST GNC/non-binary', and that 'the argument could definitely be made that Anne would be a trans man were the resources available'.[51] Other Twitter responses note the irony of opposing groups on the identity spectrum each claiming Lister for themselves, which makes Lister both central to the conversation about identity politics and a flashpoint for disagreement.[52] While the overt presentism in these debates may be frustrating to some, they show how the past can invade the present and both affirm and redefine it. They also expose the extent to which the figure of Lister generates in fans a *desire for identity*, even as Lister herself can never be firmly identified.

One of the series' distinctive features is how it pays close attention to Lister's politics in a way the *Secret Diaries* film did not; we see Lister responding to the implications of the 1832 Reform Bill as well as her commenting on her tenants and competing with Rawson, the local coal baron. At the same time, Lister's conservative political stance and her engagement in an aggressive form of capitalism is reconfigured through a proto-feminist lens as having the courage to stand up to the boys, as when she vies for her own coal mine. Lister's gender nonconformity is celebrated in ways that allow her to behave like the men rather than questioning the terms of their privilege, in both her personal and her public life. Yet Wainwright, herself from a working-class background, also reminds us that Lister 'wasn't even landed gentry – more like the level below, yeomanry, because the Shibden estate isn't that big, only about 400 acres'.[53] Until her inheritance, Lister was also struggling for money, 'always ... borrow[ing] and wait[ing] for handouts'.[54] Wainwright also suggestively gives Lister's sister, Marian – whom Lister generally ignores and overrides – more progressive views than Lister herself – as when they are discussing the 1832 Reform Bill – subtly pointing to Lister's investment in the political *status quo*. At the same time, Lister, unlike Marian, is the one being harassed and attacked on country roads on account of her gender nonconformity. In refusing conventional femininity, Lister is placing herself permanently at risk and, as Susan. S. Lanser has argued, her class allegiance and upward mobility can be read as engaging in a mode of self-protection and as a 'compensatory conservatism ... and classism'.[55] Lister foregrounds what Lanser terms the 'status risk' of her 'gender transgressions' by overdetermining her class status.[56]

Although the majority of fans see Lister as transformative for her time and for theirs, their primary response to her remains intensely personal and privileges an affective over a political engagement with her narrative. There is a focus on Lister's romantic individualism that is matched by an almost total silence concerning her Tory politics, her upward mobility and her landlord status. We see only the occasional critical entry, such as Tumblr's deandykery, who writes: 'when the class war comes [Lister] will not be spared'.[57] While it is a paradox of the show that a figure who defines herself through her uniqueness and her exceptionalism has become a harbinger for contemporary community building, this also speaks to the anachronistic effect of translating the past into the present. Fans see in Lister's refusal to remain isolated and her determination to participate in the privileges afforded her, despite her outlier status, the possibilities of a queer future. In addition, Jones's performance arguably generates feelings of desire and/or identification that obfuscate Lister's political conservatism. What fans fail to attend to is therefore as telling as what they highlight.

The most compelling scene for the fanbase has been the marriage proposal and the wedding day in season one's final episode. The Lister diaries themselves, as Simon Joyce points out, 'are full of quasi-matrimonial rituals in which she exchanges symbolic tokens with lovers as signs of "marital commitment": rings, locks of hair, and in one striking moment, pubic hair'.[58] Lister was obsessed with marriage as well as acutely aware of her exclusion from it. The marriage proposal scene takes place on top of a hill overlooking the lush Yorkshire countryside, with a subtly romantic musical score that crescendos with the sealing kiss, Walker in a powder-blue dress that echoes the sky, and Lister in her signature black overcoat studded with brass buttons. As Lister says to Walker, 'but we're not alive. Are we? If we're not taking the odd risk now and again,' a risk which is dramatised in the representation of this queer historical couple being shown in a prime-time slot.[59] The marriage proposal scene was posted by the BBC as a stand-alone YouTube clip, which has received close to a million (805,650) views to date, with 1,165 comments.

In the diaries, however, there is no hilltop proposal scene and the description of the wedding day is minimal, as Lister writes on 30 March 1834: 'At Goodramgate church at 10 35; Miss W – and I and Thomas staid [for] the sacrament ... *The first time I ever joined Miss W – in my prayers – I had prayed that our union might be happy – she had not thought of doing as much for me.*'[60] Lister had already proposed and made plans for attending a church service in lieu of a wedding ceremony as early as 14 December 1832: '*Miss W – told me in the hut if she said "Yes" again it should be binding. It should be the same as a marriage and she would give me no cause to be jealous – made no objection to what I proposed, that is, her declaring it on the Bible & taking the sacrament with me at Shibden or Lightcliffe church.*'[61] This entry shows how the wedding vows were themselves in a state of instability, having been made once, then rebuffed, then reconfirmed. This highlights the complexities of enacting a public ceremony as a private event and fully believing in it as a valid speech act. While Wainwright takes on some of this hesitancy by having Walker initially refuse Lister before the final episode, this serves primarily as a build-up to the romantic hilltop scene.

Responding to this final episode, the *Gentleman Jack* fanbase has fully endorsed the reality of Lister marrying her beloved, and there are now lesbian marriage ceremonies being performed at Shibden Hall and many pilgrimages to Holy Trinity Church, which also boasts the aforementioned heritage plaque of the Lister–Walker union signalling the first lesbian marriage. For the fans, Lister's marriage is a further confirmation of her authenticity, in that she is seen following her nature through this quasi-public ritual.

Yet it is precisely at the intersection of these opposing positions that the queerness of historical time comes into play. The original fiction, after all, belongs to Lister herself. It is she who was repeatedly staging and performing marital rituals with her lovers as a way of claiming social belonging and asserting her desire and her relationships in a world that was rendering them invisible. Wainwright's response has been to foreground, rather than to mask, this fantasy element as an integral part of the Lister narrative. By following the classic courtship and romance model of conventional costume drama, yet peopling it with queer protagonists, Wainwright creates belonging and recognition across time, while arguably honouring, rather than simply fictionalising, Lister's stated desires in her diary entries. In this sense, Wainwright gives Lister, and the fans, 'the marriage she (and they) always wanted'.[62]

While this collapse of the historical into the fictional can certainly be read as historically inaccurate, it is also a form of queer authenticity, what Jose Esteban Muñoz has theorised as a mode of 'queer utopianism'.[63] The marital scene dramatises what could have been, blending the affects of nostalgia and sentimentalism and offering what Heather Hogan describes as 'the latitude to contain multitudes in stories'.[64] Indeed, this moment of infidelity to the original diaries strikes a particular chord with Lister's own Don Juan-esque capacity for sexual infidelity, which Wainwright explores in season two. By the time she courts Walker, Lister has had eleven lovers that we know of, some of them overlapping, yet her goal throughout the diaries, as she says in 1817, is to 'have some female companion whom I could love & depend upon'.[65] Wainwright follows what James Harold describes as a 'thematic fidelity' to Lister's aspirational domestic romance narrative, but leaves room for the continued possibility of infidelity, both on Lister's part and in terms of Wainwright's own interpretation of the source material.[66]

While much of the fanbase has foregrounded the ways in which *Gentleman Jack* has generated new possibilities for global community building among lesbian and queer subjects – as illustrated in Lea's book – this productive relationality has been accompanied by complicated affective responses of loss and nostalgia as well as fulfilment, all of which speak to the ambivalent legacy of queer history-making. Among claims of transformation, fulfilment and community, there are also feelings of loss and grief, which point to a more convoluted relationship to the *Gentleman Jack* effect. Louise Alexander, a clergywoman from the United States, sums up her response as follows: 'Seeing the authentic portrayal of Anne Lister and Ann Walker stirred up grief and longing: grief for what I had missed and not allowed myself to feel for a very long time, and longing for the passion and the wholeness that Anne Lister represents.'[67] Such reactions complicate narratives of transition and transformation and gesture towards an affect more closely tied to trauma and injury rather than to completion and fulfilment.

While on viewing *Gentleman Jack*, fans have described a feeling of *coming* home, they are also describing the nostalgic quality of a *longing for* home, from the Greek roots 'algia' meaning 'longing' and 'nostos' meaning 'return home'. Svetlana Boym describes nostalgia as both 'a sentiment of loss and displacement' and 'a romance with one's own fantasy',[68] in that it can generate a longing for something that could have been rather than something that once was. This is the temporality of the perfect conditional and it articulates a form of desire that claims missed opportunities and possibilities from the past, rather than opening up potentialities for the future, the latter being the mainstay of the fanbase response. The perfect conditional instead designates a wistful, contemplative and melancholic subject position, one which is also present in certain of the fans' discourse on *Gentleman Jack* and which points to the convoluted trajectory of queer history itself.

One example of this melancholic response is Rachael Biggs's personal essay on *Gentleman Jack*, 'How *Gentleman Jac*k Changed My Life Forever', which appeared in Britain's *Diva* magazine on 20 August 2019. As with many of Lea's interviewees, Biggs is British and describes herself as a teacher and mother of three girls living in rural England, with a doctor wife. Biggs offers one of the earliest published responses to season one of *Gentleman Jack*, the final episode of which aired on 7 July 2019. In her opening paragraph, Biggs describes her viewing experience as 'the most magnificent (and scary) journey' and explains how it threw off her concentration at work and made her feel 'grief' and feelings of 'utter sadness' which 'knocked [her] sideways'.[69] Following season one's finale, Biggs was 'struggling to concentrate at work' and felt 'desperate to understand why [she] felt so much pain . . . it literally made [her] heart ache'.[70] Not only was her response overwhelming, but in contrast to many of Lea's interviewees, Biggs experienced intense feelings of hurt rather than fulfilment. The experience of watching *Gentleman Jack* positioned her as a mourner, as having lost something.

As with Kate Brown, who is brought back to her youth after watching the show, Biggs feels validated in her present while also recognising, as she says, 'what me as a little girl and me as a teenager and me as a young woman missed out on'.[71] In Biggs's case, Lister's story brings to the fore the failed past, revealing what could have been and acknowledging what can now never be fully recovered. In knocking Biggs off-course, the show disrupts her forward movement, creating a different pathway, in Sara Ahmed's terms, 'by bringing what is "behind" to the front'.[72] While, as for other fans, *Gentleman Jack* was equally transformative and, as Biggs says, gave her the 'confidence to express my innermost thoughts and my ability to just simply be me', the transformation required a painful form of regression.[73]

Biggs's article succinctly articulates the fusing of the personal and the historical past, which speaks to the affective force of Wainwright's vision in creating *Gentleman Jack*. As with other fans, a large part of Biggs's emotional response lies in the fact that Lister and Walker were real historical figures: 'it is not at all make-believe. It's based on a real-life story, a story dating back almost 200 years.'[74] Here, the historical past supports, validates and gives shape to the personal past. Biggs then decides to make a pilgrimage to Shibden Hall and explains that '[v]isiting Ann Walker's burial site was one of the most profound moments of my life'.[75] She feels as though Ann Walker 'was a relative of mine, almost as if I was discovering part of my long lost family tree'.[76] As with Kate Brown, what Biggs glimpses here is the possibility of a lineage, of a past that can be traced, recognised and celebrated up to the present moment, and that incorporates her own childhood and her own past in the process. She undergoes a kind of reverse trauma; rather than having a painful suppressed memory rise to the surface, she experiences the filling of a gap that she never knew was there. What she grieves is the paradoxical presence, rather than absence, of Lister and Walker, as figures who have always been present, yet who have been obscured and ghosted by the heterosexual historical narrative. Queer history, in this sense, is both discovered and occluded in the same moment.

At the core of this affective response is once again the mix of existential and historical authenticity. For Biggs, it is the fact of 'a historic figure, who almost 200 years ago, stayed true to herself and married another woman', that drives her profound attachment to the narrative.[77] And it is this authenticity that now enables Biggs, as she says, 'to be exactly who I am', a feeling she claims she did not have before seeing the show.[78] What *Gentleman Jack* offers fans is a historical connection created through affinity rather than kinship ties and that depends on affective longing rather than archival accuracy. The figures of Lister and Walker are both/and, rather than either/or, both real and fictional, both history and story, both authentic and idealised. They offer a queer history that fans did not know they wanted or needed, yet one that seems to resonate with them in multiple ways.

Biggs's *Diva* article garnered thirty-two responses, the majority of which echo her sentiments of loss and grief in the wake of viewing *Gentleman Jack*, with comments such as 'You have written exactly how I feel,' 'I was left feeling empty, full of anguish, not knowing why,' 'I identify with everything you write ... I thought I was the only woman who felt like this,' 'I wept as I read this article as well,' 'I spent many hours pondering why this show wouldn't let me go' and so on. Other comments focus on the question of authenticity: 'This piece ... speaks my truth as a gay woman,' 'The show validates everything I am,' 'I grieve for a lifetime of hiding my very essence,' and they also touch lesbian subjects further afield, with one woman writing: 'I had to watch the show by myself, alone in my room, on a non-official website knowing that in my country there's no same-sex marriage.' And finally: 'Here these two groundbreaking women have been dead all these years, and I am still grieving about them.'[79] We see here the emergence of a collective response, which in turn generates an empathetic mode of identification. The last comment in particular speaks to the heart of the affective conundrum, in that *Gentleman Jack* brings Lister and Walker to life in a way that projects them into the future, while simultaneously reminding us that they belong to the past. Lister and Walker create an almost untenable queer temporality, in that the experience of grieving is built into the narrative to the extent that the discovery of their existence is itself a form of loss. The two questions to which the fans are implicitly responding are: (1) How did we not know about this before? and (2) Can this story really be real?

The Lister diaries have generated an alternative queer historical trajectory beyond normative scholarly parameters in a way that simultaneously reconfigures the notion of authenticity. Wainwright, who knows the diaries intimately, has shaped them into a narrative that communicates a particular kind of attachment, one that produces a form of longing, as well as a desire for identification and queer lineage. For the fans, this desire exists in the inseparable merging of the real and the fictional; in terms of their viewing experience, Suranne Jones and Sophie Rundle *are* Anne Lister and Ann Walker, yet this leads fans such as Biggs to make the pilgrimage to Shibden Hall in order to validate the historical 'realness' of the *Gentleman Jack* narrative.

The location of the fans' desire is therefore complicated, for it is a desire for the fiction to be true and to some degree for the truth to be fictional (or at least, for the truth to follow Wainwright's script). But what emerges from a parsing of the fans' responses, above all, is a desire for affirmation and for the making real of queer lives and queer pasts. The question is less how close to the original diaries is *Gentleman Jack*, than how successful has the series been in generating a belief in that past? The fans' semantic field of lack, loss and grieving reveals the failure of history proper to make room for queer histories and therefore brings to the surface the inauthenticity of queer existence. The fact that Biggs and other fans link the public story of Lister and Walker to their own private narratives of the self points to the broader question, posed by Judith Butler, of what lives are worth remembering and what lives are grievable.[80] *Gentleman Jack* makes possible a new kind of grieving, for a past that has been repeatedly desired and repeatedly suppressed, as with the history of the Lister diaries themselves.

In David L. Eng and David Kazanjian's collection of essays, *Loss*, the authors argue that loss can be 'a creative process' rather than simply reactive, 'a field in which the past is brought to bear witness to the present – as a flash of emergence, an instant of emergency, and a moment of production'.[81] For these fans, *Gentlemen Jack* functions as this 'flash of emergence', a glimpse of another possible account of history that is outside 'history's victorious hegemonies'.[82] In this sense, Lister is made present yet remains elusive, graspable only through a kind of 'melancholic excess'.[83] The journey Wainwright takes us on is one both of recovery and of an anticipatory nostalgia for what could have been. As a romanticising of and a romance with the scholarly archive, *Gentleman Jack* calls into question the boundaries between the scholarly and the fictional in ways that allow us to imagine a more elastic and capacious relationship between stories and history, and queer pasts and the queer present.

Notes

1 For a discussion of *Gentleman Jack Saved My Life*, see the following article from the BBC Media Centre: www.bbc.com/mediacentre/2022/gentleman-jack-changed-my-life, accessed 9 May 2022.

2 S. E. Maier and R. M. Friars, 'Stoically Sapphic: Gentlemanly Encryption and Disruptive Legibility in Adapting Anne Lister', *Neo-Victorian Studies* 13.1 (2020), 125–52; E. Ng, 'The "Gentleman-Like" Anne Lister on *Gentleman Jack*: Queerness, Class, and Prestige in "Quality" Period Drama', *International Journal of Communication* 15 (2021), 2397–417; J. Lea, The *Gentleman Jack* Effect: Lessons in Breaking Rules and Living Out Loud (Santa Fe: Laurel House, 2021).

3 R. Biggs, 'How *Gentleman Jack* Changed My Life Forever', *Diva* Magazine (20 August 2019), https://divamag.co.uk/2019/08/20/the-longread-how-gentleman-jack-changed-my-life-forever/, accessed 23 December 2021.

4 L. Hutcheon with S. O'Flynn, *A Theory of Adaptation* (New York: Routledge, 2013), p. xiv.
5 Ibid., p. xvii.
6 Ibid., p. 6.
7 Ibid., p. 16.
8 Ibid., p. 111.
9 S. Wainwright, 'The Life and Legacy of Anne Lister', University of York, 21 October 2021, www.york.ac.uk/news-and-events/events/public-lectures/autumn-2021/gentleman-jack/?fbclid=IwAR2gjsd4IRS5CKg5ldklTbkKboO9FRtKbSKVqQ_xkXtv2luXmsS9miFAcbs, accessed 23 December 2021.
10 See Chapter 13, this volume.
11 I have discussed Wainwright's direct use of the diaries at greater length in 'From Text to Screen: Gentleman Jack Then and Now', in J. Reed and E. B. Hagai (eds.), *Gentleman Jack and the (Re)Discovery of Anne Lister*, special issue of *Journal of Lesbian Studies* 26.4 (2022), 309–22.
12 C. Monk, 'Sexuality and Heritage', *Sight and Sound* 5.10 (1995), 32–34; K. Harris, '"Part of the Project of That Book Was Not To Be Authentic": Neo-Historical Authenticity and its Anachronisms in Contemporary Historical Fiction', *Rethinking History* 21.2 (2017), 193–212.
13 Harris, 'Neo-Historical Authenticity', 194.
14 Ibid., 197.
15 M. Wolf, 'Love, Infidelity and Commitment in Bloomsbury', *New York Times* (19 July 1992).
16 See H. Hogan, '*Gentleman Jack*'s Finale Was One of the Finest Hours in Lesbian Cinematic History', *Autostraddle* (14 July 2019), www.autostraddle.com/gentleman-jacks-finale-was-one-of-the-finest-hours-in-lesbian-cinematic-history/, accessed 23 December 2021.
17 Ng, 'Queerness, Class and Prestige', 2400.
18 C. Brunsdon, 'Problems with Quality', *Screen* 31.1 (1990), 77–90, 86.
19 J. Leggott and J. Taddeo (eds.), Upstairs and Downstairs: British Costume Drama Television from *The Forsythe Saga* to *Downton Abbey* (London: Rowman and Littlefield, 2015), p. ix.
20 Ng, 'Queerness, Class and Prestige', 2399.
21 Jen Carter, in Lea, *The* Gentleman Jack *Effect*, p. 44.
22 Maier and Friars, 'Stoically Sapphic', 132.
23 P. Blank, 'The Proverbial "Lesbian": Queering Etymology in Contemporary Critical Practice', *Modern Philology* 109.1 (August 2011), 108–34, 123, https://doi.org/10.1086/661977, accessed 2 February 2022; M. Menon, *Unhistorical Shakespeare: Queer Theory in Shakespearean Literature and Film* (New York: Palgrave Macmillan, 2008), p. 1; C. Dinshaw, *Getting Medieval: Sexualities and Communities, Pre- and Postmodern* (Durham, NC: Duke University Press, 1999).
24 Blank, 'Queering Etymology', 119.

25 C. Freccero, *Queer/Early/Modern* (Durham, N.C.: Duke University Press, 2006), p. 70.
26 Maier and Friars, 'Stoically Sapphic', 130.
27 For an analysis of how the *Gentleman Jack* fanbase engages with Lister scholarship to create a 'paratextual' online narrative, see E. Ng, '"What Unholy Chart Is This?!": Paratextual Intertextuality in Gentleman Jack Fan Posts of Scholarship on Anne Lister', in J. Reed and E. B. Hagai (eds.), *Gentleman Jack and the (Re)Discovery of Anne Lister*, special issue of *Journal of Lesbian Studies* 26.4 (2022), 458–67.
28 Lea, *The* Gentleman Jack *Effect*, p. 4.
29 The concept of authenticity forms part of the continental philosophical tradition that culminates in existentialist philosophy and includes philosophers such as Søren Kierkegaard, Friedrich Nietzsche, Martin Heidegger, Hannah Arendt, Jean-Paul Sartre and Simone de Beauvoir, among others.
30 Fiona Evered, in Lea, *The* Gentleman Jack *Effect*, p. 17.
31 Diane Miller, in ibid., p. 14.
32 Inna Clawsette, in ibid., p. 34.
33 Jenny Corkett, in ibid., p. 21.
34 Ibid., p. i.
35 Kate Brown, in ibid., p. 13.
36 Patience, in ibid., p. 8.
37 Patience, in ibid., p. 9.
38 Patience, in ibid., p. 8.
39 Patience, in ibid., p. 10.
40 Ibid., p. 41.
41 It is important to note that India's criminalisation of homosexuality was initially the result of colonial-era sodomy laws devised by the British.
42 Jen Carter, in Lea, *The* Gentleman Jack *Effect*, p. 42.
43 Jen Carter, in ibid., p. 44.
44 Jen Carter, in ibid., p. 43.
45 Jen Carter, in ibid., p. 46.
46 Harris, 'Neo-Historical Authenticity', 208.
47 See Chapter 13, this volume.
48 Michaela Dresel, in Lea, *The* Gentleman Jack *Effect*, p. 24.
49 Katherina Oh, in ibid., p. 38.
50 Isaac Fellman, 27 July 2019, Twitter.
51 All Cal-lows EVE, 1 July 2020, Twitter.
52 Tiger Lantern, 20 December 2020, Twitter.
53 See Chapter 13, this volume.
54 Ibid.
55 S. S. Lanser, 'Befriending the Body: Female Intimacies as Class Acts', *Eighteenth-Century Studies* 32.2 (1998–9), 179–98, 190.
56 Ibid. See Lanser's development of these ideas in Chapter 6, this volume, in particular her suggestion that Lister's sexuality could be read as constitutive of her political conservatism.

57 Deandykery, 9 May 2022, Tumblr.
58 S. Joyce, 'The Perverse Presentism of Rainbow Plaques: Memorializing Anne Lister', *Nineteenth-Century Contexts* 41.5 (2019), 601–10, 602.
59 S. Wainwright, *Gentleman Jack*: Episodes 1–8 shooting script (Lookout Point Limited, 2019), episode 8, 50; www.bbc.co.uk/writersroom/scripts/tv-drama/gentleman-jack, accessed 3 January 2022.
60 Quoted in J. Liddington, *Female Fortune: Land, Gender and Authority. The Anne Lister Diaries and Other Writings, 1833–36* (London: Rivers Oram, 1998), p. 100.
61 Quoted in Liddington, *Female Fortune*, p. 69.
62 Roulston, 'From Text to Screen', 18.
63 J. E. Muñoz, *Cruising Utopia: the Then and There of Queer Futurity* (New York: New York University Press, 2009), p. 13.
64 Hogan, '*Gentleman Jack*'s Finale'.
65 11 July 1817, in H. Whitbread (ed.), *The Secret Diaries of Miss Anne Lister* (London: Virago Press, 2010), p. 19.
66 J. Harold, 'The Value of Fidelity in Adaptation', *British Journal of Aesthetics* 58.1, (January 2018), 89–100, 94; https://doi.org/10.1093/aesthj/ayx041, accessed 20 May 2022.
67 Louise Alexander, in Lea, *The* Gentleman Jack *Effect*, p. 50.
68 S. Boym, *The Future of Nostalgia* (New York: Basic Books, 2001), p. xiii.
69 Biggs, 'How *Gentleman Jack* Changed My Life Forever', 6.
70 Ibid.
71 Ibid., 7.
72 S. Ahmed, *Queer Phenomenology: Orientations, Objects, Others* (Durham, NC: Duke University Press, 2006), p. 4.
73 Biggs, 'How *Gentleman Jack* Changed My Life Forever', 7.
74 Ibid., 8.
75 Ibid., 9.
76 Ibid., 9.
77 Ibid., 9.
78 Ibid., 7.
79 Responses to Biggs, 'How *Gentleman Jack* Changed My Life Forever'.
80 See J. Butler, *Undoing Gender* (London: Routledge, 2004), pp. 17–39.
81 D. L. Eng and D. Kazanjian (eds.), *Loss* (Berkeley: University of California Press, 2003), p. 5.
82 Ibid., p. 2.
83 Ibid., p. 5.

CHAPTER 13

Emma Donoghue in Conversation with Sally Wainwright

An interview with Sally Wainwright OBE, creator/screenwriter/director of the Bafta-nominated BBC/HBO series *Gentleman Jack* (2019–)

EMMA DONOGHUE Having written biography and biographical fiction as well as screenplays, I'm very aware of the gulf that can exist between those forms. Frankly, I'm in awe of you for creating such an artistically and popularly successful TV series, drawing on a vast archive and staying true to its spirit and texture. Could you talk me through the long development of *Gentleman Jack*?

SALLY WAINWRIGHT From growing up in Halifax, I've always known about Anne Lister. My first real introduction to her was Jill [Liddington's] book [*Female Fortune: Land, Gender and Authority. The Anne Lister Diaries and Other Writings, 1833–36* (1998)]. It was life-changing, I suppose, in that for the first time it gave me this massive hit of just who Anne was. And then I went off to try and find out everything about her – this is pre-Google. I met Helena [Whitbread]. Both Jill and Helena were really generous with their time, and I just binged on Anne Lister. I'd been writing telly for over ten years, so my natural reaction to being obsessed with something was, how can I turn this into a TV show?

I started by reading the diaries myself. I worked out how to use the code one afternoon. In Jill's *Presenting the Past: Anne Lister of Halifax, 1791–1840* (1994) there's a tiny bit of code – it says something about Tib's 'racing calendar' – so I worked it out letter by letter. It was a bit torturous, but it meant it sank in because I had to work it out myself rather than just being handed a key. So I did a massive amount of my own transcription. This was in 2001; the diaries [at West Yorkshire Archive Service] had actually been photographed and I paid for the whole thing to be put on to a disk. I printed off lots and lots of 1830s diary. But I wanted to go farther back. Where Jill starts basically is in 1834 when Anne Lister and Ann Walker get married, and she didn't really touch much on the courtship from 1832 on, so I went backwards and transcribed that.

I took six months off around 2003. For the first time I had too much work and I also had two little boys. I just decided to stop. All I did was paint, and transcribe the Lister diaries. It was for fun. At the time I thought the show probably wouldn't ever get made because nobody wanted to know about somebody who wasn't famous. It was a real conundrum, that Anne Lister had been trapped in obscurity for so long simply because she was gay.

I wrote a treatment that was based very much on Jill's *Female Fortune*, but it was far too long and convoluted. I found it very hard to pin it down to something that was simple and sellable and people would get very quickly. Looking back, I think I didn't know myself what I wanted to say. I just wanted to dramatise Anne and get into her head and live in her world and make stories out of it. It went through various iterations. I kept on pitching the idea, but everybody turned it down, the BBC, Channel 4 . . . Helena told me she'd once talked to a TV producer who'd said, 'There'll only ever be one film made about Anne Lister.' Which was probably true at that time, but now I can imagine any number of films about Anne being made.

It was a long journey. But I've had so many shows like that – germs of ideas that have been in there for years. I never stopped working on *Gentleman Jack*. I even thought about trying a contemporary version.

ED Did you consider other titles for the series?

SW An early one was *The Trick of Debauching Miss Walker* – a quote from the journal. Then, when *Downton Abbey* [2010–15] was very successful, I thought of a version called *Shibden Hall* – the hierarchy of upstairs-downstairs. Obviously that was the wrong way to go because Anne is so central to her own journal – surprise surprise! – that she overtakes, she dominates everything.

ED Were there other shows or films you found helpful as models of how to make a biographical drama closely based on written sources?

SW None that I can remember. People call *Gentleman Jack* an adaptation of the diaries. For want of a better word, fine, but the word just doesn't do the process justice. There's some invention, but really it's a dramatisation of a real life. I find it a bit frustrating, because when we think of an adaptation we think of something Andrew [Davies] has adapted, say *War and Peace*, *Pride and Prejudice*, where you've already got a story, plot, characters . . . so, you know, what's left to do? [laughs]

ED You have a long and notable record of creating gritty shows about rebellious women, British and often Yorkshire ones in particular. What previous experience of yours was most crucial in making you the right person – I'd say the only possible person – to create *Gentleman Jack*?

SW When I was writing *Happy Valley* I'd basically wanted to do my own version of *Nurse Jackie* (2009–15), my all-time favourite show. I had to disguise it, obviously, so my protagonist's a policewoman. I wanted it to be very dark, but very funny. And I think it was that idea of writing a show that's a portrait – because I'd never quite thought of TV as that before – that helped me get away from the *Downton Abbey* paradigm when writing *Gentleman Jack*. What I hadn't really taken on board until getting down to the nitty-gritty of writing the damn thing was, given the time constraints of an eight-hour series, it had to be a portrait of Anne. The fictional story about the Sowdens [Anne's tenants] to my mind is the weakest part of the show because it's one of the only times we go away from her.

ED What enabled *Gentleman Jack* to finally get commissioned? Did you just find the right people to work with, or was it a matter of your own growing muscle, or the changing times?

SW The show was greenlit in 2016, after *Happy Valley* had been massive for the BBC at home and globally. Charlotte Moore [BBC Director of Content since early 2016] asked me, 'What do you want to do next?' It was the first time I'd heard that, rather than 'Tell us what you've got.' It was a combination of the fact that my star had risen and changing attitudes. Now nobody was going to think *Gentlemen Jack* was too fringey. The show could be a portrait of this woman, *one* of whose characteristics was that she was gay.

ED There's a cliché about historians doing scrupulous, unpaid, unnoticed research, and then 'Hollywood' coming along and simplifying or distorting it to win it a wide audience. Your collaborative relationships with historians and librarians couldn't present more of a contrast. Jill Liddington credits your endless curiosity with pushing her back to the archives to edit and publish a second book of excerpts, this time from 1832 (*Nature's Domain*), and I was also deeply impressed that when you won the Wellcome Screenwriting Fellowship in 2016 you funded the restoration and digitisation of Lister's diaries.

SW It was only when I started writing that I realised I'd possibly bitten off more than I could chew. In October 2016 we rented a villa in the hills of Majorca, really secluded, and I remember thinking, this is great, I've got two weeks, I can really get my head into it. But I soon realised I couldn't write the show just based on Jill's *Female Fortune* and a little bit of the diary. I needed to transcribe the whole period I was covering, to make my own selections. I transcribed for four or five months, then I realised how long it was going to require, so I took Anne Choma on to transcribe for me. I wanted to know everything. When Anne [Choma] was starting out, she said, 'Well, I won't include things like the day's temperature,' but I said, 'No, do, it might be sunny that day, or rainy, and that could make a difference to the mood!' I wanted to get immersed, every tiny detail. You only get to know Anne when you get into that level of detail day after day. And I think I do know her, in a way I didn't when I started pitching this project twenty years ago.

ED How do you think *Gentleman Jack* might have been different or received differently if you'd managed to make it in the early 2000s?

SW Back then, I don't know if I'd have had the confidence to say this is going to take longer than I thought. I'd have been more dependent on Jill's book rather than having the confidence to own the material myself.

Also, *The Crown* [2016–] was ground-breaking in that it was this massive co-production with Netflix, and everybody was trying to get co-pros with

America. We went over and had meetings with big companies, and then HBO came on board. We had the kind of budget that you just didn't get in TV before. So again, *Gentleman Jack* happened at the right time. It was actually great that we hadn't got it greenlit earlier when it would have had a more limited budget. Now we could really go to town. The arrival on the high flyer [carriage] in Episode 1 – I'd wondered how to introduce Anne, a character as big as Anne Lister – that was shot with a Russian arm. Basically it's an SUV with a crane on top with a camera attached. Really expensive bits of kit that you would normally only get in film.

ED Did you always plan to focus on the 1832–4 period, and why?

SW I really didn't want to do a linear biopic. I wanted to start at the point where she was most fascinating – because I could always work backwards, use flashbacks. When Anne came back from Hastings in 1832 after the breakup with Vere Hobart, it was a real low ebb and a turning point. She deliberately looked around her and thought, 'What woman will I pick?' She decided to turn her estate around and make it somewhere worthy to invite her aristocratic friends. She became this formidable and exciting person. So that seemed like a really good place to start, when she was forty-two. I was fifty-three when I began writing this. Twenty-year-olds are boring! Starting earlier in her life, you'd be in this thing of, it's all about sex and romance, and apart from it being gay, it just isn't that different. Starting in 1832 gave me a much more layered character. In that period Anne's got some real agency, at a time when women just didn't, in a world where they were constantly infantilised. In season two, she decides to turn Northgate House into a hotel and casino. You're thinking, '*How* did you get the idea for a hotel in Halifax?' She was a real entrepreneur. Unlike what a lot of people think, she wasn't using Ann Walker's money. She was borrowing lots from people like Mr Waterhouse. She was ridiculously ambitious. The vision! The balls!

ED What genres were you aware of drawing on? I'm thinking of the romance, the eccentric-family drama, the prestige period drama, suspense/crime, comedy . . .

SW I never really thought about genre. I just wanted to tell Anne's story. But I didn't want it to be another BBC costume drama, dressing-up box, namby-pamby Jane Austen stuff – I'd do anything to undermine that. So the comedy, silly bits of surreal stuff, her talking to camera . . . which to me was a no-brainer because it's just like the immediacy of reading the journal. In her diary Anne presents herself as she'd like to be portrayed. Not consciously – she never tells us lies, in fact quite the opposite, is brutally frank. I don't think she thought anybody else was going to read it, really it was an *aide-mémoire* – so she could be as frank as she wanted, which is endearing and engaging in itself, because you can trust her.

ED Tell me about the work of shaping story arcs from this material you were already so familiar with.

SW I have a lot of support at Lookout Point [production company]. We're working to strict deadlines and I have to churn out an episode every two months, whereas on other shows it would normally take me one. My script editors and producers – basically there's a team who meet and discuss the diaries, how we're going to turn them into TV. You try to develop a process, but the process develops all the time. It's so mercurial, the content of the diaries, it can slip through your fingers when you try to dramatise it. So, if we are lucky enough to get a third season commissioned, we've got a new plan for how we'd approach it, to save a little bit of time . . . But it's just a very hard process. In the diaries there are almost no stories with a beginning, middle and end. There are shaggy dog stories where I'd get really excited, thinking ooh, this could run right across from Episode 3 to 7. . . and then Anne just stops mentioning whatever it was.

I think going forward I might start letting myself take a few liberties. Borrow bits from earlier in the journal, which will still reflect the truth. But then again, there might be so much stuff to use as we move forward.

ED Is it ever uncomfortable for you as a writer with a working-class background to be writing from the side of the landlords?

SW One of the misconceptions from some viewers is that Anne was an aristocrat, and of course she wasn't even landed gentry – more like the level below, yeomanry, because the Shibden estate isn't that big, only about 400 acres. Until she inherited it, she never had any money – always had to borrow or wait for handouts. When Anne got the estate, she had to work really hard. She was so careful with money. She was very good to her tenants, for that period, and paid for one boy to go to a good school. I know she had children working down her coal pit, which is weird, but it's what people did then. We have to see them in their own time, their own context. In season two she's trying to influence every vote she can for the Tories, and I've tried to make it funny rather than diss her for it. And it kind of works, because Halifax was really radicalised, so she was never going to win! It's about presenting the complexities of someone who isn't always likeable. There's no drama in people who are just worthy and good.

The show's a bit . . . is picaresque the right word? It's episodic, and Anne's roguish, and you feel quite ambivalent about her. I mean, I'm basically in love with her, but I can see that she's horrible sometimes. That's why she's interesting to dramatise, because she's so complex. So Machiavellian – I think she had to be. So profoundly intelligent, every page there's something that surprises you. So eloquent and witty and resourceful.

I love Suranne [Jones] in the part. She's got this very modern energy, and Anne Lister was born out of her time, and almost like from another planet. But also Suranne's physical energy. She can be all angular – not in real life, she's very feminine, which is a bit of a shock when you meet her. There are very few people who can carry a TV show. I now can't imagine anyone else who could play Anne.

ED Was there material you found you needed to leave out because it might disgust or shock viewers? Or because there just wasn't room for everything?

SW I've not come across anything in the 1830s diaries that I wouldn't include in the show. In season two, Anne comes out of her watercloset and says, 'My bowels are all wrong again.' This is how meticulous a diarist she is! I'd love to have a little running joke that every episode we find out what's going on with her bowels. But that's the problem with only having eight hours per season, it's just not enough. We covered about eighteen months in season one and the same in season two. It's heart-breaking how many scenes we shot and had to drop: there's the editing when you're writing the script, then the editing to get the page count down, then the editing of the stuff you've shot, and what tend to go are the incidental gems. There aren't as many flashbacks in season two because we realised, having made season one, that they tended to be the things that got cut out because they weren't germane to the plot, they were just little luxuries. Like a massive scene in season one that Suranne was really glad we dropped, because it was a five-pager of her talking French with Cuvier [the French naturalist]. I was really sad about that.

ED Given that Lister has had quite a lot of attention paid to her since the 1980s, but specifically for her love life, I was thrilled by your series' equal attention to her other prodigious 'oddities' – timing and measuring, long-distance walking, autopsy-attending, coal mining, quarrying . . . Given that she had her finger in so many pies, how did you decide which of her activities to focus the story on?

SW I've tried to show all Anne's interests. I keep saying to Suranne that I want her to learn to juggle so I can include a scene where Anne's doing about ten things and also juggling.

One of the things I love about Anne is her optimism, her belief that life is for living. She always seems to bounce back, move on, put it behind her. That's something I find captivating about her because, like most people, I can obsess and worry about things and be miserable till the cows come home. If I'm down, I ask myself, 'What would Anne Lister say to you?' Pick yourself up off the floor and do something outside!

ED I want to finish by talking about the extraordinary response to the series worldwide. *Gentleman Jack* has finally brought Anne Lister to a mass audience, with effects ranging from plaques and statues and buildings named after her, to fan art and cosplay, to charity fundraising in Ann Walker's name . . .

SW I'm very proud of the show. They're making a documentary about the fans. I get these letters from all over the world, predominantly gay women but not all, about how it's made them feel validated. Often it's women who are already out, but the show's made them feel more confident about who they are. Hopefully that's because it doesn't just concentrate on Anne's sexuality. She was this fantastic polymath, so capable, so fascinated by everything. It presents a portrait that's more holistic – not just her romance with Ann Walker, but her as an estate manager. I think people have responded so strongly because she's this strong, complex, clever woman – *and* she's gay.

Ann Walker was absolutely besotted with Anne Lister, starstruck, and I think there's no doubt that she was gay too and didn't know what to do with it. I think that accounted for a lot of her inability to engage with the world or go out in the world. The only language they had was very private, like 'dinky' when they were talking about orgasm. So I imagine that must have been very compromising mentally, to live like that and not have the courage, the bizarre courage, of Anne Lister, who said, 'This is me! Let's get on with it.' For all the furore about the blue plaque in York, they could have fixed something more about it: two people took part in that marriage, yet only one has their name in capital letters.

ED Was it hard to write season two given your awareness of this fandom – how many people out there are longing for such different things from it?

SW No, the pressures are all internal.

ED And now *Gentleman Jack* has prompted hundreds of volunteers to train themselves to contribute to a crowdsourced transcription, not only of the diaries, but of the huge cache of letters as well. As far as I know, this kind of virtuous feedback loop between a TV creator and the archive on which she's drawing is unprecedented.

SW The whole thing is a unique situation. How rare it is to find such a fabulous historical document that hasn't even been transcribed yet. It's like suddenly going, 'Look, this guy called Shakespeare wrote all these plays four hundred years ago and here they all are.' Can we even imagine not knowing them? To me, Anne Lister is on that level – an extraordinary writer. One of my greatest fantasies is to have a published collection of her diaries on my bookshelf. That's why I put money into the archive and that sort of thing. I can't make it happen by myself, but I hope someday it will happen.

I do sometimes wonder, if I was given the chance to make an art film about Anne Lister, how different would it be from *Gentleman Jack*? Because the TV show is a conceit. It's very accurate in many ways, but I sometimes have this notion, I'd love the chance to make a film where I could just represent what I have in my head about who Anne really was, in a more realistic way. If I made Anne Lister in the style of *Portrait of a Lady on Fire*, would that be more like stepping back into the past? I've got this fantasy that I travel back in time and end up in 1832 at Shibden Hall, and I've got nowhere to go because obviously nobody knows me, and obviously Anne won't speak to me, I'm far too common . . .

This interview of 31 January 2022 has been edited for length and clarity.

Select Bibliography on Anne Lister

Anderson, O. 'The Anne Lister Papers'. *History Workshop Journal.* 40 (1995), 190–2.

Anne Lister Papers. Online Transcriptions. West Yorkshire Archive Service, Calderdale. www.catalogue.wyjs.org.uk/CalmView/Record.aspx?src=CalmView.Catalog&id=CC00001. Accessed 23 July 2022. [Referenced as *Lister Papers.*]

Anne Lister Research Summit. www.annelisterresearchsummit.org/home. Accessed 23 July 2022.

'Anne Lister: Reworded York Plaque for "first lesbian."' BBC News, 28 February 2019. https://www.bbc.com/news/uk-england-york-north-yorkshire–47404525. Accessed 23 July 2022.

'The Anne Lister Story'. Youtube Video. www.youtube.com/watch?v=HWMMdnzojbY&t=3s. Accessed 23 July 2022.

'Anne Lister's Diary, Tour of North Wales, 11–27 July 1822'. Transcribed with an introduction by Kirsty McHugh and edited by Elizabeth Edwards. In *Curious Travellers Digital Editions.* editions.curioustravellers.ac.uk/doc/0023. Accessed 15 February 2023.

Aston, J., A. Capern and B. McDonagh. 'More than Bricks and Mortar: Female Property Ownership as Economic Strategy in Mid-Nineteenth Century Urban England'. *Urban History.* 46.4 (2019), 695–721.

Baylis-Green, C. 'Queer Subjectivities, Closeting and Non-Normative Desire in Nineteenth-Century Women's Poetry and Life Writing'. Unpublished PhD thesis. Manchester Metropolitan University, 2016.

'BBC Factual Announces New BBC One Documentary, Gentleman Jack Changed My Life'. BBC Media Centre. 9 May 2022. www.bbc.com/mediacentre/2022/gentleman-jack-changed-my-life. Accessed 15 February 2023.

Berg, T. 'Reading Amazon Fragments: Queering *Shirley*'. *Brontë Studies.* 41.3 (2016), 216–28.

Beyer, J. and D. Orr. '"Wrote the Above of Today" – Anne Lister's Writings'. https://youtu.be/s9qY3ap5T74. Accessed 23 July 2022.

Birch, D. 'Grubbling'. *London Review of Books.* 21.2 (21 January 1999), 10–11.

Bray, A. 'Friendship and Modernity'. In *The Friend.* Chicago: University of Chicago Press, 2003. Pp. 205–88.

Brothers, H. '*Framing the Shibden Hall Portraits*: a Commission Fulfilled by Anne Lister during an Awkward Stay in London, 1833'. *Transactions of Halifax Antiquarian Society*. 4 (1996).

Burda, J. M. 'The Role Wills and Estate Planning Played in Anne Lister's Life'. In J. Reed and E. B. Hagai. (eds.). *Gentleman Jack and the (Re)Discovery of Anne Lister*. Special issue of *Journal of Lesbian Studies*. 26.4 (2022), 428–48.

Campbell, J. 'Can We Call Anne Lister a Lesbian?' In J. Reed and E. B. Hagai. (eds.). *Gentleman Jack and the (Re)Discovery of Anne Lister*. Special issue of *Journal of Lesbian Studies*. 26.4 (2022), 354–66.

Castle, T. 'The Diaries of Anne Lister'. In *The Apparitional Lesbian: Female Homosexuality and Modern Culture*. New York: Columbia University Press, 1993. Pp. 92–106.

Choma, A. 'Anne Lister and the Split Self (1791–1840): a Critical Study of her Diaries'. Unpublished Masters dissertation. University of Leeds, 1994.

Gentleman Jack: the Real Anne Lister. London: BBC Books, 2019.

Clare, A. *Anne Lister of Shibden Hall*. Halifax: Calderdale Museum Service, 2018.

'Dressing Gentleman Jack'. *Somewhere Magazine*. 5–6 (October 2021/February 2022).

Clark, A. *Alternative Histories of the Self*. London: Bloomsbury, 2017.

'Anne Lister's Construction of Lesbian Identity'. *Journal of the History of Sexuality*. 7.1 (July 1996), 23–50.

'Gender and Politics in the Long Eighteenth Century'. *History Workshop Journal*. 48.1 (1999), 252–7.

Colclough, S. *Consuming Texts: Readers and Reading Communities, 1695–1870*. Basingstoke: Palgrave, 2007.

'"Do You Not Know the Quotation?" Reading Anne Lister, Anne Lister Reading'. In J. C. Beynon and C. Gonda (eds). *Lesbian Dames: Sapphism in the Long Eighteenth Century*. Farnham: Ashgate, 2010. Pp. 159–72.

Council Minute Book of the Halifax Literary and Philosophical Society, 1831–39. Calderdale, West Yorkshire Archive Service.

Crampton, C. 'The Lesbian Dead Sea Scrolls'. *New Statesman*. 29 November 2013.

Damon, A.-B. 'Anne Lister, "A Sundial in the Shade": a Gifted Woman in the Nineteenth Century'. *Women's Studies*. 49.2 (2020), 130–48. DOI: 10.1080/00497878.2020.1729762.

Donoghue, E. 'Anne Lister'. In B. Zimmerman (ed.). *Lesbian Histories and Cultures: an Encyclopedia*. New York: Garland, 2000. P. 471.

'Liberty in Chains: the Diaries of Anne Lister (1817–24)'. In K. Lano and C. Parry (eds.). *Breaking the Barriers to Desire*. Nottingham: Five Leaves Press, 1995. Pp. 79–86.

Dubois de Montpéreux, F. *Voyage autour du Caucase, chez les Tcherkesses et les Abkhases, en Colchide, en Géorgie, en Arménie et en Crimée. Avec un Atlas géographique, pittoresque, archéologique, géologique etc.* 6 vols. Paris: Librairie de Gide, 1839–43.

Eisner, C. L. 'Shifting the Focus: Anne Lister as Pillar of Conservatism'. *a/b: Auto/Biography Studies*. 17.1 (2001), 28–42.

Emberson, C. and I. Emberson. 'A Missing Link: the Brontës, the Sowdens and the Listers'. *Brontë Studies*. 32.2 (2007), 116–24.

Euler, C. 'Moving between Worlds: Gender, Class, Politics, Sexuality and Women's Networks in the Diaries of Anne Lister of Shibden Hall, Halifax, Yorkshire, 1830 to 1840'. Unpublished PhD thesis. University of York, 1995.

Evans, C. 'Average Height, Dark and Handsome: Sexuality, Self-Presentation and Independence in the Life and Times of Anne Lister (1791–1840), c. 1816–1826'. Dissertation, Department of History, University of Sussex. May 2022. https://drive.google.com/file/d/1L2fjT76KLgEbCp7ZbcA41Ujt9fWQ5XbB/view. Accessed 15 February 2023.

Furness, C. *Unmarried Women of the Country Estate: Four Stories from 17th–20th Century*. Barnsley: Pen and Sword, 2022.

Goddard, C. 'The Anne Lister Walk'. Brochure. 2019.

Gonda, C. 'Writing Lesbian Desire in the Long Eighteenth Century'. In J. Medd (ed.). *The Cambridge Companion to Lesbian Literature*. Cambridge: Cambridge University Press, 2015. Pp. 107–21.

Green, M. (ed.). *Miss Lister of Shibden Hall: Selected Letters, 1800–1840*. Lewes: Book Guild, 1992.

Green, M. 'A Spirited Yorkshirewoman: the Letters of Anne Lister of Shibden Hall, b. 1791–d. 1840'. Library Associations Honours Diploma, 1938.

Halberstam, J. *Female Masculinity*. Durham, NC: Duke University Press, 1998.

'A (K)night of a Thousand Butches'. Blog post, May 21, 2019. https://bullybloggers.wordpress.com/2019/05/21/a-knight-of-a-thousand-butches-by-jack-halberstam/. Accessed 23 July 2022.

'Preface to the Twentieth Anniversary Edition'. In *Female Masculinity*. Durham, NC: Duke University Press, 2018.

Hamilton, R. '"Impossibility of its Being Deciphered": Anne Lister, her "Crypt Hand" Diaries, and the Contrast between Voicing and Silencing'. In J. Reed and E. B. Hagai. (eds.). *Gentleman Jack and the (Re)Discovery of Anne Lister*. Special issue of *Journal of Lesbian Studies*. 26.4 (2022), 338–53. www.tandfonline.com/doi/full/10.1080/10894160.2022.2107601. Accessed 15 February 2023.

Heyam, K. *Before We Were Trans: a New History of Gender*. London: Basic Books, 2022. Pp. 84–90.

Historic England's 'Pride of Place Project'. historicengland.org.uk/research/inclusive-heritage/lgbtq-heritage-project/. Accessed 3 March 2022.

Hogan, H. '*Gentleman Jack*'s Finale Was One of the Finest Hours in Lesbian Cinematic History'. *Autostraddle* (14 July 2019). www.autostraddle.com/gentleman-jacks-finale-was-one-of-the-finest-hours-in-lesbian-cinematic-history/. Accessed 23 July 2021.

Hughes, P. *Anne Lister's Secret Diary for 1817*. Ebook: Hues Books, 2014.

Gentleman Jack: the Early Life of Miss Anne Lister and the Curious Tale of Miss Eliza Raine. N.p.: Lulu.com, 2019.

Miss Anne Lister's Early Life and the Curious Tale of Eliza Raine. 2nd ed. Ebook: Hues Books, 2015.

'Was Eliza Raine the Real Mrs Rochester'. *Brontë Studies.* 29.1 (2004), 85–7.

Ingham, V. 'Anne Lister in the Pyrenees'. *Transactions of the Halifax Antiquarian Society.* (1969).

'Anne Lister's Ascent of Vignemale'. *Alpine Journal.* 73 (1968), 199–204.

Jagose, A.-M. *Inconsequence: Lesbian Representation and the Logic of Sexual Sequence.* Ithaca: Cornell University Press, 2002.

Jolly, M. 'Beyond Hagiography: New Books on Gay and Lesbian Life Writing'. *Women's History Review.* 10.4 (2011), 721–8.

Joyce, S. *LGBT Victorians: Sexuality and Gender in the Nineteenth-Century Archives.* Oxford: Oxford University Press, 2022.

'The Perverse Presentism of Rainbow Plaques: Memorializing Anne Lister'. *Nineteenth-Century Contexts.* 41.5 (2019), 601–10.

Kadlec, J. 'The 19th Century Lesbian Made for 21st Century Consumption'. *Longreads* (June 2019). https://longreads.com/2019/06/06/the-19th-century-lesbian-made-for-21st-century-consumption/. Accessed 23 July 2022.

Lang, D. 'Georgia in 1840: the Lister Diaries'. *Bulletin of the School of Oriental and African Studies.* 53.1 (1990), 115–20.

Lanser, S. S. 'Befriending the Body: Female Intimacies as Class Acts'. *Eighteenth-Century Studies* 32.2 (1998/9), 179–98.

'"Queer to Queer": the Sapphic Body as Transgressive Text'. In K. Kittredge (ed.). *Lewd and Notorious: Female Transgression in the Eighteenth Century.* Ann Arbor: University of Michigan Press, 2003. Pp. 21–46.

The Sexuality of History: Modernity and the Sapphic, 1565–1830. Chicago: University of Chicago Press, 2014.

'Tory Lesbians: Economies of Intimacy and the Status of Desire'. In J. C. Beynon and C. Gonda (eds). *Lesbian Dames: Sapphism in the Long Eighteenth Century.* Farnham: Ashgate, 2010. Pp. 173–89.

Lawrence, N. L. and S. Bertekap. '"Pink-Tinted Glasses": Looking and Affirmation in *Gentleman Jack.*' In J. Reed and E. B. Hagai. (eds.). *Gentleman Jack and the (Re)Discovery of Anne Lister.* Special issue of *Journal of Lesbian Studies.* 26.4 (2022), 323–37.

Lea, J. *The* Gentleman Jack *Effect: Lessons in Breaking Rules and Living Out Loud.* Santa Fe: Laurel House, 2021.

Liddington, J. 'Anne Lister and Emily Brontë, 1838–39: Landscape with Figures'. *Brontë Society Transactions.* 26.1 (2013), 46–67.

'Anne Lister of Shibden Hall, Halifax (1791–1840): Her Diaries and the Historians'. *History Workshop Journal.* 35 (1993), 45–77.

As Good as a Marriage: The Anne Lister Diaries 1836–38. Manchester: Manchester University Press, 2023.

'Beating the Inheritance Bounds: Anne Lister (1791–1840) and her Dynastic Identity'. *Gender and History.* 7.2 (1995), 260–74.

Female Fortune: Land, Gender and Authority. The Anne Lister Diaries and Other Writings, 1833–36. London: Rivers Oram, 1998.

'Gender, Authority and Mining in an Industrial Landscape: Anne Lister, 1791–1840'. *History Workshop Journal.* 42.1 (Autumn 1996), 56–86.

Nature's Domain: Anne Lister and the Landscape of Desire. Hebden Bridge: Pennine Pens, 2003.

Presenting the Past: Anne Lister of Halifax, 1791–1840. Halifax: Pennine Pens, 1994.

Liddington, J. and A. Oram. 'Decoding Anne Lister: "United in Heart and Purpose"'. *Herstoria Magazine*. (Spring 2010).

Lim, A. *In the Footsteps of Anne Lister: Travels of a Remarkable English Gentlewoman in France, Germany and Denmark in 1833*. 2 vols. Independently published, 2021–2.

Lister, J. 'Coal Mining in Halifax'. *Old Yorkshire*. (1885).

The Concord Fight: Being So Much of the Narrative of Ensign Jeremy Lister of the 10th Regiment of Foot as Pertains to His Services on the 19th of April, 1775, and to His Experiences in Boston during the Early Months of the Siege. Ed. H. Milford. Cambridge, MA: Harvard University Press, 1931.

'Shibden Hall History'. *Transactions of the Halifax Antiquarian Society*. (1907, 1910, 1915–17, 1921, 1926).

Longmuir, A. 'Anne Lister and Lesbian Desire in Charlotte Brontë's *Shirley*'. *Brontë Studies*. 31.2 (2006), 145–55.

Maier, S. E. and R. M., Friars. 'Stoically Sapphic: Gentlemanly Encryption and Disruptive Legibility in Adapting Anne Lister'. *Neo-Victorian Studies*. 13.1 (2020), 125–52.

McDowell, C. 'Staffing the Big House: Country House Domestic Service in Yorkshire, 1800–1903'. Unpublished thesis. University of Ottawa, 2012.

McHenry, J. Seven Entries from Anne Lister's Diary that were Key to Writing *Gentleman Jack*. *Vulture*. 7 May 2019. www.vulture.com/2019/05/gentleman-jack-anne-lister-diaries-sally-wainwright.html. Accessed 23 July 2022.

McHugh, K. 'Sightseeing, Social Climbing, Steamboats and Sex: Anne Lister's 1828 Tour of Scotland'. *Studies in Travel Writing*, 22.4 (2018), 420–35.

Marcus, S. *Between Women: Friendship, Desire, and Marriage in Victorian England*. Princeton: Princeton University Press, 2007.

Matthews, C. '"I Feel the Mind Enlarging Itself": Anne Lister's Gendered Reading Practices.' In J. Reed and E. B. Hagai. (eds.). *Gentleman Jack and the (Re)Discovery of Anne Lister*. Special issue of *Journal of Lesbian Studies*. 26.4 (2022), 367–81.

Maury, L. 'Le premier séjour d'Anne Lister aux Pyrénées: 11 août, 2 octobre 1830. Une ascension au Mont Perdu le jeudi 26 août 1830'. *Le Bulletin de la Société Ramond*. (1990), 91–126.

Moore, L. '"Something More Tender Still than Friendship": Romantic Friendship in Early-Nineteenth-Century England'. *Feminist Studies*. 18.3 (1992), 499–520.

Ng, E. 'The "Gentleman-Like" Anne Lister on *Gentleman Jack*: Queerness, Class, and Prestige in "Quality" Period Drama'. *International Journal of Communication*. 15 (2021), 2397–417.

'"What Unholy Chart Is This?!" Paratextual Intertextuality in *Gentleman Jack* Fan Posts of Scholarship on Anne Lister'. In J. Reed and E. B. Hagai. (eds.). *Gentleman Jack and the (Re)Discovery of Anne Lister*. Special issue of *Journal of Lesbian Studies*. 26.4 (2022), 458–67.

Oliveira, M. 'A Matter of Perspective: Anne Walker through her Lens and those of her Contemporaries'. In J. Reed and E. B. Hagai. (eds.). *Gentleman Jack and the (Re)Discovery of Anne Lister.* Special issue of *Journal of Lesbian Studies.* 26.4 (2022), 415–27.

Oram, A. 'Sexuality in Heterotopia Time Space and Love between Women in the Historic House'. *Women's History Review.* 21.4 (2012), 533–51.

Oram, A. and A. Turnbull. *The Lesbian History Sourcebook: Love and Sex between Women in Britain from 1780 to 1970*. London: Routledge, 2001.

Orr, D. '"I Tell Myself to Myself": Homosexual Agency in the Journals of Anne Lister (1791–1840)'. *Women's Writing.* 11.2 (2004), 201–22.

'A Sojourn in Paris, 1824–25: Sex and Sociability in the Manuscript Writings of Anne Lister (1791–1840)'. Unpublished PhD thesis. Murdoch University, 2007.

'Packed with Potential' website. www.packedwithpotential.org/projects/anne-lister-sex-guide.

Pryce, A. 'Anne Lister: the Mountaineer'. 'Packed with Potential' website, 20 December 2020. https://storymaps.arcgis.com/stories/3428e82114dd43fe810e814c09610f7e. Accessed 23 July 2022.

Ramsden, P. and V. Ingham (eds.). Anne Lister unpublished transcriptions. West Yorkshire Archive Services, Halifax, UK.

Rawson, C. 'Journal of an Inland Voyage through No. Wales AD 1817 & Others'. 1817–1822. Calderdale, West Yorkshire Archive Service. WYC: 1525/6/5/2.

Reed, J. and E. Ben Hagai. 'Gentleman Jack and the (Re)Discovery of Anne Lister'. In J. Reed and E. B. Hagai. (eds.). *Gentleman Jack and the (Re) Discovery of Anne Lister.* Special issue of *Journal of Lesbian Studies.* 26.4 (2022), 303–8.

Roulston, C. 'From Text to Screen: *Gentleman Jack* Then and Now'. In J. Reed and E. B. Hagai. (eds.). *Gentleman Jack and the (Re)Discovery of Anne Lister.* Special issue of *Journal of Lesbian Studies.* 26.4 (2022), 309–22.

'Interpreting the Thin Archive: Anne Lister, Eliza Raine and Telling School Tales'. *Eighteenth-Century Studies.* 55.2 (2022), 191–213.

'Marriage and its Queer Identifications in the Anne Lister Diaries'. In K. Leydecker and J. DiPlacidi (eds.). *After Marriage in the Long Eighteenth Century: Literature, Law and Society.* Cham: Palgrave Macmillan, 2018. Pp. 181–203.

'The Revolting Anne Lister: the UK's First Modern Lesbian'. In K. Browne et al. (eds.). *Revolting Bodies: Desiring Lesbians.* Special issue of *Journal of Lesbian Studies.* 17.3–4 (Spring 2013), 267–78.

'Sexuality in Translation: Anne Lister and the Ancients'. *Journal of the History of Sexuality.* 30.1 (January 2021), 112–35.

Rowanchild, A. '"Everything Done for Effect:" Georgic, Gothic and Picturesque in Anne Lister's Self-Production'. *Women's Writing.* 7.1 (2000), 89–104.

'"My Mind on Paper": Anne Lister and Literary Self-Construction in Early-Nineteenth-Century Halifax'. Unpublished PhD thesis. Open University, 1999.

'"Peeping behind the Curtain": the Significance of Classical Texts in the Sexual Self-Construction of Anne Lister'. In R. Pearson (ed.). *The Victorians and the Ancient World: Archaeology and Classicism in Nineteenth-Century Culture.* Newcastle: Cambridge Scholars, 2006. Pp. 139–51.

'Skirting the Margins: Anne Lister, Self-Representation, and Lesbian Identity in Early Nineteenth-Century Yorkshire'. In R. Phillips et al. (eds.). *De-Centering Sexualities: Politics and Representations beyond the Metropolis.* London: Taylor and Francis, 2000. Pp. 145–58.

Ryan, M. 'In *Gentleman Jack*, Sally Wainwright Brings a Fascinating Life from Diary to Screen'. *New York Times.* 18 April 2019.

Santos, C. ,Um diário para Anne Lister e Ann Walker (A Diary for Anne Lister and Ann Walker)'. Unpublished thesis. Universidade de Brasília, 2020.

Shibden Hall Guidebook. Calderdale Museum Service, 2010.

Shibden Hall – Virtual Tour. https://museums.calderdale.gov.uk/visit/shibden-hall/virtual-tour. Accessed 23 July 2022.

'Shibden Hall: 500 Years of History'. YouTube Video. www.youtube.com/watch?v=kIB-oRh8gYU. Accessed 23 July 2022.

Sjölin, M. H. 'Adapting the Queer Language of Anne Lister's Diaries'. In J. Reed and E. B. Hagai. (eds.). *Gentleman Jack and the (Re)Discovery of Anne Lister.* Special issue of *Journal of Lesbian Studies.* 26.4 (2022), 382–99.

Slater, S. J. 'Deviant Desires: Gender Resistance in Romantic Friendships between Women during the Late-Eighteenth and Early-Nineteenth Centuries in Britain'. Unpublished PhD thesis. Minnesota State University, 2012.

Stanley, L. 'Romantic Friendship? Some Issues in Researching Lesbian History and Biography'. *Women's History Review.* 1.2 (1992), 193–216.

Steidele, A. *Anne Lister. Eine erotische Biographie.* Berlin: Matthes & Seitz, 2017.

Gentleman Jack: a Biography of Anne Lister: Regency Landowner, Seducer and Secret Diarist. Translated by Katy Derbyshire. London: Serpent's Tail, 2018.

Transactions of the Halifax Literary and Philosophical Society, 1831–39. Calderdale, West Yorkshire Archive Service.

Tuite, C. 'The Byronic Woman: Anne Lister's Style, Sociability and Sexuality'. In G. Russell and C. Tuite (eds.). *Romantic Sociability: Social Networks and Literary Culture in Britain, 1770–1840.* Cambridge: Cambridge University Press, 2002. Pp. 186–210.

Turton, S. '"Improper words": Silencing Same-Sex Desire in Eighteenth-Century General English Dictionaries'. *Oxford Research in English.* 8 (2019), 9–36.

'The Lexicographical Lesbian: Remaking the Body in Anne Lister's Erotic Glossary'. *Review of English Studies.* 73.310 (2022), 537–51.

Ulph, C. '"Under the Existing Rules": Anne Lister and the Halifax Literary and Philosophical Society'. *Nineteenth-Century Literature.* 73.4 (2019), 462–85.

Upchurch, C. 'Following Anne Lister: Continuity and Queer History before and after the Late Nineteenth Century'. In J. Reed and E. B. Hagai. (eds.). *Gentleman Jack and the (Re)Discovery of Anne Lister.* Special issue of *Journal of Lesbian Studies.* 26.4 (2022), 400–14.

Valladares, S. 'An Introduction to the "Literary Person(s)" of Anne Lister and the Ladies of Llangollen'. *Literature Compass.* 10.3 (2013), 353–68.

Vermeer, L. 'Tiny Symbols Tell Big Stories: Naming and Concealing Masturbation in Diaries (1650–1940)'. *European Journal of Life Writing.* 6 (2007), 101–34.

Vicinus, M. 'Lesbian History: All Theory and No Facts or All Facts and No Theory?' *Radical History Review.* 60 (1994), 57–75.

'A Scheme of Romantic Friendship: Love and Same-Sex Marriage'. In *Intimate Friends: Women who Loved Women, 1778–1928.* Chicago: University of Chicago Press, 2004. Pp. 5–30.

Wainwright, S. *Gentleman Jack*: Episodes 1–8 shooting script. Lookout Point Limited, 2019. www.bbc.co.uk/writersroom/scripts/tv-drama/gentleman-jack. Accessed 23 July 2022.

'The Life and Legacy of Anne Lister'. University of York, 21 October 2021. www.york.ac.uk/news-and-events/events/public-lectures/autumn–2021/gentleman-jack/?fbclid=IwAR2gjsd4IRS5CKg5ldklTbkKboO9FRtKbSKVqQ_xkXtv2luXmsS9miFAcbs. Accessed 23 July 2022.

Whitbread, H. 'Initiations, Explanations, Discriminations: Anne Lister's Strategies of Seduction'. In M. McAuliffe and S. Tiernan (eds.). *Tribades, Tommies, and Transgressives: History of Sexualities.* Newcastle: Cambridge Scholars, 2008. Pp. 109–27.

Whitbread, H., (ed.) *I Know My Own Heart: the Diaries of Anne Lister, 1791–1840*. London, Virago, 1988; New York: New York University Press, 1992. Reprinted in the following editions: H. Whitbread (ed.) *The Secret Diaries of Miss Anne Lister*. London: Virago, 2010; *The Secret Diaries of Miss Anne Lister, vol. I: I Know My Own Heart.* London: Virago, 2010; *The Secret Diaries of Miss Anne Lister, 1791–1840*. New York: New York University Press, 2010.

(ed.). *No Priest but Love: the Journals of Anne Lister from 1824–1826*. Otley: Smith Settle, 1992; New York: New York University Press, 1993. Reprinted as H. Whitbread (ed.). *The Secret Diaries of Miss Anne Lister, vol. II: No Priest but Love*. London: Virago, 2020.

Whitbread, H. and N. Holme. *Secret Diaries Past and Present: Q&A With Helena.* N.p.: CreateSpace, 2016.

White, P.. '"Gentleman Jack": HBO and BBC Renew Sally Wainwright's Suranne Jones-Fronted Period Drama for Season 2'. *Deadline.* 23 May 2019.

Wingrove, S. 'Queer Pilgrimage: Anne Lister, Gentleman Jack and Locating Community.' In J. Reed and E. B. Hagai. (eds.). *Gentleman Jack and the (Re)Discovery of Anne Lister.* Special issue of *Journal of Lesbian Studies.* 26.4 (2022), 449–57.

Index

Milton Keynes UK
Ingram Content Group UK Ltd.
UKHW022143110823
426767UK00008B/167

9 781009 280730